Rita Schneider-Sliwa (Ed.)
with Mihir Bhatt

Recovering Slums

Determinants of poverty and upward social mobility in urban slums

Technical report for the funding agencies, submitted 2005

ISBN: 978-3-7965-2564-3
© R. Schneider-Sliwa, Department of Geography, University of Basel, with
   M. Bhatt, All India Disaster Mitigation Institute, Ahmedabad
   2008
All rights reserved

Satellite image processing / GIS base-map: Jörg Wendel
Databank management: Vipal Shah, Deepesh Sinha, Jörg Wendel
GIS-map assistance: Jörg Wendel, Fiona Wieland
Verification of survey results: Hasmukh Sadhu
Editorial assistance: Katharina Conradin, Nadezhda Sliwa, Fiona Wieland
Layout: Katharina Seider, Jennifer Whitebread, Charlotte Ciprian
Cover Design: Nadezhda Sliwa, Selin Ciprian

This research was funded by: The National Center of Competence in Research North – South Partnerships (NCCR North-South) of the Swiss National Science Foundation, the Swiss Agency for Development and Cooperation and the Swiss Academy of Sciences Commission for Research Partnerships with Developing Countries. The editors wish to thank Government authorities in Ahmedabad, Gandhinagar, the District of Kutch and the City of Bhuj, particularly: Government of Gujarat Labour and Employment Department, Gujarat State Disaster Management Authority, Kutch District and Bhuj Collectorate, Bhuj Area Development Authority.

Table of Contents

1 Slums, urban poverty and local strengths 1
R. Schneider-Sliwa with Mihir Bhatt

1.1 Introduction 1
1.2 The objectives of the project 3
1.3 The relevance of GIS-based social science research in the process of
    development 3
1.4 Application of findings in the Indian planning context 5
1.5 Transfer of methods and results to capacity building in other regional
    contexts 6

**2 Slums – most important form of urban living in the
21st century 7**
A. Staub, P. Thum, J. Whitebread

2.1 Introduction 7
2.2 Definition of the term "slum" 7
2.3 Slums of hope and slums of despair 8
2.4 Slum location 11
2.5 Slums as global risk areas 11
2.6 Slums in India 12

3 Urban policy in India and Gujarat 13
V. Babbar

3.1 Vision statement 13
3.2 Overarching principles and objectives 13
3.3 Definition of "slum" in Gujarat, India 16
3.4 Motivation of community by mobilizing support of NGOs and CBOs 18
3.5 Financing mechanisms 19
3.6 Availing of national and state funds 20
3.7 Operation and maintenance 20
3.8 Shelter improvement 20
3.9 Land use classification 20
3.10 Special purpose vehicle (SPV) and its role 21
3.11 Residents' association 21
3.12 Transfer of titles to slum dwellers 21
3.13 Relaxation in rules for building permission 23
3.14 Creating of housing stock for urban poor 23
3.15 Legal reforms 24

4 Differences in slums and poverty structures 25
R. Schneider-Sliwa

4.1 The slum communities under study 25
4.2 Religious and caste affiliation.. 26
4.3 Livelihood security, incomes and poverty 28
4.4 Ownership issues and shelter information 32
4.5 Access to health 32
4.6 Assistance/relief received 33
4.7 Own contributions, willingness to pay for services 33
4.8 Felt needs 34
4.9 Summary 34

5 Income differentials – household livelihood security 45
K. Conradin, R. Schneider-Sliwa, F. Wieland

5.1 Introduction 45
5.2 Occupation 46
5.3 Average daily wage of household members 49
5.4 Livelihood affected 51
5.5 Monthly savings 53
5.6 Amount of debts (in Rs.) 59
5.7 Conclusion 64

6 The structure of slum housing 73
K. Conradin, F. Wieland

6.1 Introduction 73
6.2 Type of house 73
6.3 Post earthquake housing status 76
6.4 Current housing status 79
6.5 Living in the same house as before the earthquake 80
6.6 Precautions to make the house earthquake proof 80
6.7 Precautions have been efficient 82
6.8 Investment to make shelter earthquake proof 83
6.9 Conclusion 84

7 Ownership and tax bill 95
B. Lietzke, D. Michel, N. Sliwa

7.1 Introduction 95
7.2 Ownership document 95
7.3 Tax bill ownership 99
7.4 Conclusion 103

8 Food security 117
K. Conradin, B. Lietzke, D. Michel, F. Wieland

8.1 Introduction 117
8.2 Able to feed the family 117
8.3 Ration Card 118
8.4 Conclusion 120

9 Health issues and occupational hazards 125
K. Conradin, F. Wieland

9.1 Introduction 125
9.2 Places for health check-up 125
9.3 Purpose of visiting the health centre 129
9.4 Illness/death of a family member in the last year 131
9.5 Illness 134
9.6 Monthly expenses for medicines 136
9.7 Conclusion 140

10 Demographic determinants – child bearing and age structure 153
S. Eichenberger, M. Gysi, C. Saalfrank, N. Sliwa

10.1 Introduction 153
10.2 Number of children 153
10.3 Number of dependant old people 164
10.4 Conclusion 170

11 Educational achievements – occupational structure and political participation 183
A. Staub, N. Sliwa, S. Waldburger

11.1 Introduction 183
11.2 Education 183
11.3 Occupation 189
11.4 Home based occupation 193
11.5 Election Card 197
11.6 Conclusion 199

12 Problems of addiction 205
A. Cavelti, N. Sliwa, J. Whitebread

12.1 Introduction 205
12.2 Type of addiction 205
12.3 Expenses for addiction 209
12.4 Conclusion 211

13 Willingness to contribute towards infrastructural services 213
A. Cavelti, N. Sliwa, J. Whitebread

13.1 Introduction 213
13.2 Type of services available at home 213
13.3 Priority of improvements of services at home 235
13.4 Willingness to contribute for better drinking water 241
13.5 Conclusion 245

14 Willingness to pay for the legalization of land 285
M. Barmettler, R. Schneider-Sliwa, P. Thum

14.1 Introduction 285
14.2 Good drinking water, drainage/sanitation, solid waste removal 285
14.3 Affordable amount of money to legalize the land (in Rs.) 290
14.4 Willingness to pay property tax 291
14.5 Willingness to pay property tax (in Rs. per month) 293
14.6 Willingness to pay water tax (in Rs. per month) 294
14.7 Willingness to invest in house when land is legalized 295
14.8 Priority benefit in new government scheme – compensations for loss of earnings 296
14.9 Priority benefit in new government scheme – improving housing conditions 298
14.10 Conclusion 299

15 Willingness to relocate 319
B. Lietzke, D. Michel

15.1 Introduction 319
15.2 Acceptance for relocation with land and services 319
15.3 Willingness to move with own family and other families 324
15.4 Conclusion 331

16 Help received – help perceived 345
N. Sliwa, S. Wehrli

16.1 Introduction 345
16.2 Receiving some form of relief 345
16.3 Receiving help with the reconstruction of the house 348
16.4 Receiving different types of help 352
    16.4.1 Material 352
    16.4.2 Cash 353
    16.4.3 Information 354
16.5 Receiving relief from the government 355
16.6 Receiving relief from AIDMI 358
16.7 General linkages with AIDMI 359

    16.8 Evaluation: role of relief donors 362
    16.9 Conclusion 363

17 Basic infrastructure – basic problems – the case of drinking water supplies 385
F. Wieland

    17.1 Introduction 385
    17.2 Used methodology 386
    17.3 Religion 388
    17.4 Caste 389
    17.5 Number of family members 391
    17.6 Case of illness or death in the last year 392
    17.7 Place for health check-up 393
    17.8 Monthly expenses for medicine 394
    17.9 Monthly income of the family 395
    17.10 Knowledge of the relation between hygiene and health 396
    17.11 Improvement of drinking water supply: most urgent need 398
    17.12 Water facilities in the house 399
    17.13 Willingness to get involved towards achieving better
          drinking water 400
    17.14 Water treatment 402
    17.15 Toilet facilities in the house 404
    17.16 Sewerage facility in the house 406
    17.17 Slum 407
    17.18 Type of house 409
    17.19 Analysis of water treatment methods 410
    17.20 Filtration 411
    17.21 Clorination 412
    17.22 Solar disinfection (SODIS) 415
    17.23 Conclusion 418

18 GIS applications as tools in urban poverty reduction – methodological aspects 425
J. Wendel

    18.1 Methodology 425
    18.2 Problems and solutions 427
    18.3 Conclusion 433
    References 435

19 Socially differentiated urban slums – findings, problems, options for intervention 437
R. Schneider-Sliwa

    19.1 Introduction 437

19.2 Major findings – determinants of poverty and upward
    social mobility 439
19.3 Implications of socially differentiated urban slums 444
    19.3.1 What do we *not* know of sufficiently in terms of degrees of
        social differentiation, objective slum conditions and social
        realities? 445
    19.3.2 What is a matter of debate? 447
    19.3.3 What should be decided upon by public administration? What
        is being overemphasized? What is being insufficiently
        emphasized? 448
19.4 What are the leverages in terms of public policies? 449

List of Tables 453

List of Maps 462

List of Figures 467

1 Slums, urban poverty and local strengths

R. Schneider-Sliwa, University of Basel with
M. Bhatt, All India Disaster Mitigation Institute, Ahmedabad

1.1
Introduction

This report assumes that urban poverty, reality of hundreds of millions of people in the developing world, is not a given, uninfluencable condition. This, of course, has not gone unrecognized as is evident by the fact that development policy by international, national and nongovernmental agencies, metropolitan planning authorities and public administrations have for a long time targeted urban poverty conditions. This study, however, reflects on *the local forces and processes in the slums themselves that help move people out of urban poverty.* It is assumed that whether or not urban poverty persists and how it manifests itself at the local level is not only dependent on planning efforts from the outside or from the top down. Rather, *local forces, processes and individual initiatives and adaptive capacities in urban slum areas are also instrumental in the alleviation of poverty.*

Urban poverty and life in slums, thus, is not seen as a situation in which there exist only losers and by which no winners could possibly emerge. Rather, the phenomenon of urban poverty and slum living may be seen as a spectrum along which there exist to varying degrees opportunities to beak out of a situation, even if one is born into it. Some of these local opportunities may pertain to initial conditions of slums, be it better housing and infrastructural provision on part of planning agencies, or be it the social and economic conditions of the inhabitants. Some of the local strengths may derive from behavioural factors that relate to the motivation to achieve in education in order to have better employment and wages, to seek and use health care, to contribute to the provision of infrastructural services, to pay for the legalization of illegally occupied land, or to actively seek and receive help from governmental and nongovernmental sources.

The power of theses local forces and adaptive capacities is demonstrated by slum communities in which local people have and use their strengths and potentials for development in different ways. The question of *how do people move themselves out of urban poverty* is, of course, also relevant in terms of the planning question of how to move people out of urban poverty. Slum communities, their population and their endogenous potential, then, are at the core of this book. Their interests, social economic conditions and development patterns are not easily grasped conceptually, nor understood. Commonly, slums are vast islands in seas of unplanning, at best they are administered marginal settlements, at worst they are settlements that are marginalized by public administration. As spaces of exclusion of professionalized bureaucracy, they rarely have a dense network of infrastructure. They are rarely part of political advocacy, and only recently they have become the focus of non governmental development efforts of NGOs.

Apart from visible infrastructure disparities, slums do, however, distinguish themselves among and from each other greatly, as noticeable differences do exist within the communities. This is one of the reasons why case studies are so important. *There are no simple solutions to complex problems* in the field of disaster management and development research. Every case is special, and solutions that worked in one situation will not necessarily be applicable in a different context. Even if the underlying conditions determining poverty are the same in different contexts, solutions must be adapted to different cases. A second reason why case studies are so crucial is that disasters, perceived as an interaction between nature and society, have a profound impact on people who are *social actors*: They process social experience in their response, and their different histories and life worlds lead to different interpretations of situations (Hilford 2007:54,56). Thus, *multiple realities emerge* (Hilford 2007:56) that are more complex to deal with, but that enhance custom-made solutions based on endogenous potentials and capacities. Third, case studies as conceived in this book are based on a *participatory approach* that places the poor at the center. "People affected by an emergency are the best judges of their own interest…It is their home, their family and their world that have been turned upside down." (Oxfam 2007:17).

When spaces of exclusion do exhibit great socio-economic disparities, one must conclude that there are powerful forces and adaptive capacities within the slums themselves that account for these. As spaces with inherent development potentials and capacities, slum communities themselves, then, deserve detailed analysis in order to identify the forces and potentials for betterment of living conditions from within. The general research question, whether or not and how slum communities differ in their internal structure and how this relates to development and the amelioration of living conditions, is of paramount importance for the understanding of how to assist slums, which leverages to use and where the greatest impact can be made. As such, socioeconomic slum analysis can yield results that can be transferred to the general context of slums worldwide.

In the following case studies of four slums in the Indian City of Bhuj, Gujarat, particular attention is given to the *local forces originating from slums, that are part of the central process of change and that work for or against improvement of living conditions*. In sum, these lead to considerable qualitative and quantitative differences in the development processes of slum communities. Understanding this will assist in identifying what leverages need to be activated in order to accelerate development.

1.2
The objectives of the project

In order to pursue the notion that *local forces and processes in the slums themselves are agents of change that help move people out of urban poverty situations*, this project addressed the living conditions and potentials embodied in slum communities. Particular emphasis was given to both differences in socioeconomic structures which represent initial conditions in the slum communities, and to behavioral aspects such as the willingness to contribute to the betterment of conditions, which is crucial for sustained development.

Using the City of Bhuj, Gujarat, as an example, the specific objectives were to
- analyse socio-economic structural conditions of slum communities at the household level
- identify the factors likely to affect living and health conditions in the slums and the determinants and processes of change and improvements in slums using a GIS-based social science approach. This involved creating a GIS-base map from a satellite image, the verification of the base map through house to house surveying in the four slum communities of Mustuffanagar, Bhimraonagar, Jayprakashnagar and Shantinagar of the City of Bhuj
- carry out a social science survey of each slum household in the four communities, a total of 657 slum households yielding data on about 2 800 persons. There are various ways in which local people cope with emergencies, and participatory action research can therefore be a powerful tool (Tyler 2006:4). It is fundamental to "ask people how *they* feel and what *they* want to see happen as a result", because "when people are not involved, a response can miss its mark, leave out vulnerable groups, waste money and add to suffering" (Oxfam 2007:17).
- The relevance of this research is seen with respect to the process of development, planning for slum communities and transferability of results to capacity building in other regional and cultural contexts as is outlined in points 1.3 to 1.5.

1.3
The relevance of GIS-based social science research in the process of development

If anybody wants to improve living conditions in slums, information about basic facilities like housing and water supply is needed to identify areas of greatest need. If one wants to bring about long lasting improvements in slums, the characteristics of the slum population, too, need to be understood. Some households may be hindered by their own levels of education or training or caste affiliation or aspirations to achieve betterments or to contribute to services. Other households may by means of their own initiative seek and receive training and help. Thus, obstacles to development may be overcome at the micro level of the household and this may improve development levels at the macro level of the community. If authorities want to understand both the needs of the slums and the development potentials embedded in the slum population, communities and households must be given a voice in the issues of slum upgrading.

How does GIS assist in this matter? Stated simply: GIS puts people on a map and once they are there, authorities and NGOs can determine what kind of help is needed and what the appropriate course of action is. As such, GIS serves to empower people and development agencies.

Generally, GIS is essential for all planning and development tasks since Geographic Information Systems offer the opportunity to take inventory of geographic realities easily and to link spatial data with household surveys or official statistics. Using GIS tools, this wealth of information can be computed and spatially analyzed and interpreted. The results can be visualized in thematic maps, easily understandable for everyone. In slums, the population themselves may even hand-draw GIS-type maps ('participation GIS') with relevant data that can be transferred into official GIS data bases. GIS applications offer a quick overview over which conditions are located where. A household and its specific situation which is neither documented on a cadastral nor on a GIS map would go unnoticed by authorities or NGOs and might not receive needed assistance. As a result, GIS applications are uniquely useful in poverty reduction since only precise and problem oriented relief will lead to sustained development. This is especially true for urban poverty areas due to two reasons: First, urban poverty areas are predominantly slums and illegal settlements. These ever growing slums are neither surveyed nor mapped nor registered by local authorities. Thus, maps or detailed household information are generally not available for most slums. Conventional cadastral mapping cannot possibly catch up with the rapidly growing slum areas. GIS maps based on high resolution satellite images can give precise base map information that has the advantage of being able to be linked with social survey data yielding household characteristics. Such information is urgently needed to optimize public and private sector relief. Second, most of the existing topographical maps and city plans are older than 25 years and therefore useless as base for modern planning. In this context, GIS in combination with remote sensing technologies is the cheapest way to generate new and easy to update topographic and overview maps as well as thematic maps on different scale in a short time, providing relevant and reliable information to all actors involved in fighting poverty. Consider, for example, that after the earthquake of 26th of January 2001, a GIS base information centre was installed at Bhuj that was recognized as the most powerful decision support system to various agencies involved in rescue, relief, rehabilitation and reconstruction.

Last, it is of note that although the creation of a comprehensive GIS-data base is time consuming and costly, a GIS has two major advantages in comparison to conventional maps: first, the continuous updating of geographical data (possible from satellite images) and social science data linked with geographical information that guarantees, indeed, up to date maps. Second, the time series of GIS maps allows comparisons and empowers authorities and NGOs to monitor whether or not and how development proceeds, thus, to evaluate the efficiency of their own activities. As such, Geographic Information Systems are a milestone in documenting and giving further impulse to development that starts at the grassroots level.

1.4
Application of findings in the Indian planning context

The detailed results in the following technical report provide a benchmark for further assessment of development. The technical report provides for the first time a complete account of a number of socioeconomic variables that one can use in order to track development of these (and similar) communities.

The GIS-application used in this report will be useful for the following types of development work in India and elsewhere. *Advocacy Work:* Basic facilities (like water, sanitation etc.) are fundamental human rights which should be accessible to everyone. With maps showing deficiencies in these facilities, authorities can be more easily convinced to involve the slum areas in the urban planning and reconstruction process. In a country like India, where computer skills are highly valued, the use of participatory GIS maps is a particularly powerful tool for the enhancement of development. *Implementation of other projects of nongovernmental organizations:* In India, All India Disaster Mitigation Institute (AIDMI), for example, is working for the long term recovery of communities, as many communities were affected by various disasters and also live with a lack of facilities and basic necessities. To reduce their vulnerability, AIDMI addresses their needs from various angles with a view to appropriate support measures. If community members are covered by various AIDMI projects, their lives become more stable and they are more prepared to overcome the effects of any type of disaster. For better co-operation between AIDMI`s implementation projects, the GIS data generated is useful. *Educational, awareness raising and participation processes:* AIDMI is running four information centres in Bhuj slums which serve as community meeting and learning centres. Print-outs of the GIS maps are used for Community Focus Group Meetings as well as for PRA-Tools (Participatory Rural Appraisal), which have been adapted by AIDMI also to the urban context. The tools (e.g. community drawing of needed slum facilities, slum time graphs, daily time use, grouping within the community etc.) are a standard instrument in AIDMI's ongoing work. Instead of using hand-drawn, unscaled maps, GIS maps are much more accurate and can together with the PRA-tools help to find suitable locations for facilities and thus improve living conditions. The exercises are especially helpful to create a higher awareness of their situation and possible solutions as well as raising the overall confidence of the slum dwellers. GIS training is also a way of capacity building: People learn what it takes to document their situation and needs with the help of thematic GIS maps. These maps help them address their issues also at an official level. *Slum Planning:* By the initiative of AIDMI, slum communities have initialised slum area committees which function as informal self-governments and take up issues of the slums. The GIS maps will be very helpful for planning and to launch further activities like small scale insurance or micro-financing. *Public Distribution System:* People in India below the poverty line have a right to obtain certain services. With the help of the GIS- and social science survey data, households in need can be identified easier and steps be taken to alleviate their situation. As part of the transfer of results and tools to government and non-government agencies, the results will be shared with the Ahmedabad Municipal Corporation and Bhuj Housing and Area Development Authority (BHADA), which may encourage the institutions to involve the slum dwellers in the town planning process. AIDMI is one of India's leading organisations promoting learning in the humanitarian sector. Findings of the project will be of use in AIDMI's local capacity cycles, national course series, preparedness pocket-book series, experience learning series and the monthly publication of *Afat Nivaran* (in Gujarati) and the quarterly *Vipada Nivaran* (in Hindi). Furthermore, it will be used for leaflets, information sheets and websites.

1.5
Transfer of methods and results to capacity building in other regional contexts

The methodology used in these case studies (satellite and GIS-based methods and complementary social science surveys) can be transferred to any context. Although Participation-GIS is a well established area of work and research, the use of satellite images for the mapping of slum areas in India has not been done widely in the past, even though it presents a relatively fast way of obtaining accurate GIS data upon which social science surveys on relevant questions can be carried out. The combination of these specific tools applied by a joint research project between a university and a grassroots NGO is rather new. Also, the application of GIS in slums is relatively novel approach as AIDMI involves slum dwellers on issues of planning and local people produce their own hand drawn Geographic Information Systems showing local conditions. Thus, this research enhances capacity building in the slums and supports a process of self sustained participatory community planning.

2 Slums – most important form of urban living in the 21st century

A. Staub, P. Thum, J. Whitebread
University of Basel

2.1
Introduction

Since the 1940s the world population experienced a rapid growth which has become primarily urban growth. No longer are all cities able to support the population growth that has been unprecedented in history (UNITED NATIONS HUMAN SETTLEMENT PROGRAMME, 2003: 5). Living in the slums has become a reality for a majority of the urban population in cities of the developing countries. According to UNHABITAT the slum population worldwide is estimated at 923 986 000 which in 2001 was 31.6% of the word's population.

What are slums and what does living in the slums mean? Taking a look at the etymology of the word "slum" reveals: *SLUM - 1845, from back slum "back alley, street of poor people" (1825), originally a slang word meaning "room," especially "back room" (1812), of unknown origin. Go slumming is from 1884, pastime popularized by East End novels. Slumlord first attested 1953, from slum landlord (1893)"* (Harper, 2001). Since 1812 the term slum was extended to mean "neglected parts of cities where housing and living conditions are appallingly lacking" (THE WORLD BANK GROUP, 2001: 24).

2.2
Definition of the term "slum"

The term slum is very imprecise as it literally combines everything, from the simplest shanty town to permanently constructed slum settlements. Apart from the different shelter construction, the available infrastructure (water, electricity, sanitation etc.) varies significantly, too. What also contributes to the confusion of the term are all the other terms which are used additionally like "squatter", "low-income housing", "shanty town" or terms of other languages like "favelas" (Portuguese), "barraca" (Spanish) or "chawls" (in Ahmedabad) (UNITED NATIONS HUMAN SETTLEMENT PROGRAMME, 2003: 9). The lack of one consistent term makes the work of urban developers and also of researchers very difficult, because what is not defined will not be measured and compared, and most importantly will not be taken serious enough. The problem of definition has been observed by many people but solving the problem of definition seems to be as difficult as solving the problem of slums as such. In the words of B. K. Prasad: "Variations in definitions not only cause confusions but also come in the way of comparing data from different sources" (PRASAD, 2003: 220). Consequently, figures on the dimension of slums can only be estimated.

The UN had the following problems when looking for a definition and a way to measure slums:
1. Slums are too complex to define according to one single parameter.
2. Slums are a relative concept and what is considered as a slum in one city will be regarded as adequate in another city – even in the same country.
3. Local variations among slums are too wide to define universally applicable criteria.
4. Slums change too fast to render any criterion valid for a reasonably long period of time.
5. The spatial nature of slums means that the size of particular slum areas is vulnerable to changes in jurisdiction or spatial aggregation.

[UNITED NATIONS HUMAN SETTLEMENT PROGRAMME, 2003: 11]

The UN classification points out the important characteristics of slums that can be measured (Fig. 2.1).

2.3
Slums of hope and slums of despair

According to the UN population growth, migration and the trends of globalization are all at the core of slum development in developing countries. These are, however, not the only problems, rather, urban development policy and misguided national policy that does not give due respect to the concerns of slums are also part of the problem (UNITED NATIONS HUMAN SETTLEMENT PROGRAMME, 2003: 5). The different causes are presented in Figure 2.2.

In sum, they imply different potentials for slum development, making some "slums of despair" and some "slums of hope"

There are important differences between slums. To implement effective planning strategies, these differences need to be taken into account. One way to categorize slums is into slums of hope and slums of despair. *Slums of hope* refer to those slum communities with certain potentials to alleviate their conditions, whereas *slums of despair* refer to slums which are exposed to bad conditions like pollution and dilapidation of building fabric.

Figure 2.1 Indicators and thresholds for defining slums. Source: UNITED NATIONS HUMAN SETTLEMENT PROGRAMME, 2003: 12 (modified).

Characteristic	Indicator	Definition
Access to water	Inadequate drinking water supply	A settlement has an inadequate drinking water supply if less than 50% of households have an improved water supply: • household connection • access to public stand pipe • rainwater collection with at least 20 liters/person/day available *within an acceptable collection distance*
Access to sanitation	Inadequate sanitation	A settlement has inadequate sanitation if less than 50% of households have improved sanitation: • public sewer • septic tank • pour-flush latrine • ventilated improved pit latrine The excreta disposal system is considered adequate if it is private or shared by a *maximum of two households*.
Structural quality of housing	a. Location	Proportion of households residing on or near a hazardous site. The following locations schould be considered: • housing in geologically hazardous zones (landslide/earthquake and flood areas) • housing on or under gargage mountains • housing around high-industrial pollution areas • housing around other unprotected high-risk zones (e.g. railroads, airports, energy transmission lines).
	b. Permanency of structure	Proportion of households living in temporary and/or dilapidated structures. The following factors should be considered when placing a housing unit in these categories: • quality of construction (e.g. materials used for wall, floor and roof) • compliance with local building codes, standards and bylaws.
Overcrowding	Overcrowding	Proportion of households with more than two persons per room. The alternative is to set a minimum standart for floor area per person (e.g. 5 square meters).
Security of tenure	Security of tenure	• Proportion of households with formal title deeds to both land and residence • Proportion of households with formal title deeds to either one of land or residence • Proportion of households with enforceable agreements or any document as a proof of a tenure arrangement

Figure 2.2 Inequality, poverty and slum formation. Source: UNITED NATIONS HUMAN SETTLEMENT PROGRAMME, 2003: 17 (modified).

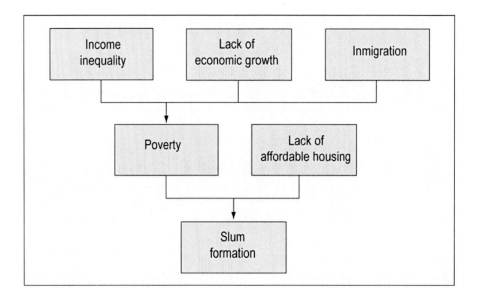

Other classifications are the following:

Inner-city slums: Immigrants who seek work in the cities rent cheap flats and through overcrowding and lack of building maintenance the process of dilapidation takes its course.

Slum estates: These were mostly public housing estates or built by mines and factories for industrial workers. Overcrowding, lack of infrastructure and emergence of social problems like crime quickly lead to slumification.

Squatter settlements: The squatter settlements are built illegally and are a major problem for urban planning, particularly when needed infrastructure cannot be as easily provided. The formation of a squatter settlement is mostly a gradual process but can also happen very quickly, as in most developing countries. Some slum settlements are legalized later and others are demolished by planning agencies.

Semi-legal subdivisions: Land owners divide their property and sell cheap land to build on. These land owners are often farmers who neglect the fact that there is no infrastructure for settlement and that construction on these sites is illegal. The land is usually very densely populated to make the most profit and make the land affordable for the poorest. Mostly unclear land rights between traditional and new federal regulations lead to the fact that settlements are not registered by the government (UNITED NATIONS HUMAN SETTLEMENT PROGRAMME 2003: 81-87).

2.4
Slum location

The location has an influence on the structure and the development of the slums.

Central: Characteristics for central locations are high concentrations and proximity of employment, especially for unskilled and short term jobs. The most common living form is to rent; through overcrowding the infrastructure is insufficient or damaged.

Scattered slum islands: These islands are very small and use up space in cities which is not used by the government. There is no infrastructure and they are often surrounded by pipe lines, railway tracks, and airport runways.

Outer city slums: These settlements are mostly illegal squatter settlements. The land is cheap and the living quality mostly better than in the inner-cities but infrastructure is low. As the costs of transport to workplaces are high, the slum dwellers often do home-based work such as handicraft (UNITED NATIONS HUMAN SETTLEMENT PROGRAMME 2003: 88-90).

2.5
Slums as global risk areas

There are many sources of risk for people living in slum areas. Mostly the *location* is unsuitable or even very dangerous. The risk varies from landslides, marshes, fire, pollution through solid waste disposal or industries to highly frequented railway lines, roads or runways of airports. The *health risks* and illnesses are mainly due to lacking clean water facilities. But also bad sanitation facilities, waste disposals, insects and animals, air pollution (cheap fuel which emits particles) and lack of medical services are sources for illnesses (UNITED NATIONS HUMAN SETTLEMENT PROGRAMME 2003: 69-71, 113-114).

Another risk factor is the poor *education standard* of the inhabitants, especially of women, as often child labour prevents children from going to school. In slums there is very often a concentration of various social problems which lead to *crime* and civil commotions. Sometimes these social conflicts have their source in the *insecurity* with which the people have to live. Insecurity includes not only material livelihood but also the right to stay on the land and to have employment, moreover access to health facilities and good educational prospects for the children and the right to be protected from domestic violence (UNITED NATIONS HUMAN SETTLEMENT PROGRAMME 2003: 75-77).

Further the *urban planning agencies* often lack the necessary know-how, experience and resources to direct population growth within the urban context. The planning agencies have to acknowledge that the slums are an urban phenomenon and that they have to take up responsibilities and implement actions such as sustainable and affordable housing, basic infrastructure and legal security (http://www.bbr.bund.de/staedtebau/ download/praesentation.pdf).

2.6
Slums in India

In India, unsatisfactory *economic* conditions for millions of people translate into unsatisfactory *living* conditions, as evident in slums and enormous numbers of pavement dwellers and street sleepers in Indian cities which is nowhere in the world as high as here. The slums seem to spread uncontrolled through vast areas of cities, and there are hardly enough solutions to significantly reduce the problem (Desai and Pillai 1990, Prasad 2003).

While Indian slums still are major problem areas awaiting improvement, they are by no means a homogenous phenomenon. Rather, there is great variety and social differentiation. Indian slums, for example, are organized along cultural lines: Castes with similar cultures and traditions group together and influence the social life and the atmosphere to a great extent. As such, in India there are great differences between slums in appearance and living conditions, and social stratification. This makes research on the internal structure of slums at the micro level of the household and the question why and how some manage to move out of poverty conditions especially interesting. Such research can aid India's local Government's plans and visions for alleviating slum situations. The vision for doing this will be presented next.

Literature
DESAI A.R., DEVADAS PILLAI, S. (1990): Slums and Urbanization. London: Sangam Books Limited.
PRASAD, B.K. (2003): Urban Development. A New Perspective? New Delhi, Sarup & Sons. 296 S.
UNITED NATIONS HUMAN SETTLEMENT PROGRAMME (Hrsg.) (2003): The Challenge of Slums. Global Report on Human Settlement. London and Sterling: VA Earthscan Publications Ltd. 310 S.
THE WORLD BANK GROUP (2001): Upgrading Urban Communities – A Resource Framework. In: Shelter. Cities without Slums. Vol.4 No.3 (October, 2001), S.24-36.

Internet Sources
HARPER, D. (2001): Online Etymology Dictionary. URL:
    http://www.etymonline.com/index.php?term=slum, (7th .Jan .2005)
http://www.bbr.bund.de/staedtebau/download/praesentation.pdf (11th Jan 2005)

3 Urban policy in India and Gujarat

V. Babbar
Department of Labour and Employment, State of Gujarat

The problematic status of slums and of slum living is also an issue with the local politicians at the Government of Gujarat. In 2005, the Government of Gujarat has developed a plan how to reduce urban poverty in slum areas (Fig. 3.1).

3.1
Vision statement

Cities without slums will be the vision of all the urban local bodies (ULBs) and the State. The State and the ULBs shall endeavour to ensure:
a) A planned growth of urban areas integrating the slum dwellers into the mainstream of the society by up-grading of all eligible slums, with due regard to the wider public interest.
b) The proliferation of slums will be prevented by making available serviced and semi-serviced lands, and facilitating low cost housing in the public and private sectors, especially by means of Economically Weaker Section Housing (EWSH).

3.2
Overarching principles and objectives

It is widely recognised that slums dwellers live in slums due to non availability of low cost housing at locations close to their place of employment. It is also widely recognised that slums contribute significantly to the state economy through their labour market contributions and informal production activities. Slum dwellers require, as a fundamental right, access to basic civic amenities such as safe drinking water and sanitation and social infrastructure. Accordingly, State Policy is based on the following overarching principles and objectives:

Systematic Provision for the Urban Poor. The housing requirements of the urban poor will be a major factor to be considered when preparing development plans and town planning schemes. Cities and areas having 20% slum dwellers (as a proportion of urban population) will reserve 10% of the total area of the town planning scheme for the Economically Weaker Housing Section. Cities and areas having less than 20% slum dwellers will reserve 3% of the total areas of the town planning scheme for such housing. The Urban Local Bodies will endeavour to provide water and sanitation within 2 years of such reservations.

Figure 3.1 Comprehensive approach to slum improvement.

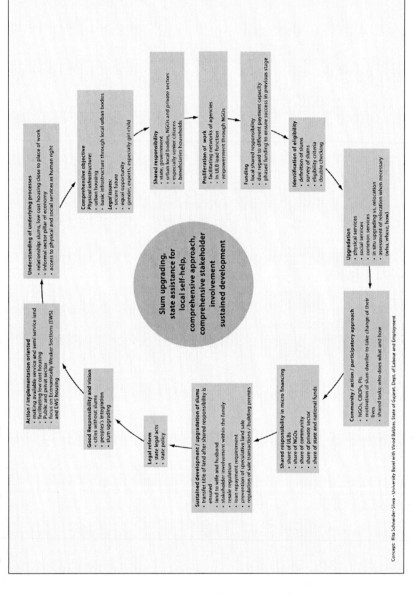

Security Tenure and equity. It is now widely recognised that security of tenure is an essential condition for slum upgrading and especially for motivating the slum dwellers to invest in housing improvements. State Policy provides for permanent tenure and related measures which would minimize misuse of this provision. The State and ULBs will ensure that all citizens get equal opportunity to share public resources without any discrimination between various sections of the society. ***Gender equity.*** Gender equity is to be ensured by allotting the land in the name of both husband and wife. Special care will be taken to meet the needs of women and children, particularly the girl child, by taking up health programmes in the initial phase as an entry point, covering all nearby schools under medical programmes. ***Promoting Partnerships.*** In order to scale-up the current pace of slum improvement, ULBs and the state government will solicit cooperation and active participation of the community. NGOs, social institutions and the private sector will promote the basic tenants of true partnership by organizing and empowering community based organizations. A list of architects and engineers (including senior citizens) would be prepared by NGOs, so that detailed layouts of infrastructure can be prepared on a voluntary basis. This ensures that the CBOs (Community Based Organisations) are competent to lay out the infrastructure themselves. The cost of infrastructure lines within the slums is estimated to be Rs.6000 per household and is expected to be borne by the beneficiaries themselves. Once this amount is collected by the CBO, the ULBs will commence the work of trunk lines as a priority. ***Networking of various agencies.*** The ULBs and the State Government will facilitate networking among all its agencies working for the urban poor so as to bring in synergy towards achievement of goals. Urban local bodies will take the lead role, and work in collaboration with the communities. In absence of NGOs and/or partners, the ULB will, within their means, set up CBOs and empower them. ***Financing mechanisms for provision of services.*** Slum dwellers are expected to pay Rs.6000 towards the cost of physical and social infrastructure. The ULBs are expected to pay for the trunk infrastructure lines (estimated cost is 3000 Rs.) and for the toilet (4500 Rs.). If the slum dwellers are unable to pay 6000 Rs., the alternative is that slum dwellers pay 3000 Rs., ULBs pay 3000 Rs. and toilets are left to be constructed by the household. The other infrastructures such as internal roads or street lighting will be provided in Phase 2, i.e. after water and sanitation was made available and the household has become liable for water and sanitation charges.

Table 3.1 The sequencing and phasing of slum improvements

Phase.	Event/ Process	Agency	Duration (days)
1	Identification of slums where households are willing to pay Rs.6000	NGOs	30
2	Organisation of preventive health programmes in identified slums, explaining the schemes, establishing the CBO	ULBs + NGOs	30
3	Training of CBOs for 3 days (incl. visit to sccessful slum projects	ULBs + NGOs	15
4	Survey by architects, detailed layouting	Architect	30
5	Collection of Rs.6000 from households, opening bank account as joint account of 2 CBO members	CBO +NGOs	30
6	Preparation of estimates of internal lines	ULBs + NGOs	30
7	Awarding work to contractor by CBOs from list of eligible contractors (incl. negotiation)	ULBs + NGOs	30
8.	Providing truck infrastructure line	ULBs	180
9	Making the household liable for water/ sanitation charges	ULBs	30
10	Providing for land, including legal title	ULBs	30
11	Covering slums with roads / street lights	ULBs	180

CBO: community based organization, ULB: urban local bodies

3.3
Definition of "slum" in Gujarat, India

A 'slum' shall mean a high-density settlement, having a cluster of a minimum 50 dwelling units in Class 1 cities or a minimum of 25 dwelling units for towns with a population of below 100 000, and where at least 50% dwelling units have semi-permanent structures of less than 25 sq. mts. area, principally made of materials such as mud, bricks, wooden planks, polyethylene sheets, tin sheets, or a combination of such materials, and where such settlements are lacking in basic infrastructure and amenities such as water supply, sanitation, toilets, regular pathways etc., and when they are mainly inhabited by low income group residents not having a legal title of the land.

A residential area having more than 50% of permanent, (*pucca*) structures will not be considered a slum. ***Registration of slums.*** All slums existing prior to December, 2000 will be surveyed and comprehensively listed by the respective urban local boards and ward-wise, slum-wise details of the dwelling units, amenities available, socio-economic conditions of the inhabitants, tenural status and eligibility of getting basic services as per this policy will be compiled by all urban local boards.

All people residing in the listed slums will be registered with the urban local boards and suitable ID cards will be issued to all households in listed slums. It will have details of address, household size, family members etc. The cost of preparing identity cards may be recovered by the urban local boards from such enlisted persons if so desired. *Eligibility for upgradation*. All slums other than those situated on

- public streets
- the bank of rivers-lakes
- lands situated in known disaster-prone areas or on the locations which are hazardous in nature
- environmentally sensitive areas, and
- on plots critically required by the urban local boards for providing essential services, will be eligible to be covered. The urban local boards may prepare a list of such eligible slums and publish the same suitably.

Slums situated on public streets and at other locations mentioned above, will be re-located in other slums, preferably within 2 km from the original location. If possible, 3 choices would be given to such slum dwellers.

The urban local bodies will re-examine reservation and consider varying the scheme, especially if slums are more than 10 years old. If land is required for public purpose, then alternative sites owned by the ULCs will be examined, and if no alternative site is available, then the minimum area required for the public purpose will be divided and the houses affected would be re-located into the area available for slum upgradation.

The Municipal Commissioner / Chief Officer will consider such cases within 3 months and report to the State Government. *Upgradation of slums.* 'Upgradation' would mean provision of a package of physical services at the household level, comprising water supply, sewerage, disposal of solid waste matter and toilets. Street-lighting, street-paving, storm water drainage are not considered as essential for upgrading of slums and are to be taken up later. Upgradation would also include provision of social services such as health, education, income generation activities, etc and facilitating electric connections. Where individual services are not possible, common services will be provided.

At places where individual toilets cannot be provided, pay & use community toilet facilities will be provided especially by repairing community toilets constructed earlier. National schemes such as Nirmal Bharat Abhiyan sanitation scheme of maintenance of community toilet blocks by community based groups and family passes for one or two households at Rs 20 per month per family for daily use of such toilets, will be considered. Such charges will be subject to change from time to time to meet the costs of services rendered. In situ upgradation will be preferred to relocation. All efforts will be made by ULBs to upgrade the slums at the same sites. *Layout Planning.* Where in situ-upgradation projects are taken up, proper layout planning including plot realignment and equalization of land may be undertaken as necessary in consultation with local residents. All relocation processes will be carried out in consultation with the affected slum dwellers, keeping in mind the distance from workplace and other livelihood facilities after the State Governments considers such re-location as unavoidable. Re-location will be carried out wherever necessary, when in situ upgradation is not possible when houses need to be removed from their present locations because of widening of streets or making provision for community hall and community open space. Relocation may also be considered in rare situations where slums are situated on very expensive plots that could be commercially developed to raise city finances. In such cases, the slum dwellers will be relocated to the interior areas so that the frontage is available for commercial development. In cases where slums are ineligible for upgradation at the existing location, the urban local boards may consider relocating the slum dwellers from the existing ineligible sites in consultation with slum dwellers. Where slum dwellers are to be re-located, they will be given shifting assistance of 1000 Rs. and alternate site within 2 km from their original site.

3.4
Motivation of community by mobilizing support of NGOs and CBOs

NGOs, Community based organizations (CBOs) and People Institutions (PIs) will be mobilized and supported by the urban local bodies (ULBs) to motivate slum dwellers to participate in the slum upgradation process. Women's groups will be encouraged to actively participate in the process. NGOs not having sufficient experience and expertise to work in the informal sector will be trained so as to involve as many urban NGOs as possible in the partnership.

Role of NGOs/PIs

- NGOs/PIs would be encouraged and supported to play a key role in providing socio-economic inputs as follows: form Neighbourhood Committees
- motivate the community to participate in the project and take interest in all developmental works in the slums
- capacity building programs for the committee of slum dwellers to manage the funds and carry out community development activities
- promote income generation activities within a community to improve their financial conditions through micro enterprise creation and the formation of savings groups.
- promote linkages with micro-finance institutions for shelter upgradation and income generating activities
- create and manage at the slum level a corpus of funds by raising monthly or annual contribution from the slum dwellers
- facilitate slum dwellers' access to social services such as primary health care, primary education etc.

Urban policy in India and Gujarat

- assist in the formulation of policies, support the same and bring out policy issues
- carry out micro-level research and documentation on aspects of slum improvement
- assist in the implementation of slum policy and improvise implementation strategies from time to time
- assist the urban local bodies in the surveying work and issuing identity cards
- assist the urban local bodies in consultation processes for relocation.

3.5
Financing mechanisms

The financing mechanisms will be participatory in nature. Urban local bodies shall endeavour to create partnerships between communities, NGOs, social and charitable institutions, business houses and ULBs (urban local bodies) to meet the costs of the projects. This will be in addition to raising finances through levies and other charges for slum improvement. *Share of ULBs.* The municipal corporations and municipalities will meet their share of cost for slum upgradation within their means. For this purpose, each urban local board shall set apart a minimum of 10% of the revenues and capital budget available for developmental work, for slum upgradation activities after meeting the establishment cost and other fixed costs. The Bombay Provinicial Municipal Corporation Act of 1949 (BPMC Act) will be suitably amended. The Act will also be amended to enable local bodies to levy access for slum improvement for a period of 5 years and utilize the amount to meet the share of ULBs for this purpose. These funds shall be utilized to meet partly the cost of provision of internal infrastructure in slums and creating linkages with city infrastructure. *Share of the community*. The slum dwellers will share the cost of internal infrastructure to the extent of 100% of the cost of the basic infrastructure per dwelling unit (i.e. 6000 Rs. per dwelling unit as per 2003 market rates). *Micro-Finance*. Micro -finance facilities will be made available through NGO-organized financial institutions. *Share of NGOs*. NGOs will be motivated to share a part of the cost to perform their role and for providing social services in the slums. *Share of Private Sector.* Private sector and social institutions will also be encouraged to join as a partner and share a minimum of 2000 Rs. per dwelling unit or a higher amount up to one-third cost of internal infrastructure as may be determined from time to time by concerned ULBs.

Sharing of other sources. The finances available with the Members of Parliament, Members of Local Authorities and municipal councillors for providing infrastructure facilities in their constituencies will be dovetailed with this project and they could be made partners. They could be encouraged to contribute a fixed amount of 1000 Rs. per dwelling unit.

3.6
Availing of national and state funds

Urban local bodies (ULBs) will avail of the funds from the National Slum Development program of Government of India. All central government and state government schemes and grants for the urban poor will be channelized through ULBs to get optimum advantage of the resources available. The loan-cum-subsidy central sector scheme, the Valmiki Ambedkar Awas Yojana (VAMBAY) for construction of dwelling units, having a provision for slum upgradation, will be dovetailed with state level finance mechanisms. The State Government may make an endeavour to provide some matching grants to ULBs to support early completion of slum upgradation activities in the urban areas in the state.

3.7
Operation and maintenance

The ULB will carry out regular O&M of services laid within the slums as done in other parts of the city or facilitate provision of operation and maintenance through private sector and/or NGOs.

3.8
Shelter improvement

Shelter improvement shall be the responsibility of individual settlers. The urban local body may facilitate through NGOs, economic empowerment through formation of local self-help groups (SHGs), particularly women's groups, and train them for savings and thrift mechanisms so as to make such SHGs cognizable by micro-finance institutions for extending further financial support. The ULBs may also promote NGOs to establish material banks to facilitate shelter upgradation.

3.9
Land use classification

Land use for in situ upgradation projects will be designated as high density mixed use. This will be subject to the condition that any commercial/trading ventures existing on such lands shall only be those that are non-polluting, environment friendly and which provide services and employment opportunities to local slum dwellers.

3.10
Special purpose vehicle (SPV) and its role

If the CBO (Community Based Organisation) agree, a SPV (special purpose vehicle) may be created as a nodal agency for networking with all concerned departments and for implementing the slum upgradation process in the cities with NGOs and CBOs and community participation.

The SPV may comprise all stakeholders and have powers to implement programs and projects within the broad policy framework of the state and ULBs. The state government will encourage this mechanism for expeditious implementation of slum upgradation projects.

3.11
Residents' association

It will be a pre-requisite for the residents to form an association or a cooperative housing society that must be recognized by the concerned urban local body. This association or society will normally consist of all resident families in that area where at least 33% families will be represented by women and it will have at least 33% women in their governing council. Its office bearers will have the authority to interact with the ULBs and other governmental agencies for the well being of the slum dwellers.

3.12
Transfer of titles to slum dwellers

Private land. As the slum dwellers are to be given title of land which they occupy they will have to collectively buy the private land under their occupation. Cases where there is adverse possession of 12 years or more, will be taken up in the initial phase. In other cases, the ULBs shall endeavour to facilitate transfer of the land through negotiated settlement with the owner at a price not exceeding 33% of the market value as may be ascertained from the stamp duty records. The representatives of all the stakeholders will be invited to participate in the negotiations to promote transparency. Such a transfer will be in favour of a registered association or housing cooperative society of the slum dwellers. Slum dwellers will be required to pay the amount up front by taking loans from micro finance institutions, if need be. The contribution of each dwelling units will be worked out after adding the proportionate cost of open land, streets, etc., to each square meter of land occupied by the slum dwellers.

- The association or cooperative society of slum dwellers may allot sub plots in the joint name of the wife first and then the husband. If such an arrangement is not possible, the same may be done in the joint name of the main earning member and a female member of the family.

- The sub-plot allotment will be for the portion of the land occupied.

In such cases, the slum dwellers will have a right to sell their dwelling unit along with land to any other low-income group person anytime with prior approval of the association or cooperative society. It will be open for the slum dwellers to raise finance from banks and other financial institutions. ***Government***. If the eligible slum dwellers desire to have ownership rights on government land they occupy, such rights will be given to slum dwellers after payment of charges as may be determined by the State Government. If the slum dwellers desire to have title of municipal land which they occupy they will have to collectively buy such land under their occupation. In such cases, the ULBs shall endeavour to facilitate transfer of municipal land through negotiated settlement with the slum dwellers at a price not exceeding 33% of the market value as may be ascertained from the stamp duty records. The representatives of all the stakeholders will be invited to participate in the negotiations to promote transparency. Such a transfer will be in favour of a registered association or housing cooperative society of the slum dwellers. Slum dwellers will be required to pay the amount up front by taking loans from micro finance institutions, if need be. The contribution of each dwelling units will be worked out after adding the proportionate cost of open land, streets, etc., to each square meter of land occupied by the slum dwellers. The sub-plot allotment will be for the portion of the land occupied and will be made after charging the actual cost per square meter of land occupied by the slum dweller and the proportionate cost of open lands. The slum dwellers who have paid the cost of land as above shall have a right to sell their dwelling unit with land to any other low-income group person anytime with prior approval of the association or society and four neighbours living in the vicinity. ***Ban on sale of land to higher income groups***. The society or association will have no right to sell entire land or parts thereof for non-residential purposes or even for residential purposes to anyone who does not fall into low-income groups as categorized under the EWS scheme (Economically Weaker Section), without the prior permission of the ULB. This is to ensure that the slum dwellers are not lured by private estate developers to sell away their lands situated on prime locations at a higher price. ***Other forms of tenure***. Other forms of tenure may also be considered, if so desired by the community. This may include: group tenure, collective tenure, co-operative tenure etc. ***Transfer Fees***. The association or cooperative society of slum dwellers will consider levying a transfer fee on all sales proposed to be made by slum dwellers in favour of other eligible buyers, and utilize this amount only for maintenance of internal infrastructure services and for the provision of social infrastructure for slum dwellers. Accounts of such income and expenditure shall be maintained by the association/society in the proforma that may be prescribed by the state government. ***Regularization of sales transactions invade without a valid sale deed***. The state government will make suitable amendments by law to the effect that the documents made on plain paper or stamp paper of any low denomination for the sale of land on which eligible slums are situated, or for the sale of dwelling units with or without land situated in the eligible slums, shall be treated as valid. The short fall in stamp duty payable for such transactions shall be either waived or an amount as may be prescribed by the state government shall be levied for regularising such transactions from time to time, and that any further sale of such property in favour of slum dwellers will be made on a stamp paper of a lower value as may be prescribed by the government.

3.13
Relaxation in rules for building permission

Once a slum is upgraded or the title of the land is transferred under this policy in favour of the slum dwellers' association or cooperative housing society, it will be permissible for the slum dwellers to upgrade their built environment and/or shelter by following the guidelines that may be prescribed from time to time by the state government without insisting on obtaining the permission for construction of building under the Municipal Act or Town Planning Act.

Slum dwellers shall have to ensure structural safety and stability of the facilities and they shall have to get a certificate from registered structural engineers or qualified civil engineers.

They will not be allowed to raise the height of the building beyond one floor above the ground floor, and the height of the building shall not exceed 22 feet. In case the building height exceeds 22 feet, prior building permission would be required from the Municipal Authority.

3.14
Creating of housing stock for urban poor

Migration of people from rural to urban areas is not likely to stop and the estimated housing gap in Gujarat by 2010 is expected to be 160 000 units. To bridge this gap, the government will promote the construction of housing stock by the private sector for the Economically Weaker Sections.

To realize Gujarat's Social Sector vision for urban housing, mechanisms will be worked out to expedite preparation and implementation of town planning schemes. The state government will allot all the lands that have been rendered surplus under the Urban Land Ceiling Act for housing the slum dwellers preferably.

In the town planning schemes, maximum permissible land will be reserved for weaker sections of the society and shall be made available to slum dwellers preferably. Delivery mechanisms to provide for the poor and access to such land acquired will be evolved. Such land will be made available at a concessional rate to housing cooperatives or associations of urban poor. Such land, as far as practical, would be identified at locations where provision of infrastructure could be made easily. *De-Notification*. Once basic amenities and services are provided in a slum pocket, it shall be de-notified.

3.15
Legal reforms

To achieve the goals of this policy, the state will endeavour to bring about amendments to the various acts, rules and regulations that shall include, among others, the following:
a. Gujarat Slum Act, 1973
b. Bombay Land Revenue Code, 1879
c. Bombay Provincial Municipal Corporation Act, 1949
d. Bombay Stamp Act, 1958
e. The Gujarat Town Planning and Urban Development Act, 1976
f. Government policies in form of various resolutions.

Low-cost housing policy. For optimising the benefits of this policy, the state government will endeavour to frame policies for low-cost housing policy for the poor.

4 Differences in slums and poverty structures

R. Schneider-Sliwa
University of Basel

4.1
The slum communities under study

This chapter provides an overview of the general situation in the four slum communities under study in the City of Bhuj (Map 4.1 at the end of this chapter). Bhuj is the capital city of the Kutch region in Western Gujarat and is close to the Pakistani border. To the North and West, Bhuj is surrounded by the Rann of Kutch, which is a salty desert in the dry season but is flooded by the sea during monsoon, which enables salt harvesting. The city is situated among some small hills, the most prominent of them being Bhujia Hill in the Eastern part of the city. Another landmark is the Hamirsar-Tank in the West, a lake with an island, which hardly contains any more water.

The four slum communities under study are shown in Map 4.2. These are the communities of Bhimraonagar, Jayprakashnagar, Shantinagar and Mustuffanagar (Maps 4.3 through 4.8). These were chosen because of their similarities, being illegal settlements, rather poor, of lower social status within the Indian society (in Western countries commonly known as the "untouchables"), but offering a large spectrum of social stratification within and between the communities. In order to analyze these communities, satellite based GIS-maps were produced (for example Maps 4.5, 4.8) and verified on the ground. Although the IKONOS satellite image that served as base has a resolution of 60 cm, certain conditions (shadows, trees, distinction between storage places and living quarters) made ground verification necessary. The resulting, corrected GIS-base maps were a necessary element, serving almost like a cadastral survey of houses and households. Based on this a social science survey could be taken of households and data could be analyzed both statistically and in terms of their spatial distributions and patterns within and among communities. The following sections outline some of the differences in socioeconomic conditions between communities.

4.2
Religious and caste affiliation

The slum communities selected in the City of Bhuj, Gujarat, India (see Map 4.1) consisted of a total of 165 households in Bhimraonagar, 71 in Jayprakashnagar, 209 in Mustuffanagar, and 212 in Shantinagar. The predominantly Muslim community of Mustuffanagar and the mixed community of Shantinagar were the largest communities, with over two thirds of the households surveyed. In general, Hindu families (43.7%) and Muslim families (55.9%) dominated the sample; other religious groups were rather insignificant (Tabs. 4.1 and 4.2).

Table 4.1 Religion of family head, by slum.

Slum \ Religion	Bhimraonagar in % (n=130)	Jayprakashnagar in % (n=53)	Mustuffanagar in % (n=158)	Shantinagar in % (n=154)	Total in % (n=495)
Hindu	75.4	88.7	10.1	36.4	43.8
Muslim	24.6	11.3	89.9	63.6	56.2
Total	100.0	100.0	100.0	100.0	100.0

SOURCE: UNIVERSITY OF BASEL, DEPT. OF GEOGRAPHY AND ALL INDIA DISASTER MITIGATION INSTITUTE, AHMEDABAD, INDIA 2005. SOCIAL SCIENCE SURVEY IN SELECTED SLUM COMMUNITIES IN THE CITY OF BHUJ, GUJARAT, INDIA.

Table 4.2 Religion, by slum.

Slum \ Religion	Bhimraonagar in % (n=626)	Jayprakashnagar in % (n=237)	Mustuffanagar in % (n=926)	Shantinagar in % (n=839)	Total in % (n=2628)
Hindu	76.8	86.5	10.2	29.6	39.1
Muslim	23.2	13.5	89.8	70.4	60.9
Total	100.0	100.0	100.0	100.0	100.0

SOURCE: UNIVERSITY OF BASEL, DEPT. OF GEOGRAPHY AND ALL INDIA DISASTER MITIGATION INSTITUTE, AHMEDABAD, INDIA 2005. SOCIAL SCIENCE SURVEY IN SELECTED SLUM COMMUNITIES IN THE CITY OF BHUJ, GUJARAT, INDIA.

All four communities belonged to the lower castes. The four castes are the Scheduled Tribe Castes (STC) which have been the target of special Indian development policy, as are the Scheduled Castes (SC) and the so called Other Backward Classes (OBC) in the Muslin communities that do not actually know the caste system by their Islamic faith but are socially stratified as part of their Indian culture (Tabs 4.3 and 4.4).

Table 4.3 Caste of family head, by slum.

Slum Caste	Bhimraonagar in % (n=130)	Jayprakashnagar in % (n=53)	Mustuffanagar in % (n=158)	Shantinagar in % (n=155)	Total in % (n=496)
SC	42.3	11.3	8.2	7.7	17.3
ST	27.7	15.1	1.9	6.5	11.5
OBC	3.1	5.7	40.5	70.3	36.3
General	26.9	67.9	49.4	15.5	34.9
Total	100.0	100.0	100.0	100.0	100.0

SOURCE: UNIVERSITY OF BASEL, DEPT. OF GEOGRAPHY AND ALL INDIA DISASTER MITIGATION INSTITUTE, AHMEDABAD, INDIA 2005. SOCIAL SCIENCE SURVEY IN SELECTED SLUM COMMUNITIES IN THE CITY OF BHUJ, GUJARAT, INDIA.

Table 4.4 Caste, by slum

Slum Caste	Bhimraonagar in % (n=626)	Jayprakashnagar in % (n=237)	Mustuffanagar in % (n=923)	Shantinagar in % (n=845)	Total in % (n=2631)
SC	41.7	11.8	7.7	7.9	16.2
ST	28.6	11.4	1.4	6.2	10.3
OBC	4.3	6.3	41.2	72.2	39.2
General	25.4	70.5	49.7	13.7	34.2
Total	100.0	100.0	100.0	100.0	100.0

SOURCE: UNIVERSITY OF BASEL, DEPT. OF GEOGRAPHY AND ALL INDIA DISASTER MITIGATION INSTITUTE, AHMEDABAD, INDIA 2005. SOCIAL SCIENCE SURVEY IN SELECTED SLUM COMMUNITIES IN THE CITY OF BHUJ, GUJARAT, INDIA.

The General Castes refer to *all other lower caste groups* within the highly stratified Indian cultural system. In terms of the social science survey it is of note that the households surveyed rank very low in the cultural system and are target groups of government schemes. However, a considerable internal differentiation is noticeable.

Number of children. In terms of household structure, 50% of the households have between 3 and 6 family members, only 12% are small one to two person households. About 14% have more than 7 household members. A total of 42.8% of the households have children and youth up to age 17 to take care of (Tab. 4.5), with Jayprakashnagar having a total of 30.9% and Shantinagar 46.5% of their respective population in those age brackets.

Table 4.5 Age, by slum

Age \ Slum	Bhimraonagar in % (n=631)	Jayprakashnagar in % (n=236)	Mustuffanagar in % (n=925)	Shantinagar in % (n=844)	Total in % (n=2636)
0-1	2.9	0.4	2.5	3.9	2.8
2-7	14.1	10.6	16.4	18.0	15.9
8-17	26.0	19.9	23.5	24.6	24.1
18-25	17.9	19.1	14.2	17.3	16.5
26-35	14.1	15.3	19.5	13.7	16.0
36-50	16.2	23.3	13.3	14.0	15.1
51+	8.9	11.4	10.7	8.4	9.6
Total	100.0	100.0	100.0	100.0	100.0

SOURCE: UNIVERSITY OF BASEL, DEPT. OF GEOGRAPHY AND ALL INDIA DISASTER MITIGATION INSTITUTE, AHMEDABAD, INDIA 2005. SOCIAL SCIENCE SURVEY IN SELECTED SLUM COMMUNITIES IN THE CITY OF BHUJ, GUJARAT, INDIA.

Dependent old people. Generally, most families have at least one dependent old person to take care of, the percentage who do not is rather small (5.7%, table not shown). Close to 48% have 1-3 elderly and 31% have 4-5 old persons in the household. One cannot, however, conclude that the elderly in the household are necessarily dependent financially, as many may rather support the family income by their pension (particularly former government employees), or generate additional income from craft work.

Migrant status. The majority of the slum dwellers are local in the sense that they are from Gujarat and do not or have not migrated. Less than 10% travel for certain occasions such as festivals or family meetings. Past migration is not a significant issue that would account for living. There is, however, a small poverty group of tribals in Shantinagar, for which migratory status is a reason for living conditions that differ considerably from the average of that slum.

4.3
Livelihood security, incomes and poverty

In terms of occupations, there are considerable differences that may account for the visible different degrees of development or poverty: Whereas in Bhimraonagar, the largest share of employment (14.8%) is in construction (Tab. 4.6, 4.7), it is vendors and service sector employment in Jayprakashnagar (13.8%, 14.5%), textiles and construction in Mustuffanagar (23.1%, 11.9%). With 20.3% casual laborers and only 10.5% in textile industry as largest shares of employment, Shantinagar has the highest proportion of working age population with unstable earnings.

Table 4.6 Occupation, by slum.

Slum / Occupation	Bhimraonagar in % (n=352)	Jayprakashnagar in % (n=152)	Mustuffanagar in % (n=523)	Shantinagar in % (n=448)	Total in % (n=1475)
textile/ industry	8.2	2.0	23.1	5.1	11.9
government	0.3	3.9	1.1	0.4	1.0
casual labour	9.4	0.0	2.3	20.3	9.2
construction	14.8	7.2	11.9	10.5	11.7
Farming	0.9	1.3	1.0	2.7	1.5
automotive related job	5.4	3.9	4.8	5.6	5.1
vendor/ shop	7.1	13.8	4.4	3.3	5.7
Crafts	6.8	2.0	4.8	2.7	4.3
service sector	8.8	14.5	9.0	4.9	8.3
retiree/ housewife/ unemployed	38.4	50.7	37.5	44.4	41.2
unclear/ indian	0.0	0.7	0.2	0.0	0.1
Total	100.0	100.0	100.0	100.0	100.0

SOURCE: UNIVERSITY OF BASEL, DEPT. OF GEOGRAPHY AND ALL INDIA DISASTER MITIGATION INSTITUTE, AHMEDABAD, INDIA 2005. SOCIAL SCIENCE SURVEY IN SELECTED SLUM COMMUNITIES IN THE CITY OF BHUJ, GUJARAT, INDIA.

Table 4.7 Occupation of family head, by slum.

Slum / Occupation	Bhimraonagar in % (n=662)	Jayprakashnagar in % (n=254)	Mustuffanagar in % (n=979)	Shantinagar in % (n=902)	Total in % (n=2797)
textile/ industry	4.4	1.2	12.4	2.5	6.3
government	0.2	2.4	0.6	0.2	0.5
casual labour	4.8	0.0	1.2	10.1	4.8
construction	8.0	4.3	6.3	5.2	6.2
Farming	0.5	0.8	0.5	1.3	0.8
automot. related job	2.9	2.4	2.6	2.8	2.7
vendor/ shop	3.8	8.3	2.3	1.7	3.0
Crafts	3.6	1.2	2.6	1.3	2.3
service sector	4.2	8.7	4.8	2.5	4.3
Retiree	2.3	2.8	2.7	1.6	2.2
Housewife	17.5	25.2	16.4	18.1	18.0
unemployed	0.5	2.4	0.9	2.4	1.4
unclear/ indian	0.0	0.4	0.1	0.0	0.1
no answer	47.4	40.2	46.6	50.2	47.4
Total	100.0	100.0	100.0	100.0	100.0

SOURCE: UNIVERSITY OF BASEL, DEPT. OF GEOGRAPHY AND ALL INDIA DISASTER MITIGATION INSTITUTE, AHMEDABAD, INDIA 2005. SOCIAL SCIENCE SURVEY IN SELECTED SLUM COMMUNITIES IN THE CITY OF BHUJ, GUJARAT, INDIA.

Poverty is wide spread. Household income as measured by average daily wages of all household members (n=2321, Tab. 4.8) is rather low.

Table 4.8 Daily wages, by slum.

Slum Wage	Bhimraonagar in % (n=585)	Jayprakashnagar in % (n=234)	Mustuffanagar in % (n=677)	Shantinagar in % (n=825)	Total in % (n=2321)
0-10 Rs.	65.8	68.4	57.5	71.5	65.7
11-20 Rs.	1.9	1.3	6.1	1.9	3.1
21-30 Rs.	3.2	1.3	2.4	1.5	2.2
31-40 Rs.	1.5	2.1	3.1	2.2	2.3
41-50 Rs.	6.5	2.1	6.5	6.8	6.2
51-70 Rs.	7.2	9.4	5.3	6.5	6.6
71-100 Rs.	11.3	9.0	11.7	7.8	9.9
>100 Rs.	2.6	6.4	7.5	1.8	4.1
Total	100.0	100.0	100.0	100.0	100.0

SOURCE: UNIVERSITY OF BASEL, DEPT. OF GEOGRAPHY AND ALL INDIA DISASTER MITIGATION INSTITUTE, AHMEDABAD, INDIA 2005. SOCIAL SCIENCE SURVEY IN SELECTED SLUM COMMUNITIES IN THE CITY OF BHUJ, GUJARAT, INDIA.

It becomes evident that a majority in Bhimraonagar is having rather low daily wages (65.8% with less than 10 Rs. per day) and that only construction generates incomes of about 70-100 Rs. per day. In Jayprakashnagar, too, the majority has rather low wages, but over 25% make more than 50 Rs. per day; apparently from vending and service sector jobs. Mustuffanagar has the lowest proportion of low wage earners, taking the daily average wages of individual household members. It appears then, that employment in textile industries and construction account for the rather favorable income situation, as compared to other communities. Last, the poor conditions of Shantinagar stand out quite well when considering average daily wages. Here, the highest proportion of lowest income earners is evident, with 71.5% of the wage earners making only up to 10 Rs. per day, mostly in casual labor.

It should be noted how education relates to occupation and incomes (Tab. 4.9). Whereas Jayprakashnagar has around 50% of the households with educational levels grades 7-12, Bhimraonagar has 47% with grades 4-9 and Mustuffanagar 50% with grades 4-9, Shantinagar has only 27% with grades 1-6 and 57% illiterates. Among the medium level of schooling of grades 4-9, Mustuffanagar shows the highest percentage of those with continued or continuing education (Tab. 4.10), indicating that potentials for further development are actively sought after. This may also be indicated by the fact that Mustuffanagar has a higher proportion of households with election cards than Bhimraonagar or Shantinagar (Tab. 4.11). There, the percentage of election card holders is lowest, possibly due to poor education or illiterate status. Although there are different degrees in poverty between the slum communities, still, all are rather poor.

Table 4.9 Education, by slum

Slum / Education	Bhimraonagar in % (n=541)	Jayprakashnagar in % (n=219)	Mustuffanagar in % (n=798)	Shantinagar in % (n=736)	Total in % (n=2294)
Std. 1-3	15.2	10.0	15.4	13.5	14.2
Std. 4-6	22.4	16.9	23.9	13.7	19.6
Std 7-9	24.6	35.6	25.9	12.5	22.2
Std. 10-12	7.2	13.7	11.0	2.9	7.8
completed diploma	0.2	0.5	0.1	0.0	0.1
completed graduation	1.1	3.7	1.4	0.4	1.2
illiterate	29.4	19.6	22.2	57.1	34.8
Total	100.0	100.0	100.0	100.0	100.0

SOURCE: UNIVERSITY OF BASEL, DEPT. OF GEOGRAPHY AND ALL INDIA DISASTER MITIGATION INSTITUTE, AHMEDABAD, INDIA 2005. SOCIAL SCIENCE SURVEY IN SELECTED SLUM COMMUNITIES IN THE CITY OF BHUJ, GUJARAT, INDIA.

Table 4.10 Study continue, by slum.

Slum / Study continue	Bhimraonagar in % (n=602)	Jayprakashnagar in % (n=217)	Mustuffanagar in % (n=817)	Shantinagar in % (n=759)	Total in % (n=2395)
yes	24.8	22.1	29.6	16.9	23.7
no	75.2	77.9	70.4	83.1	76.3
Total	100.0	100.0	100.0	100.0	100.0

SOURCE: UNIVERSITY OF BASEL, DEPT. OF GEOGRAPHY AND ALL INDIA DISASTER MITIGATION INSTITUTE, AHMEDABAD, INDIA 2005. SOCIAL SCIENCE SURVEY IN SELECTED SLUM COMMUNITIES IN THE CITY OF BHUJ, GUJARAT, INDIA.

Table 4.11 Election card, by slum.

Slum / Election card	Bhimraonagar in % (n=586)	Jayprakashnagar in % (n=216)	Mustuffanagar in % (n=789)	Shantinagar in % (n=754)	Total in % (n=2345)
yes	43.7	56.0	49.6	38.9	45.2
no	56.3	44.0	50.4	61.1	54.8
Total	100.0	100.0	100.0	100.0	100.0

SOURCE: UNIVERSITY OF BASEL, DEPT. OF GEOGRAPHY AND ALL INDIA DISASTER MITIGATION INSTITUTE, AHMEDABAD, INDIA 2005. SOCIAL SCIENCE SURVEY IN SELECTED SLUM COMMUNITIES IN THE CITY OF BHUJ, GUJARAT, INDIA.

It is, therefore, of no surprise that 80.4% of the households do not report any savings at all (Tab. 5.11) and that only 8% have up to 100 Rs. in savings, 3.2% having 125 – 200 Rs., 5.2% 250 – 500 Rs. and only 3% having in excess of 700 Rs. saved. It is of note that although 95% of the households have medical expenses fewer than 500 Rs. Equally high amounts have little or no savings at all. This is not to suggest that medical expenses may prevent savings but given that poor people do set priorities for medical expenses and that money is tight to begin with there is not enough let for significant savings. It is remarkable, however, that close to 60% have not debts either, almost 41% had their livelihood affected and therefore do have debts of varying degrees.

4.4
Ownership issues and shelter information

95.6% a self-owned house, however, 60.4% do not have an ownership document of the house (Tab. 7.1). A property card is held by 14.4% and an ownership document on 10, 20, or 50 Rupees stamp paper by another 20%. Concerning a tax bill, half of the households surveyed reported to have one (Tab. 7.9), almost half had none.

Minor and major earthquake damages were suffered by 33.8% and 21.9%, respectively, with 35.1% reporting that their houses had been completely destroyed (Tab. 6.6). At the time of the survey, however, 82.8% lived in the same house as before the disaster (Tab. 6.7). This can be understood as living in a repaired, reconstructed or completely new house on the same site. Whereas 67.8% of the houses were regarded as safe, 33.6% still were reported to have minor damages (Tab. 6.7). It is noteworthy that whereas more than 84% did report damages, 48% did not get help at all from any side, 23% could rely on help from the government and 9% from NGOs, 5.2% from friends and relatives.

It is clear, that local forces, own initiative to apply for and seek help from NGOs, relatives or friends were decisive in half of the cases where help was received. That help was not sufficient or that not sufficient amounts of people had asked for help is evidenced by the fact that over 51% stated that at the time of the survey, a high proportion of the interviewed households indicated that their earthquake precaution had not been sufficient (Tab. 6.15). That improvements are major issues is shown by the fact that cost estimations for shelter improvements ranking from 6000 Rs to 50 000 Rs are fairly evenly spread. Moreover 90.2% could not or had not taken special measures to make their homes earthquake proof. Quite striking is the fact that even with land, cash, services and built up only 23.3% would want to relocate. Almost two thirds would not. Of those who would want to relocate about 70% would only relocate if other families, presumably of their present surroundings, would relocate. Even then, the maximum distance people are willing to relocate is just barley outside their own communities. This attests to the strength of local community ties, also it suggests that governmental programs may not promote relocation schemes so much but rather the strengthening and support of local communities, local initiatives in reconstructing and stabilizing their communities.

4.5
Access to health

Access to governmental health services seems to be good as 68.8% report going to the government hospital for health check ups, medicines at reasonable rates and vaccinations see Chap. 9, (Tab. 9.6). Private hospitals and private practitioners are being used by around 30%. Regarding the types of vaccinations most persons have the standard (B.C.G., Polio, Triple MMR - mumps, measles, rubella). Health problems did not figure prominently in the self reporting. If ill, malaria (3.3%), tuberculosis (4.9%), diabetes, blood pressure (10.7%), asthma (5.7%) and other diseases (21.3%) were mentioned (Tab. 9.14).

Generally, access to government health facilities and health problems resulting from lack of access do not seem to be major problems (Tab. 9.1 to 9.5), as can be concluded from the fact that 80.8% reported no deaths, including child deaths, in their families within in the past year and that medical expenses were rather low and affordable. This also attests to the general care provided for by the government.

4.6
Assistance/relief received

Whereas 48.1% had reported not to have received any help for reconstructing the house, 67.3% reported to have received no relief (of any type).With respect to AIDMI, other NGO and family assistance as well as government relief the responses differ quite significantly from those given with respect to help received for reconstructing the house. Reasons for these responses vary. Whether or not these figures were deliberately understated (no help received) in order to gain an advantage, or overstated to please the interviewers (from AIDMI) or the government (that might read the report) cannot be stated with certainty. Clearly, government help figured prominently in the statistic as the government assisted almost everyone affected. To the extent that people reported not to have received any assistance (not even from the government), one can conclude that they had not been affected by the earthquake either. Next to the government, NGOs were seen as the most helpful, which attests to the complementary role of NGOs in assisting with the reconstruction of livelihood and shelter. In terms of the type of relief material assistance to promote self help was the most important relief after cash assistance (by the government). It is of no surprise that loan assistance is low given that incomes and repayment capacity are low as well. It is of note, however, that relief in the form of knowledge, information, training was not received by almost 99%, or not recognized as such. This appears clearly as a deficit for the agencies interested in providing knowledge and for the households that did not realize that information was provided. For those who did get cash assistance, the amount was around 2000 Rs. which was a start up but not sufficient capital when considering the actual damage.

4.7
Own contributions, willingness to pay for services

Water was regarded as a critical issue for slum dwellers, therefore, acceptance was high to pay for safe drinking water. 21% would pay up to 100 Rs, over 1/3 (36.6%) would pay up to 200 Rs, 4.6% wanted to pay between 250 and 500 Rs. Given the small shares of people who would pay up to 16000 Rs leads one to the conclusion that these amounts were understood as a one-time-investment, whereas the other categories were rather meant as monthly payments. Clearly noticeable is the fact that everyone was willing to pay, according to financial capacity (Tab.

13.52 to 13.55). The same holds true for the acceptance of cost sharing with respect to sanitation and solid waste removal. Almost a third and more than half would pay the minimum amounts of 50 Rs. for drainage and waste removal, respectively. Medium amounts of 160 - 500 Rs. for sanitation and 30-100 Rs. for waste removal are no problem for 42% and 21.6% of the households, respectively. These results must be carefully interpreted in view of the fact that the question did not explicitly ask for monthly or one-time-investments. Given the fact that a majority earns only up to 3000 Rs. per month the accumulated contributions to paying for services may not mean monthly contributions, since these would easily add up to one third of the monthly income.

4.8
Felt needs

Services offered by AIDMI in terms of microcredits, or small scale assistance through a chamber of commerce are not at the moment widely used as information about these options was generally low in communities and with AIDMI just having started these activities. There was probably a need for intensifying AIDMI's efforts because poverty was widespread. Close to half of the households had the governmental BPL (below poverty line) card. 61.4% got food from the ration shop, 86.8% did not see a reason for complaining at the food and found supplies timely, there were, however, clearly expressed needs: whereas only about one third found improvements in the housing substance necessary, more than 2/3 found improvements in sanitation important. Legal water facilities in the house were still important for 68.4% because more than 2/3 had to purchase water from nearby places, 30.8% found the treatment of water by filtering with cloth necessary and 80.5% were willing to pay for better drinking water.

4.9
Summary

Although the four communities were all rather poor and of lower status in the Indian social hierarchy, there was a noticeable internal stratification mostly along educational background that translated into differential opportunities for creating well being of the household. Educational achievements, for example, were lowest and illiteracy was highest among the tribal population of one community which allowed only for casual day labor, low wages, insecurity and a general lack of ability to access services. Where educational attainment was higher, people would fend for themselves better by obtaining employment in better paying construction or industrial activities. Still, the better paying jobs generated only poverty level incomes (for example, 20 days at 70 Rs. per day). However, at 8-10 Rs. per day, casual day labor yields no hope of improvement even if several household members work. It was noteworthy that no matter what the educational and income levels were, most households showed a capacity to contribute towards services, based on their financial capacity. No matter what educational levels, the needs were clearly voiced, depending on deficits in infrastructure such as sanitation and water facilities, whereas improvement of food supplies on BPL (below poverty line) cards were not considered an important issue. Additional services provided by NGO-work, such as membership in a small business chamber of commerce or microcredit schemes, although not understood widely, have a greater acceptance among households with higher educational attainment. In general, educational level emerges as a factor important in social differentiation even at poverty levels, and of upward social mobility.

Map 4.1 The City of Bhuj, District of Kutch, Gujarat India viewed from the IKONOS satellite image

Differences in slums and poverty structures 37

Map 4.2 The four study areas in the City of Bhuj, Gujarat - The slum communities of Bhimraonagar, Jayprakashnagar, Shantinagar and Mustuffunagar

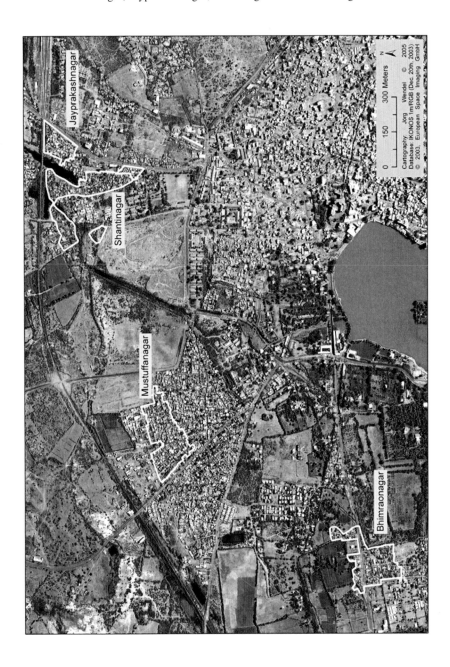

Map 4.3 The slum community of Bhimraonagar, as viewed from the satellite (City of Bhuj, Gujarat)

Map 4.4 The slum community of Jayprakashnagar, as viewed from the satellite (City of Bhuj, Gujarat)

Map 4.5 The slum community of Jayprakashnagar after verification of the satellite based GIS-Map by means of *in situ* surveying

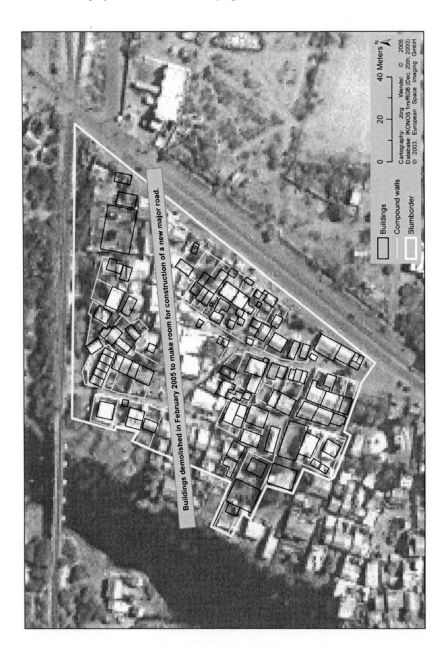

Map 4.6 The slum community of Shantinagar, as viewed from the satellite (City of Bhuj, Gujarat)

Map 4.7   The slum community of Mustuffunagar, as viewed from the satellite (City of Bhuj, Gujarat)

Differences in slums and poverty structures 43

Map 4.8 The slum community of Mustuffunagar, after verification of the satellite based GIS-Map by means of in situ surveying

5 Income differentials – household livelihood security

K. Conradin, R. Schneider-Sliwa, F. Wieland
University of Basel

5.1 Introduction

Following the general overview of social differentiation within and among slums, the issues of income and livelihood security are discussed in greater detail. Attention is given to the economic situation of the slum dwellers, how the 2001 earthquake affected the livelihoods and livelihood security of the slum dwellers and how well they were able to cope with this catastrophe. Data was also collected to assess the financial situation (such as savings and debts) of the households. The data was collected based on household questionnaires (n=657), where also details on the individual household members (n=2636), in particular occupation and average wages, were asked for. The following questions were of prime interest:

- How do the occupations of the slum dwellers affect their income?
- What are the factors that influence the average daily wages of a family?
- In what different ways were the livelihoods of the people affected through the 2001 earthquake?
- How is the financial situation of the slum dwellers almost five years after the earthquake?
- What influences factors such as debts and monthly savings?
- In general, do social / societal factors such as caste or religion appear as prominent determinants of poverty?

Where it was of importance, the fact whether the information was given by the family head for the whole household, or whether it was information on individual persons, was mentioned before the respective chapter.

5.2
Occupation

By slum (Tab. 5.1). The distribution of the occupation by slum shows some remarkable facts. Since textile products can mainly be manufactured at home, one can see a relation between jobs in the textile sector and the home-based occupation sector by slum. 23.5% of the home-based occupation could be found in Mustuffanagar. Most of the persons declaring to work as casual labourers, namely 19.8%, are living in Shantinagar, whereas in Jayprakashnagar, comparatively many people are working as vendors or own a shop.

Other observations are a higher amount of people from Jayprakashnagar working in the service sector or a slightly higher percentage of farmers in Shantinagar, due to the fact that there are higher proportions of Scheduled Tribe families engaged in animal husbandry. Explanations for the concentration of employment categories are difficult to find. Employment does relate to educational attainment, which differs within and between slums, but this in itself does not explain the apparent specialization of communities in different employment categories.

Table 5.1 Occupation, by slum.

Slum Occupation	Bhimraonagar in % (n=272)	Jayprakashnagar in % (n=127)	Mustuffanagar in % (n=413)	Shantinagar in % (n=344)	Total in % (n=1156)
textile/industry	8.5	2.4	23.5	4.7	12.0
government	0.4	4.7	1.2	0.6	1.2
casual labour	11.0	0.0	2.7	19.8	9.4
construction	17.3	7.1	13.8	11.3	13.1
farming	1.1	1.6	0.7	3.2	1.6
automotive related job	7.0	4.7	5.3	6.7	6.1
vendor/shop	5.9	15.0	4.8	2.6	5.5
crafts	4.4	2.4	5.3	2.3	3.9
service sector	9.2	16.5	9.7	5.5	9.1
retiree	1.5	0.8	2.2	0.9	1.5
housewife	32.7	40.9	30.0	38.7	34.4
unemployed	1.1	3.9	0.7	3.8	2.1
Total	100.0	100.0	100.0	100.0	100.0

SOURCE: UNIVERSITY OF BASEL, DEPT. OF GEOGRAPHY AND ALL INDIA DISASTER MITIGATION INSTITUTE, AHMEDABAD, INDIA 2005. SOCIAL SCIENCE SURVEY IN SELECTED SLUM COMMUNITIES IN THE CITY OF BHUJ, GUJARAT, INDIA.

By sex (Tab. 5.2). The rank for the women's occupation is as follows: With 70.8%, most women work as housewives, 14.1% in the textile sector and 5.5% in the service sector. It is not true for the context of the study area that more women than man are working in the service sector. The highest percentage of the male population is working in construction (21.7%), but high values are also visible for the service sector (12.3%) and automotive related jobs (11.3%). The distribution of occupation reveals a picture of a relatively traditional society.

Table 5.2 Occupation, by sex.

Occupation \ Sex	female in % (n=545)	male in % (n=612)	Total in % (n=1157)
textile/industry	14.1	10.1	12.0
government	0.2	2.1	1.2
casual labour	1.7	16.5	9.5
construction	3.5	21.7	13.1
farming	0.7	2.5	1.6
automotive related job	0.2	11.3	6.1
vendor/shop	1.3	9.3	5.5
crafts	1.7	5.9	3.9
service sector	5.5	12.3	9.1
retiree	0.0	2.8	1.5
housewife	70.8	2.0	34.4
unemployed	0.4	3.6	2.1
Total	100.0	100.0	100.0

SOURCE: UNIVERSITY OF BASEL, DEPT. OF GEOGRAPHY AND ALL INDIA DISASTER MITIGATION INSTITUTE, AHMEDABAD, INDIA 2005. SOCIAL SCIENCE SURVEY IN SELECTED SLUM COMMUNITIES IN THE CITY OF BHUJ, GUJARAT, INDIA.

By religion (Tab. 5.3). There is a distinct pattern: Muslim households are to a larger degree engaged in the textile industry (14.8%), construction (13.2%) as compared to the Hindu households (7.8% in textiles, 9.7% in construction) who have a lighter share in casual labour (11.5%). The former (textile industry) seems to be a particular characteristic of the Mustuffanagar slum, where there is a high number of families involved in the textile industry for which there is no obvious reason.

By caste (Tab. 5.4). Scheduled castes are concentrated mainly in construction (16.3%), whereas Scheduled Tribes more in casual labour (15.4%) than in construction (12.5%) Also other backward castes are employed as casual labourers, in textiles and in construction this pattern is corresponding to the fact that the Scheduled Tribe/Other Backward Classes population usually has a low degree of education and is thus usually not employed in jobs which require high skills. General castes are involved in service activities to a higher degree than the other castes. Additionally, a higher degree of the Scheduled Tribe women do not indicate that they are housewives – they are probably also engaged in farming work more often than the women of other castes.

Table 5.3 Occupation, by religion.

Occupation \ Religion	Hindu in % (n=1007)	Muslim in % (n=1574)	Sikh in % (n=3)	Christian in % (n=6)	Total in % (n=2590)
textile/ industry	8.1	9.5	0.0	100.0	9.2
government	4.0	2.0	0.0	0.0	2.7
casual labour	22.4	14.7	0.0	0.0	17.7
construction	16.2	19.3	0.0	0.0	18.0
farming	0.5	4.5	0.0	0.0	2.9
automotive related job	10.7	7.9	0.0	0.0	9.0
vendor/ shop	10.0	5.5	0.0	0.0	7.3
crafts	4.8	3.4	0.0	0.0	3.9
service sector	9.1	8.9	0.0	0.0	9.0
retiree	8.1	13.7	100.0	0.0	11.6
rousewife	3.7	6.6	0.0	0.0	5.4
unemployed	2.3	3.9	0.0	0.0	3.2
Total	100.0	100.0	100.0	100.0	100.0

SOURCE: UNIVERSITY OF BASEL, DEPT. OF GEOGRAPHY AND ALL INDIA DISASTER MITIGATION INSTITUTE, AHMEDABAD, INDIA 2005. SOCIAL SCIENCE SURVEY IN SELECTED SLUM COMMUNITIES IN THE CITY OF BHUJ, GUJARAT, INDIA.

Table 5.4 Occupation, by caste.

Occupation \ Caste	SC in % (n=245)	ST in % (n=136)	OBC in % (n=553)	General in % (n=533)	Total in % (n=1467)
textile/ industry	5.7	8.8	11.0	16.7	12.0
government	0.8	0.0	1.4	0.9	1.0
casual labour	6.1	15.4	14.5	3.6	9.2
construction	16.3	12.5	11.8	9.6	11.8
farming	0.8	0.0	2.0	1.7	1.5
automotive related job	4.9	4.4	4.7	5.8	5.1
vendor/ shop	6.5	11.0	3.6	6.2	5.7
crafts	6.1	3.7	2.5	5.6	4.4
service sector	8.6	8.1	5.8	10.3	8.1
retiree	2.4	5.1	3.8	5.1	4.2
housewife	39.6	27.9	35.3	32.5	34.3
unemployed	2.0	2.9	3.6	2.1	2.7
Total	100.0	100.0	100.0	100.0	100.0

SOURCE: UNIVERSITY OF BASEL, DEPT. OF GEOGRAPHY AND ALL INDIA DISASTER MITIGATION INSTITUTE, AHMEDABAD, INDIA 2005. SOCIAL SCIENCE SURVEY IN SELECTED SLUM COMMUNITIES IN THE CITY OF BHUJ, GUJARAT, INDIA.

5.3
Average daily wage of household members

As maps 5.1 through 5.4 show, poverty is rather wide spread. Generally, average daily wages of household members are low, but they are not equally low, and there are pockets of low wage earners and higher wage earners in each slum community.

By caste (Tab. 5.5). Though there is no statistically significant relation between the income and caste membership, there are differences between the individual castes and their respective incomes. Especially the General Castes more often belong to the higher income groups than Scheduled Castes and Scheduled Tribes. The Scheduled Tribes in the survey are most often found among the lowest income classes. Only 1.8% of them belong to the two highest income categories, compared to 8.4% of the members of the General Castes in this income classes. The same observations emerge: precarity and poverty are not evenly distributed, but affect the lower castes selectively.

Table 5.5 Average daily wages of household members (in Rs.), by caste.

Caste / Wage	SC in % (n=84)	ST in % (n=55)	OBC in % (n=174)	General in % (n=166)	Total in % (n=479)
0 to 9 Rs.	7.1	10.9	9.2	6.6	8.1
10 to 19 Rs.	32.1	36.4	39.1	29.5	34.2
20 to 29 Rs.	34.5	30.9	27.6	27.7	29.2
30 to 39 Rs.	13.1	18.2	10.9	19.9	15.2
40 to 49 Rs.	4.8	1.8	5.2	7.8	5.6
50 to 89 Rs.	6.0	1.8	6.9	7.8	6.5
90 to 130 Rs.	2.4	0.0	1.1	0.6	1.0
Total	100.0	100.0	100.0	100.0	100.0

SOURCE: UNIVERSITY OF BASEL, DEPT. OF GEOGRAPHY AND ALL INDIA DISASTER MITIGATION INSTITUTE, AHMEDABAD, INDIA 2005. SOCIAL SCIENCE SURVEY IN SELECTED SLUM COMMUNITIES IN THE CITY OF BHUJ, GUJARAT, INDIA.

By religion (Tab. 5.6). The relation between the total daily wages of a family and their religion is not statistically significant – however, trends are visible. While only 37.5% of the Hindu families are found in the lower income classes (0-9 and 10-19 Rs. per person per day), almost half of the Muslim population are among the lower income classes. The distribution among the middle income classes (20-29 and 30-39 Rs. per person per day) is about equal for Hindus and Muslims, but there are more Hindus in the higher income classes: 9.6% are in the two highest income classes (50-130 Rs. per person per day), compared to only 5.9% of the Muslims.

Table 5.6 Average daily wages of household members (in Rs.), by religion.

Wage / Religion	Hindu in % (n=208)	Muslim in % (n=269)	Total in % (n=477)
0 to 9 Rs.	4.3	11.2	8.2
10 to 19 Rs.	33.2	34.9	34.2
20 to 29 Rs.	29.8	29.0	29.4
30 to 39 Rs.	16.8	13.8	15.1
40 to 49 Rs.	6.3	5.2	5.7
50 to 89 Rs.	8.2	5.2	6.5
90 to 130 Rs.	1.4	0.7	1.0
Total	100.0	100.0	100.0

SOURCE: UNIVERSITY OF BASEL, DEPT. OF GEOGRAPHY AND ALL INDIA DISASTER MITIGATION INSTITUTE, AHMEDABAD, INDIA 2005. SOCIAL SCIENCE SURVEY IN SELECTED SLUM COMMUNITIES IN THE CITY OF BHUJ, GUJARAT, INDIA.

By slum (Tab. 5.7). Although the information obtained from this table is not statistically significant, there are some interesting observations. Generally, the income levels are higher in Jayprakashnagar (20.3% in the higher income classes, 40-130 Rs. per person per day) and in Mustuffanagar, while they are slightly lower in Bhimraonagar and noticeably lower in Shantinagar – 78.8% of the family members there earn between 0 and 29 Rs. a day.

Table 5.7 Average daily wages of household members (in Rs.), by slum.

Wage / Slum	Bhimraonagar in % (n=128)	Jayprakashnagar in % (n=49)	Mustuffanagar in % (n=156)	Shantinagar in % (n=146)	Total in % (n=479)
0 to 9 Rs.	4.7	6.1	7.7	12.3	8.1
10 to 19 Rs.	33.6	26.5	33.3	38.4	34.2
20 to 29 Rs.	32.0	32.7	26.9	28.1	29.2
30 to 39 Rs.	19.5	14.3	17.3	9.6	15.2
40 to 49 Rs.	4.7	12.2	6.4	3.4	5.6
50 to 89 Rs.	3.9	6.1	7.1	8.2	6.5
90 to 130 Rs.	1.6	2.0	1.3	0.0	1.0
Total	100.0	100.0	100.0	100.0	100.0

SOURCE: UNIVERSITY OF BASEL, DEPT. OF GEOGRAPHY AND ALL INDIA DISASTER MITIGATION INSTITUTE, AHMEDABAD, INDIA 2005. SOCIAL SCIENCE SURVEY IN SELECTED SLUM COMMUNITIES IN THE CITY OF BHUJ, GUJARAT, INDIA.

By occupation (Tab. 5.8). There is a highly significant relation between the daily wages per person and the occupation of the family head. The lowest income class (0-9 Rs. per person per day) is mostly employed in construction (7.3%), works as vendors (9.8%), in the service sector (8.7%), and is retired and unemployed (17.4%). Family heads situated in a middle income class (30-39 Rs.) work in the (textile) industry (20.0%), in automotive related jobs (19.0%), in farming (25.0%) and are casual labourers (18.1%) and vendors (19.5%). But also a large group are still the housewives, retired and unemployed persons (17.4%). The two highest income classes, which earn about 50-130 Rs. a day, are mostly working for the government (27.3%), in the industry (11.4%), in handicraft sector (29.4%) but also belong to the retired and unemployed people (9.8%) – this seeming discrepancy could probably be explained by the fact that those who are retired and still have a large income, have children or relatives who have well paid jobs. In every income class a wide range of occupations is represented. Except for government jobs, all occupations are distributed over the different classes of daily wages per person. A clear trend is therefore hard to establish.

5.4
Livelihood affected

Maps 5.5 through 5.8 show that the communities have been impacted differently by the earthquake. Whereas livelihoods were affected to some degree in all communities, Jayprakashnagar showed rather little impact because of the high proportion of persons in government or service sector jobs. The high proportion of households whose livelihood was affected in Shantinagar relates in part to the extremely poor housing of tribal families depending on animal husbandry and their compounds for keeping the animals.

By post earthquake housing status (Tab. 5.9). A large proportion of the households stated that their livelihood was affected by the earthquake, although they still considered their dwellings safe (56.1%). In addition, 43.5% of the inhabitants of houses which only suffered minor damage stated that their livelihood was affected. This peculiarity is easily explained by the fact that a stable and safe house is only part of a livelihood. The high percentage of families who answered that their livelihood was affected can be related to changes in their income opportunities or health status, rather than their respective housing status.

Table 5.9 Livelihood affected, by post earthquake housing status.

Post earthquake housing status Livelihood affected	safe in % (n=41)	minor damage in % (n=154)	severe damage in % (n=97)	completely destroyed in % (n=155)	Total in % (n=447)
Yes	56.1	43.5	74.2	69.0	60.2
No	43.9	56.5	25.8	31.0	39.8
Total	100.0	100.0	100.0	100.0	100.0

SOURCE: UNIVERSITY OF BASEL, DEPT. OF GEOGRAPHY AND ALL INDIA DISASTER MITIGATION INSTITUTE, AHMEDABAD, INDIA 2005. SOCIAL SCIENCE SURVEY IN SELECTED SLUM COMMUNITIES IN THE CITY OF BHUJ, GUJARAT, INDIA.

By slum (Tab. 5.10). Livelihoods were affected to different degrees depending on the slum location. The highest share of families or individuals (75.6%) who say that their livelihoods were affected by the earthquake lives in Bhimraonagar. Also, the livelihoods of the dwellers of Mustuffanagar (60.5%) and Shantinagar (55.3%) were adversely affected. The number of families affected in Jayprakashnagar is surprisingly low, only 28.3% answered this question in the affirmative. This can either be explained by the better housing structure in Jayprakashnagar (see Tab. 6.1), or by the fact that other livelihood factors (income possibilities, health etc.) were not affected as badly as in the other slums.

Table 5.8 Average daily wages of household members (in Rs.), by occupation of family head.

Occupation Wage	textile/ industry in % (n=35)	govern- ment in % (n=11)	casual labour in % (n=83)	construc tion in % (n=82)	farming in % (n=12)	automotive related job in % (n=42)	vendor/ shop in % (n=41)	crafts in % (n=17)	service sector in % (n=46)	retiree/ housewife/ unemployed in % (n=92)	unclear/ indian in % (n=12)	Total in % (n=473)
0 to 9 Rs.	5.7	0.0	4.8	7.3	8.3	2.4	9.8	0.0	8.7	17.4	8.3	8.2
10 to 19 Rs.	34.3	0.0	43.4	42.7	33.3	28.6	26.8	29.4	30.4	29.3	41.7	34.0
20 to 29 Rs.	25.7	36.4	27.7	30.5	25.0	38.1	31.7	29.4	30.4	22.8	50.0	29.4
30 to 39 Rs.	20.0	9.1	18.1	7.3	25.0	19.0	19.5	0.0	15.2	17.4	0.0	15.0
40 to 49 Rs.	2.9	27.3	2.4	9.8	0.0	7.1	4.9	11.8	6.5	3.3	0.0	5.7
50 to 89 Rs.	11.4	18.2	3.6	2.4	8.3	4.8	4.9	29.4	6.5	7.6	0.0	6.6
90 to 130 Rs.	0.0	9.1	0.0	0.0	0.0	0.0	2.4	0.0	2.2	2.2	0.0	1.1
Total	100.0	100.0	100.0	100.0	100.0	100.0	100.0	100.0	100.0	100.0	100.0	100.0

SOURCE: UNIVERSITY OF BASEL, DEPT. OF GEOGRAPHY AND ALL INDIA DISASTER MITIGATION INSTITUTE, AHMEDABAD, INDIA 2005. SOCIAL SCIENCE SURVEY IN SELECTED SLUM COMMUNITIES IN THE CITY OF BHUJ, GUJARAT, INDIA.

Table 5.10 Livelihood affected by earthquake, by slum.

Slum Livelihood affected	Bhimraona-gar in % (n=127)	Jayprakashna-gar in % (n=53)	Mustuffanagar in % (n=157)	Shantinagar in % (n=150)	Total in % (n=487)
Yes	75.6	28.3	60.5	55.3	59.3
No	24.4	71.7	39.5	44.7	40.7
Total	100.0	100.0	100.0	100.0	100.0

SOURCE: UNIVERSITY OF BASEL, DEPT. OF GEOGRAPHY AND ALL INDIA DISASTER MITIGATION INSTITUTE, AHMEDABAD, INDIA 2005. SOCIAL SCIENCE SURVEY IN SELECTED SLUM COMMUNITIES IN THE CITY OF BHUJ, GUJARAT, INDIA.

5.5
Monthly savings

The analysis of the monthly savings is based on the accumulated data for the family, shown for the family head - in other words, the values represent the savings of the whole family, not the contribution of a single family member to savings.

By slum (Tab. 5.11). The table on the distribution of the monthly savings by slum reflects also personal impressions from working in the slums: 80.4% indicated not to be able to save any money. Further tables support this notion. In other words, the people do not have a financial reserve for a crisis and are not able to invest into projects, be it personal or infrastructural, that could lift them out of poverty. This again causes a permanent vulnerability of the people. The few that can save a little of the monthly earning (up to 100 Rs.) are mostly from Bhimraonagar, with 16.2% and 10% being able to save between 201 and 700 Rs. every month.

Table 5.11 Monthly savings (in Rs.) of household, by slum.

Slum Monthly savings	Bhimraona-gar in % (n=130)	Jayprakashna-gar in % (n=53)	Mustuffanagar in % (n=158)	Shantinagar in % (n=155)	Total in % (n=496)
0	66.2	83.0	83.5	88.4	80.4
1-100	16.2	5.7	5.1	5.2	8.1
101-200	4.6	3.8	3.8	1.3	3.2
201-700	10.0	3.8	5.1	2.6	5.4
> 700	3.1	3.8	2.5	2.6	2.8
Total	100.0	100.0	100.0	100.0	100.0

SOURCE: UNIVERSITY OF BASEL, DEPT. OF GEOGRAPHY AND ALL INDIA DISASTER MITIGATION INSTITUTE, AHMEDABAD, INDIA 2005. SOCIAL SCIENCE SURVEY IN SELECTED SLUM COMMUNITIES IN THE CITY OF BHUJ, GUJARAT, INDIA.

By age of the family head (Tab. 5.12). Monthly savings are by and large impossible, irrespective of age. Small savings of up to 100 Rs. per month, however, are reported by those in the age groups of 20-29, which is the age of getting ready for marriage and establishing a household and a family. Again, those aged 40-49 are to a larger degree able to save. This is the age group when the children are grown up and establishing their own households. The small proportion of families in the age group of 30-39 clearly indicates that the family situation itself and the priorities a family requires, prevents savings and more secure situations. It appears that if governmental or non-governmental agencies want to increase the propensity to save, one must target the families with younger children, not only for the financial stability of such families but also because savings habits are passed onto children who thus are enabled to help themselves in the future.

Table 5.12 Monthly savings (in Rs.) of household, by age of family head.

Age Monthly savings	0-19 in % (n=1)	20-29 in % (n=56)	30-39 in % (n=134)	40-49 in % (n=130)	50-59 in % (n=69)	60-69 in % (n=69)	70-79 in % (n=24)	80-89 in % (n=7)	> 90 in % (n=5)	Total in % (n=495)
0	0.0	82.1	85.1	72.3	78.3	88.4	83.3	71.4	80.0	80.4
1-100	0.0	14.3	5.2	9.2	8.7	7.2	0.0	14.3	20.0	8.1
101-200	100.0	0.0	2.2	6.2	1.4	1.4	8.3	0.0	0.0	3.2
201-700	0.0	1.8	6.0	7.7	5.8	1.4	8.3	14.3	0.0	5.5
> 700	0.0	1.8	1.5	4.6	5.8	1.4	0.0	0.0	0.0	2.8
Total	100.0	100.0	100.0	100.0	100.0	100.0	100.0	100.0	100.0	100.0

SOURCE: UNIVERSITY OF BASEL, DEPT. OF GEOGRAPHY AND ALL INDIA DISASTER MITIGATION INSTITUTE, AHMEDABAD, INDIA 2005. SOCIAL SCIENCE SURVEY IN SELECTED SLUM COMMUNITIES IN THE CITY OF BHUJ, GUJARAT, INDIA.

By sex of the family head (Tab. 5.13). The ability for monthly savings is not gender specific.

Table 5.13 Monthly savings (in Rs.) of household, by sex of family head.

Sex Monthly savings	female in % (n=65)	male in % (n=430)	Total in % (n=495)
0	87.7	79.3	80.4
1-100	4.6	8.6	8.1
101-200	1.5	3.5	3.2
201-700	4.6	5.6	5.5
> 700	1.5	3.0	2.8
Total	100.0	100.0	100.0

SOURCE: UNIVERSITY OF BASEL, DEPT. OF GEOGRAPHY AND ALL INDIA DISASTER MITIGATION INSTITUTE, AHMEDABAD, INDIA 2005. SOCIAL SCIENCE SURVEY IN SELECTED SLUM COMMUNITIES IN THE CITY OF BHUJ, GUJARAT, INDIA.

By education (Tab. 5.14). Though most households indicate that they are not able to put any money aside, there are differences between levels of education. One would expect that the illiterate group would save the least money compared to the other education standards based on the assumption that a higher education level leads to a better financial foresight due to a better information basis. This assumption is proven wrong: While 85.3% of the illiterates indicated not to be able to save any money, this figure does not differ much from the group of people who finished school between the 7th and the 9th standards. Striking, however, is the fact that most groups tend to save according to their capacity, when they *do* save: 13% of those with little education (1st-3rd Standard) or no education (7.4% of the illiterate) do save up to 100 Rs. per month.

The higher the educational level obtained the higher are the savings: 9.8% of these with standards 4-6 and 5.6% of these 7-9 standards and 8.3% of these with 10-12 standards save intermediate amounts (201-700Rs. per month). The highest educated 10-12 standards, furthermore, save in two categories, the 1-100Rs. per month (13.9%) and the 201-700 Rs. per month.

By occupation (Tab. 5.15). Though most families are not able to save anything, savings seem to be related to the occupational structure of the household members: Secure government jobs apparently offer better options for savings than in other occupational categories such as casual labourers or construction workers. Care has to be taken, however: since this is only a general trend based on the small number of government employees this is not necessarily highly representative.

It is an important finding that all occupational groups seem to attempt to come up with some savings. Savings up to 100 Rs. per month are found in all occupations.

By average daily wages of household members (Tab. 5.16). Generally, the families belonging to the income class of 50 to 89 Rs. per person per day are able to save the most money per month, but it has to be considered, that the income classes from 40 Rs. on upwards are statistically not significant as the numbers of families in that group are low (n=26, n=30, n=5).

The first glance gives the impression that the more a family earns, the more they can save. This assumption is confirmed: The income class of 20 to 29 Rs. can mostly save 1 to 100 Rs. (13.6%), 7.7% of those in the income class of 40 to 49 Rs. are able to save 101 to 200 Rs., in the income category of 50 to 89 Rs., the percentage is at 23.3% for savings between 201 and 700 Rs. In general, the values indicate the willingness of the families to save some money: all income classes manage to save a little amount of their income.

Table 5.16 Monthly savings (in Rs.) of household, by average daily wages of household members (in Rs.).

Wages / Monthly savings	0 to 9 Rs. in % (n=39)	10 to 19 Rs. in % (n=164)	20 to 29 Rs. in % (n=140)	30 to 39 Rs. in % (n=73)	40 to 49 Rs. in % (n=26)	50 to 89 Rs. in % (n=30)	90 to 130 Rs. in % (n=5)	Total in % (n=437)
0	94.8	90.2	76.4	71.2	80.8	53.3	80.0	80.7
1-100	0.0	6.7	13.6	11.0	0.0	3.3	0.0	8.2
101-200	2.6	1.2	3.6	5.5	7.7	6.7	0.0	3.4
201-700	2.6	1.2	5.7	8.2	3.8	23.3	20.0	5.5
>700	0.0	0.6	0.7	4.1	7.7	13.4	0.0	2.3
Total	100.0	100.0	100.0	100.0	100.0	100.0	100.0	100.0

SOURCE: UNIVERSITY OF BASEL, DEPT. OF GEOGRAPHY AND ALL INDIA DISASTER MITIGATION INSTITUTE, AHMEDABAD, INDIA 2005. SOCIAL SCIENCE SURVEY IN SELECTED SLUM COMMUNITIES IN THE CITY OF BHUJ, GUJARAT, INDIA.

Table 5.14 Monthly savings (in Rs.) of household, by education standard of family head

Education / Monthly Savings	Hrs. 1-3 in % (n=46)	Hrs. 4-6 in % (n=82)	Hrs. 7-9 in % (n=107)	Hrs. 10-12 in % (n=36)	Completed Diploma in % (n=1)	Completed Graduation in % (n=6)	Illiterate in % (n=217)	Total in % (n=495)
0 Rs.	73.9	74.4	83.2	69.4	100.0	50.0	85.3	80.4
1-100 Rs.	13.0	9.8	4.7	13.9	0.0	0.0	7.4	8.1
101-200 Rs.	2.2	4.9	2.8	5.6	0.0	0.0	2.8	3.2
201-700 Rs.	4.3	9.8	5.6	8.3	0.0	0.0	3.7	5.5
>700 Rs.	6.5	1.2	3.7	2.8	0.0	50.0	0.9	2.8
Total	100.0	100.0	100.0	100.0	100.0	100.0	100.0	100.0

Table 5.15 Monthly savings (in Rs.) of household, by occupation of family head.

Occupation / Monthly Savings	textile/industry in % (n=35)	government in % (n=13)	casual labour in % (n=84)	construction in % (n=84)	farming in % (n=13)	automotive related job in % (n=43)	vendor/shop in % (n=42)	crafts in % (n=17)	service sector in % (n=47)	retiree/housewife/unemployed in % (n=98)	Total in % (n=476)
0 Rs	74.3	46.2	79.8	86.9	76.9	81.4	85.7	58.8	78.7	85.7	80.7
1-100 Rs	8.6	7.7	14.3	7.1	15.4	9.3	4.8	11.8	4.3	4.1	8.0
101–200 Rs	5.7	0.0	1.2	3.6	0.0	4.7	2.4	5.9	2.1	4.1	3.2
201-700 Rs	5.7	30.8	2.4	1.2	7.7	4.7	4.8	17.6	10.6	4.1	5.5
>700 Rs.	5.7	15.4	2.4	1.2	0.0	0.0	2.4	5.9	4.3	2.0	2.7
Total	100.0	100.0	100.0	100.0	100.0	100.0	100.0	100.0	100.0	100.0	100.0

SOURCE: UNIVERSITY OF BASEL, DEPT. OF GEOGRAPHY AND ALL INDIA DISASTER MITIGATION INSTITUTE, AHMEDABAD, INDIA 2005. SOCIAL SCIENCE SURVEY IN SELECTED SLUM COMMUNITIES IN THE CITY OF BHUJ, GUJARAT, INDIA.

By religion (Tab. 5.17). Fewer Muslim households tend to save (86.3%) compared to Hindus (72.8%). Savings up to 100 Rs. are possible for only for 5.1% of the Muslims whereas 12.0% of the Hindus indicated to save a bigger amount. The reasons for these differences are not exactly clear.

Table 5.17 Monthly savings (in Rs.) of household, by religion.

Religion / Monthly savings	Hindu in % (n=217)	Muslim in % (n=277)	Total in % (n=494)
0	72.8	86.3	80.4
1-100	12.0	5.1	8.1
101-200	4.1	2.5	3.2
201-700	7.4	4.0	5.5
> 700	3.7	2.2	2.8
Total	100.0	100.0	100.0

SOURCE: UNIVERSITY OF BASEL, DEPT. OF GEOGRAPHY AND ALL INDIA DISASTER MITIGATION INSTITUTE, AHMEDABAD, INDIA 2005. SOCIAL SCIENCE SURVEY IN SELECTED SLUM COMMUNITIES IN THE CITY OF BHUJ, GUJARAT, INDIA.

By caste (Tab. 5.18). It is striking that though Scheduled Tribes are usually among the income group with the smallest income, there is a comparatively high percentage of households (36.1%) indicating to save at least something, compared to figures between roughly 10% and 25% for the other castes. In the category of savings up to 100 Rs., 22.8% belong to the Scheduled Tribes group, compared to figures between roughly 9.3% and 2% for the other three groups. No obvious explanation emerges for this.

More easily explained is the fact that General Caste households are able to save higher amounts, with about 10% indicating to save more than 200 Rs. per month. This might be due to the fact that General Castes are generally economically better off than Scheduled Castes and Scheduled Tribes.

Table 5.18 Monthly savings (in Rs.) of household, by caste.

Caste / Monthly Savings	SC in % (n=86)	ST in % (n=57)	OBC in % (n=180)	General in % (n=172)	Total in % (n=495)
0	77.9	64.9	90.0	76.7	80.4
1-100	9.3	22.8	2.2	8.7	8.1
101-200	2.3	5.3	1.1	5.2	3.2
201-700	9.3	7.0	3.9	4.7	5.5
> 700	1.2	0.0	2.8	4.7	2.8
Total	100.0	100.0	100.0	100.0	100.0

SOURCE: UNIVERSITY OF BASEL, DEPT. OF GEOGRAPHY AND ALL INDIA DISASTER MITIGATION INSTITUTE, AHMEDABAD, INDIA 2005. SOCIAL SCIENCE SURVEY IN SELECTED SLUM COMMUNITIES IN THE CITY OF BHUJ, GUJARAT, INDIA.

5.6
Amount of debts (in Rs.)

By slum (Tab. 5.19). Jayprakashnagar is the slum with the best situation considering the amount of debts: 71.7% of the families are free of debts, but 13.2% has a rather high sum on debts, namely 20.001 to 50.000 Rs. To get a clear picture, one would have to compare this fact to the income situations (Tab. 5.7) of the households. Generally, the incomes in Jayprakashnagar are higher – and households can probably afford higher debts more easily. Mustuffanagar has a comparatively low amount of household who have no debts (50.0%). Maybe this can be explained by the relatively good housing structure in Mustuffanagar, which may be he result of previous credit-financed investments. Additionally, on a general impression, the economic situation in Mustuffanagar seems to be better than in other slums – and people with a higher income can usually afford higher debts. The figure for Shantinagar is similar, where only 55.5% of the households are free of debts – this corresponds to the general situation in Shantinagar, where the families are usually rather poor in comparison with the other four slums.

Table 5.19 Amount of debt (in Rs.) of household, by slum.

Slum Amount of debt	Bhimraonagar in % (n=129)	Jayprakashnagar in % (n=53)	Mustuffanagar in % (n=158)	Shantinagar in % (n=154)	Total in % (n=494)
0	66.7	71.7	50.0	54.5	58.1
1-5000	9.3	3.8	8.9	12.3	9.5
5001-10000	10.1	3.8	12.0	10.4	10.1
10001-20000	7.0	3.8	7.0	10.4	7.7
20001-50000	3.9	13.2	14.6	7.8	9.5
> 50000	3.1	3.8	7.6	4.5	5.1
Total	100.0	100.0	100.0	100.0	100.0

SOURCE: UNIVERSITY OF BASEL, DEPT. OF GEOGRAPHY AND ALL INDIA DISASTER MITIGATION INSTITUTE, AHMEDABAD, INDIA 2005. SOCIAL SCIENCE SURVEY IN SELECTED SLUM COMMUNITIES IN THE CITY OF BHUJ, GUJARAT, INDIA.

By age of the family head (Tab. 5.20). The incidence of not having debt is related to the age of the household head. Household heads of younger families are to a greater extent free of debts (66.1% of the age 20-29) than other age groups. Among those who report debts of more than 20.000 Rs., various reasons could apply. In the case of young family heads, these debts can be explained with the expenses for housing. The high percentage among the age group of 40 to 49 years (10.9%) is most likely due to the fact that this is the age for family heads when their children move out, and thus they probably have to assist them. Also, one must not forget the financial burden of marrying a daughter. The high amount of elderly people above 60 (in total almost 50% of those who have debts between 20.000 Rs and 50.000 Rs. are older than 60 years) can probably be explained by the fact that people accumulate their debts over the years, and with high interest rates and a declining income, the amount of debt rises steadily.

Table 5.20 Amount of debt (in Rs.) of household, by age of family head.

Age / Amount of debt	0-19 in % (n=1)	20-29 in % (n=56)	30-39 in % (n=133)	40-49 in % (n=129)	50-59 in % (n=69)	60-69 in % (n=69)	70-79 in % (n=24)	80-89 in % (n=7)	>90 in % (n=5)	Total in % (n=493)
0	100.0	66.1	63.2	52.7	56.5	53.6	62.5	42.9	60.0	58.2
1-5000	0.0	8.9	12.0	8.5	5.8	10.1	12.5	14.3	0.0	9.5
5001-10000	0.0	10.7	5.3	7.8	17.4	14.5	8.3	28.6	0.0	9.9
10001-20000	0.0	1.8	9.0	12.4	4.3	5.8	0.0	14.3	20.0	7.7
20001-50000	0.0	12.5	6.0	10.9	7.2	11.6	16.7	0.0	20.0	9.5
> 50000	0.0	0.0	4.5	7.8	8.7	4.3	0.0	0.0	0.0	5.1
Total	100.0	100.0	100.0	100.0	100.0	100.0	100.0	100.0	100.0	100.0

SOURCE: UNIVERSITY OF BASEL, DEPT. OF GEOGRAPHY AND ALL INDIA DISASTER MITIGATION INSTITUTE, AHMEDABAD, INDIA 2005. SOCIAL SCIENCE SURVEY IN SELECTED SLUM COMMUNITIES IN THE CITY OF BHUJ, GUJARAT, INDIA.

By sex, education and occupation of family head (Tab. 5.21, 5.22, 5.23). There is a gender component to debts: 16.9% of all women but only 8.9% of the men have debts of 5001 to 10.000 Rs. whereas 10% of the males and only 6.2% of the females have debts in excess of 20.000Rs. One might assume that the credits are taken for different purposes: with women it is smaller amounts to establish small businesses, with men it may be a credit for the family's house or investments in the house. This notion is supported by the fact that an amount of debt smaller than 20.000Rs., is not apparently related to education and occupation with the exception of government employees and crafts/trades persons. The former have higher debts possibly because they can afford larger homes and the latter possibly because they invested in commercial space where they can perform their trade/crafts.

Table 5.21 Amount of debt (in Rs.) of household, by sex of family head.

Sex / Amount of debt	female in % (n=65)	male in % (n=428)	Total in % (n=493)
0	63.1	57.5	58.2
1-5000	7.7	9.8	9.5
5001-10000	16.9	8.9	9.9
10001-20000	6.2	7.9	7.7
20001-50000	6.2	10.0	9.5
> 50000	0.0	5.8	5.1
Total	100.0	100.0	100.0

SOURCE: UNIVERSITY OF BASEL, DEPT. OF GEOGRAPHY AND ALL INDIA DISASTER MITIGATION INSTITUTE, AHMEDABAD, INDIA 2005. SOCIAL SCIENCE SURVEY IN SELECTED SLUM COMMUNITIES IN THE CITY OF BHUJ, GUJARAT, INDIA.

Table 5.22 Amount of debt (in Rs.) of household, by education standard.

Education Amount of debt	Hrs. 1-3 in % (n=45)	Hrs. 4-6 in % (n=82)	Hrs. 7-9 in % (n=107)	Hrs. 10-12 in % (n=36)	Completed Diploma in % (n=1)	Completed Graduation in % (n=6)	Illiterate in % (n=216)	Total in % (n=493)
0 Rs.	55.6	53.7	66.4	66.7	0.0	83.3	54.6	58.2
1-5000 Rs.	11.1	15.9	6.5	2.8	0.0	0.0	9.7	9.5
5001-10000 Rs.	6.7	9.8	2.8	2.8	0.0	0.0	15.7	9.9
10001-20000 Rs.	2.2	7.3	9.3	2.8	0.0	0.0	9.3	7.7
20001-50000 Rs.	13.3	11.0	9.3	13.9	0.0	16.7	7.4	9.5
> 50000 Rs.	11.1	2.4	5.6	11.1	100.0	0.0	3.2	5.1
Total	100.0	100.0	100.0	100.0	100.0	100.0	100.0	100.0

Table 5.23 Amount of debt (in Rs.) of household, by occupation of family head.

Occupation Amount of debt	textile/industry in % (n=35)	government in % (n=3)	casual labour in % (n=82)	construction in % (n=82)	farming in % (n=13)	automotive related job in % (n=42)	vendor/shop in % (n=41)	crafts in % (n=17)	service sector in % (n=47)	retiree/housewife/unemployed in % (n=98)	Total in % (n=470)
0 Rs	57.1	61.5	64.6	57.3	46.2	66.7	61.0	52.9	57.4	54.1	58.7
1 - 5000 Rs	17.1	0.0	9.8	12.2	0.0	0.0	2.4	11.8	8.5	7.1	8.1
5001 - 10000 Rs	2.9	0.0	9.8	8.5	0.0	7.1	14.6	0.0	17.0	14.3	10.0
10001 -20000 Rs	5.7	15.4	4.9	8.5	30.8	9.5	4.9	11.8	2.1	10.2	8.1
20001 -50000 Rs	5.7	23.1	6.1	12.2	7.7	11.9	9.8	23.5	8.5	8.2	9.8
> 50000 Rs	11.4	0.0	4.9	1.2	15.4	4.8	7.3	0.0	6.4	6.1	5.3
Total	100.0	100.0	100.0	100.0	100.0	100.0	100.0	100.0	100.0	100.0	100.0

SOURCE: UNIVERSITY OF BASEL, DEPT. OF GEOGRAPHY AND ALL INDIA DISASTER MITIGATION INSTITUTE, AHMEDABAD, INDIA 2005. SOCIAL SCIENCE SURVEY IN SELECTED SLUM COMMUNITIES IN THE CITY OF BHUJ, GUJARAT, INDIA.

By average daily wages of household members (Tab. 5.24). A clear pattern emerges in the three low income groups. Here, it is apparent that amount of debt rises with average daily income. 31.6% of those with average daily incomes of 0 to 9 Rs. report debts up to 10.000Rs., a total of 20.8% of those with daily income of 10 to 19 Rs. report debt from 5.000 to 20.000 Rs. and a total of 17.9% of those with average daily income of 20 to 29 Rs. Clearly, a higher daily income gives the opportunity of higher investments which may be made through credit financing (see also Tab. 5.19).

Table 5.24 Amount of debt (in Rs.) of household, by average daily wages of household members (in Rs.).

Amount of debt	0 to 9 Rs. in % (n=38)	10 to 19 Rs. in % (n=164)	20 to 29 Rs. in % (n=140)	30 to 39 Rs. in % (n=72)	40 to 49 Rs. in % (n=27)	50 to 89 Rs. in % (n=30)	90 to 130 Rs. in % (n=5)	Total in % (n=476)
0	52.6	53.0	59.3	68.1	63.0	76.7	80.0	59.5
1 - 5000 Rs.	15.8	14.0	6.4	1.4	3.7	3.3	0.0	8.6
5001 - 10000 Rs.	15.8	10.4	10.0	12.5	7.4	0.0	0.0	10.1
10001 - 20000 Rs.	0.0	10.4	7.9	6.9	3.7	3.3	0.0	7.4
20001 - 50000 Rs.	13.2	7.9	12.1	4.2	18.5	6.7	20.0	9.7
> 50000 Rs.	2.6	4.3	4.3	6.9	3.7	10.0	0.0	4.8
Total	100.0	100.0	100.0	100.0	100.0	100.0	100.0	100.0

SOURCE: UNIVERSITY OF BASEL, DEPT. OF GEOGRAPHY AND ALL INDIA DISASTER MITIGATION INSTITUTE, AHMEDABAD, INDIA 2005. SOCIAL SCIENCE SURVEY IN SELECTED SLUM COMMUNITIES IN THE CITY OF BHUJ, GUJARAT, INDIA.

By caste (Tab. 5.25). The table is not statistically significant, nevertheless one can observe certain trends: Members of the Scheduled Castes and Scheduled Tribes mostly have debts of only up to 10.000 (12.8% and 5.4%) and 20.000 Rs. (12.8% and 7.1%) while the amount of the debt for the Other Backward Classes and General Castes is higher: 10.6% have debts up to 50.000 Rs. and 10.5% of more than 50.000Rs. Again, this can be explained by the fact that Scheduled Castes and Scheduled Tribes are the ones that generally have the smallest income – and as shown above (Tab. 5.24), a high income often also leads to a high debt. Still, the fact that the Scheduled Castes and Scheduled Tribes have smaller debts must not lead to the misconception that they are financially better of. Even a small debt is a huge financial burden for a family who does not have a regular income, and the tables on occupation show that especially Scheduled Castes and Scheduled Tribes often only work as casual labourers with no regular income.

Table 5.25 Amount of debt (in Rs.) of household, by caste.

Caste Amount of debt	SC in % (n=86)	ST in % (n=56)	OBC in % (n=179)	General in % (n=172)	Total in % (n=493)
0	53.5	69.6	58.1	56.4	58.0
1 - 5000 Rs.	8.1	10.7	10.1	9.3	9.5
5001 - 10000 Rs.	12.8	5.4	10.6	9.9	10.1
10001 - 20000 Rs.	12.8	7.1	5.6	7.6	7.7
20001 - 50000 Rs.	9.3	3.6	10.6	10.5	9.5
> 50000 Rs.	3.5	3.6	5.0	6.4	5.1
Total	100.0	100.0	100.0	100.0	100.0

SOURCE: UNIVERSITY OF BASEL, DEPT. OF GEOGRAPHY AND ALL INDIA DISASTER MITIGATION INSTITUTE, AHMEDABAD, INDIA 2005. SOCIAL SCIENCE SURVEY IN SELECTED SLUM COMMUNITIES IN THE CITY OF BHUJ, GUJARAT, INDIA.

By religion (Tab. 5.26). It is of note that more Hindus than Muslims are free of debt (67.3% and 50.5% respectively). This corresponds to table 5.6 which indicates more Muslims among the lower income classes. A smaller income usually implies smaller savings, and thus an increased need for credits if investments need to be done. There is quite a high percentage of Muslims (11.6%) who have debts between 20.000 and 50.000 Rs. In some Muslim households, this was explained by the high dowries that have to be paid when marrying off a daughter. However, the question remains why Hindu households that have to manage dowry payments as well are to a greater extent free of debts, as compared to the Muslim households.

Table 5.26 Amount of debt (in Rs.) of household, by religion.

Religion Amount of debt	Hindu in % (n=217)	Muslim in % (n=275)	Total in % (n=492)
0	67.3	50.5	57.9
1 - 5000 Rs.	7.8	10.9	9.6
5001 - 10000 Rs.	7.4	12.4	10.2
10001 - 20000 Rs.	5.5	9.5	7.7
20001 - 50000 Rs.	6.9	11.6	9.6
> 50000 Rs.	5.1	5.1	5.1
Total	100.0	100.0	100.0

SOURCE: UNIVERSITY OF BASEL, DEPT. OF GEOGRAPHY AND ALL INDIA DISASTER MITIGATION INSTITUTE, AHMEDABAD, INDIA 2005. SOCIAL SCIENCE SURVEY IN SELECTED SLUM COMMUNITIES IN THE CITY OF BHUJ, GUJARAT, INDIA.

5.7 Conclusion

Concerning the occupations of the slum dwellers, the high amount of people who work in the casual labour and construction sectors is striking. This fact can mainly be ascribed to the low educational standard of the slum dwellers. It must also be considered that casual labour generates casual income and thus makes families more vulnerable to changing situations; especially members of the Scheduled Castes, the Scheduled Tribes and Other Backward Castes are often engaged in casual labour – focus must be laid on these groups especially to give them greater opportunities for a regular income.

The importance of schooling and education for all members of society (see Chapter 11) must once again be mentioned. Moreover, the general livelihoods of the people depend to a large extent upon the occupation, hence, the income of the slum dwellers.

Moreover, the occupation and thus income have a major impact on the financial behaviour of the inhabitants – there were highly significant relations between the amount people earn and their debts, as well as their respective savings. The monthly savings value is an indicator which allows drawing conclusions on the foresight, rationality and financial possibilities of a family. Savings are of paramount importance allowing to absorb losses, crisis situations, illnesses and so on, when there is no guaranty to receive immediate help from the government. Concerning the savings behaviour of the slum dwellers, it is remarkable that only a very small percentage of the interviewed households are able to save small amounts. This situation creates a high vulnerability in the case of unforeseen expenses such as illnesses, accidents, or – as happened in 2001 – in the case of catastrophes.

As for the debts of the households, the following must be pointed out: There is a relation between the amount of debts and the income of a family, families with a lower income tend to have smaller debts, whereas families with a higher income tend to have higher debts. Though the debts seem to be comparatively small for families with a lower income, they represent a huge financial burden for these families; often it is exactly those families who only have a casual income and thus have to struggle continuously to come up with the money for the interest payments. The high proportion of families who are indebted strongly indicates the need for (small) credits, and thus also for small and locally based financing agents, such as slum-based saving groups, micro-financing institutes etc. and, last but not least, savings self-help efforts such as rotating credit schemes that are set up with the help of NGO's.

Map 5.1 Average daily wages of household members in Bhimraonagar

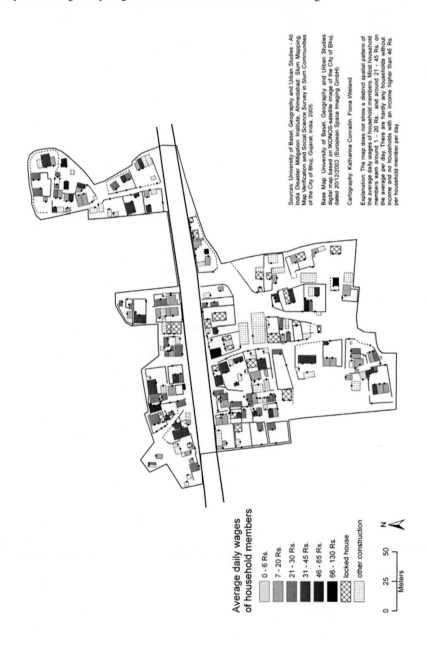

Income differentials – household livelihood security

Map 5.2 Average daily wages of household members in Jayprakashnagar

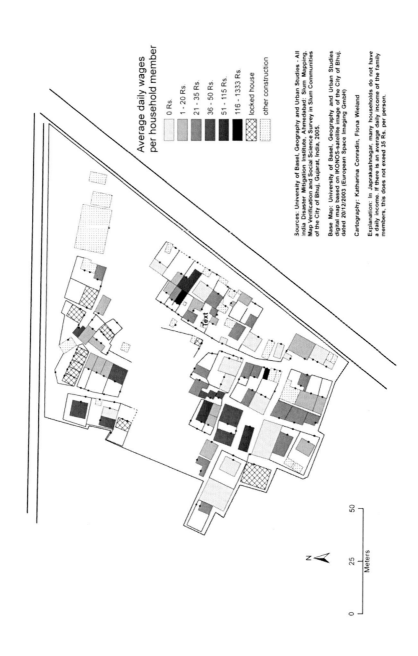

Map 5.3 Average daily wages of household members in Mustuffanagar

Map 5.4 Average daily wages of household members in Shantinagar

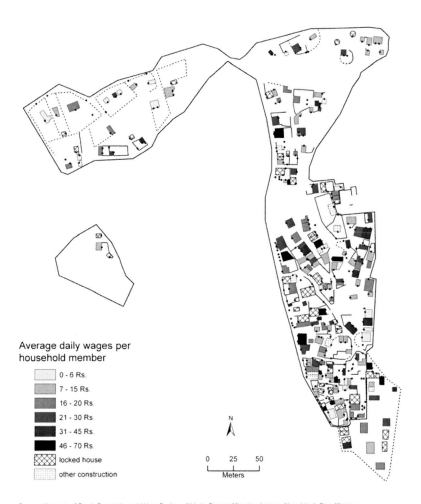

Sources: University of Basel, Geography and Urban Studies - All India Disaster Mitigation Institute, Ahmedabad: Slum Mapping, Map Verification and Social Science Survey in Slum Communities of the City of Bhuj, Gujarat, India, 2005.

Base Map: University of Basel, Geography and Urban Studies digital map based on IKONOS-satellite image of the City of Bhuj, dated 20/12/2003 (European Space Imaging GmbH)

Cartography: Katharina Conradin, Fiona Wieland

Explanation: In most households in Shantinagar the family members earn around 7 - 22 Rs. per day, on average. Even if there are households with a higher daily income per person, the highest of these daily wages per family member is around 67 Rs. Compared to the other four slums, this is very low.

Map 5.5 Households with livelihood affected by the earthquake in Bhimraonagar

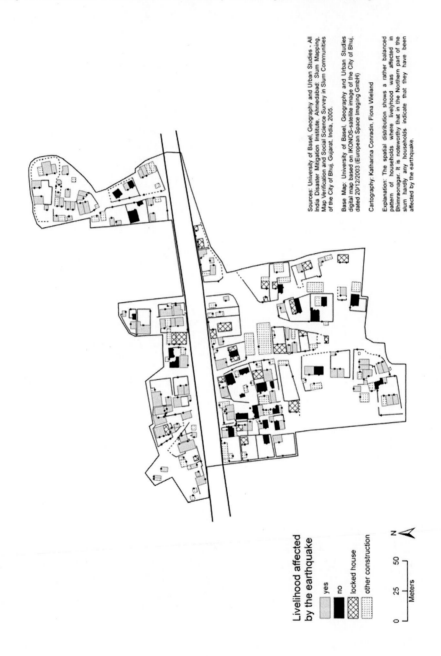

Income differentials – household livelihood security 69

Map 5.6 Households with livelihood affected by the earthquake in Jayprakashnagar

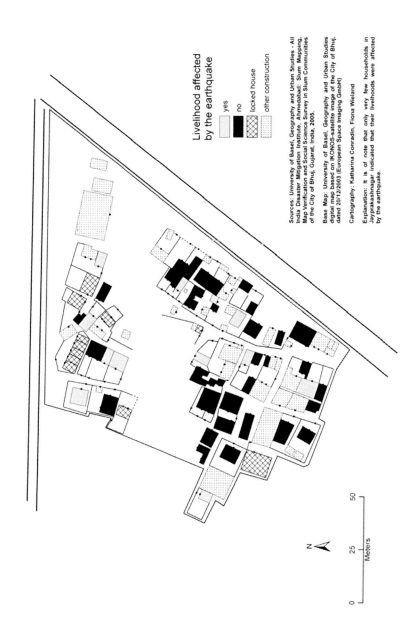

Map 5.7 Households with livelihood affected by the earthquake in Mustuffanagar

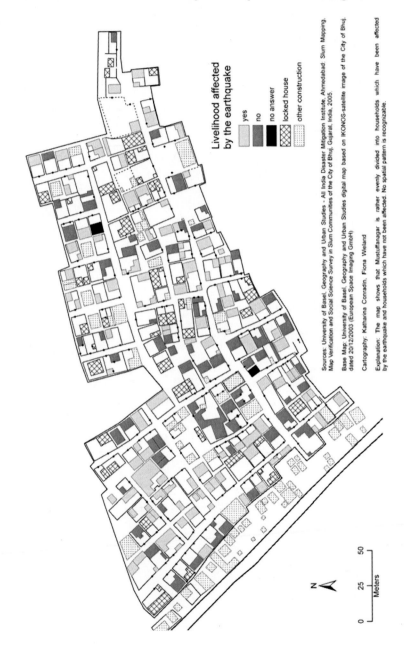

Income differentials – household livelihood security 71

Map 5.8 Households with livelihood affected by the earthquake in Shantinagar

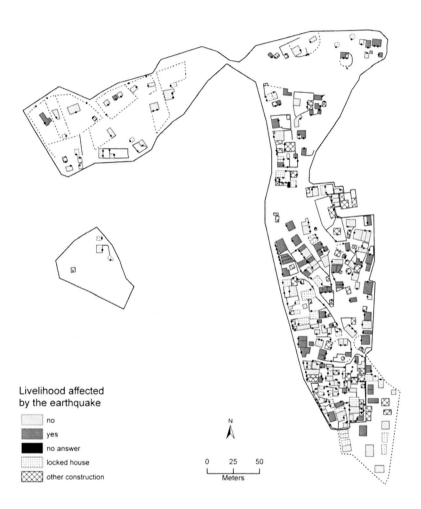

Sources: University of Basel, Geography and Urban Studies - All India Disaster Mitigation Institute, Ahmedabad: Slum Mapping, Map Verification and Social Science Survey in Slum Communities of the City of Bhuj, Gujarat, India, 2005.

Base Map: University of Basel, Geography and Urban Studies digital map based on IKONOS-satellite image of the City of Bhuj, dated 20/12/2003 (European Space Imaging GmbH)

Cartography: Katharina Conradin, Fiona Wieland

Explanation: As the map shows, many households had their livelihoods affected by the earthquake, supporting the general finding that disasters usually affect those already vulnerable the most.

6 The structure of slum housing

K. Conradin, F. Wieland
University of Basel

6.1
Introduction

Analysing the structure of slum housing yields information on the interrelationship between different housing structures, general living conditions, economic situations of the slum dwellers and their general livelihoods. Main questions were:

- Does the type of house reveal details on the livelihoods/economic situation of the slum dwellers?
- What are the differences in housing and is there a connection between the house types and the year when they were built?
- How did the earthquake affect the housing structures in the different slums?
- What are the housing conditions of the families now? Are there still remnants of the 2001 earthquake?
- Did the households take precautions against further earthquakes, and are they perceived to be efficient?
- Has the general knowledge on earthquake-proof shelters increased after 2001?

The information for these questions was obtained by a household-based survey, as well as by observations made by the interviewers. This does not only reveal visible information on the physical state of the slums after the earthquake, but also allows to draw conclusions on the housing status and livelihood in general. Additionally, this chapter also gives information on how the housing structures of people were affected by the earthquake and how the families have arranged themselves with this situation four years after the actual catastrophe.

6.2
Type of house

By slum (Tab. 6.1). The houses were classified into three different types: ***Kachcha*** houses are the traditionally built houses, usually made of mud or clay, sticks and other materials, and have a thatched roof. Generally, they have the lowest price. *Semi-pucca* houses have walls made out of brick, although the type of bricks varies: there are clay bricks (baked or air-dried), stone bricks, or concrete bricks. Semi-pucca houses are one-storied buildings, where the roof is not accessible, i.e. it is not made of cement or concrete. *Pucca* houses are the most stable of the three types and generally have the highest quality. They are made of bricks and are at least two-storied or have a walkable roof. As shown by Maps 6.1 through 6.4, all three types of houses occur in all communities, with Kachcha houses being the smallest proportion and mostly inhabited by Scheduled Tribe households in Shantinagar. The house types vary greatly depending on the slum. The highest proportion of the Kachcha houses are in Bhimraonagar (25.4%), but also a significant fraction of the families in Shantinagar live in Kachcha houses (13.5%). Only a negligible quantity of households resides in Kachcha houses in Jayprakashnagar (1.9%). This is not surprising, as it is the community which is most developed in general. 83.0% of the families in Jayprakashnagar live in semi-pucca houses. The largest percentage of pucca houses is situated in Mustaffanagar (34.6%). This can be explained by the fact that comparatively many families in Mustaffanagar are economically better off, being engaged in textile industries or construction, and can thus afford a brick shelter.

Table 6.1 Type of house, by slum.

Slum Type of house	Bhimraonagar in % (n=130)	Jayprakashnagar in % (n=53)	Mustuffanagar in % (n=159)	Shantinagar in % (n=155)	Total in % (n=497)
Kachcha house	25.4	1.9	11.3	13.5	14.7
Pucca house	16.9	15.1	34.6	10.3	20.3
Semi-Pucca house	57.7	83.0	54.1	76.1	65.0
Total	100.0	100.0	100.0	100.0	100.0

SOURCE: UNIVERSITY OF BASEL, DEPT. OF GEOGRAPHY AND ALL INDIA DISASTER MITIGATION INSTITUTE, AHMEDABAD, INDIA 2005. SOCIAL SCIENCE SURVEY IN SELECTED SLUM COMMUNITIES IN THE CITY OF BHUJ, GUJARAT, INDIA.

By average daily wages of household members (Tab. 6.2). The type of house and the family income did not show a statistically relevant relationsship. Still, there is a trend that few families of the two highest income classes (average daily income per person of whole family) live in a kachcha houses (2.8%). Kachcha house dwellers are more frequent among the lower income classes (12.7% of the people living in kachcha houses are member of the lowest income class). The opposite trend emerges with pucca houses: more families of the higher income classes tend to be living in pucca houses – 20.0% of the members of the highest income class live in pucca houses. The proportion of people living in semi-pucca houses does not vary greatly among all income classes. This might be due to the fact that the quality of semi-pucca houses differs strongly, and the definition of this housing type is quite wide.

Table 6.2 Average daily wages of household members (in Rs.), by type of house.

Type of house Wage	Kachcha house in % (n=71)	Pucca house in % (n=95)	Semi-Pucca house in % (n=313)	Total in % (n=479)
0 to 9 Rs.	12.7	5.3	8.0	8.1
10 to 19 Rs.	36.6	34.7	33.5	34.2
20 to 29 Rs.	33.8	21.1	30.7	29.2
30 to 39 Rs.	11.3	18.9	15.0	15.2
40 to 49 Rs.	2.8	9.5	5.1	5.6
50 to 89 Rs.	1.4	8.4	7.0	6.5
90 to 130 Rs.	1.4	2.1	0.6	1.0
Total	100.0	100.0	100.0	100.0

SOURCE: UNIVERSITY OF BASEL, DEPT. OF GEOGRAPHY AND ALL INDIA DISASTER MITIGATION INSTITUTE, AHMEDABAD, INDIA 2005. SOCIAL SCIENCE SURVEY IN SELECTED SLUM COMMUNITIES IN THE CITY OF BHUJ, GUJARAT, INDIA.

By year of arrival at this house (Tab. 6.3). The underlying idea of the relation between the arrival at the house and the type of house was to show if there was a trend to build more stable houses in the last decades, or if more households had managed to construct for themselves more stable houses. Regardless of the decade in which they were built, most houses were constructed in the semi-pucca style. But there was a slight trend to build fewer semi-pucca houses in favour of pucca houses. Whereas in the years between 1940 and 1970 70% of all new houses were semi-pucca houses, in the years between 2000 and 2005 there were only 53.5% semi-pucca houses. Accordingly, there was a trend to build more pucca houses. In the years 1940-1958 only 14.3% of all new build houses were pucca houses, but between 2000 and 2005 there were already 30.3% new pucca houses. Regarding the trend of building kachcha houses over the indicated period of 65 years no trend can be recognised. The percentage of kachcha house varied from 10-20% without any further significant information.

Table 6.3 Type of house, by year of arrival at this house.

Year of arrival at this house Type of house	1940-1958 in % (n=21)	1960-1969 in % (n=42)	1970-1979 in % (n=56)	1980-1989 in % (n=135)	1990-1999 in % (n=144)	2000-2005 in % (n=99)	Total in % (n=497)
kachcha house	14.3	9.5	12.5	20.7	10.4	16.2	14.7
pucca house	14.3	19.0	10.7	19.3	19.4	30.3	20.3
semi-pucca house	71.4	71.4	76.8	60.0	70.1	53.5	65.0
Total	100.0	100.0	100.0	100.0	100.0	100.0	100.0

SOURCE: UNIVERSITY OF BASEL, DEPT. OF GEOGRAPHY AND ALL INDIA DISASTER MITIGATION INSTITUTE, AHMEDABAD, INDIA 2005. SOCIAL SCIENCE SURVEY IN SELECTED SLUM COMMUNITIES IN THE CITY OF BHUJ, GUJARAT, INDIA.

By livelihood affected (Tab. 6.4). There are no statistically significant relationships between the type of house and whether the livelihood was affected or not. This is easily explained by the fact that the livelihood of a person does not only consist in a stable/good shelter, but does also include other aspects such as an occupation with a regular income, health etc.

Table 6.4 Affected livelihood through earthquake, by type of house.

Type of house Livelihood affected	Kachcha house in % (n=71)	Pucca house in % (n=100)	Semi-Pucca house in % (n=316)	Total in % (n=487)
Yes	67.6	55.0	58.9	59.3
No	32.4	45.0	41.1	40.7
Total	100.0	100.0	100.0	100.0

SOURCE: UNIVERSITY OF BASEL, DEPT. OF GEOGRAPHY AND ALL INDIA DISASTER MITIGATION INSTITUTE, AHMEDABAD, INDIA 2005. SOCIAL SCIENCE SURVEY IN SELECTED SLUM COMMUNITIES IN THE CITY OF BHUJ, GUJARAT, INDIA.

6.3
Post earthquake housing status

By type of house (Tab. 6.5). Not surprisingly, the largest proportion of the houses which were completely destroyed, are kachcha houses (45.6%). An additional fifth of these houses (22.1%) are severely damaged, and only 5.9% of them were still considered safe. Of pucca houses, which are built in a more stable way, almost two thirds (64.7%) were safe or showed only minor damages. It is of note that quite a high proportion of the semi-pucca houses were also severely damaged or completely destroyed (60.7%). This is explained partly by the fact that semi-pucca houses have no cement of concrete roofing. Those roofs are thus more prone to collapse. Additionally, semi-pucca houses are probably the cheapest and first option a family chooses if they do not build a kachcha house. Thus, the quality of the houses is probably not always very good, since people might still not have enough money to build a stable and safe shelter. To be able to interpret this aspect fully, information on the building material (especially of the semi-pucca houses) would have to be obtained – which was not the case in this survey.

Table 6.5 Post earthquake housing status, by type of house.

Type of house Post earthquake housing status	Kachcha house in % (n=68)	Pucca house in % (n=85)	Semi-Pucca house in % (n=303)	Total in % (n=456)
Safe	5.9	21.2	6.6	9.2
minor damage	26.5	43.5	32.7	33.8
severe damage	22.1	17.6	23.1	21.9
completely destroyed	45.6	17.6	37.6	35.1
Total	100.0	100.0	100.0	100.0

SOURCE: UNIVERSITY OF BASEL, DEPT. OF GEOGRAPHY AND ALL INDIA DISASTER MITIGATION INSTITUTE, AHMEDABAD, INDIA 2005. SOCIAL SCIENCE SURVEY IN SELECTED SLUM COMMUNITIES IN THE CITY OF BHUJ, GUJARAT, INDIA.

By slum (Tab. 6.6). Not all slums were affected equally by the 2001 earthquake, as shown by Maps 6.5 through 6.8. This is mostly explained by the different housing structures and the quality of the respective buildings. The gravest consequences were suffered in Shantinagar and Bhimraonagar, where almost three quarters of the houses were severely damaged or completely destroyed (76.0% and 69.9%, respectively). In Jayprakashnagar on the other hand, 78.4% of the dwellings are still considered safe after the earthquake, or show only minor damages. The case is similar in Mustaffanagar, where 63.5% of the houses are safe or have only minor damages. Analysing these figures, one must keep in mind the different types of houses prevalent in the individual slums and the stability of each type of building – kachcha houses are clearly less stable than pucca houses.

Table 6.6 Post earthquake housing status, by slum.

Slum Post earth-quake housing status	Bhimraona-gar in % (n=126)	Jayprakashna-gar in % (n=51)	Mustuffana-gar in % (n=129)	Shantina-gar in % (n=150)	Total in % (n=456)
Safe	2.4	3.9	24.0	4.0	9.2
minor damage	27.8	74.5	39.5	20.0	33.8
severe damage	30.2	7.8	26.4	16.0	21.9
completely destroyed	39.7	13.7	10.1	60.0	35.1
Total	100.0	100.0	100.0	100.0	100.0

SOURCE: UNIVERSITY OF BASEL, DEPT. OF GEOGRAPHY AND ALL INDIA DISASTER MITIGATION INSTITUTE, AHMEDABAD, INDIA 2005. SOCIAL SCIENCE SURVEY IN SELECTED SLUM COMMUNITIES IN THE CITY OF BHUJ, GUJARAT, INDIA.

By living in the same house as before the earthquake (Tab. 6.7). A highly significant relation can be observed between the post earthquake housing status and the question if the household members are still living in the same house as before the earthquake. It is interesting to note that 81.6% of the households with a safe or only minor damaged house do not live in the same house as before the earthquake. Only 6.2% of the household considering their house after the earthquake as safe still live in it. But in 37.6% of the completely destroyed houses the same families are still living in. This seems to be a contradiction: At first sight, it is not clear why the families who live in safe houses leave them and the families in completely damages houses stay.

However, comparing this with table 6.2 sheds light onto this matter. Most of the completely destroyed houses were kachcha houses. As households living in kachcha houses most frequent belong to lower income classes they will not have the same financial means to rebuild their houses as the pucca and semi-pucca households. In place of the old house families of more means could therefore build a new one. Poorer families had to stay in their old house and try to renovate it as good as possible.

Table 6.7 Post earthquake housing status, by living in the same house as before the earthquake.

Post earthquake Housing status \ Living in the same house as before the earthquake	Yes in % (n=404)	No in % (n=49)	Total in % (n=453)
Safe	6.2	34.7	9.3
minor damage	31.9	46.9	33.6
severe damage	24.3	4.1	22.1
completely destroyed	37.6	14.3	35.0
Total	100.0	100.0	100.0

SOURCE: UNIVERSITY OF BASEL, DEPT. OF GEOGRAPHY AND ALL INDIA DISASTER MITIGATION INSTITUTE, AHMEDABAD, INDIA 2005. SOCIAL SCIENCE SURVEY IN SELECTED SLUM COMMUNITIES IN THE CITY OF BHUJ, GUJARAT, INDIA.

By current housing status (Tab. 6.8). The significant relation between the post earthquake status and the current housing status shows that the current housing status is not depending on the post earthquake status. Only 12.5% of the houses now considered as safe were also in a safe status after the earthquake. But also 36.3% of the completely damaged houses are now indicated as safe. Besides, 98% of the households indicate that they are now living in a safe or minor damaged house. This shows that most houses regardless of their post earthquake status appear to have a better status, or that improvements were made, irrespective of the impact received by the earthquake.

Table 6.8 Post earthquake housing status, by current housing status.

Post earthquake housing status \ Current housing status	safe in % (n=303)	minor damage in % (n=144)	severe damage in % (n=7)	completely destroyed in % (n=2)	Total in % (n=456)
Safe	12.5	2.8	0.0	0.0	9.2
minor damage	30.0	43.1	0.0	50.0	33.8
severe damage	21.1	24.3	14.3	0.0	21.9
completely destroyed	36.3	29.9	85.7	50.0	35.1
Total	100.0	100.0	100.0	100.0	100.0

SOURCE: UNIVERSITY OF BASEL, DEPT. OF GEOGRAPHY AND ALL INDIA DISASTER MITIGATION INSTITUTE, AHMEDABAD, INDIA 2005. SOCIAL SCIENCE SURVEY IN SELECTED SLUM COMMUNITIES IN THE CITY OF BHUJ, GUJARAT, INDIA.

6.4
Current housing status

By average daily wages of household members (Tab. 6.9). The assumption that members of the higher income classes tend to have better houses (and thus suffer less damage) cannot be proven here, as the relation is not statistically significant. Nevertheless, the tendency can be made out that the share of safe houses is generally larger among the higher income classes. This is backed by the impression that there are more severely damaged houses among the lower income classes.

Table 6.9 Current housing status, by average daily wages of household members (in Rs.).

Current housing status \ Wage	0 to 9 Rs. in % (n=39)	10 to 19 Rs. in % (n=163)	20 to 29 Rs. in % (n=139)	30 to 39 Rs. in % (n=73)	40 to 49 Rs. in % (n=27)	50 to 89 Rs. in % (n=31)	90 to 130 Rs. in % (n=5)	Total in % (n=477)
safe	61.5	67.5	66.9	69.9	74.1	71.0	80.0	67.9
minor damage	33.3	30.1	33.1	28.8	25.9	25.8	20.0	30.4
severe damage	5.1	2.5	0.0	0.0	0.0	0.0	0.0	1.3
completely destroyed	0.0	0.0	0.0	1.4	0.0	3.2	0.0	0.4
Total	100.0	100.0	100.0	100.0	100.0	100.0	100.0	100.0

SOURCE: UNIVERSITY OF BASEL, DEPT. OF GEOGRAPHY AND ALL INDIA DISASTER MITIGATION INSTITUTE, AHMEDABAD, INDIA 2005. SOCIAL SCIENCE SURVEY IN SELECTED SLUM COMMUNITIES IN THE CITY OF BHUJ, GUJARAT, INDIA.

6.5
Living in the same house as before the earthquake

By average daily wages of household members (Tab. 6.10). The place of living after the earthquake (same or different house) shows no relation with the income of the surveyed households. The number of people who live in the same house after the earthquake is even higher among the lower income classes. This might be explained as follows: Though there are more severely or completely destroyed houses among the lower income classes – 5.1% severely damaged houses among the lowest income class, compared to 0.0% among the highest five classes (see Tab. 6.9) – those people probably do not have the money to build up a completely new structure. Rather, they reconstruct or repair their damaged shelter – and thus state in the survey, that they still live in the same house. Among the higher income classes, the case is different: Though there are fewer houses which show damages, the people of the higher income classes can afford to move somewhere else into a new and safe shelter or rebuilt on site. This would explain why more people of the lower income classes than of the higher income classes still live in the same houses, although their shelters got destroyed more often.

Table 6.10 Living in the same house as before the earthquake, by average daily wages of household members (in Rs.).

Wage / Living in the same house as bef. the earthq.	0 to 9 Rs. in % (n=39)	10 to 19 Rs. in % (n=163)	20 to 29 Rs. in % (n=140)	30 to 39 Rs. in % (n=72)	40 to 49 Rs. in % (n=27)	50 to 89 Rs. in % (n=31)	90 to 130 Rs. in % (n=5)	Total in % (n=477)
yes	87.2	84.7	81.4	83.3	70.4	77.4	80.0	82.4
no	12.8	15.3	18.6	16.7	29.6	22.6	20.0	17.6
Total	100.0	100.0	100.0	100.0	100.0	100.0	100.0	100.0

SOURCE: UNIVERSITY OF BASEL, DEPT. OF GEOGRAPHY AND ALL INDIA DISASTER MITIGATION INSTITUTE, AHMEDABAD, INDIA 2005. SOCIAL SCIENCE SURVEY IN SELECTED SLUM COMMUNITIES IN THE CITY OF BHUJ, GUJARAT, INDIA.

6.6
Precautions to make the house earthquake proof

By average daily wages of household members (Tab. 6.11). There was no significant relation between the precautions a person took against earthquakes and the income level. Still, it can be observed that independent of income classes, almost no one took any precautions against future earthquakes (total only 9.6%). This is probably due to a lack of knowledge of how to build earth-quake proof shelters, since only a very small percentage of households were even introduced to measures how to make a house earthquake proof.

Table 6.11 Precaution to make the house earthquake proof, by average daily wages of household members (in Rs.)

Wage / Precaution to make the house earthquake proof	0 to 9 Rs. in % (n=24)	10 to 19 Rs. in % (n=118)	20 to 29 Rs. in % (n=104)	30 to 39 Rs. in % (n=54)	40 to 49 Rs. in % (n=20)	50 to 89 Rs. in % (n=21)	90 to 130 Rs. in % (n=4)	Total in % (n=345)
yes	8.3	5.9	9.6	14.8	15.0	14.3	0.0	9.6
no	91.7	94.1	90.4	85.2	85.0	85.7	100.0	90.4
Total	100.0	100.0	100.0	100.0	100.0	100.0	100.0	100.0

SOURCE: UNIVERSITY OF BASEL, DEPT. OF GEOGRAPHY AND ALL INDIA DISASTER MITIGATION INSTITUTE, AHMEDABAD, INDIA 2005. SOCIAL SCIENCE SURVEY IN SELECTED SLUM COMMUNITIES IN THE CITY OF BHUJ, GUJARAT, INDIA.

By education of family head (Tab. 6.12). Also the relation between precaution measures to make a house earthquake proof and the education of the family head are not statistically significant. Again, only a very small number had taken precautions anyway.

Table 6.12 Precaution to make the house earthquake proof, by education standard of family head.

Education / Precaution to make the house earthquake proof	3rd Standard in % (n=34)	4th – 6th Standard in % (n=54)	7th – 9th Standard in % (n=82)	10th – 12th Standard in % (n=24)	completed graduation / diploma in % (n=5)	Illiterate in % (n=158)	Total in % (n=357)
Yes	20.6	3.7	11.0	8.3	0.0	9.5	9.8
No	79.4	96.3	89.0	91.7	100.0	90.5	90.2
Total	100.0	100.0	100.0	100.0	100.0	100.0	100.0

SOURCE: UNIVERSITY OF BASEL, DEPT. OF GEOGRAPHY AND ALL INDIA DISASTER MITIGATION INSTITUTE, AHMEDABAD, INDIA 2005. SOCIAL SCIENCE SURVEY IN SELECTED SLUM COMMUNITIES IN THE CITY OF BHUJ, GUJARAT, INDIA.

By caste (Tab. 6.13). It must first be stated that again, only a small percentage of the surveyed households have taken precautions – but concerning castes, there are significant discrepancies. While roughly 8% of the Scheduled Castes and Scheduled Tribe families (8.9% and 8.0%, respectively) took precaution measures, only 5% of the Other Backward Caste families answered this question in the affirmative – 16.4% of the General Caste families had taken precautions. Maybe this can be explained by the fact that the General Caste families are generally economically better off and can thus afford to take precaution measures. There was no significant relation between the precaution measures taken and the religious affiliation.

Table 6.13 Precaution to make the house earthquake proof, by caste.

Caste Pre-caution to make the house earthquake proof	SC in % (n=79)	ST in % (n=50)	OBC in % (n=119)	General in % (n=110)	Total in % (n=358)
Yes	8.9	8.0	5.0	16.4	9.8
No	91.1	92.0	95.0	83.6	90.2
Total	100.0	100.0	100.0	100.0	100.0

SOURCE: UNIVERSITY OF BASEL, DEPT. OF GEOGRAPHY AND ALL INDIA DISASTER MITIGATION INSTITUTE, AHMEDABAD, INDIA 2005. SOCIAL SCIENCE SURVEY IN SELECTED SLUM COMMUNITIES IN THE CITY OF BHUJ, GUJARAT, INDIA.

By slum (Tab. 6.14). The percentage of precautionary measures taken varies greatly between the individual slums – though one must keep in mind the small number of families who did take precautionary measures. The highest percentage of households who took measures is located in Mustuffanagar (28.0%). This corresponds to the findings of table 6.13, since most households in Mustuffanagar are Muslims belonging to the Other Backward Castes.

Table 6.14 Precaution to make your house earthquake proof, by slum.

Slum Pre-caution to make the house earthquake proof	Bhimraonagar in % (n=130)	Jayprakashnagar in % (n=53)	Mustuffanagar in % (n=50)	Shantinagar in % (n=125)	Total in % (n=358)
Yes	2.3	13.2	28.0	8.8	9.8
No	97.7	86.8	72.0	91.2	90.2
Total	100.0	100.0	100.0	100.0	100.0

SOURCE: UNIVERSITY OF BASEL, DEPT. OF GEOGRAPHY AND ALL INDIA DISASTER MITIGATION INSTITUTE, AHMEDABAD, INDIA 2005. SOCIAL SCIENCE SURVEY IN SELECTED SLUM COMMUNITIES IN THE CITY OF BHUJ, GUJARAT, INDIA.

6.7
Precautions have been efficient

By education of family head (Tab. 6.15). Whether the precautionary measures taken are perceived as efficient is not significantly related to the education of the family head. This is most probably due to the fact that the largest proportion of households did not take precautionary measures at all – among the small number who did, a regular pattern did not emerge.

The structure of slum housing 83

Table 6.15 Perception of efficiency of precautions measures, by education standard of family head.

Education / Efficient precautions	Hrs. 1-3 in % (n=13)	Hrs. 4-6 in % (n=17)	Hrs. 7-9 in % (n=25)	Hrs. 10-12 in % (n=8)	completed graduation / diploma in % (n=1)	Illiterate in % (n=37)	Total in % (n=101)
Yes	61.5	17.6	32.0	25.0	0.0	37.8	34.7
No	38.5	82.4	68.0	75.0	100.0	62.2	65.3
Total	100.0	100.0	100.0	100.0	100.0	100.0	100.0

SOURCE: UNIVERSITY OF BASEL, DEPT. OF GEOGRAPHY AND ALL INDIA DISASTER MITIGATION INSTITUTE, AHMEDABAD, INDIA 2005. SOCIAL SCIENCE SURVEY IN SELECTED SLUM COMMUNITIES IN THE CITY OF BHUJ, GUJARAT, INDIA.

6.8
Investment to make shelter earthquake proof

By average daily wages of household members (Tab. 6.16). There was no statistically relevant relation between the income of a family and the sum they invested in making their shelter earthquake proof. This is, on one hand to be attributed to the small number of households who have taken precautionary measures, and on the other hand also on the fact that very few families have been instructed about how to make their shelter earthquake proof. One should note, however, that the base number of those who made investments to make their shelter earthquake proof is quite small (31 in total). Thus, the findings only give an impression and are not necessarily representative.

Table 6.16 Investment to make shelter earthquake proof, by average daily wages of household members (in Rs.).

Wage / Investment	0 to 9 Rs. in % (n=39)	10 to 19 Rs. in % (n=164)	20 to 29 Rs. in % (n=140)	30 to 39 Rs. in % (n=73)	40 to 49 Rs. in % (n=27)	50 to 89 Rs. in % (n=31)	90 to 130 Rs. in % (n=5)	Total in % (n=479)
<5000	94.9	90.9	93.6	90.4	88.9	90.3	100.0	91.9
5000-9999	2.6	5.5	0.7	4.1	3.7	0.0	0.0	3.1
10000-19999	2.6	2.4	1.4	1.4	0.0	0.0	0.0	1.7
20000-49999	0.0	1.2	2.9	0.0	3.7	6.5	0.0	1.9
50000-199999	0.0	0.0	0.7	0.0	3.7	0.0	0.0	0.4
200000-350000	0.0	0.0	0.7	4.1	0.0	3.2	0.0	1.0
Total	100.0	100.0	100.0	100.0	100.0	100.0	100.0	100.0

SOURCE: UNIVERSITY OF BASEL, DEPT. OF GEOGRAPHY AND ALL INDIA DISASTER MITIGATION INSTITUTE, AHMEDABAD, INDIA 2005. SOCIAL SCIENCE SURVEY IN SELECTED SLUM COMMUNITIES IN THE CITY OF BHUJ, GUJARAT, INDIA.

By slum (Tab. 6.17). There was no relation between the individual slums and the investments that their respective inhabitants made in order to make their shelters earthquake proof. Although one would expect that the inhabitants of the wealthier slums areas such as Jayprakashnagar and Mustuffanagar, (Tab. 5.5) invest more.

Table 6.17 Investment to make shelter earthquake proof, by slum (in Rs.).

Slum Investment	Bhimraonagar in % (n=130)	Jayprakashnagar in % (n=53)	Mustuffanagar in % (n=159)	Shantinagar in % (n=155)	Total in % (n=497)
<5'000	95.4	88.7	90.6	91.0	91.8
5'000-9'999	2.3	5.7	3.8	1.9	3.0
10'000-19'999	0.8	1.9	1.9	2.6	1.8
20'000-49'999	1.5	1.9	1.3	2.6	1.8
50'000-199'999	0.0	0.0	0.6	1.3	0.6
200'000-350'000	0.0	1.9	1.9	0.6	1.0
Total	100.0	100.0	100.0	100.0	100.0

SOURCE: UNIVERSITY OF BASEL, DEPT. OF GEOGRAPHY AND ALL INDIA DISASTER MITIGATION INSTITUTE, AHMEDABAD, INDIA 2005. SOCIAL SCIENCE SURVEY IN SELECTED SLUM COMMUNITIES IN THE CITY OF BHUJ, GUJARAT, INDIA.

6.9 Conclusion

The interrelations between the housing structures and the slums revealed some noteworthy details. The housing types (kachcha, pucca and semi-pucca) show a relationship with the general economic status of the slum areas; especially Shantinagar, which has the highest Scheduled Tribe population, had a large number of kachcha houses. The reverse was true for more developed slums such as Jayprakashnagar, where only a very small part of the houses was of the traditional kachcha type. As a deplorable fact, the kachcha houses were the one group that was worst affected by the earthquake, thus most households who were already living in very poor circumstances also suffered the biggest impact from the earthquake. Additionally, a very high percentage of semi-pucca houses were severely damaged or completely destroyed. The reason for this is that though semi-pucca houses have brick walls, their roofing structure is not always very stable and very likely consists of corrugated iron or other materials which collapse easily. Additionally, though semi-pucca houses are less expensive than pucca houses, many families still lack the proper financing to build a truly stable house – and the houses are more prone to suffer damages or collapse during an earthquake. Thus, it was the "poorer" slums (Shantinagar, Bhimraonagar) which were affected worst during the earthquake.

The assumption that fewer kachcha houses are built today was not confirmed – kachcha houses are still built today. This is most likely due to the fact that kachcha houses are significantly cheaper than the brick pucca or semi-pucca houses – and still offer a comparably higher living standard than temporary shelters made from cloth, corrugated iron or plastic sheets.

Though most of the families have very limited financial means, they have mostly been able to rebuild their housing structures – almost all of them live in houses which they consider safe or which only show minor damages. Regarding Tab. 6.7, an interesting trend could be made out: While families with a higher income were living in different houses than before the earthquake, families with a lower income were mainly still living in the same houses – which means that they have rebuilt their houses from the rubble, whereas wealthier families could move to another, new place or newly rebuild *in situ*.

Map 6.1 Types of houses in Bhimraonagar

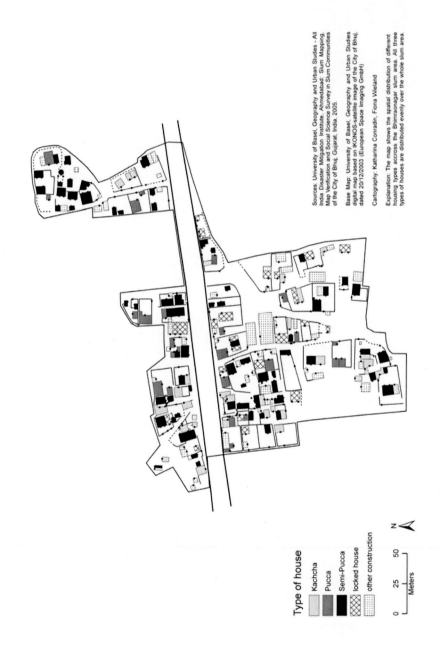

Map 6.2 Types of houses in Jayprakashnagar

Map 6.3 Types of houses in Mustuffanagar

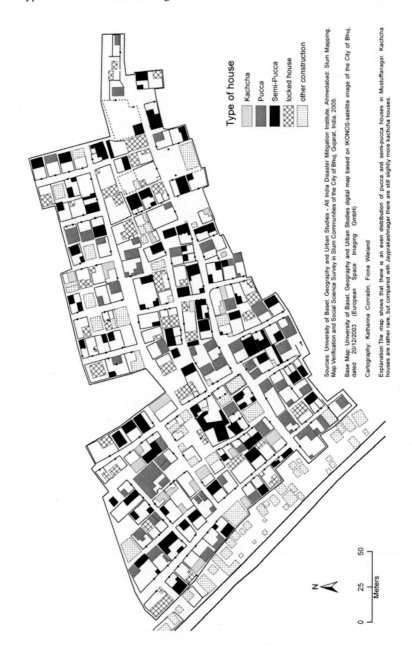

The structure of slum housing

Map 6.4 Types of houses in Shantinagar

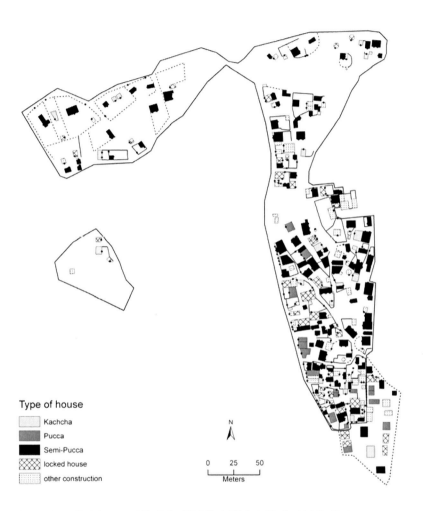

Sources: University of Basel, Geography and Urban Studies - All India Disaster Mitigation Institute, Ahmedabad: Slum Mapping, Map Verification and Social Science Survey in Slum Communities of the City of Bhuj, Gujarat, India, 2005.

Base Map: University of Basel, Geography and Urban Studies digital map based on IKONOS-satellite image of the City of Bhuj, dated 20/12/2003 (European Space Imaging GmbH)

Cartography: Katharina Conradin, Fiona Wieland

Explanation: Semi-pucca houses are the prevailing type of house in this slum, but also pucca and kachcha houses occur. The latter type of house is particularly inhabited by the scheduled tribes, which are strongly represented in the southern and nothern part of this slum.

90 The structure of slum housing

Map 6.5 Post earthquake housing status in Bhimraonagar

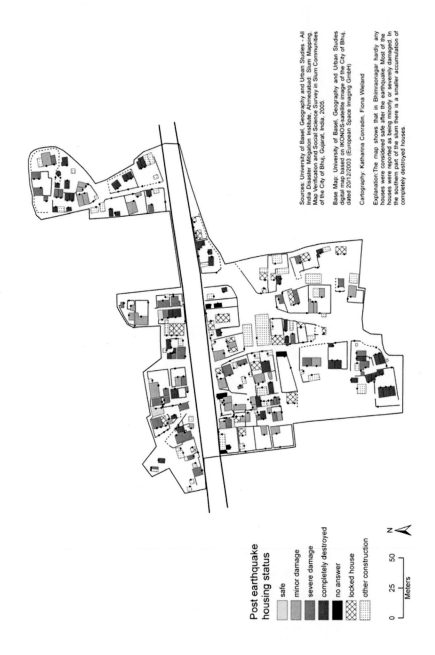

The structure of slum housing 91

Map 6.6 Post earthquake housing status in Jayprakashnagar

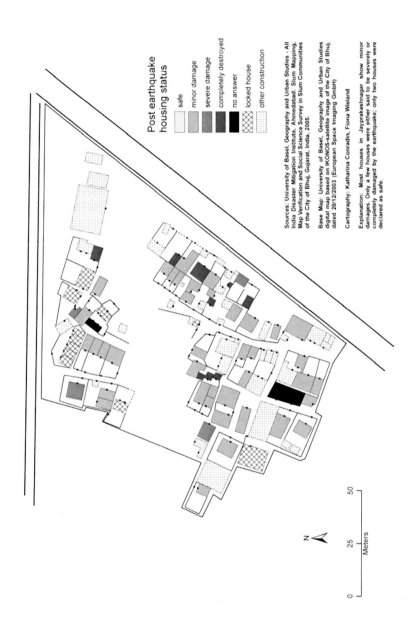

Map 6.7 Post earthquake housing status in Mustuffanagar

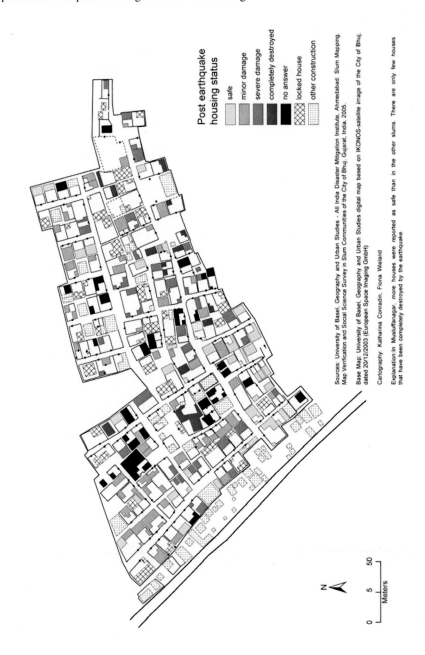

The structure of slum housing 93

Map 6.8 Post earthquake housing status in Shantinagar

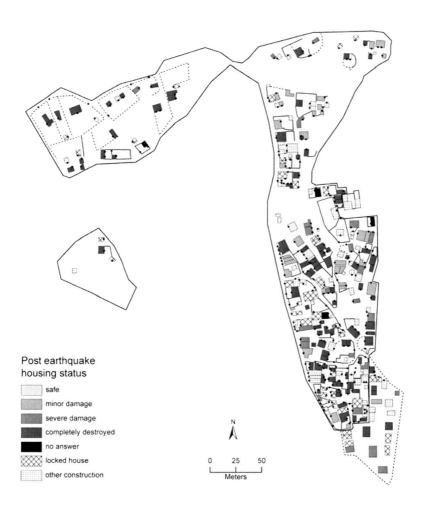

Sources: University of Basel, Geography and Urban Studies - All India Disaster Mitigation Institute, Ahmedabad Slum Mapping, Map Verification and Social Science Survey in Slum Communities of the City of Bhuj, Gujarat, India, 2005.

Base Map: University of Basel, Geography and Urban Studies digital map based on IKONOS-satellite image of the City of Bhuj, dated 20/12/2003 (European Space Imaging GmbH)

Cartography: Katharina Conradin, Fiona Wieland

Explanation: The spatial pattern shows that most houses were completely destroyed by the earthquake. This indicates that the housing substance in Shantinagar was worse than in the other four slums.

7 Ownership and tax bill

B. Lietzke, D. Michel, N. Sliwa
University of Basel

7.1
Introduction

This chapter explores tax bill ownership as an indicator of willingness to make an own contribution to the government's efforts for the betterment of living conditions. Shared responsibility that expresses itself in paying one's fair share of taxes is a concept not understood easily even in developed countries. Even in high income countries there is a general tendency to have high expectations on what government should provide with low acceptance for one's own share of responsibility. In the context of development deficiencies, the expectations may even be higher that government should provide for central services without having to contribute at all. Whether or not people are willing to share, the burden largely depends on the degree of their willingness to pay for taxes. As such, tax bill ownership serves as an approximation of acceptance to share financial responsibility in efforts in what is perceived as a government duty.

7.2
Ownership document

Remarkably in view of the general poverty is the fact that in all communities the degree of house ownership is quite high (see Maps 7.1 through 7.4). Rather astonishing, however, is that there is a fair number of households in all communities who do not have ownership documents, and that there are people who do not know whether they are owners or not (see Maps 7.1 through 7.4).

Roughly one third of all households state that they possess an ownership document for their house. There are more households with an ownership document on stamp paper (20%) than with a property card (14.4%).

By age of the family head (Tab. 7.1). Roughly one fifth of the questioned 20 to 59 year old household heads state that they possess an ownership document on stamp paper for their house. Slightly lower is the value (13.2%) among the group of the 60-69 year old people, whereas approximately one third of the 70-89 year old possesses an ownership document on stamp paper. These intergenerational differences may reflect family traditions (the eldest being the owner), furthermore economic situations (the working age household heads being the owner) or different administrative policies requiring ownership proof to a greater degree in some years but not in others.

Table 7.1 Ownership document, by age of family head

Ownership document \ Age	20-29 in % (n=55)	30-39 in % (n=33)	40-49 in % (n=125)	50-59 in % (n=68)	60-69 in % (n=68)	70-79 in % (n=24)	80-89 in % (n=7)	>90 in % (n=5)	Total in % (n=485)
No	72.7	66.2	54.4	57.4	63.2	45.8	28.6	40.0	60.4
yes, property card	7.3	12.8	17.6	16.2	13.2	20.8	14.3	20.0	14.4
yes, on 10/20/50 Rs. Stamp paper	18.2	18.8	21.6	23.5	13.2	29.2	28.6	20.0	20.0
yes, other	1.8	0.0	1.6	0.0	2.9	0.0	14.3	20.0	1.4
do not know	0.0	2.3	4.8	2.9	7.4	4.2	14.3	0.0	3.7
Total	100.0	100.0	100.0	100.0	100.0	100.0	100.0	100.0	100.0

SOURCE: UNIVERSITY OF BASEL, DEPT. OF GEOGRAPHY AND ALL INDIA DISASTER MITIGATION INSTITUTE, AHMEDABAD, INDIA 2005. SOCIAL SCIENCE SURVEY IN SELECTED SLUM COMMUNITIES IN THE CITY OF BHUJ, GUJARAT, INDIA.

By slum name (Tab. 7.2). Great differences concerning the ownership situation exist between the different slum areas. While 83.8 % of the households of Bhimraonagar and 65.1 % in Shantinagar do not have any ownership document, in Jayprakashnagar only one third does not have one. In Mustuffanagar, the percentage of those having no ownership document is 46.1%. In Shanti- (23%) and Jayprakashnagar (60%), property cards are the common ownership document, whereas in Mustuffanagar (46.8%), stamp papers are widely spread.

Table 7.2 Ownership document, by slum.

Ownership document \ Slum	Bhimraonagar in % (n=130)	Jayprakashnagar in % (n=50)	Mustuffanagar in % (n=154)	Shantinagar in % (n=152)	Total in % (n=486)
no	83.8	30.0	46.1	65.1	60.5
yes, property card	0.8	60.0	2.6	23.0	14.4
yes, on 10/20/50 Rs. Stamp paper	7.7	6.0	46.8	7.9	20.0
yes, other	0.8	0.0	2.6	1.3	1.4
do not know	6.9	4.0	1.9	2.6	3.7
Total	100.0	100.0	100.0	100.0	100.0

SOURCE: UNIVERSITY OF BASEL, DEPT. OF GEOGRAPHY AND ALL INDIA DISASTER MITIGATION INSTITUTE, AHMEDABAD, INDIA 2005. SOCIAL SCIENCE SURVEY IN SELECTED SLUM COMMUNITIES IN THE CITY OF BHUJ, GUJARAT, INDIA.

By religion (Tab. 7.3). 66.8% of the Hindu and 55.7% of the Muslim households do not have any ownership document for their house. While the distribution of property cards is quite the same (15.6% and 13.6%), there is almost the same difference between the Hindus (12.3%) and the Muslim (25.6%) who have an ownership document on stamp paper as between those who have no document at all. This relates more to location than to religion. For example, there are more Muslims than Hindus living in Mustuffanagar where the distribution of stamp papers is dominant.

Table 7.3 Ownership document, by religion.

Ownership document / Religion	Hindu in % (n=211)	Muslim in % (n=273)	Total in % (n=484)
no	66.8	55.7	60.5
yes, property card	15.6	13.6	14.5
yes, on 10/20/50 Rs. Stamp paper	12.3	25.6	19.8
yes, other	0.5	2.2	1.4
do not know	4.7	2.9	3.7
Total	100.0	100.0	100.0

SOURCE: UNIVERSITY OF BASEL, DEPT. OF GEOGRAPHY AND ALL INDIA DISASTER MITIGATION INSTITUTE, AHMEDABAD, INDIA 2005. SOCIAL SCIENCE SURVEY IN SELECTED SLUM COMMUNITIES IN THE CITY OF BHUJ, GUJARAT, INDIA.

By caste (Tab. 7.4). There is a striking difference between the different castes. The majority of scheduled caste (85.9%) and scheduled tribe (70.2%) members does not possess any ownership document. Other backward caste (OBC) members have distinctively lower shares (62.4%). This may show that access to and information about ownership documents depends on caste affiliation. The high percentage of ownership documents held in the OBC is probably related to the high percentage of Muslims in these castes (see Tab. 3). Most stamp papers are held by people of the general castes (37.6%).

Table 7.4 Ownership document, by caste.

Ownership document / Caste	SC in % (n=85)	ST in % (n=57)	OBC in % (n=178)	General in % (n=165)	Total in % (n=485)
No	85.9	70.2	62.4	42.4	60.6
yes, property card	2.4	8.8	21.3	15.2	14.4
yes, on 10/20/50 Rs. Stamp paper	7.1	7.0	14.0	37.6	20.0
yes, other	0.0	1.8	1.1	1.8	1.2
do not know	4.7	12.3	1.1	3.0	3.7
Total	100.0	100.0	100.0	100.0	100.0

SOURCE: UNIVERSITY OF BASEL, DEPT. OF GEOGRAPHY AND ALL INDIA DISASTER MITIGATION INSTITUTE, AHMEDABAD, INDIA 2005. SOCIAL SCIENCE SURVEY IN SELECTED SLUM COMMUNITIES IN THE CITY OF BHUJ, GUJARAT, INDIA.

By average daily income, education standard and sex of household members (Tab. 7.5 – 7.7). The possession of an ownership document has no relation to the average family income, nor with education or with the sex of the head of the family, which leaves the question for further exploration why some favour ownership documents and others do not, also what the implication or perceived advantages are of having an ownership document or not.

Table 7.5 Ownership document, by average daily wages of household members (in Rs.).

Ownership document	Wage 0 to 9 Rs. in % (n=39)	10 to 19 Rs. in % (n=163)	20 to 29 Rs. in % (n=137)	30 to 39 Rs. in % (n=70)	40 to 49 Rs. in % (n=25)	50 to 89 Rs. in % (n=30)	90 to 130 Rs. in % (n=5)	Total in % (n=469)
no	53.8	68.1	62.0	45.7	56.0	50.0	60.0	59.9
yes, property card	12.8	14.7	13.1	17.1	16.0	10.0	20.0	14.3
yes, on 10/20/50 Rs. Stamp paper	23.1	13.5	19.7	28.6	24.0	36.7	20.0	20.5
yes, other	5.1	0.0	0.7	4.3	4.0	0.0	0.0	1.5
do not know	5.1	3.7	4.4	4.3	0.0	3.3	0.0	3.8
Total	100.0	100.0	100.0	100.0	100.0	100.0	100.0	100.0

SOURCE: UNIVERSITY OF BASEL, DEPT. OF GEOGRAPHY AND ALL INDIA DISASTER MITIGATION INSTITUTE, AHMEDABAD, INDIA 2005. SOCIAL SCIENCE SURVEY IN SELECTED SLUM COMMUNITIES IN THE CITY OF BHUJ, GUJARAT, INDIA.

Table 7.6 Ownership document, by education standard of family head.

Ownership document	Education Hrs. 1-3 in % (n=46)	Hrs. 4-6 in % (n=81)	Hrs. 7-9 in % (n=103)	Hrs. 10-12 in % (n=33)	Completed Diploma in % (n=1)	Completed Graduation in % (n=6)	Illiterate in % (n=215)	Total in % (n=485)
No	41.3	60.5	57.3	54.5	0.0	33.3	67.9	60.4
yes, property card	15.2	11.1	20.4	3.0	0.0	16.7	14.4	14.4
yes, on 10/20/50 Rs. Stamp paper	39.1	23.5	18.4	39.4	100.0	50.0	11.2	20.0
yes, other	2.2	1.2	1.0	3.0	0.0	0.0	1.4	1.4
do not know	2.2	3.7	2.9	0.0	0.0	0.0	5.1	3.7
Total	100.0	100.0	100.0	100.0	100.0	100.0	100.0	100.0

SOURCE: UNIVERSITY OF BASEL, DEPT. OF GEOGRAPHY AND ALL INDIA DISASTER MITIGATION INSTITUTE, AHMEDABAD, INDIA 2005. SOCIAL SCIENCE SURVEY IN SELECTED SLUM COMMUNITIES IN THE CITY OF BHUJ, GUJARAT, INDIA.

Table 7.7 Ownership document, by sex of family head.

Ownership document	Sex female in % (n=65)	male in % (n=420)	Total in % (n=485)
no	58.5	60.7	60.4
yes, property card	15.4	14.3	14.4
yes, on 10/20/50 Rs. Stamp paper	16.9	20.5	20.0
yes, other	1.5	1.4	1.4
do not know	7.7	3.1	3.7
Total	100.0	100.0	100.0

SOURCE: UNIVERSITY OF BASEL, DEPT. OF GEOGRAPHY AND ALL INDIA DISASTER MITIGATION INSTITUTE, AHMEDABAD, INDIA 2005. SOCIAL SCIENCE SURVEY IN SELECTED SLUM COMMUNITIES IN THE CITY OF BHUJ, GUJARAT, INDIA.

By occupation of family head (Tab. 7.8). Comparing Tab. 7.8 to Tab. 7.5, it seems that the ownership of a document can be better explained by occupation than by family income. As mentioned in Tab. 3 and Tab. 4, there is obviously no relation between the possession of an ownership document and the question whether or not one can afford it. Roughly three fourths of the casual labour and construction workers do not possess any ownership document whereas only 35.3% of the "crafts" category do not have one. However, the significance of an ownership document and occupation of the family head remains weak because of the low numbers of households in several occupational categories.

7.3
Tax bill ownership

There is a noticeable difference in tax bill ownership among the four communities (see Maps 7.9 through 7.12) with the highest proportion of tax bill owners in Jayprakashnagar, where there is also a high share of government services. The overall distribution of heads of families having a tax bill as compared to those who do not is almost 50% to 50%.

By age of the family head (Tab. 7.9). The majority of the people aged 20 to 29 (64.8%) do not possess any tax bill, whereas among those aged 40-49, an equally high share (65.6%) have one. Among the other categories one can find an almost balanced distribution of tax bill owners and non owners. Still, the number of households without tax bill is strikingly high which leads to the question what the perceived advantages of not having a tax bill are and also, what disadvantages there are for the government when people do not have a tax bill. An additional question is how to raise the acceptance among the population for having a tax bill.

Table 7.9 Tax bill ownership, by age of family head.

Age Tax bill	0-19 in % (n=1)	20-29 in % (n=54)	30-39 in % (n=129)	40-49 in % (n=125)	50-59 in % (n=68)	60-69 in % (n=68)	70-79 in % (n=24)	80-89 in % (n=7)	>90 in % (n=5)	Total in % (n=481)
yes	0.0	35.2	48.8	65.6	48.5	44.1	50.0	71.4	20.0	50.9
no	100.0	64.8	51.2	34.4	51.5	55.9	50.0	28.6	80.0	49.1
Total	100.0	100.0	100.0	100.0	100.0	100.0	100.0	100.0	100.0	100.0

SOURCE: UNIVERSITY OF BASEL, DEPT. OF GEOGRAPHY AND ALL INDIA DISASTER MITIGATION INSTITUTE, AHMEDABAD, INDIA 2005. SOCIAL SCIENCE SURVEY IN SELECTED SLUM COMMUNITIES IN THE CITY OF BHUJ, GUJARAT, INDIA.

Table 7.8 Ownership document, by occupation of family head.

Occupation / Ownership document	textile/ industry in % (n=35)	govern- ment in % (n=13)	casual labour in % (n=83)	construc- tion in % (n=84)	farming in % (n=12)	automotive related job in % (n=42)	vendor/ shop in % (n=39)	crafts in % (n=17)	service sector in % (n=46)	retiree/ housewife/ unemployed in % (n=95)	unclear/ indian in % (n=13)	Total in % (n=479)
No	45.7	53.8	72.3	73.8	66.7	61.9	53.8	35.3	52.2	50.5	84.6	60.3
yes, property card	8.6	23.1	16.9	9.5	16.7	16.7	23.1	5.9	13.0	15.8	15.4	14.6
yes, on 10/20/50 Rs. Stamp paper	45.7	23.1	9.6	16.7	8.3	14.3	17.9	52.9	17.4	24.2	0.0	19.8
yes, other	0.0	0.0	0.0	0.0	0.0	4.8	2.6	0.0	2.2	3.2	0.0	1.5
do not know	0.0	0.0	1.2	0.0	8.3	2.4	2.6	5.9	15.2	6.3	0.0	3.8
Total	100.0	100.0	100.0	100.0	100.0	100.0	100.0	100.0	100.0	100.0	100.0	100.0

Table 7.16 Tax bill ownership, by occupation of family head

Occupation / Tax bill	textile/ industry in % (n=36)	govern- ment in % (n=13)	casual labour in % (n=81)	construc- tion in % (n=81)	farming in % (n=11)	automotive related job in % (n=41)	vendor/ shop in % (n=40)	crafts in % (n=17)	service sector in % (n=46)	retiree/ housewife/ unemployed in % (n=96)	unclear/ indian in % (n=13)	Total in % (n=475)
Yes	25.0	69.2	55.6	44.4	81.8	63.4	60.0	58.8	60.9	41.7	53.8	51.2
No	75.0	30.8	44.4	55.6	18.2	36.6	40.0	41.2	39.1	58.3	46.2	48.8
Total	100.0	100.0	100.0	100.0	100.0	100.0	100.0	100.0	100.0	100.0	100.0	100.0

SOURCE: UNIVERSITY OF BASEL, DEPT. OF GEOGRAPHY AND ALL INDIA DISASTER MITIGATION INSTITUTE, AHMEDABAD, INDIA 2005. SOCIAL SCIENCE SURVEY IN SELECTED SLUM COMMUNITIES IN THE CITY OF BHUJ, GUJARAT, INDIA.

By slum (Tab. 7.10). In the areas of Bhimrao- and Shantinagar approximately two thirds own a tax bill. The distribution of tax bill owners in percentage in Mustuffa- and Jayprakashnagar is almost exactly opposite. While in Jayprakashnagar 86.3% have a tax bill, 85.7% of the dwellers in Mustuffanagar have none. Mustuffanagar, therefore, is the only slum with a majority without tax bills. The reason for this is not yet clear. More information about the meaning of tax bills, how people receive one and what role the government plays in this case is necessary.

Table 7.10 Tax bill ownership, by slum.

Slum Tax bill	Bhimraonagar in % (n=130)	Jayprakashnagar in % (n=51)	Mustuffanagar in % (n=154)	Shantinagar in % (n=147)	Total in % (n=482)
Yes	61.5	86.3	14.3	67.3	50.8
No	38.5	13.7	85.7	32.7	49.2
Total	100.0	100.0	100.0	100.0	100.0

SOURCE: UNIVERSITY OF BASEL, DEPT. OF GEOGRAPHY AND ALL INDIA DISASTER MITIGATION INSTITUTE, AHMEDABAD, INDIA 2005. SOCIAL SCIENCE SURVEY IN SELECTED SLUM COMMUNITIES IN THE CITY OF BHUJ, GUJARAT, INDIA.

By religion (Tab. 7.11). Two thirds of the Hindus interviewed have a tax bill, whereas two thirds of the Muslims have none. This is related to the fact that in the Muslim dominated area of Mustuffanagar the tax bill ownership is low (see Tab. 7.10) although the share of those with ownership documents is higher (see Tab. 7.3). What role religion per se, and in particular Islam, plays in tax bill ownership can not be ascertained, however.

Table 7.11 Tax bill ownership, by religion.

Religion Tax bill	Hindu in % (n=212)	Muslim in % (n=268)	Total in % (n=482)
Yes	65.6	39.6	51.0
No	34.4	60.4	49.0
Total	100.0	100.0	100.0

SOURCE: UNIVERSITY OF BASEL, DEPT. OF GEOGRAPHY AND ALL INDIA DISASTER MITIGATION INSTITUTE, AHMEDABAD, INDIA 2005. SOCIAL SCIENCE SURVEY IN SELECTED SLUM COMMUNITIES IN THE CITY OF BHUJ, GUJARAT, INDIA.

By caste (Tab. 7.12). For the Scheduled Castes and Scheduled Tribe groups, there are slightly higher percentages of tax bill owners (57.6% and 56.1%). This indicates that there may be advantages in having a tax bill if one belongs to these households (and would not have to pay much tax or would not pay tax at all) and have access to other government benefits if a household is registered through its tax bill.

Table 7.12 Tax bill ownership, by caste.

Caste Tax bill	SC in % (n=85)	ST in % (n=57)	OBC in % (n=171)	General in % (n=168)	Total in % (n=481)
Yes	57.6	56.1	47.4	48.8	50.7
No	42.4	43.9	52.6	51.2	49.3
Total	100.0	100.0	100.0	100.0	100.0

SOURCE: UNIVERSITY OF BASEL, DEPT. OF GEOGRAPHY AND ALL INDIA DISASTER MITIGATION INSTITUTE, AHMEDABAD, INDIA 2005. SOCIAL SCIENCE SURVEY IN SELECTED SLUM COMMUNITIES IN THE CITY OF BHUJ, GUJARAT, INDIA.

By average daily income of household members (Tab. 7.13). Although Scheduled Castes and Scheduled Tribes have a higher propensity to have a tax bill, it is noteworthy that the poor income groups have a rather low share of tax bill owners. This may relate to their status as Casual day labourers and the fact that at such low income, one does not pay taxes anyway.

Table 7.13 Tax bill ownership, by average daily wages of household members (in Rs.).

Wage Tax bill	0 to 9 Rs. in % (n=38)	10 to 19 Rs. in % (n=163)	20 to 29 Rs. in % (n=133)	30 to 39 Rs. in % (n=71)	40 to 49 Rs. in % (n=25)	50 to 89 Rs. in % (n=30)	90 to 130 Rs. in % (n=5)	Total in % (n=465)
yes	36.8	52.1	49.6	53.5	60.0	56.7	40.0	51.0
no	63.2	47.9	50.4	46.5	40.0	43.3	60.0	49.0
Total	100.0	100.0	100.0	100.0	100.0	100.0	100.0	100.0

SOURCE: UNIVERSITY OF BASEL, DEPT. OF GEOGRAPHY AND ALL INDIA DISASTER MITIGATION INSTITUTE, AHMEDABAD, INDIA 2005. SOCIAL SCIENCE SURVEY IN SELECTED SLUM COMMUNITIES IN THE CITY OF BHUJ, GUJARAT, INDIA.

By education standard (Tab. 7.14). Above the education standard 3, the ownership of a tax bill shows no further relation to the education standard. Almost one third of the people with an education standard 1-3 have a tax bill for reasons discussed above. This supports the notion that among the poorest and least educated, tax bill ownership is of advantage in accessing government programs. Within the group of illiterates, the percentage of people owning a tax bill (55.9%) is again higher than the percentage of people without (44.1%).

Table 7.14 Tax bill ownership, by education standard of family head.

Education Tax bill	Hrs. 1-3 in % (n=46)	Hrs. 4-6 in % (n=80)	Hrs. 7-9 in % (n=104)	Hrs. 10-12 in % (n=33)	Completed Diploma in % (n=1)	Completed Graduation in % (n=6)	Illiterate in % (n=211)	Total in % (n=481)
yes	28.3	43.8	55.8	48.5	100.0	66.7	55.9	50.9
no	71.7	56.3	44.2	51.5	0.0	33.3	44.1	49.1
Total	100.0	100.0	100.0	100.0	100.0	100.0	100.0	100.0

SOURCE: UNIVERSITY OF BASEL, DEPT. OF GEOGRAPHY AND ALL INDIA DISASTER MITIGATION INSTITUTE, AHMEDABAD, INDIA 2005. SOCIAL SCIENCE SURVEY IN SELECTED SLUM COMMUNITIES IN THE CITY OF BHUJ, GUJARAT, INDIA.

By sex of family head (Tab. 7.15). The gender specific distribution of tax bill owners shows that more male (52.2%) than female family heads (43.1%) have a tax bill. However, the absolute number of male family heads is much larger (n=416) than the number of female (n=65), so that this distribution is not significant.

Table 7.15 Tax bill ownership, by sex of family head.

Tax bill \ Sex	female in % (n=65)	male in % (n=416)	Total in % (n=481)
Yes	43.1	52.2	50.9
No	56.9	47.8	49.1
Total	100.0	100.0	100.0

SOURCE: UNIVERSITY OF BASEL, DEPT. OF GEOGRAPHY AND ALL INDIA DISASTER MITIGATION INSTITUTE, AHMEDABAD, INDIA 2005. SOCIAL SCIENCE SURVEY IN SELECTED SLUM COMMUNITIES IN THE CITY OF BHUJ, GUJARAT, INDIA.

By occupation of family head (Tab. 7.16 – see page 100). The most remarkable difference in distribution is to be noted in the categories 'textile/industry' and 'farming'. Three fourths of the 'textile/industry' workers state that they have no tax bill, whereas the majority of farming workers (81.8%) state that they have one. Again, farming workers being poorer and most vulnerable may derive certain benefits from tax bill registration. The distribution among the other groups varies between two thirds having a tax bill and two thirds having none.

7.4 Conclusion

Tax bill ownership does not seem to follow clear patterns with the exception that poorer households such as Scheduled Tribe households may have more to gain (and not much to lose) from having a tax bill registration. If the government is interested in larger proportions of the slum dwellers being registered with a tax bill, it is important to determine first what benefits are to be had from tax bill ownership and for what segments of the population they are of greatest relevance. This demand side perspective, however, that is based on the question as to what slum dwellers may gain from having a tax bill, is, of course, only one side, and a very limited one, too. The real question is how to raise awareness for accepting one's duty of having a tax bill, even if one is a poor slum dweller and possibly residing on land which is not legalized yet. In other words, a key problem is to raise acceptance for sharing responsibilities, even if the government has not given everything (away) yet (legalization of land). If each partner in the development game – slum communities and government – waits for the other to make the first move, stagnation will result, and not the desired process.

Map 7.1 Households reporting ownership of house, Bhimraonagar

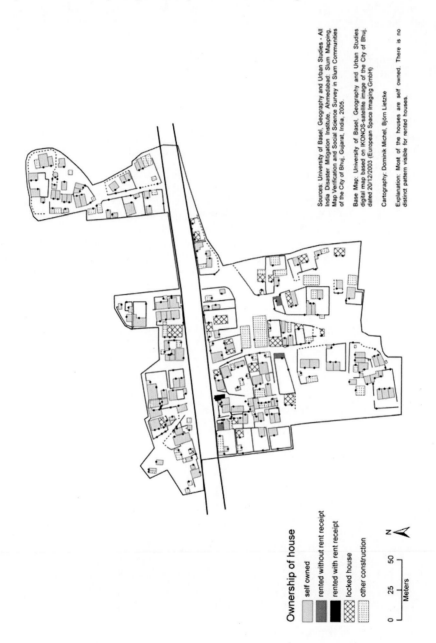

Ownership and tax bill 105

Map 7.2 Households reporting ownership of house, Jayprakashnagar

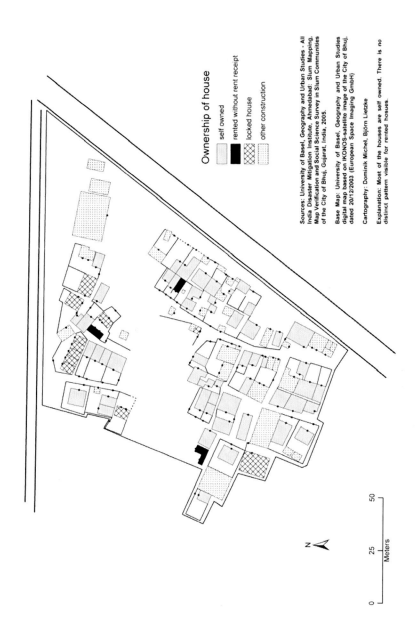

Map 7.3 Households reporting ownership of house, Mustuffanagar

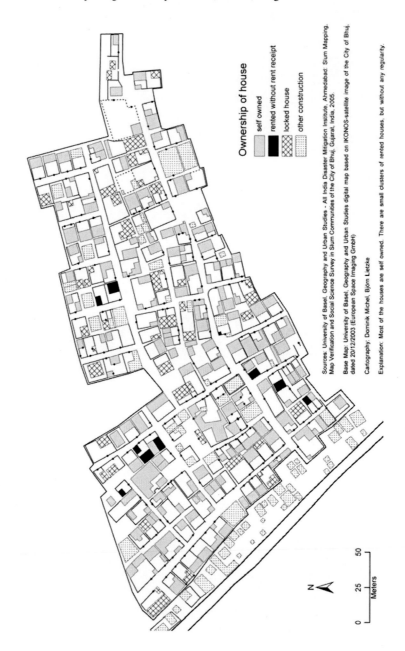

Map 7.4 Households reporting ownership of house, Shantinagar

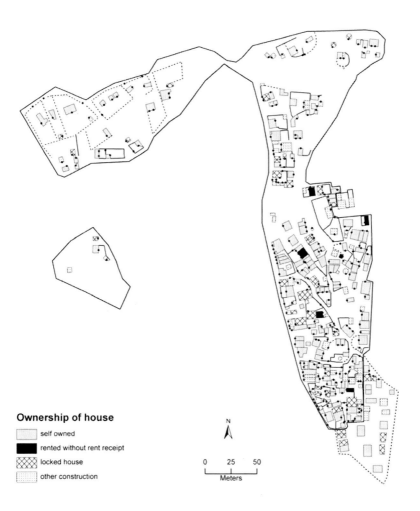

Ownership of house
- self owned
- rented without rent receipt
- locked house
- other construction

Sources: University of Basel, Geography and Urban Studies - All India Disaster Mitigation Institute, Ahmedabad: Slum Mapping, Map Verification and Social Science Survey in Slum Communities of the City of Bhuj, Gujarat, India, 2005.

Base Map: University of Basel, Geography and Urban Studies digital map based on IKONOS-satellite image of the City of Bhuj, dated 20/12/2003 (European Space Imaging GmbH)

Cartography: Dominik Michel, Björn Lietzke

Explanation: Most houses of Shantinagar are self-owned, which is remarkable given the general degree of poverty.

Map 7.5 Households reporting ownership document of the house, Bhimraonagar

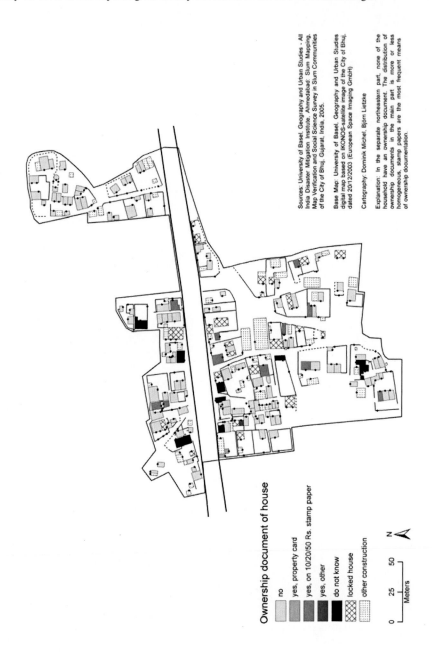

Ownership and tax bill 109

Map 7.6 Households reporting ownership document of the house, Jayprakashnagar

Map 7.7 Households reporting ownership document of the house, Mustuffanagar

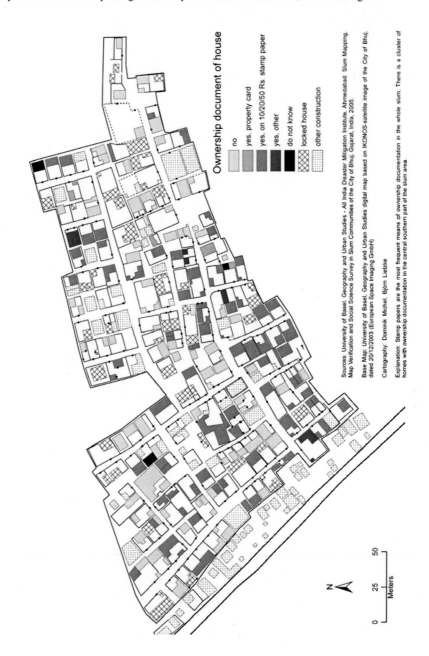

Ownership and tax bill 111

Map 7.8 Households reporting ownership document of the house, Shantinagar

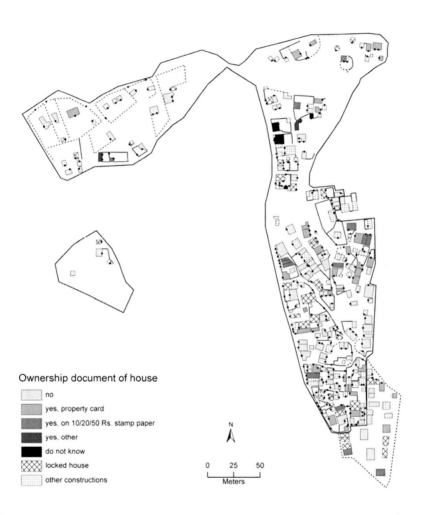

Sources: University of Basel, Geography and Urban Studies - All India Disaster Mitigation Institute, Ahmedabad: Slum Mapping, Map Verification and Social Science Survey in Slum Communities of the City of Bhuj, Gujarat, India, 2005.

Base Map: University of Basel, Geography and Urban Studies digital map based on IKONOS-satellite image of the City of Bhuj, dated 20/12/2003 (European Space Imaging GmbH)

Cartography: Dominik Michel, Björn Lietzke

Explanation: There is no distinct spatial pattern visible concernign the distribution of ownership documents.

112   Ownership and tax bill

Map 7.9 Households reporting tax bill ownership, Bhimraonagar

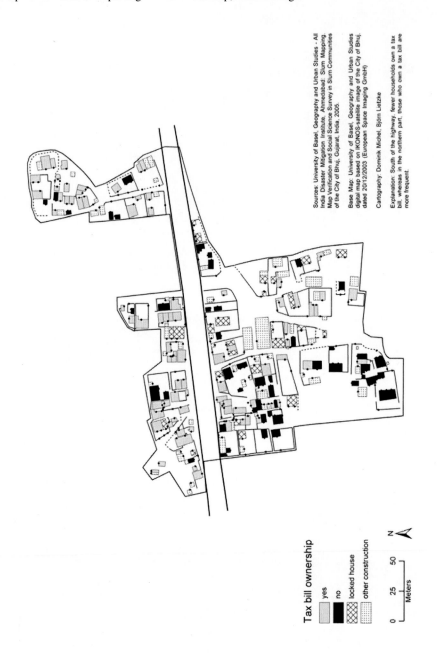

Map 7.10 Households reporting tax bill ownership, Jayprakashnagar

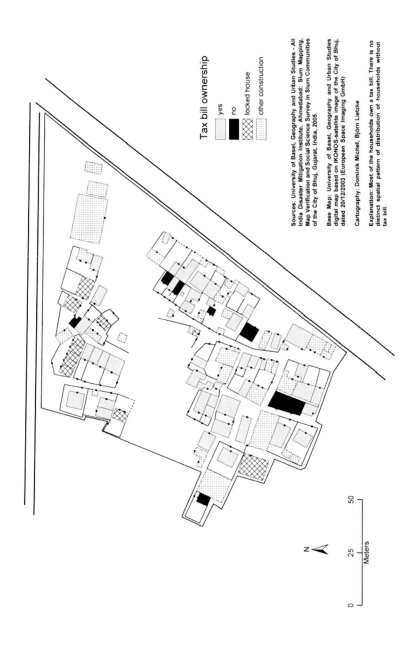

Map 7.11 Households reporting tax bill ownership, Mustuffanagar

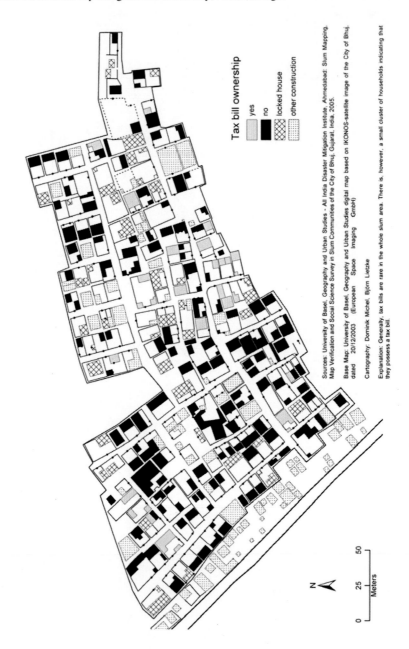

Ownership and tax bill 115

Map 7.12 Households reporting tax bill ownership, Shantinagar

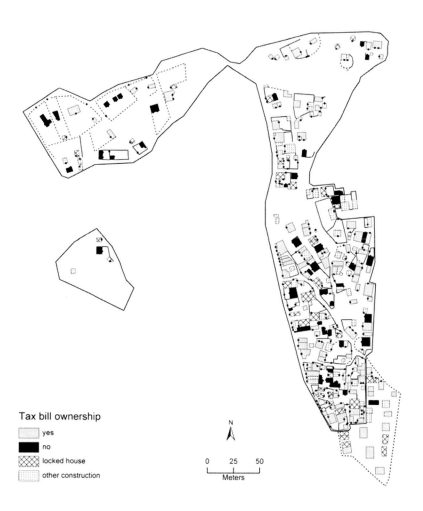

8 Food security

K. Conradin, B. Lietzke, D. Michel, F. Wieland
University of Basel

8.1
Introduction

In this chapter, the issue of food security of the people of Bhimraonagar, Jayprakashnagar, Mustuffanagar and Shantinagar will be looked at more closely. Next to housing, food availability and food security are most important in daily survival and also when considering the question whether or not a household can afford to save (deferred consumption) or has to consume right away, by the necessities given through hunger and malnutrition. Whether or not households can get ahead and provide for their future does depend to a large degree on present food security. To identify the extent to which food availability is a problem or not, the main questions were:

- What is the distribution of general ration cards and Below Poverty Line (BPL) cards?
- What is the relationship between General/BPL card and income?
- Are there differences in the possession of General/BPL cards concerning caste or religion?

The data for these questions was gathered in a household based survey, where one person (usually the family head) answered.

8.2
Able to feed the family

It is of note that a very high percentage (97.8%) of the families stated that they were able to feed their family. This indicates that although the families are generally rather poor, they can nourish themselves. However, since there was no medical staff there to examine how well nourished people were, this is, to a certain degree, a subjective judgement. Signs of malnutrition are often not perceived by those affected.

8.3
Ration Card

By average daily wages of household members (Tab. 8.1). Because some goods as petrol and gas are subject to rationing in India, the Indian government distributes a general ration card to every citizen. This card entitles each citizen to obtain a certain amount of these special goods. In addition, there is another card for the very poor people. This BPL (Below Poverty Line) card makes it possible for these people to get food in special stores. The official definition of the poverty line is marked by a monthly income of less than 1200 Rs. per person. Food and other goods of daily use which can be obtained by this card are also rationed. Coupons are distributed on a monthly basis and can then be used in special stores. Given that every household is entitled to a general card and the general degree of poverty in the communities, it is not surprising that almost all households have one or the other, with Bhimraonagar and Shantinagar having the highest number of below poverty line cards (see Maps 8.1 through 8.4).

BPL cards are given based on need. In families with lower daily wages per person (0-19 Rs.), more than 51% possess a BPL card. It is of note, however, that it is not a higher percentage of poor households that have BPL cards. While in the middle daily wage classes (20-39 Rs.) around 44% still have a BPL card, only about 30% of the families with higher daily wages per person (40-130 Rs.) own a BPL card.

Table 8.1 Ration card, by average daily wages of household members (in Rs.).

Wage / Ration card	0 to 9 Rs. in % (n=39)	10 to 19 Rs. in % (n=164)	20 to 29 Rs. in % (n=139)	30 to 39 Rs. in % (n=73)	40 to 49 Rs. in % (n=27)	50 to 89 Rs. in % (n=31)	90 to 130 Rs. in % (n=5)	Total in % (n=478)
no	7.7	7.3	11.5	6.8	14.8	9.7	20.0	9.2
yes, BPL card	51.3	57.3	46.0	47.9	29.6	32.3	0.0	48.3
Yes, general card	38.5	35.4	41.7	45.2	55.6	54.8	80.0	41.8
lost	0.0	0.0	0.7	0.0	0.0	3.2	0.0	0.4
dont know	2.6	0.0	0.0	0.0	0.0	0.0	0.0	0.2
Total	100.0	100.0	100.0	100.0	100.0	100.0	100.0	100.0

SOURCE: UNIVERSITY OF BASEL, DEPT. OF GEOGRAPHY AND ALL INDIA DISASTER MITIGATION INSTITUTE, AHMEDABAD, INDIA 2005. SOCIAL SCIENCE SURVEY IN SELECTED SLUM COMMUNITIES IN THE CITY OF BHUJ, GUJARAT, INDIA.

By castes (Tab. 8.2). This distribution is also reflected with respect to caste. 69.9% of households interviewed from the Scheduled Castes and 73.2% of those from the Scheduled Tribes possess a BPL card. In the Other Backward Classes, there were only 47.2%, the general group showing even less with 32.6%. This detail correlates with the distribution of income between the different castes (see Tab. 8.7). The connection between poverty and the affiliation to a caste is statistically significant.

Table 8.2 Ration card, by caste.

Caste / Ration card	SC in % (n=84)	ST in % (n=56)	OBC in % (n=180)	General in % (n=172)	Total in % (n=492)
no	7.1	5.4	11.1	9.9	9.3
yes, BPL card	69.0	73.2	47.2	32.6	48.8
yes, general card	23.8	21.4	41.7	57.6	41.9
Total	100.0	100.0	100.0	100.0	100.0

SOURCE: UNIVERSITY OF BASEL, DEPT. OF GEOGRAPHY AND ALL INDIA DISASTER MITIGATION INSTITUTE, AHMEDABAD, INDIA 2005. SOCIAL SCIENCE SURVEY IN SELECTED SLUM COMMUNITIES IN THE CITY OF BHUJ, GUJARAT, INDIA.

By religion (Tab. 8.3). The relation between the possession of a BPL card and religion, however, is not significant. Nevertheless, there is a slight trend that Hindu households more often have a BPL card (53.0%) than Muslim households (45.7%). As there were only a few Christian and Sikh households, they were not considered in the analysis.

Table 8.3 Ration card, by religion.

Religion / Ration card	Hindu in % (n=215)	Muslim in % (n=276)	Total in % (n=491)
no	8.8	9.8	9.4
yes, BPL card	53.1	45.7	48.8
yes, general card	38.1	44.5	41.8
Total	100.0	100.0	100.0

SOURCE: UNIVERSITY OF BASEL, DEPT. OF GEOGRAPHY AND ALL INDIA DISASTER MITIGATION INSTITUTE, AHMEDABAD, INDIA 2005. SOCIAL SCIENCE SURVEY IN SELECTED SLUM COMMUNITIES IN THE CITY OF BHUJ, GUJARAT, INDIA.

By illness of a family member in the last year (Tab. 8.4). The illness of a family member in the last year and the possession of a BPL card have no apparent connection.

Table 8.4 Ration card, by illness of a family member in the last year.

Illness / Ration card	no, nobody in % (n=372)	died from serious illness in % (n=10)	been seriously ill in % (n=78)	Total in % (n=460)
no	8.9	10.0	11.5	9.3
yes, BPL card	49.5	50.0	50.0	49.6
yes, general card	41.7	40.0	38.5	41.1
Total	100.0	100.0	100.0	100.0

SOURCE: UNIVERSITY OF BASEL, DEPT. OF GEOGRAPHY AND ALL INDIA DISASTER MITIGATION INSTITUTE, AHMEDABAD, INDIA 2005. SOCIAL SCIENCE SURVEY IN SELECTED SLUM COMMUNITIES IN THE CITY OF BHUJ, GUJARAT, INDIA.

By slum (Tab. 8.5). The four different slums exhibit a highly significant difference concerning the possession of a ration card. While in Bhimraonagar 71.9% of all households own a BPL card, in Shantinagar there are still 53.5%. In the "richer" slums Mustuffanagar and Jayprakashnagar only 32.1% and 30.6% of the households possess such a card. This distribution fits itself well into the general picture of the four surveyed slums and is well represented by Maps 8.1 through 8.4.

Table 8.5 Ration card, by slum.

Slum Ration card	Bhimraonagar in % (n=128)	Jayprakashnagar in % (n=53)	Mustuffanagar in % (n=157)	Shantinagar in % (n=155)	Total in % (n=493)
no	7.0	5.7	9.6	12.3	9.3
yes, BPL card	71.9	32.1	30.6	53.5	48.7
yes, general card	21.1	62.3	59.9	34.2	42.0
Total	100.0	100.0	100.0	100.0	100.0

SOURCE: UNIVERSITY OF BASEL, DEPT. OF GEOGRAPHY AND ALL INDIA DISASTER MITIGATION INSTITUTE, AHMEDABAD, INDIA 2005. SOCIAL SCIENCE SURVEY IN SELECTED SLUM COMMUNITIES IN THE CITY OF BHUJ, GUJARAT, INDIA.

8.4
Conclusion

It is striking that a large number of families own a BPL card – roughly half of the population (48.5%). In almost half of the families, the individual members have to get on with less than 1200 Rs. per person. BPL cards are thus very important for a large share of the slum dwellers. The food the families got from the special stores was mostly rated as average (86.6%). As stated in the introduction, only 2.2% of the family heads indicated that they were not able to feed their family. However, considering the high amount of families who live below the poverty line, further research would be necessary to determine whether all of the families whose heads answered that they were able to feed were also well-nourished, i.e. showed no signs of malnutrition or lack of certain minerals/vitamins etc.

The distribution of the BPL card reaffirms the general picture of the slum communities – the highest percentage of those who own a BPL card lives in Shantinagar, and Jayprakashnagar features the lowest number. To draw a conclusion on the general issue whether or not food insecurity is a problem that needs to be resolved with priority in order to ameliorate poverty, it can be stated that due to the government rationing system the basic need of food security seems to be met. With all households having basic food security or the possibility thereof through BPL cards, the question of how to move out of poverty does not relate much to food and food expenses, but must strongly depend on other factors, such as educational attainment and occupation.

Food security 121

Map 8.1 Households with ration card, Bhimraonagar

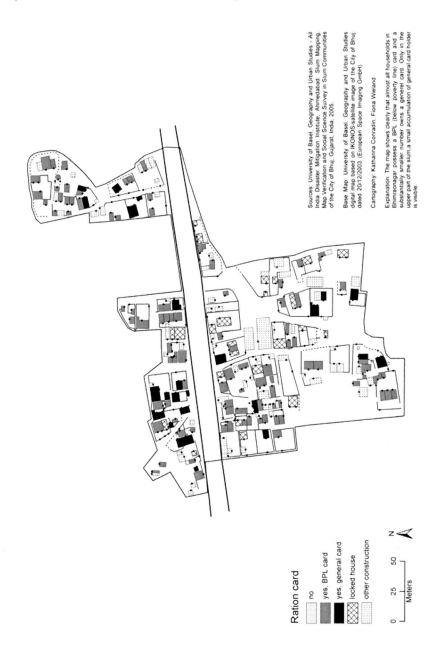

Map 8.2 Households with ration card, Jayprakashnagar

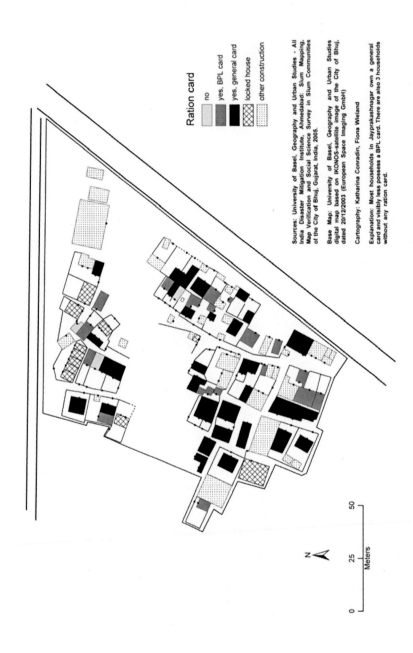

Food security

Map 8.3 Households with ration card, Mustuffanagar

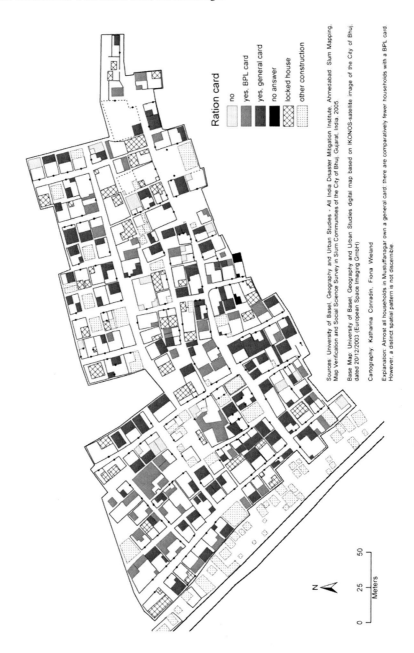

124 Food security

Map 8.4 Households with ration card, Shantinagar

Sources: University of Basel, Geography and Urban Studies - All India Disaster Mitigation Institute, Ahmedabad: Slum Mapping, Map Verification and Social Science Survey in Slum Communities of the City of Bhuj, Gujarat, India, 2005.

Base Map: University of Basel, Geography and Urban Studies digital map based on IKONOS-satellite image of the City of Bhuj, dated 20/12/2003 (European Space Imaging GmbH)

Cartography: Katharina Conradin, Fiona Wieland

Explanation: In Shantinagar, most households possess a BPL card. The households with a general card are scattered over the whole slum area without a visible pattern.

9 Health issues and occupational hazards

K. Conradin, F. Wieland
University of Basel

9.1
Introduction

In this chapter, the general state of health of the slum dwellers will be looked at more closely. The goal of the study was not only to find out simple health patterns, but also to find relations between livelihood factors (occupation, education, income) and health status. The main questions asked were:

- What are the factors that influence where people go for health check-ups?
- Do the reasons why people visit health centres differ by family background?
- Are there recognizable patterns in the distribution and occurrence of illnesses?
- Are there visible patterns in the distributions of different kinds of illnesses?
- What factors influence the occurrence of illnesses?
- How much do people spend on medicine – and does this behaviour show a relation to their respective living circumstances?

The information for these questions was obtained by a door to door household-based survey. Due to the fact that no medical staff was involved, the answers of the interviewees are to a certain degree subjective. Nevertheless, the interrelations, especially between economic factors and health states, proved to be highly significant.

9.2
Places for health check-up

By average daily wages of household members (Tab. 9.1). The relation between the place for health check-up and the average income was not statistically significant. Most of the slum dwellers make use of the government hospital services in all income classes which attests to the fact that access to health centers and obtaining basic health care is not a problem. However, perception of what is an illness might be lacking as well as awareness of when medical care would be needed. It appears that some diseases, like coughing, skin rashes and diarrhoea seemed to be so widespread and normal that they might not be considered as illness and cure, therefore, is not sought. Still, there is a tendency that the higher income classes call on private hospitals or practitioners more often than those belonging to lower income classes.

Table 9.1 Place for health check-up, by average daily wages of household members.

Wage Place for health check-up	0 to 9 Rs. in % (n=39)	10 to 19 Rs. in % (n=164)	20 to 29 Rs. in % (n=140)	30 to 39 Rs. in % (n=73)	40 to 49 Rs. in % (n=27)	50 to 89 Rs. in % (n=31)	90 to 130 Rs. in % (n=5)	Total in % (n=479)
government hospital	74.4	75.0	72.9	57.5	59.3	54.8	60.0	69.3
private hospital	15.4	19.5	20.7	28.8	29.6	25.8	40.0	22.1
private practiner	10.3	3.7	3.6	13.7	11.1	16.1	0.0	6.9
private health centre	0.0	1.2	1.4	0.0	0.0	3.2	0.0	1.0
ayurvedic/homepethic practitioner	0.0	0.6	0.0	0.0	0.0	0.0	0.0	0.2
other	0.0	0.0	1.4	0.0	0.0	0.0	0.0	0.4
Total	100.0	100.0	100.0	100.0	100.0	100.0	100.0	100.0

SOURCE: UNIVERSITY OF BASEL, DEPT. OF GEOGRAPHY AND ALL INDIA DISASTER MITIGATION INSTITUTE, AHMEDABAD, INDIA 2005. SOCIAL SCIENCE SURVEY IN SELECTED SLUM COMMUNITIES IN THE CITY OF BHUJ, GUJARAT, INDIA.

By education of family head (Tab. 9.2). Most of the slum dwellers make use of the government hospitals, independent of their education. Nevertheless, there are clear differences between those with a completed graduation/diploma and those who are illiterate. While the former access the services of private hospitals more often (57.1%), the latter mainly go to the government hospitals (77.3%). Only a small proportion of the illiterates make use of the services of private hospitals or private practitioners (21.8%)

Table 9.2 Place for health check-up, by education standard of family head.

Education Place for health check-up	Hrs. 1-3 in % (n=44)	Hrs. 4-6 in % (n=82)	Hrs. 7-9 in % (n=108)	Hrs. 10-12 in % (n=36)	completed graduation / diploma in % (n=7)	Illiterate in % (n=216)	Total in % (n=493)
government hospital	63.6	58.5	67.6	55.6	42.9	77.3	68.8
private hospital	31.8	24.4	24.1	36.1	57.1	15.3	22.3
private practitioner	4.5	14.6	7.4	8.3	0.0	5.1	7.3
private health centre	0.0	1.2	0.9	0.0	0.0	1.4	1.0
ayurvedic/homepethic practitioner	0.0	0.0	0.0	0.0	0.0	0.5	0.2
other	0.0	1.2	0.0	0.0	0.0	0.5	0.4
Total	100.0	100.0	100.0	100.0	100.0	100.0	100.0

SOURCE: UNIVERSITY OF BASEL, DEPT. OF GEOGRAPHY AND ALL INDIA DISASTER MITIGATION INSTITUTE, AHMEDABAD, INDIA 2005. SOCIAL SCIENCE SURVEY IN SELECTED SLUM COMMUNITIES IN THE CITY OF BHUJ, GUJARAT, INDIA.

By caste (Tab. 9.3). Although all castes mainly go to the hospitals run by the government (69% of the total population), there are disparities among the individual castes. The Scheduled Tribes are the ones with the highest proportion of families who make use of the government hospital services (80.7%). Moreover, only 17.5% of them go to a private hospital, and none of them consult private practitioners. This is most probably due to the fact that the government services are the cheapest health services available. Interestingly, 34.9% of the Scheduled Caste families interviewed go to either private hospitals or private practitioners – a figure which is almost equal to the member of the General Castes, where 34.7% make use of either private hospitals or private practitioners. The reason for this is not immediately apparent. There may, however, be a correlation with income: members of the Scheduled Castes in the surveyed slum area are generally poor, but still better off than Scheduled Tribes. Hardly any of all the castes make use of the traditional Ayurvedic services or use homeopathy – though this can be explained by the fact that they do not need to consult a practitioner for traditional medicines – but rather make use of these techniques themselves.

Table 9.3 Place for health check-up, by caste.

Caste Place for health check-up	SC in % (n=86)	ST in % (n=57)	OBC in % (n=177)	General in % (n=173)	Total in % (n=493)
government hospital	64.0	80.7	73.4	63.0	69.0
private hospital	32.6	17.5	20.9	19.7	22.1
private practioner	2.3	0.0	4.5	15.0	7.3
private health centre	1.2	1.8	0.0	1.7	1.0
ayurvedic/homepethic practioner	0.0	0.0	0.0	0.0	0.2
other	0.0	0.0	0.6	0.6	0.4
Total	100.0	100.0	100.0	100.0	100.0

SOURCE: UNIVERSITY OF BASEL, DEPT. OF GEOGRAPHY AND ALL INDIA DISASTER MITIGATION INSTITUTE, AHMEDABAD, INDIA 2005. SOCIAL SCIENCE SURVEY IN SELECTED SLUM COMMUNITIES IN THE CITY OF BHUJ, GUJARAT, INDIA.

By religion (Tab. 9.4). There are no striking differences between Muslim and Hindu households and the place where they go for health services. Slightly more Muslims make use of the government hospitals (72%), whereas slightly fewer Hindu households use this service (65%). As opposed to this, 32.3% of the Hindus consult private hospitals/practitioners, whereas only 27.3% of the Muslims make use of private health services. Both Muslims and Hindus hardly ever use the services of Ayurvedic doctors or homeopathy – again, this might be due to the fact that these treatments are generally applied at home, and not in a health centre.

Table 9.4 Place for health check-up, by religion.

Place for health check-up	Religion	Hindu in % (n=217)	Muslim in % (n=275)	Total in % (n=492)
government hospital		65.0	72.0	68.9
private hospital		24.9	20.0	22.2
private practioner		7.4	7.3	7.3
private health centre		1.8	0.4	1.0
ayurvedic/homepethic practioner		0.0	0.4	0.2
other		0.9	0.0	0.4
Total		100.0	100.0	100.0

SOURCE: UNIVERSITY OF BASEL, DEPT. OF GEOGRAPHY AND ALL INDIA DISASTER MITIGATION INSTITUTE, AHMEDABAD, INDIA 2005. SOCIAL SCIENCE SURVEY IN SELECTED SLUM COMMUNITIES IN THE CITY OF BHUJ, GUJARAT, INDIA.

By slum (Tab. 9.5). Although most of the slum dwellers use the services of government hospitals anyway, the percentage varies greatly between the individual communities. The highest proportion of dwellers who use government services is in Shantinagar (82.5%), and only 16.2% of them consult private institutions. This can probably be explained to a large extent by the generally lower income level in Shantinagar and the high proportion of liberal people, who are a target group of the government. In the other three slum areas, the percentage of those who access government hospitals is always roughly 60%, and the proportion of families who make use of private hospitals/practitioners varies only slightly around 35%.

Table 9.5 Place for health check-up, by slum.

Place for health check-up	Slum	Bhimraonagar in % (n=130)	Jayprakashnagar in % (n=53)	Mustuffanagar in % (n=157)	Shantinagar in % (n=154)	Total in % (n=494)
government hospital		63.1	58.5	63.7	82.5	68.8
private hospital		34.6	22.6	25.5	8.4	22.3
private practioner		0.8	15.1	9.6	7.8	7.3
private health centre		1.5	1.9	0.6	0.6	1.0
ayurvedic/ homepathic practioner		0.0	0.0	0.6	0.0	0.2
other		0.0	1.9	0.0	0.6	0.4
Total		100.0	100.0	100.0	100.0	100.0

SOURCE: UNIVERSITY OF BASEL, DEPT. OF GEOGRAPHY AND ALL INDIA DISASTER MITIGATION INSTITUTE, AHMEDABAD, INDIA 2005. SOCIAL SCIENCE SURVEY IN SELECTED SLUM COMMUNITIES IN THE CITY OF BHUJ, GUJARAT, INDIA.

9.3
Purpose of visiting the health centre

By average daily wages of household members (Tab. 9.6). There was no significant relation between the purpose of visiting the health centre and the average daily income of the family members. The reason for visiting the health centre does not seem to depend on the income.

Table 9.6 Purpose of visiting health centre, by average daily wages of household members (in Rs.).

Wage / Purpose of visiting health centre	0 to 9 Rs. in % (n=39)	10 to 19 Rs. in % (n=162)	20 to 29 Rs. in % (n=140)	30 to 39 Rs. in % (n=73)	40 to 49 Rs. in % (n=27)	50 to 89 Rs. in % (n=30)	90 to 130 Rs. in % (n=5)	Total in % (n=476)
for check-up	55.2	47.7	51.5	50.0	36.4	46.5	60.0	49.3
for vaccination	25.8	24.5	22.8	18.4	18.2	14.0	0.0	22.0
for medicines at reasonable rate	19.0	27.8	25.7	31.6	45.4	39.5	40.0	28.7
Total	100.0	100.0	100.0	100.0	100.0	100.0	100.0	100.0

SOURCE: UNIVERSITY OF BASEL, DEPT. OF GEOGRAPHY AND ALL INDIA DISASTER MITIGATION INSTITUTE, AHMEDABAD, INDIA 2005. SOCIAL SCIENCE SURVEY IN SELECTED SLUM COMMUNITIES IN THE CITY OF BHUJ, GUJARAT, INDIA.

By education of family head (Tab. 9.7). There was no significant relation between the purpose of visiting the health centre and the education of the family head. The reason for visiting the health centre does not seem to depend on the education of the family head.

Table 9.7 Purpose of visiting health centre, by education standard of family head.

Education / Purpose of visiting health centre	Hrs. 1-3 in % (n=61)	Hrs. 4-6 in % (n=122)	Hrs. 7-9 in % (n=160)	Hrs. 10-12 in % (n=48)	completed graduation / diploma in % (n=9)	Illiterate in % (n=297)	Total in % (n=697)
for check-up	54.1	45.1	43.1	45.8	66.7	53.2	49.2
for vaccination	18.0	21.3	26.9	25.0	11.1	20.5	22.1
for medicines at reasonable rate	27.9	33.6	30.0	29.2	22.2	26.3	28.7
Total	100.0	100.0	100.0	100.0	100.0	100.0	100.0

SOURCE: UNIVERSITY OF BASEL, DEPT. OF GEOGRAPHY AND ALL INDIA DISASTER MITIGATION INSTITUTE, AHMEDABAD, INDIA 2005. SOCIAL SCIENCE SURVEY IN SELECTED SLUM COMMUNITIES IN THE CITY OF BHUJ, GUJARAT, INDIA.

By caste (Tab. 9.8). Whereas Scheduled Castes and Scheduled Tribes mainly visit health centres for medical checkups (67.9%, 70%), only 39.6% of the members of Other Backward Classes use it for medical checkups. Opposed to this, a higher number of OBC/General castes families stated that they go to health centres to purchase medicines at reasonable rates (37.3%/31.4%). Only 11.9% of the interviewed members of the Scheduled Castes and 12.9% of the Scheduled Tribes go there for this reason. The figures concerning vaccination do not differ strongly: roughly 20% of all castes visit the health centres for vaccination. This might be due to the fact that Other Backward Classes and General Caste families generally among the higher income classes and can therefore afford to buy medicines – whereas especially the Scheduled Tribes, which are economically worst off, can not afford to buy any medicine.

Table 9.8 Purpose of visiting health centre, by caste.

Purpose of visiting health centre	Caste SC in % (n=109)	ST in % (n=70)	OBC in % (n=260)	General in % (n=258)	Total in % (n=697)
for check-up	67.9	70.0	39.6	45.3	49.2
for vaccination	20.2	17.1	23.1	23.3	22.1
for medicines at reasonable rate	11.9	12.9	37.3	31.4	28.7
Total	100.0	100.0	100.0	100.0	100.0

SOURCE: UNIVERSITY OF BASEL, DEPT. OF GEOGRAPHY AND ALL INDIA DISASTER MITIGATION INSTITUTE, AHMEDABAD, INDIA 2005. SOCIAL SCIENCE SURVEY IN SELECTED SLUM COMMUNITIES IN THE CITY OF BHUJ, GUJARAT, INDIA.

By religion (Tab. 9.9). More Hindu households visit the health centre for check-ups (54%), as compared to Muslim households (45.3%). On the other hand, Muslim households seem to access health centres more often to buy medicines at reasonable rates (31.3%), as compared to Hindus, where only 25.2% state that they go there to buy medicines at reasonable rates. Maybe this is due to the fact that Hindus often tend to make use of and prepare in their homes the traditional medical practices, and thus buy less medicine in general.

Table 9.9 Purpose of visiting health centre, by religion.

Purpose of visiting health centre	Religion Hindu in % (n=309)	Muslim in % (n=386)	Total in % (n=695)
for check-up	54.0	45.3	49.2
for vaccination	20.7	23.3	22.2
for medicines at reasonable rate	25.2	31.3	28.6
Total	100.0	100.0	100.0

SOURCE: UNIVERSITY OF BASEL, DEPT. OF GEOGRAPHY AND ALL INDIA DISASTER MITIGATION INSTITUTE, AHMEDABAD, INDIA 2005. SOCIAL SCIENCE SURVEY IN SELECTED SLUM COMMUNITIES IN THE CITY OF BHUJ, GUJARAT, INDIA.

By slum (Tab. 9.10). Although there are no great differences in the distribution of reasons for which people visit the health centres, there are some points of interest: There is a smaller percentage of inhabitants of Bhimraonagar who consult the health centres in order to buy medicines (16.3%) – this figure is roughly 30% in the other three slums. This could be due to the fact that a high percentage of people in Bhimraonagar state that they have no illness (See Tab. 21). Additionally, due to the more traditional (village like) living structure in

Bhimraonagar, people there probably draw more on traditional medical practices at home (Ayurveda). Fewer people in Jayprakashnagar call on the health centres for vaccination (13.0%, compared to roughly 23% in the other three slums). This might be ascribed to the fact that more people are already vaccinated, since there are fewer children and youth in the community and the slum is more advanced in development in general.

Table 9.10 Purpose of visiting health centre, by slum.

Slum Purpose of visiting health centre	Bhimraona-gar in % (n=166)	Jayprakashna-gar in % (n=69)	Mustuffana-gar in % (n=227)	Shantina-gar in % (n=236)	Total in % (n=698)
for check-up	62.6	50.7	44.5	44.1	49.3
for vaccination	21.1	13.0	22.9	24.5	22.1
for medicines at reasonable rate	16.3	36.3	32.6	31.4	28.6
Total	100.0	100.0	100.0	100.0	100.0

SOURCE: UNIVERSITY OF BASEL, DEPT. OF GEOGRAPHY AND ALL INDIA DISASTER MITIGATION INSTITUTE, AHMEDABAD, INDIA 2005. SOCIAL SCIENCE SURVEY IN SELECTED SLUM COMMUNITIES IN THE CITY OF BHUJ, GUJARAT, INDIA.

9.4
Illness/death of a family member in the last year

By average daily wages of household members and education of the family heads (Tab. 9.11). The relation between income level and serious illnesses are striking. Whereas in the lowest income level group, one third (33.3%) of the families say that at least one person of their household has been seriously ill, only 19.4% state the same in the income class 50 to 89 Rs. per day Although there is no continuous decrease through the individual income classes, there are clearly more seriously ill people in the lower income classes – due to the fact that poor people are generally less well nourished, work in more hazardous jobs, live in less sanitary conditions and have worse buildings (see also Tab. 9.16). But additionally, poor families also have to struggle continuously to survive, and are consequently under a very high physical and psychological pressure. Concerning deaths from serious illnesses, there are no significant differences among income classes. There are no statistically significant differences between the education standard of the head of the family and deaths from serious illnesses.

By caste and religion (Tab. 9.12). It is noteworthy that the Scheduled Tribe population which lives in the poorest conditions of the four castes, showed the lowest proportion of seriously ill people (7.3%). Also, only 11.7% of the Other Backward Class families stated that someone in the family had been seriously ill during the previous year. The figures are considerably higher for Scheduled Caste families and General Caste families (19.8% and 23.8%, respectively) – this discrepancy is not clearly understandable. However, it must be kept in mind that the perception of illness varies according to how frequent a disease is. If a disease occurs often, it probably changes from "disease" to a state which is perceived as normal. This was especially striking in the case of skin diseases, respiratory problems and diarrhoea. These diseases were hardly ever mentioned, although the work in the slum areas clearly showed that a high percentage of people – especially children – were affected by these diseases. There is no statistically significant difference between the incidence of illnesses, or death from illnesses, between Hindus and Muslims.

Table 9.11 Illness/death of a family member in the last year, by average daily wages of household members (in Rs.).

Wage Illness/death	0 to 9 Rs. in % (n=36)	10 to 19 Rs. in % (n=151)	20 to 29 Rs. in % (n=134)	30 to 39 Rs. in % (n=69)	40 to 49 Rs. in % (n=25)	50 to 89 Rs. in % (n=31)	90 to 130 Rs. in % (n=4)	Total in % (n=450)
no, nobody	63.9	82.8	86.6	76.8	88.0	71.0	75.0	80.9
died from serious illness	2.8	2.0	2.2	0.0	0.0	9.7	0.0	2.2
been seriously ill	33.3	15.2	11.2	23.2	12.0	19.4	25.0	16.9
Total	100.0	100.0	100.0	100.0	100.0	100.0	100.0	100.0

SOURCE: UNIVERSITY OF BASEL, DEPT. OF GEOGRAPHY AND ALL INDIA DISASTER MITIGATION INSTITUTE, AHMEDABAD, INDIA 2005. SOCIAL SCIENCE SURVEY IN SELECTED SLUM COMMUNITIES IN THE CITY OF BHUJ, GUJARAT, INDIA.

Table 9.12 Illness/death of a family member in the last year, by caste.

Caste Illness/ death	SC in % (n=81)	ST in % (n=55)	OBC in % (n=163)	General in % (n=164)	Total in % (n=463)
no, nobody	77.8	90.9	86.5	73.8	81.0
died from serious illness	2.5	1.8	1.8	2.4	2.2
been seriously ill	19.8	7.3	11.7	23.8	16.8
Total	100.0	100.0	100.0	100.0	100.0

SOURCE: UNIVERSITY OF BASEL, DEPT. OF GEOGRAPHY AND ALL INDIA DISASTER MITIGATION INSTITUTE, AHMEDABAD, INDIA 2005. SOCIAL SCIENCE SURVEY IN SELECTED SLUM COMMUNITIES IN THE CITY OF BHUJ, GUJARAT, INDIA.

By slum (Tab. 9.13). Concerning the individual slum communities, there was no considerable difference between the incidences of serious illnesses and deaths from serious illnesses (see also Maps 9.5 through 9.12).

Table 9.13 Illness/death of a family member in the last year, by slum.

Slum Illness/ death	Bhimraonagar in % (n=129)	Jayprakashnagar in % (n=53)	Mustuffanagar in % (n=132)	Shantinagar in % (n=150)	Total in % (n=464)
no, nobody	78.3	84.9	81.1	81.3	80.8
died from serious illness	2.3	0.0	2.3	2.7	2.2
been seriously ill	19.4	15.1	16.7	16.0	17.0
Total	100.0	100.0	100.0	100.0	100.0

SOURCE: UNIVERSITY OF BASEL, DEPT. OF GEOGRAPHY AND ALL INDIA DISASTER MITIGATION INSTITUTE, AHMEDABAD, INDIA 2005. SOCIAL SCIENCE SURVEY IN SELECTED SLUM COMMUNITIES IN THE CITY OF BHUJ, GUJARAT, INDIA.

9.5
Illness

By average daily wages of household members (Tab. 9.14). There is a strong relation between income classes and the occurrence of illnesses. It is striking that of those belonging to the lowest income class (0-9 Rs. per day), 59.0% stated that they were not suffering from an illness of any kind. In all other income classes, this figure was much higher (between 60.0% and 78.6%). Moreover, 12.8% of the members of the lowest income group were suffering from Asthma, T.B. or other respiratory diseases. This figure was between 3.3% and 6.5% in all other higher income classes. Furthermore, also the incidence of Polio was much higher among the lowest income class, where 5.1% of the persons were affected, compared to figures of between 0 and 3.2% suffering from Polio.

Table 9.14 Illnesses, by average daily wages of household members (in Rs.).

Wage / Illnesses	0 to 9 Rs. in % (n=39)	10 to 19 Rs. in % (n=164)	20 to 29 Rs. in % (n=153)	30 to 39 Rs. in % (n=78)	40 to 49 Rs. in % (n=28)	50 to 89 Rs. in % (n=31)	90 to 130 Rs. in % (n=5)	Total in % (n=498)
no illness	59.0	76.2	75.8	67.9	78.6	71.0	60.0	73.1
Asthma & Respiratory Diseases	5.1	3.7	2.0	1.3	0.0	6.5	0.0	2.8
T.B.	7.7	1.2	1.3	3.8	3.6	0.0	0.0	2.2
Jaundice	0.0	1.2	0.0	0.0	0.0	0.0	0.0	0.4
Malaria	5.1	1.2	2.0	1.3	0.0	0.0	0.0	1.6
Typhoid	2.6	0.6	0.7	1.3	0.0	0.0	0.0	0.8
Blood pressure	2.6	2.4	3.9	14.1	3.6	3.2	20.0	5.0
Diabetes	0.0	1.2	4.6	2.6	3.6	0.0	0.0	2.4
Cancer	2.6	0.6	0.0	0.0	0.0	0.0	0.0	0.4
Polio	5.1	0.6	0.0	2.6	0.0	3.2	0.0	1.2
Skin Diseases	0.0	0.6	0.0	1.3	0.0	0.0	0.0	0.4
other	10.3	10.4	9.8	3.8	10.7	16.1	20.0	9.6
Total	100.0	100.0	100.0	100.0	100.0	100.0	100.0	100.0

SOURCE: UNIVERSITY OF BASEL, DEPT. OF GEOGRAPHY AND ALL INDIA DISASTER MITIGATION INSTITUTE, AHMEDABAD, INDIA 2005. SOCIAL SCIENCE SURVEY IN SELECTED SLUM COMMUNITIES IN THE CITY OF BHUJ, GUJARAT, INDIA.

By religion (Tab. 9.15). There was no relation between the incidences of illnesses and the religious affiliation of the interviewed persons. Illnesses were distributed quite evenly.

By slum (Tab. 9.16). There are differences between the occurrence of different illnesses and slums. While there are slightly higher proportions of ill people in Mustuffanagar, the rates in Shantinagar, Bhimraonagar and Jayprakashnagar did not differ greatly.

The percentage of respiratory diseases is slightly higher in Shantinagar than in the other slums (5.8%). There were also cases of T.B. in all four slums; moreover, the percentage of affected people in Shantinagar was slightly higher, with 3.9% compared to roughly 2% in the other three slums. Yet again, the question of perception of illnesses must be raised here, since the number of persons observed during the work in the slum areas who seemed to suffer from some kind of cough or respiratory problems appeared to be much higher (see Tab. 9.13). Problems with blood pressure were among the most frequently mentioned illnesses in all four slums, though the number was slightly higher in Mustuffanagar. Though there were quite a few open sewers and ponds which seemed to be ideal breeding grounds for disease carrying insects, Malaria was hardly ever mentioned.

The distribution pattern of the illnesses among the slum can also be explained regarding the general economic condition – again, in Shantinagar, which is least developed and economically worst off, the highest incidences of illnesses occur – whereas Jayprakashnagar, which is significantly better off than Shantinagar, features a smaller percentage of ill people.

Table 9.15 Illnesses, by religion.

Religion / Illnesses	Hindu in % (n=216)	Muslim in % (n=276)	Total in % (n=492)
no illness	76.9	65.9	70.7
Asthma & Respiratory Diseases	2.8	4.3	3.7
T.B.	1.9	2.9	2.4
Jaundice	0.0	0.7	0.4
Malaria	0.5	2.5	1.6
Typhoid	0.9	1.1	1.0
Blood Pressure	4.6	5.8	5.3
Diabetes	1.9	2.9	2.4
Cancer	0.0	0.7	0.4
Polio	1.4	1.1	1.2
Skin Diseases	0.0	0.7	0.4
Other	9.3	11.2	10.4
Total	100.0	100.0	100.0

SOURCE: UNIVERSITY OF BASEL, DEPT. OF GEOGRAPHY AND ALL INDIA DISASTER MITIGATION INSTITUTE, AHMEDABAD, INDIA 2005. SOCIAL SCIENCE SURVEY IN SELECTED SLUM COMMUNITIES IN THE CITY OF BHUJ, GUJARAT, INDIA.

By occupation (Tab. 9.17). Although the cross tabulation between the occupation of a person and the incidence of illness is not statistically significant, there are some points of interest: The highest proportion of those who state that they are not ill (84.6%), work for the government. This can probably be explained by the fact that government jobs do not usually include hard physical labour or a hazardous environment. Persons working as farmers or in jobs related to farming, together with retirees, housewives and unemployed, indicate the highest shares of illnesses (46.2% ill and 46.4%, respectively). Concerning the former, this is probably due to the hard physical labour and hazardous work. The high occurrence of illnesses in the latter group is probably due to the advanced age (retirees) and the psychologically difficult situation of the unemployed – both factors are known to be leading to illnesses. The latter group also shows the highest incidence of diabetes – probably also due to the higher age of the interviewees.

Table 9.16 Illnesses, by slum.

Slum \ Illnesses	Bhimraonagar in % (n=129)	Jayprakashnagar in % (n=53)	Mustuffanagar in % (n=158)	Shantinagar in % (n=154)	Total in % (n=494)
No illness	75.2	75.5	65.2	70.1	70.4
Asthma & Respiratory Diseases	1.6	3.8	3.8	5.8	3.8
T.B.	1.6	1.9	1.9	3.9	2.4
Jaundice	1.6	0.0	0.0	0.0	0.4
Malaria	2.3	0.0	1.3	1.9	1.6
Typhoid	0.0	0.0	1.9	1.3	1.0
Blood Pressure	3.9	5.7	8.2	3.2	5.3
Diabetes	3.1	1.9	3.2	1.3	2.4
Cancer	0.8	0.0	0.0	0.6	0.4
Polio	0.8	0.0	0.6	2.6	1.2
Skin Diseases	0.0	0.0	1.3	0.0	0.4
Other	9.3	11.3	12.7	9.1	10.5
Total	100.0	100.0	100.0	100.0	100.0

SOURCE: UNIVERSITY OF BASEL, DEPT. OF GEOGRAPHY AND ALL INDIA DISASTER MITIGATION INSTITUTE, AHMEDABAD, INDIA 2005. SOCIAL SCIENCE SURVEY IN SELECTED SLUM COMMUNITIES IN THE CITY OF BHUJ, GUJARAT, INDIA.

9.6
Monthly expenses for medicines

By average daily wages of household members (Tab. 9.18). Interestingly, there is no statistically significant relation between the income and the monthly expenses for medicines. There seems to be a slight tendency that members of the higher income classes (40-130 Rs. per day) spend a little more on medicines, if compared to members of the lower income classes (0-9 Rs. per day and 10-19 Rs. per day) – but the difference is small. Still, one has to keep in mind that lower income classes have higher incidences of illnesses (see Tab. 9.21). They therefore also have to buy more medicines: thus, it is likely that many illnesses among the lower income classes remain untreated (i.e. people do not buy medicine). The fact that higher income classes spend about the same amount on medicine as the lower income classes, is probably due to the fact that the fewer illnesses of the higher income classes are better treated, i.e. that they buy more medicine.

Table 9.17 Illnesses, by occupation of family head.

Occupation / Illnesses	textile/ industry in % (n=38)	government in % (n=13)	casual labour in % (n=84)	construction in % (n=84)	farming in % (n=13)	automotive related job in % (n=43)	vendor/ shop in % (n=41)	crafts in % (n=17)	service sector in % (n=47)	retiree/ housewife/ unemployed in % (n=97)	unclear/ indian in % (n=13)	Total in % (n=487)
no illness	65.7	84.6	79.8	77.4	53.8	67.4	85.4	70.6	68.1	53.6	84.6	70.6
Asthma & Respiratory Diseases	5.7	7.7	2.4	1.2	7.7	4.7	0.0	5.9	4.3	7.2	0.0	3.9
T.B.	2.9	0.0	2.4	3.6	0.0	2.3	2.4	0.0	4.3	2.1	0.0	2.5
Jaundice	0.0	0.0	0.0	1.2	0.0	0.0	0.0	0.0	0.0	1.0	0.0	0.4
Malaria	0.0	0.0	2.4	2.4	0.0	0.0	0.0	0.0	2.1	3.1	0.0	1.6
Typhoid	0.0	0.0	2.4	0.0	7.7	2.3	0.0	0.0	2.1	0.0	0.0	1.0
Blood Pressure	8.6	7.7	1.2	2.4	0.0	7.0	2.4	0.0	6.4	10.3	7.7	5.1
Diabetes	2.9	0.0	0.0	1.2	7.7	2.3	2.4	0.0	6.4	4.1	0.0	2.5
Cancer	0.0	0.0	0.0	0.0	0.0	0.0	0.0	0.0	0.0	2.1	0.0	0.4
Polio	2.9	0.0	2.4	0.0	15.4	0.0	0.0	0.0	0.0	1.0	0.0	1.2
Skin Diseases	0.0	0.0	1.2	1.2	0.0	0.0	0.0	0.0	0.0	0.0	0.0	0.4
Other	11.4	0.0	6.0	9.5	7.7	14.0	7.3	23.5	6.4	15.5	7.7	10.3
Total	100.0	100.0	100.0	100.0	100.0	100.0	100.0	100.0	100.0	100.0	100.0	100.0

SOURCE: UNIVERSITY OF BASEL, DEPT. OF GEOGRAPHY AND ALL INDIA DISASTER MITIGATION INSTITUTE, AHMEDABAD, INDIA 2005. SOCIAL SCIENCE SURVEY IN SELECTED SLUM COMMUNITIES IN THE CITY OF BHUJ, GUJARAT, INDIA.

Table 9.18 Monthly expenses for medicine (in Rs.), by average daily wages of household members (in Rs.).

Wage Monthly expenses	0 to 9 Rs. in % (n=29)	10 to 19 Rs. in % (n=110)	20 to 29 Rs. in % (n=102)	30 to 39 Rs. in % (n=56)	40 to 49 Rs. in % (n=19)	50 to 89 Rs. in % (n=21)	90 to 130 Rs. in % (n=5)	Total in % (n=342)
1-50	37.9	50.0	41.2	41.1	36.8	42.9	40.0	43.6
51-100	20.7	15.5	23.5	17.9	15.8	14.3	20.0	18.7
101-200	17.2	10.0	7.8	16.1	21.1	23.8	0.0	12.3
201-500	17.2	20.0	20.6	17.9	15.8	9.5	40.0	19.0
501-5000	6.9	4.5	6.9	7.1	10.5	9.5	0.0	6.4
Total	100.0	100.0	100.0	100.0	100.0	100.0	100.0	100.0

SOURCE: UNIVERSITY OF BASEL, DEPT. OF GEOGRAPHY AND ALL INDIA DISASTER MITIGATION INSTITUTE, AHMEDABAD, INDIA 2005. SOCIAL SCIENCE SURVEY IN SELECTED SLUM COMMUNITIES IN THE CITY OF BHUJ, GUJARAT, INDIA.

By education of family head (Tab. 9.19). Although not statistically significant, a general trend can be made out. Those who have completed their schooling with a graduation or have a diploma more often spend higher amounts per month on medicine. On the other hand, those who are illiterate mostly spend little amounts on medicine. This can probably be explained by the fact that those who have a higher education also earn more and can thus afford to spend more on medicine. Moreover, they may have more knowledge and information on illnesses, symptoms and treatments and therefore tend to be more interested in health issues and to spend more on maintaining health.

Table 9.19 Monthly expenses for medicine (in Rs.), by education standard of family head.

Education Monthly expenses	Hrs. 1-3 in % (n=32)	Hrs. 4-6 in % (n=63)	Hrs. 7-9 in % (n=76)	Hrs. 10-12 in % (n=31)	completed graduation / diploma in % (n=6)	Illiterate in % (n=147)	Total in % (n=355)
1-50 Rs.	53.1	27.0	43.4	35.5	50.0	49.7	43.4
51-100 Rs.	15.6	20.6	15.8	16.1	16.7	20.4	18.6
101-200 Rs.	9.4	20.6	11.8	9.7	0.0	10.2	12.1
201-500 Rs.	15.6	23.8	23.7	29.0	16.7	14.3	19.4
501-5000 Rs.	6.3	7.9	5.3	9.7	16.7	5.4	6.5
Total	100.0	100.0	100.0	100.0	100.0	100.0	100.0

SOURCE: UNIVERSITY OF BASEL, DEPT. OF GEOGRAPHY AND ALL INDIA DISASTER MITIGATION INSTITUTE, AHMEDABAD, INDIA 2005. SOCIAL SCIENCE SURVEY IN SELECTED SLUM COMMUNITIES IN THE CITY OF BHUJ, GUJARAT, INDIA.

By caste (Tab. 9.20). While there is a small percentage of persons among the General Castes who spend between 550-5000 Rs. per month on medicines (11.1%), the proportion who spend only 1-50 Rs. per month on medicines is comparably high (27.0%). The pattern is strikingly different for the Other Backward Classes: Among them, 62.9% spend only 1-50 Rs. per month on medicine, and only 4.3% spend between 550 and 5000 Rs. per month. Also Scheduled Tribes families are among the ones who spend less money on medicine (48.8% spend 1-50Rs/month and another 29.3% spend 60-100 Rs. per month).

Again, this fits in well with the fact that the Scheduled Tribes population is economically worst off, and members of the Other Backward Classes and General castes are usually "wealthier".

Table 9.20 Monthly expenses for medicine (in Rs.), by caste.

Caste Monthly expenses	SC in % (n=72)	ST in % (n=41)	OBC in % (n=116)	General in % (n=126)	Total in % (n=355)
1-50 Rs.	36.1	48.8	62.9	27.0	43.1
51-100 Rs.	27.8	29.3	12.9	15.1	18.6
101-200 Rs.	2.8	9.8	7.8	22.2	12.1
201-500 Rs.	29.2	9.8	12.1	24.6	19.7
501-5000 Rs.	4.2	2.4	4.3	11.1	6.5
Total	100.0	100.0	100.0	100.0	100.0

SOURCE: UNIVERSITY OF BASEL, DEPT. OF GEOGRAPHY AND ALL INDIA DISASTER MITIGATION INSTITUTE, AHMEDABAD, INDIA 2005. SOCIAL SCIENCE SURVEY IN SELECTED SLUM COMMUNITIES IN THE CITY OF BHUJ, GUJARAT, INDIA.

By religion (Tab. 9.21). Muslim households seem to spend less on medicine than Hindus. Whereas 69.3% of the Muslims spend 1-100 Rs. per month, the percentage of Hindus who are in the same spending class is lower, at 50.7%. On the other hand, 9.2% of the Hindus spend 550-5000 Rs per month. Only 4.7% of the Muslims are in the same spending class. Reasons for this are not easily apparent.

Table 9.21 Monthly expenses for medicine (in Rs.), by religion.

Religion Monthly expenses	Hindu in % (n=142)	Muslim in % (n=212)	Total in % (n=354)
1-50 Rs.	31.7	50.9	43.2
51-100 Rs.	19.0	18.4	18.6
101-200 Rs.	14.1	10.4	11.9
201-500 Rs.	26.1	15.6	19.8
501-5000 Rs.	9.2	4.7	6.5
Total	100.0	100.0	100.0

SOURCE: UNIVERSITY OF BASEL, DEPT. OF GEOGRAPHY AND ALL INDIA DISASTER MITIGATION INSTITUTE, AHMEDABAD, INDIA 2005. SOCIAL SCIENCE SURVEY IN SELECTED SLUM COMMUNITIES IN THE CITY OF BHUJ, GUJARAT, INDIA.

By slum (Tab. 9.22). As the economic situation in Jayprakashnagar is better than in other slums, it is not surprising that quite a high proportion (15.8%) of the families from there are in the highest spending class (550-5000 Rs. per month). In Mustuffanagar, where there are mainly Muslims, the same figure is down to 4.6%. This correlates with the fact that Muslims generally seem to spend less money on medicine (see Tab. 9.19). Otherwise, the spending classes are quite evenly distributed: in all slums, roughly 60% are in the two lowest spending classes.

Table 9.22 Monthly expenses for medicine (in Rs.), by slum.

Slum Monthly expenses	Bhimraona-gar in % (n=130)	Jayprakashna-gar in % (n=19)	Mustuffana-gar in % (n=130)	Shantina-gar in % (n=77)	Total in % (n=356)
1-50 Rs.	34.6	42.1	50.8	45.5	43.3
51-100 Rs.	27.7	15.8	13.1	13.0	18.5
101-200 Rs.	8.5	5.3	12.3	19.5	12.1
201-500 Rs.	23.1	21.1	19.2	14.3	19.7
501-5000 Rs.	6.2	15.8	4.6	7.8	6.5
Total	100.0	100.0	100.0	100.0	100.0

SOURCE: UNIVERSITY OF BASEL, DEPT. OF GEOGRAPHY AND ALL INDIA DISASTER MITIGATION INSTITUTE, AHMEDABAD, INDIA 2005. SOCIAL SCIENCE SURVEY IN SELECTED SLUM COMMUNITIES IN THE CITY OF BHUJ, GUJARAT, INDIA.

9.7 Conclusion

The assumption that there is a connection between income levels and the occurrence of illnesses was once again proven – and it seems to be even more striking in the slum context. All illnesses were much more frequent among the lower income classes, though there is still a pronounced difference between the lowest income classes and all other income classes. This pattern is visible across all four slum areas.

Most households depend on government institutions for their health concerns – a fact that is surely due to the generally low income level of the surveyed. Thus, since a very large number of people depend on the government hospitals, it is essential to further strengthen and support them. Most people visit the health centres for check-ups, but a significant number of people also use the government hospitals to buy medicine (due to the fact that quite a high proportion is ill and needs medicines regularly).

Quite a large number of interviewees indicated that they or their family have not been ill during the last year – though this is to some part also due to a changed perception on what the term "illness" means. While working in the slums, a very high number of people – especially children – could be seen with coughs and skin diseases. Additionally, since the sanitary conditions were quite bad, it can be assumed many people also suffered from diarrhoea and related diseases. Though the former (respiratory problems) was mentioned every now and then, skin diseases was hardly ever indicated, and diarrhoea was completely left out; probably because the affected persons do not see this as diseases any more, but regard it as a "normal" state. Thus, the figures represent a subjective state rather than an objective one – to gain objective statistical figures, more research would have to be done with skilled medical stuff. Still, these survey results are in the end not less meaningful – because the health status and well-being are always to a certain extent subjective.

The study revealed once again that economical state and health/well-being are closely linked – and therefore have to be considered jointly for further action.

Map 9.1 Households reporting on their places for health check up, Bhimraonagar

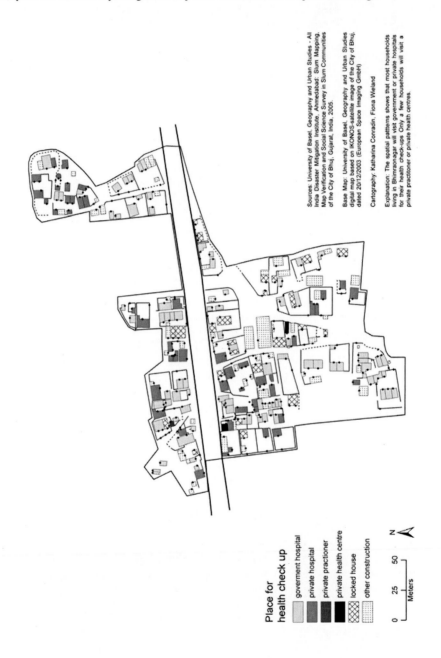

Health issues and occupational hazards 141

Map 9.2 Households reporting on their places for health check up, Jayprakashnagar

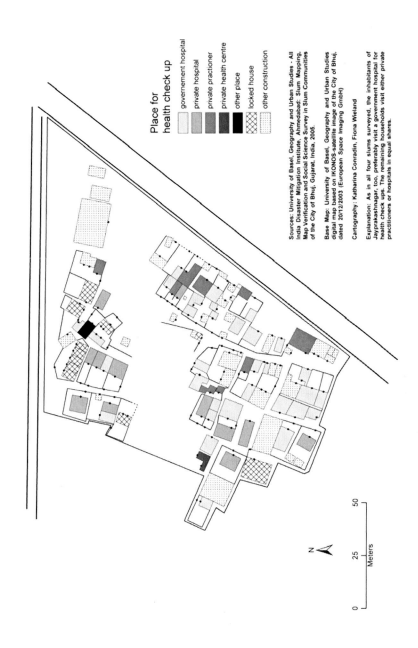

142   Health issues and occupational hazards

Map 9.3 Households reporting on their places for health check up, Mustuffanagar

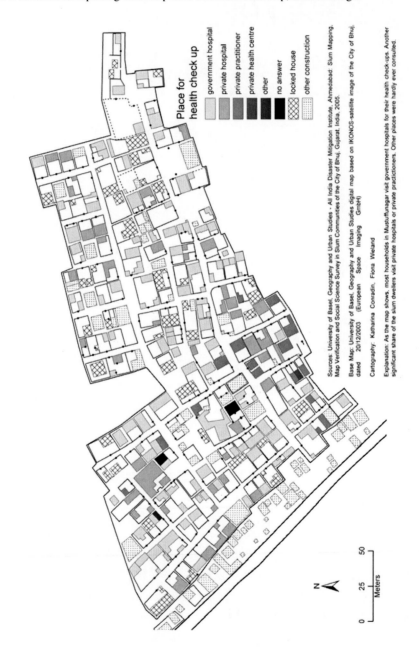

Health issues and occupational hazards 143

Map 9.4 Households reporting on their places for health check up, Shantinagar

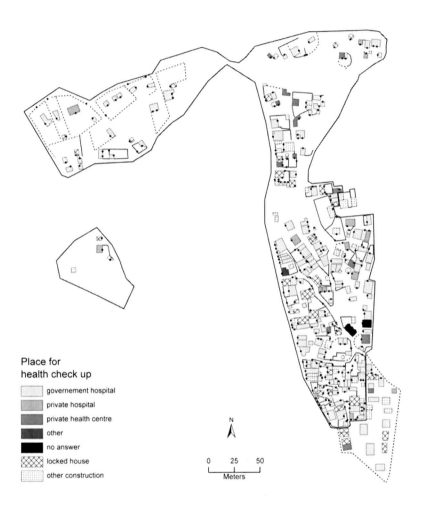

Place for health check up
- governement hospital
- private hospital
- private health centre
- other
- no answer
- locked house
- other construction

0 25 50
Meters

Sources: University of Basel, Geography and Urban Studies - All India Disaster Mitigation Institute, Ahmedabad: Slum Mapping, Map Verification and Social Science Survey in Slum Communities of the City of Bhuj, Gujarat, India, 2005.

Base Map: University of Basel, Geography and Urban Studies digital map based on IKONOS-satellite image of the City of Bhuj, dated 20/12/2003 (European Space Imaging GmbH)

Cartography: Katharina Conradin, Fiona Wieland

Explanation: In Shantinagar, almost all surveyed households visit government hospitals for health check-ups. In this slum comparatively few households visit other places for health check-ups, due to the generally low income here.

144   Health issues and occupational hazards

Map 9.5 Spatial pattern of illness or death of a family member during the past year in Bhimraonagar

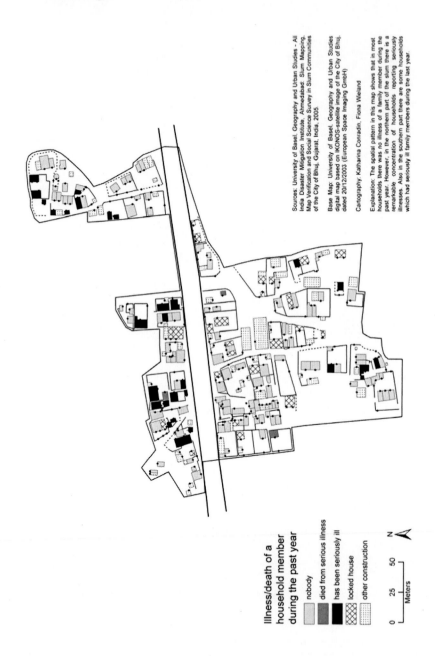

Map 9.6 Spatial pattern of illness or death of a family member during the past year in Jayprakashnagar

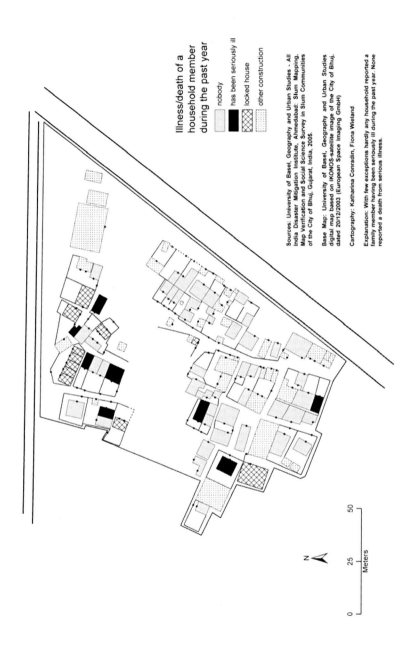

146   Health issues and occupational hazards

Map 9.7   Spatial pattern of illness or death of a family member during the past year in Mustuffanagar

Health issues and occupational hazards 147

Map 9.8   Spatial pattern of illness or death of a family member during the past year in Shantinagar

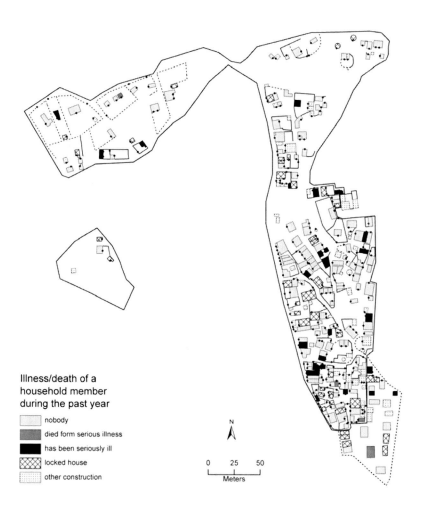

Sources: University of Basel, Geography and Urban Studies - All India Disaster Mitigation Institute, Ahmedabad: Slum Mapping, Map Verification and Social Science Survey in Slum Communities of the City of Bhuj, Gujarat, India, 2005.

Base Map: University of Basel, Geography and Urban Studies digital map based on IKONOS-satellite image of the City of Bhuj, dated 20/12/2003 (European Space Imaging GmbH)

Cartography: Katharina Conradin, Fiona Wieland

Explanation: The map shows that most households in Shantinagar did not experience any illnesses. But compared to the other slums surveyed there are still quite a few households with family members having been seriously ill during the past year.

148   Health issues and occupational hazards

Map 9.9 Households reporting illnesses in Bhimraonagar

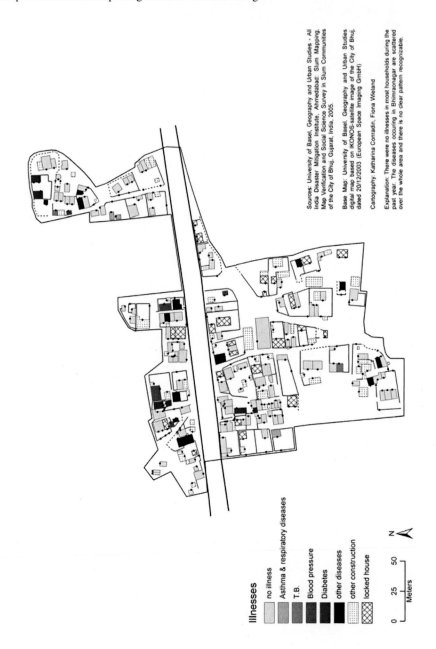

Map 9.10 Households reporting illnesses in Jayprakashnagar

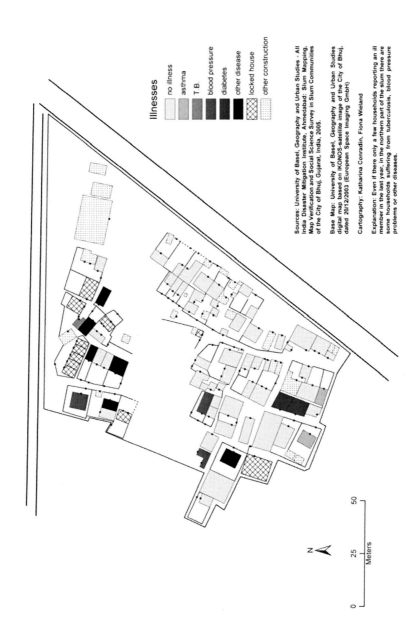

Map 9.11 Households reporting illnesses in Mustuffanagar

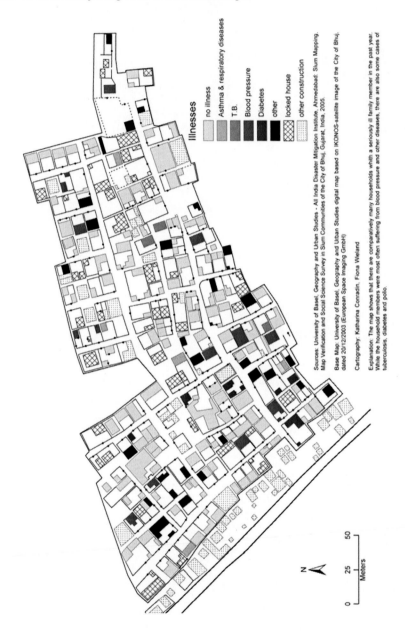

Health issues and occupational hazards 151

Map 9.12 Households reporting illnesses in Shantinagar

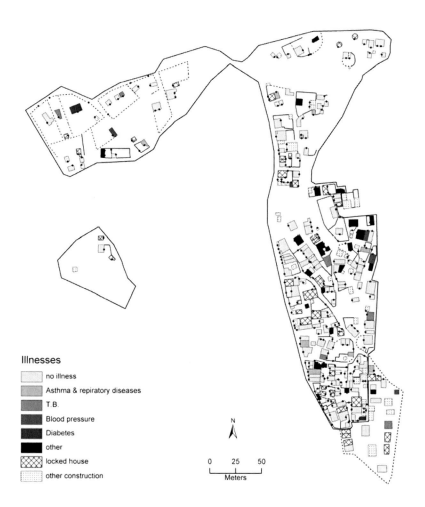

Sources: University of Basel, Geography and Urban Studies - All India Disaster Mitigation Institute, Ahmedabad: Slum Mapping, Map Verification and Social Science Survey in Slum Communities of the City of Bhuj, Gujarat, India, 2005.

Base Map: University of Basel, Geography and Urban Studies digital map based on IKONOS-satellite image of the City of Bhuj, dated 20/12/2003 (European Space Imaging GmbH)

Cartography: Katharina Conradin, Fiona Wieland

Explanation: Whereas a large number of households reported not having had a seriously ill family member during the past year, there are a number of cases of asthma and respiratory diseases, diabetes and other diseases. The central part of Shantinagar where most tribals live is particularly affected.

10 Demographic determinants – child bearing and age structure

S. Eichenberger, M. Gysi, C. Saalfrank, N. Sliwa
University of Basel

10.1
Introduction

Whether or not there is a connection between number of children, demographic structure and different levels of economic well-being is focussed upon in this chapter. The main research question of how people can move out of poverty and what factors determine an upward social mobility or stagnation in poverty was reiterated by the following aspects: Are families with many children poorer? Does the number of children depend on the education level of the family, and in what way does the combination of factors like education, occupation and number of children influence the income situation or poverty?

In order to gain an understanding of these issues, the number of children from 0-7 and from 8-17 years per household was analyzed by education standard of the family head (Tab. 10.1 and 10.2), by caste (Tab. 10.3 and 10.4), by average daily wages of household members (Tab. 10.11 and 10.12) and by occupation of the family head (Tab. 10.3 to 10.16). The analysis of the number of old people per household (Tab. 10.17 to 10.24) contributes to the understanding of the family structure in the slums and its relation to socioeconomic factors.

10.2
Number of children

By education of the family head (Tab. 10.1, 10.2). Generally, less educated people are thought to have more children than families with a higher education standard. As table 10.1 shows, there is a clear decrease in the number of young children up to seven years per household with a rising education level of the family head. Throughout all education groups, most families have between one and three children aged 0 to 7 years. Illiterates, however, show the highest percentage of four young children per household. A similar picture emerges from Tab. 10.2. Illiterates and people with the lowest education standard 1-3 are the ones that also show the highest proportions of households with four children aged 8-17 years, as compared to all other education groups. Furthermore, those two groups are the only ones that have five children from 8-17 years per household, although the percentages are low. There appears to be a relation between the education standard of the family head and the number of children per household.

Table 10.1 Number of children between 0-7 years, by education standard of family head.

Education \ Number of children	Hrs. 1-3 in % (n=46)	Hrs. 4-6 in % (n=82)	Hrs. 7-9 in % (n=108)	Hrs. 10-12 in % (n=36)	completed diploma in % (n=1)	completed Graduation in % (n=6)	Illiterate in % (n=217)	Total in % (n=496)
0	52.2	42.7	37.0	38.9	0.0	50.0	50.7	45.6
1	19.6	23.2	31.5	30.6	100.0	50.0	20.3	24.4
2	17.4	19.5	17.6	22.2	0.0	0.0	14.3	16.5
3	8.7	8.5	13.9	8.3	0.0	0.0	7.8	9.3
4	2.2	2.4	0.0	0.0	0.0	0.0	6.5	3.4
5	0.0	2.4	0.0	0.0	0.0	0.0	0.5	0.6
6	0.0	1.2	0.0	0.0	0.0	0.0	0.0	0.2
Total	100.0	100.0	100.0	100.0	100.0	100.0	100.0	100.0

SOURCE: UNIVERSITY OF BASEL, DEPT. OF GEOGRAPHY AND ALL INDIA DISASTER MITIGATION INSTITUTE, AHMEDABAD, INDIA 2005. SOCIAL SCIENCE SURVEY IN SELECTED SLUM COMMUNITIES IN THE CITY OF BHUJ, GUJARAT, INDIA.

Table 10.2 Number of children between 8-17 years, by education standard of family head.

Education \ Number of children	Hrs. 1-3 in % (n=46)	Hrs. 4-6 in % (n=82)	Hrs. 7-9 in % (n=108)	Hrs. 10-12 in % (n=36)	completed diploma in % (n=1)	completed Graduation in % (n=6)	Illiterate in % (n=217)	Total in % (n=496)
0	43.5	51.2	45.4	44.4	0.0	33.3	41.9	44.4
1	10.9	22.0	19.4	22.2	100.0	33.3	19.4	19.6
2	23.9	9.8	16.7	13.9	0.0	33.3	15.7	15.7
3	8.7	12.2	15.7	11.1	0.0	0.0	12.4	12.5
4	10.9	4.9	2.8	8.3	0.0	0.0	6.9	6.0
5	2.2	0.0	0.0	0.0	0.0	0.0	3.2	1.6
7	0.0	0.0	0.0	0.0	0.0	0.0	0.5	0.2
Total	100.0	100.0	100.0	100.0	100.0	100.0	100.0	100.0

SOURCE: UNIVERSITY OF BASEL, DEPT. OF GEOGRAPHY AND ALL INDIA DISASTER MITIGATION INSTITUTE, AHMEDABAD, INDIA 2005. SOCIAL SCIENCE SURVEY IN SELECTED SLUM COMMUNITIES IN THE CITY OF BHUJ, GUJARAT, INDIA.

By dependence of caste affiliation (Tab. 10.3, 10.4). Whereas in the categories Scheduled Castes (SC) and Scheduled Tribes (ST) - mostly Hindus - , the percentage of those without children is around 50%, it is significantly lower with the Other Backward Castes (OBC: 34.4%), who are mainly Muslims. Households of the OBC show the highest proportion of four children up to seven years (6.1%, Tab. 10.3). However, table 10.4 shows that the mainly Muslim OBC population also has the highest proportion of households with just one child aged 8 to 17 years, as compared to the other castes. The fact that families in the predominantly Muslim slum Mustuffanagar generally have a better education standard, might be reflected by the OBC population showing the highest proportion of just one older child per household. The relatively high percentage of four children aged up to seven years per OBC household, as compared to the other castes (Tab. 10.3), might be an indicator of a recent development.

Table 10.3 Number of children between 0-7 years, by caste.

Caste \ Number of children	SC in % (n=86)	ST in % (n=57)	OBC in % (n=180)	General in % (n=173)	Total in % (n=496)
0	53.5	52.6	34.4	51.4	45.8
1	20.9	19.3	28.3	23.1	24.2
2	18.6	14.0	17.8	15.0	16.5
3	4.7	12.3	12.2	7.5	9.3
4	1.2	1.8	6.1	2.3	3.4
5	1.2	0.0	1.1	0.0	0.6
6	0.0	0.0	0.0	0.6	0.2
Total	100.0	100.0	100.0	100.0	100.0

SOURCE: UNIVERSITY OF BASEL, DEPT. OF GEOGRAPHY AND ALL INDIA DISASTER MITIGATION INSTITUTE, AHMEDABAD, INDIA 2005. SOCIAL SCIENCE SURVEY IN SELECTED SLUM COMMUNITIES IN THE CITY OF BHUJ, GUJARAT, INDIA.

Table 10.4 Number of children between 8-17 years, by caste.

Caste \ Number of children	SC in % (n=86)	ST in % (n=57)	OBC in % (n=180)	General in % (n=173)	Total in % (n=496)
0	45.3	47.4	43.9	43.4	44.4
1	17.4	14.0	20.6	22.0	19.8
2	16.3	14.0	12.2	19.7	15.7
3	14.0	19.3	11.1	10.4	12.3
4	4.7	5.3	9.4	3.5	6.0
5	2.3	0.0	2.2	1.2	1.6
7	0.0	0.0	0.6	0.0	0.2
Total	100.0	100.0	100.0	100.0	100.0

SOURCE: UNIVERSITY OF BASEL, DEPT. OF GEOGRAPHY AND ALL INDIA DISASTER MITIGATION INSTITUTE, AHMEDABAD, INDIA 2005. SOCIAL SCIENCE SURVEY IN SELECTED SLUM COMMUNITIES IN THE CITY OF BHUJ, GUJARAT, INDIA.

By religion (Tab. 10.5, 10.6). A lower percentage of Muslims has no small children up to seven years (39.2%) as compared to the Hindus (53.2%). This finding is supported by the fact that Muslim households show a higher proportion with all numbers of children between 0 to 7 years than the Hindu households. The percentage of Muslim families with no or only one child between 8 and 17 years is lower than the one in Hindu households. Also, more Muslim households have four or more children in that age group than Hindu ones (Tab. 10.6).

Table 10.5 Number of children between 0-7 years, by religion.

Religion Number of children	Hindu in % (n=217)	Muslim in % (n=278)	Total in % (n=495)
0	53.5	39.2	45.5
1	22.1	26.3	24.4
2	13.4	19.1	16.6
3	8.8	9.7	9.3
4	1.8	4.7	3.4
5	0.0	1.1	0.6
6	0.5	0.0	0.2
Total	100.0	100.0	100.0

SOURCE: UNIVERSITY OF BASEL, DEPT. OF GEOGRAPHY AND ALL INDIA DISASTER MITIGATION INSTITUTE, AHMEDABAD, INDIA 2005. SOCIAL SCIENCE SURVEY IN SELECTED SLUM COMMUNITIES IN THE CITY OF BHUJ, GUJARAT, INDIA.

Table 10.6 Number of children between 8-17 years, by religion.

Religion Number of children	Hindu in % (n=217)	Muslim in % (n=278)	Total in % (n=495)
0	48.8	40.3	44.0
1	20.3	19.4	19.8
2	14.3	16.9	15.8
3	12.4	12.6	12.5
4	3.2	8.3	6.1
5	0.9	2.2	1.6
7	0.0	0.4	0.2
Total	100.0	100.0	100.0

SOURCE: UNIVERSITY OF BASEL, DEPT. OF GEOGRAPHY AND ALL INDIA DISASTER MITIGATION INSTITUTE, AHMEDABAD, INDIA 2005. SOCIAL SCIENCE SURVEY IN SELECTED SLUM COMMUNITIES IN THE CITY OF BHUJ, GUJARAT, INDIA.

By slum (Tab. 10.7, 10.8). In Mustuffanagar, only 38.5% of the families do not have children between 0 and 7 years, whereas the percentage is at 44.6% in Shantinagar, at 61.2% in Bhimraonagar and highest in Jayprakashnagar with 65.5%. Mustuffa- and Shantinagar are two slums with a Muslim majority of the population: almost 90% of the inhabitants of Mustuffa-, and around 64% of those in Shantinagar are Muslims, the other two slums being mainly Hindu. In the two predominantly Muslim communities, the percentage of households with more than three children up to seven years, respectively up to 17 years, is higher than in the other slums (Tab. 10.7, 10.8). It appears that households in predominantly Muslim communities tend to have more children in general (Tab. 10.7, 10.8). In what way this might influence the socioeconomic situation of the families (income, poverty, education), will be analyzed in the following paragraphs, but also in further detail in chapter 11.

The two communities of Shanti- and Mustuffanagar have similar percentages in the numbers of children per household (Tab. 10.7 and 10.8) and are both predominantly Muslim. Therefore, they can be compared in terms of life conditions and education standard. Whereas housing conditions and livelihood in Mustuffanagar were relatively good, the situation was apparently much worse in Shantinagar, where housing and living conditions seemed very poor. Since the two communities have the same religious background and do not differ much as to the numbers of children per household, the main reasons for the different living conditions in Mustuffa- and Shantinagar must be sought elsewhere.

As a matter of fact, Shantinagar is the slum with the highest proportion of illiterates (57%), whereas the percentage is significantly lower in Mustuffanagar with 22% (Tab. 11.1). Also, the population in Mustuffanagar generally has a better education standard than the population in Shantinagar (Tab. 11.1). One can conclude that education standards seem to determine livelihood conditions more than the number of children per household, since both communities have similar proportions to that aspect. However, as could be seen in table 10.1, the number of children per household does decrease with rising education standards of the family, but does not explain in itself different living conditions in the communities.

Table 10.7 Number of children between 0-7 years, by slum.

Slum / Number of children	Bhimraonagar in % (n=165)	Jayprakashnagar in % (n=58)	Mustuffanagar in % (n=161)	Shantinagar in % (n=157)	Total in % (n=541)
0	61.2	65.5	38.5	44.6	50.1
1	17.6	20.7	29.2	21.0	22.4
2	13.3	13.8	19.3	13.4	15.2
3	6.7	0.0	9.9	12.1	8.5
4	1.2	0.0	1.2	8.3	3.1
5	0.0	0.0	1.2	0.6	0.6
6	0.0	0.0	0.6	0.0	0.2
Total	100.0	100.0	100.0	100.0	100.0

SOURCE: UNIVERSITY OF BASEL, DEPT. OF GEOGRAPHY AND ALL INDIA DISASTER MITIGATION INSTITUTE, AHMEDABAD, INDIA 2005. SOCIAL SCIENCE SURVEY IN SELECTED SLUM COMMUNITIES IN THE CITY OF BHUJ, GUJARAT, INDIA.

Table 10.8 Number of children between 8-17 years, by slum.

Slum / Number of children	Bhimraonagar in % (n=165)	Jayprakashnagar in % (n=58)	Mustuffanagar in % (n=161)	Shantinagar in % (n=157)	Total in % (n=541)
0	57.6	60.3	40.4	43.9	48.8
1	14.5	15.5	21.1	19.7	18.1
2	10.3	13.8	17.4	15.9	14.4
3	10.9	10.3	13.7	10.2	11.5
4	5.5	0.0	6.8	6.4	5.5
5	1.2	0.0	0.6	3.2	1.5
7	0.0	0.0	0.0	0.6	0.2
Total	100.0	100.0	100.0	100.0	100.0

SOURCE: UNIVERSITY OF BASEL, DEPT. OF GEOGRAPHY AND ALL INDIA DISASTER MITIGATION INSTITUTE, AHMEDABAD, INDIA 2005. SOCIAL SCIENCE SURVEY IN SELECTED SLUM COMMUNITIES IN THE CITY OF BHUJ, GUJARAT, INDIA.

By age of the family head (Tab. 10.9, 10.10). As expected, the number of children up to seven years decreases with increasing age of the family head (10.9). Households with a family head aged 20-29 years show the highest percentage of children aged 0-7 years (36.8%). The percentage is still around 27% and 25% in the age groups 30-39 and 40-49 years and decreases with age. Households with a family head aged 30-39 years show the highest proportions of children between 8 and 17 years (10.10). Clearly, the time of founding a family is between 20 and 29 years. Under 20 years, most people do not have an own household yet, but still live with their parents. An indication is that in order to make people and their families move out of poverty, measures need to be taken early, because families are founded at a young age. If people aged between 20 and 29 already have to take care of a family and they do not have the possibilities to make a stable living, poverty will be the result and will determine the life of the next generation as well.

Table 10.9 Number of children between 0-7 years, by age of family head.

Age / Number of children	0-19 in % (n=1)	20-29 in % (n=57)	30-39 in % (n=134)	40-49 in % (n=130)	50-59 in % (n=69)	60-69 in % (n=69)	70-79 in % (n=24)	80-89 in % (n=7)	>90 in % (n=5)	Total in % (n=496)
0	100.0	17.5	26.9	58.5	59.4	58.0	58.3	71.4	60.0	45.6
1	0.0	36.8	26.9	24.6	17.4	18.8	20.8	0.0	40.0	24.4
2	0.0	28.1	23.1	8.5	13.0	15.9	12.5	14.3	0.0	16.5
3	0.0	14.0	16.4	3.8	7.2	4.3	8.3	14.3	0.0	9.3
4	0.0	1.8	5.2	3.8	2.9	2.9	0.0	0.0	0.0	3.4
5	0.0	1.8	0.7	0.8	0.0	0.0	0.0	0.0	0.0	0.6
6	0.0	0.0	0.7	0.0	0.0	0.0	0.0	0.0	0.0	0.2
Total	100.0	100.0	100.0	100.0	100.0	100.0	100.0	100.0	100.0	100.0

SOURCE: UNIVERSITY OF BASEL, DEPT. OF GEOGRAPHY AND ALL INDIA DISASTER MITIGATION INSTITUTE, AHMEDABAD, INDIA 2005. SOCIAL SCIENCE SURVEY IN SELECTED SLUM COMMUNITIES IN THE CITY OF BHUJ, GUJARAT, INDIA.

Table 10.10 Number of children between 7-17 years, by age of family head.

Age / Number of children	0-19 in % (n=1)	20-29 in % (n=57)	30-39 in % (n=134)	40-49 in % (n=130)	50-59 in % (n=69)	60-69 in % (n=69)	70-79 in % (n=24)	80-89 in % (n=7)	>90 in % (n=5)	Total in % (n=496)
0	100.0	80.7	27.6	26.9	52.2	60.9	58.3	71.4	80.0	44.4
1	0.0	12.3	28.4	18.5	17.4	15.9	16.7	0.0	20.0	19.6
2	0.0	3.5	20.9	17.7	18.8	11.6	16.7	0.0	0.0	15.7
3	0.0	3.5	15.7	23.1	4.3	7.2	0.0	14.3	0.0	12.5
4	0.0	0.0	6.7	8.5	5.8	4.3	8.3	14.3	0.0	6.0
5	0.0	0.0	0.7	5.4	0.0	0.0	0.0	0.0	0.0	1.6
7	0.0	0.0	0.0	0.0	1.4	0.0	0.0	0.0	0.0	0.2
Total	100.0	100.0	100.0	100.0	100.0	100.0	100.0	100.0	100.0	100.0

SOURCE: UNIVERSITY OF BASEL, DEPT. OF GEOGRAPHY AND ALL INDIA DISASTER MITIGATION INSTITUTE, AHMEDABAD, INDIA 2005. SOCIAL SCIENCE SURVEY IN SELECTED SLUM COMMUNITIES IN THE CITY OF BHUJ, GUJARAT, INDIA.

By average wage per person (Tab. 10.11, 10.12). The number of children up to seven years per household decreases remarkably with growing income: whereas around 20% of the households in the daily income groups 0 up to 29 Rs. have two children aged 0-7 years, it is only 6.5% of those with an average daily income of 50-130 Rs. However, lower income categories do not necessarily have small wages, but a growing number of children might reduce the average daily income per household member. As table 10.12 shows, the proportion of families with lower incomes declines as compared to the previous table once they have children aged 8 to 17 years that might contribute to the family income.

Table 10.11 Number of children between 0-7 years, by average daily wages of household members (in Rs.).

Wage / Number of children	0 to 9 Rs. in % (n=39)	10 to 19 Rs. in % (n=164)	20 to 29 Rs. in % (n=140)	30 to 39 Rs. in % (n=73)	40 to 49 Rs. in % (n=27)	50 to 89 Rs. in % (n=31)	90 to 130 Rs. in % (n=5)	Total in % (n=479)
0	28.2	34.1	40.7	60.3	74.1	74.2	80.0	44.9
1	23.1	23.2	30.7	26.0	14.8	19.4	20.0	25.1
2	23.1	20.1	19.3	9.6	3.7	6.5	0.0	16.5
3	17.9	15.9	7.1	0.0	7.4	0.0	0.0	9.4
4	5.1	6.7	1.4	1.4	0.0	0.0	0.0	3.3
5	2.6	0.0	0.7	1.4	0.0	0.0	0.0	0.6
6	0.0	0.0	0.0	1.4	0.0	0.0	0.0	0.2
Total	100.0	100.0	100.0	100.0	100.0	100.0	100.0	100.0

SOURCE: UNIVERSITY OF BASEL, DEPT. OF GEOGRAPHY AND ALL INDIA DISASTER MITIGATION INSTITUTE, AHMEDABAD, INDIA 2005. SOCIAL SCIENCE SURVEY IN SELECTED SLUM COMMUNITIES IN THE CITY OF BHUJ, GUJARAT, INDIA.

Table 10.12 Number of children between 8-17 years, by average wages per person of whole family.

Wage / Number of children	0 to 9 Rs. in % (n=39)	10 to 19 Rs. in % (n=164)	20 to 29 Rs. in % (n=140)	30 to 39 Rs. in % (n=73)	40 to 49 Rs. in % (n=27)	50 to 89 Rs. in % (n=31)	90 to 130 Rs. in % (n=5)	Total in % (n=479)
0	33.3	29.3	45.0	65.8	40.7	83.9	60.0	44.3
1	12.8	22.6	21.4	13.7	33.3	6.5	20.0	19.6
2	17.9	16.5	17.1	13.7	14.8	9.7	20.0	15.9
3	15.4	17.7	12.1	6.8	11.1	0.0	0.0	12.5
4	17.9	9.1	4.3	0.0	0.0	0.0	0.0	5.8
5	2.6	4.3	0.0	0.0	0.0	0.0	0.0	1.7
7	0.0	0.6	0.0	0.0	0.0	0.0	0.0	0.2
Total	100.0	100.0	100.0	100.0	100.0	100.0	100.0	100.0

SOURCE: UNIVERSITY OF BASEL, DEPT. OF GEOGRAPHY AND ALL INDIA DISASTER MITIGATION INSTITUTE, AHMEDABAD, INDIA 2005. SOCIAL SCIENCE SURVEY IN SELECTED SLUM COMMUNITIES IN THE CITY OF BHUJ, GUJARAT, INDIA.

By occupation of family head (Tab. 10.13, 10.14, 10.15, 10.16). Between 32.6% and 39.3% of the people employed in the second sector (textile/industry, casual labour, construction, automotive related jobs) have no children aged 0-7 years (crafts: 53%). The proportions of people working in the first and third sector that have no children of that age are higher: percentages are at around 54% for those holding governmental or farming jobs and at around 55%, respectively 62% for those working in the service sector or as vendors/in a shop (Tab. 10.13).

Households with a family head working either in a governmental job or in crafts predominantly have only one young child (30.8%, 35.3%), and only at a very low percentage two or more children up to seven years (two and three children: 7.7% government, 5.9% crafts, Tab. 10.13). Households with family heads working in automotive related jobs, in casual labour or in textile/industry show the highest proportions of two children up to seven years (20.9%, 20.2%, 22.2%, Tab. 10.13). People employed in construction show high percentages for one child up to seven years (29.8%), but also for two or three young children (14.3%, 11.9%). Although vendors had two children from 0-7 years at 16.7%, no household had more than two young children. By contrast, in households with a family head making a living on casual labour, the percentages grow in relation with a growing number of young children per household: 14.3% had only one child up to seven years, compared to 20.2% with two children and 15.5% with three children. Households with family heads employed in casual labour also show the highest proportion of four children under 8 years of all occupation categories (10.7%). Family heads employed in farming mostly have two or three children (equally 15.4%).

There is a clear difference in the number of young children up to seven years per household by occupation of the family head. Those who hold jobs that require a certain level of education or certain skills (government, crafts) tend to have less young children per household - mostly only one - whereas family heads working in jobs where specific knowledge counts to a lesser degree (some occupations of the second sector such as casual labour or construction), usually have a higher number of young children per household (Tab. 10.13). If people employed in jobs that require less education and also pay less tend to have more young children per household, the small amount of money they earn needs to support a large family and might cement poor life conditions. Again, a better education that leads to better jobs appears to be a key factor in the socio-economic situation of families. Education that enables people to make a better living must be focussed upon before founding a family at age 20 to 29 (Tab. 10.9, 10.10), so that livelihood conditions will improve for the family and the children.

Almost all occupation categories, regardless of the sector, show the highest proportions in the column "no children 8-17 years". An exception are households where the family head holds a governmental job, because here, the highest percentages are at three children between 8-17 years (38.5%, Tab. 10.15). This might explain why this occupation group also has a very high proportion of households without children under 8 years (53.8%) and mostly only one small child (Tab. 10.13). Apparently, a majority with family heads employed in governmental jobs have two or three grown children and maybe another small child, but not too many more. A similar picture emerges by looking at the number of children per household with family heads working in crafts or the service sector: they have high percentages of one to three grown children (8-17 years) and one small child (0-7 years) per household, but percentages for two or more small children per household are rather low (Tab. 10.13). Also, families in which the head of the family works as a vendor or in a shop rather have older children (61.9%, Tab. 10.15) than younger ones (38.1%, Tab. 10.13).

By contrast, households where family heads are doing casual labour or construction show high proportions both of one to three and even four small children under 8 years, and of one up to four children from 8 to 17 years (Tab. 10.13, 10.15). It seems that households where the family head works in construction or as a casual labourer generally have more children, both small and older ones. However, those jobs usually are by far more insecure in terms of illness, accidents and loss of income and job, and they affect the worker's health much more than for example governmental or crafts jobs. It is incontestable that a family's socioeconomic situation strongly depends on the family head's job that is in itself determined by education standards: in households where the one main contributor to the family income holds a job with great health or accident risks, the family itself is exposed to the risk of losing the only income. Also, social security in casual labour or construction work is low or inexistent, so that there will neither be health insurance nor a pension plan. Therefore, children are a way of securing the parents` livelihood at age. Furthermore, children might contribute to the family income from an early age on. However, a high number of children in a household where the only income is generated by an unstable, risky job, augments the probability of poverty, especially when one takes into consideration the fact that the generally poor income resulting from such jobs has to provide for a large family and that women taking care of many young children cannot contribute to the family income by working outside of the house. The vicious circle of insecurity and poverty can only be broken when family heads get into more stable, better paying jobs. But in order to improve the job and with it, the income situation, education is *the* major factor and must, for this reason, be focussed upon if one wants to make people move out of poverty.

Table 10.13: Number of children between 0-7 years, by occupation of family head (with reference to families)

Occupation / Number of children	textile/ industry in % (n=36)	govern- ment in % (n=13)	casual labour in % (n=84)	construc- tion in % (n=84)	farming in % (n=13)	automotive related job in % (n=43)	vendor/ shop in % (n=42)	crafts in % (n=17)	service sector in % (n=47)	retiree/ housewife/ unemployed in % (n=98)	unclear/ indian in % (n=13)	Total in % (n=490)
0	38.9	53.8	39.3	36.9	53.8	32.6	61.9	52.9	55.3	52.0	46.2	45.7
1	27.8	30.8	14.3	29.8	7.7	23.3	21.4	35.3	29.8	27.6	15.4	24.5
2	22.2	7.7	20.2	14.3	15.4	20.9	16.7	5.9	12.8	13.3	23.1	16.1
3	5.6	7.7	15.5	11.9	15.4	20.9	0.0	5.9	2.1	5.1	15.4	9.4
4	0.0	0.0	10.7	4.8	7.7	2.3	0.0	0.0	0.0	2.0	0.0	3.5
5	2.8	0.0	0.0	2.4	0.0	0.0	0.0	0.0	0.0	0.0	0.0	0.6
6	2.8	0.0	0.0	0.0	0.0	0.0	0.0	0.0	0.0	0.0	0.0	0.2
Total	100	100	100	100	100	100	100	100	100	100	100	100

Table 10.14 Number of children between 0-7 years, by occupation of family head (with reference to single persons)

Occupation / Number of children	textile/ industry in % (n=176)	Govern- ment in % (n=15)	casual labour in % (n=136)	construc- tion in % (n=172)	Farming in % (n=22)	automotive related job in % (n=75)	vendor/ shop in % (n=84)	Crafts in % (n=64)	service sector in % (n=122)	retiree/ housewife/ unemployed in % (n=607)	unclear/ indian in % (n=2)	Total in % (n=1475)
0	42.6	53.3	44.1	40.1	50.0	28.0	53.6	57.8	55.7	44.0	50.0	44.9
1	23.9	26.7	17.6	29.1	13.6	28.0	26.2	21.9	26.2	27.0	0.0	25.5
2	20.5	13.3	14.7	13.4	13.6	21.3	14.3	14.1	13.9	14.7	50.0	15.5
3	8.5	6.7	14.7	12.2	9.1	16.0	4.8	6.3	2.5	9.9	0.0	9.6
4	0.0	0.0	8.8	4.1	13.6	5.3	1.2	0.0	1.6	3.3	0.0	3.3
5	2.3	0.0	0.0	1.2	0.0	1.3	0.0	0.0	0.0	1.0	0.0	0.9
6	2.3	0.0	0.0	0.0	0.0	0.0	0.0	0.0	0.0	0.2	0.0	0.3
Total	100.0	100.0	100.0	100.0	100.0	100.0	100.0	100.0	100.0	100.0	100.0	100.0

SOURCE: UNIVERSITY OF BASEL, DEPT. OF GEOGRAPHY AND ALL INDIA DISASTER MITIGATION INSTITUTE, AHMEDABAD, INDIA 2005. SOCIAL SCIENCE SURVEY IN SELECTED SLUM COMMUNITIES IN THE CITY OF BHUJ, GUJARAT, INDIA.

Table 10.15 Number of children between 8-17 years, by occupation of family head (with reference to families).

Occupation Number of children	textile/ industry in % (n=36)	government in % (n=13)	casual labour in % (n=84)	construction in % (n=84)	farming in % (n=13)	automotive related job in % (n=43)	vendor/ shop in % (n=42)	crafts in % (n=17)	service sector in % (n=47)	retiree/ housewife/ unemployed in % (n=98)	unclear/ indian in % (n=13)	Total in % (n=490)
0	55.6	23.1	41.7	27.4	38.5	39.5	38.1	47.1	48.9	62.2	38.5	44.1
1	13.9	7.7	21.4	27.4	15.4	18.6	31.0	17.6	12.8	15.3	15.4	19.6
2	11.1	23.1	16.7	19.0	23.1	18.6	11.9	11.8	19.1	11.2	15.4	15.7
3	13.9	38.5	11.9	15.5	7.7	16.3	16.7	17.6	10.6	4.1	15.4	12.7
4	5.6	7.7	7.1	8.3	0.0	2.3	0.0	5.9	8.5	6.1	15.4	6.1
5	0.0	0.0	1.2	2.4	7.7	4.7	2.4	0.0	0.0	1.0	0.0	1.6
7	0.0	0.0	0.0	0.0	7.7	0.0	0.0	0.0	0.0	0.0	0.0	0.2
Total	100	100	100	100	100	100	100	100	100	100	100	100

Table 10.16 Number of children between 8-17 years, by occupation of family head (with reference to single persons).

Occupation Number of children	textile/ industry in % (n=176)	government in % (n=15)	casual labour in % (n=13)	construction in % (n=172)	farming in % (n=22)	automotive related job in % (n=75)	vendor/ shop in % (n=84)	crafts in % (n=64)	service sector in % (n=122)	retiree/ housewife/ unemployed in % (n=607)	unclear/ indian in % (n=2)	Total in % (n=1475)
0	43.8	33.3	40.4	32.6	45.5	46.7	40.5	45.3	55.7	45.3	50.0	43.7
1	19.9	6.7	20.6	23.3	9.1	20.0	27.4	17.2	17.2	18.9	0.0	19.7
2	14.8	20.0	17.6	25.6	22.7	14.7	8.3	14.1	13.1	15.0	50.0	16.1
3	14.8	33.3	12.5	11.0	4.5	10.7	13.1	17.2	8.2	11.4	0.0	12.0
4	5.7	6.7	5.9	5.8	0.0	4.0	8.3	4.7	4.9	7.4	0.0	6.3
5	1.1	0.0	1.5	1.7	9.1	4.0	2.4	1.6	0.8	1.6	0.0	1.8
7	0.0	0.0	1.5	0.0	9.1	0.0	0.0	0.0	0.0	0.3	0.0	0.4
Total	100.0	100.0	100.0	100.0	100.0	100.0	100.0	100.0	100.0	100.0	100.0	100.0

SOURCE: UNIVERSITY OF BASEL, DEPT. OF GEOGRAPHY AND ALL INDIA DISASTER MITIGATION INSTITUTE, AHMEDABAD, INDIA 2005. SOCIAL SCIENCE SURVEY IN SELECTED SLUM COMMUNITIES IN THE CITY OF BHUJ, GUJARAT, INDIA.

10.3
Number of dependant old people

By education of the family head, by caste, religion, slum, age of the family head, occupation (Tab. 10.17, 10.18, 10.19, 10.20, 10.21, 10.23, 10.24). Many households, regardless of the education standard of the family head, live together with up to four or five old people (Tab. 10.17). Neither education, nor caste, religion, slum, age or occupation seem to have a decisive influence on the number of dependant old people per household which do not differ to a great extent (Tab. 10.17-10.20, Tab. 10.23, 10.24) with one exception: The two communities of Jayprakash- and Mustuffanagar showed higher proportions of households without any old person (around 10%) than Bhimrao- and Shantinagar, where the percentage was between 2 and 3% (Tab. 10.20).

However, results show that a traditional family with grandparents living under the same roof as the grandchildren is still very common. This finding indicates that also in the coming generation, parents will be taken care of by their children and their families, probably due, among other things, to the lack of social security systems. It appears that for many people, especially in unstable job and livelihood conditions, children are still the way to secure livelihood at an old age, since in all slums, proportions of households with up to six dependant old people per household were rather high (Tab. 10.20).

Nevertheless, the more dependant people there are in a household, the larger the family becomes, which effects average daily wages per household member, too. On the other hand, with children taken care of by grandparents, mothers could contribute to the family income by a job outside of the household. Given that with increasing education standards, the number of children per household decreases as well (Tab. 10.1), there is a possibility to improve the family's socioeconomic situation by providing women the education that enables them to stabilize the family's income by holding a job, too. The fact that high proportions of all households live with old people, is a positive potential under the right circumstances: better education and better jobs for the parents, fewer children with better opportunities, taken care of by grandparents while the parents are at work, stabilizing the income situation of the whole family.

Table 10.17 Number of old people, by education standard of family head.

Education Number of old people	Hrs. 1-3 in % (n=45)	Hrs. 4-6 in % (n=78)	Hrs. 7-9 in % (n=106)	Hrs. 10-12 in % (n=35)	completed diploma in% (n=1)	completed graduation in % (n=6)	Illiterate in % (n=202)	Total in % (n=473)
0	2.2	2.6	7.5	5.7	0.0	0.0	6.9	5.7
1	22.2	10.3	6.6	20.0	0.0	0.0	13.4	12.5
2	28.9	19.2	17.0	14.3	0.0	33.3	13.9	17.1
3	8.9	21.8	23.6	17.1	100.0	16.7	15.8	18.2
4	15.6	23.1	26.4	11.4	0.0	33.3	17.8	20.1
5	4.4	10.3	13.2	5.7	0.0	16.7	12.4	11.0
6	8.9	7.7	0.9	14.3	0.0	0.0	9.4	7.4
7	6.7	2.6	3.8	5.7	0.0	0.0	4.0	4.0
8	0.0	1.3	0.9	2.9	0.0	0.0	4.0	2.3
9	2.2	0.0	0.0	2.9	0.0	0.0	1.0	0.8
10	0.0	0.0	0.0	0.0	0.0	0.0	1.5	0.6
13	0.0	1.3	0.0	0.0	0.0	0.0	0.0	0.2
Total	100.0	100.0	100.0	100.0	100.0	100.0	100.0	100.0

SOURCE: UNIVERSITY OF BASEL, DEPT. OF GEOGRAPHY AND ALL INDIA DISASTER MITIGATION INSTITUTE, AHMEDABAD, INDIA 2005. SOCIAL SCIENCE SURVEY IN SELECTED SLUM COMMUNITIES IN THE CITY OF BHUJ, GUJARAT, INDIA.

Table 10.18 Number of old people, by caste.

Caste Number of old people	SC in % (n=86)	ST in % (n=54)	OBC in % (n=161)	General in % (n=172)	Total in % (n=473)
0	1.2	7.4	5.6	7.6	5.7
1	14.0	16.7	13.0	9.3	12.3
2	20.9	13.0	14.3	19.2	17.1
3	19.8	20.4	14.3	20.9	18.4
4	23.3	18.5	18.6	20.3	20.1
5	11.6	11.1	11.8	9.9	11.0
6	4.7	11.1	9.3	5.8	7.4
7	3.5	1.9	6.2	2.9	4.0
8	0.0	0.0	4.3	2.3	2.3
9	1.2	0.0	1.2	0.6	0.8
10	0.0	0.0	1.2	0.6	0.6
13	0.0	0.0	0.0	0.6	0.2
Total	100.0	100.0	100.0	100.0	100.0

SOURCE: UNIVERSITY OF BASEL, DEPT. OF GEOGRAPHY AND ALL INDIA DISASTER MITIGATION INSTITUTE, AHMEDABAD, INDIA 2005. SOCIAL SCIENCE SURVEY IN SELECTED SLUM COMMUNITIES IN THE CITY OF BHUJ, GUJARAT, INDIA.

Table 10.19 Number of old people, by religion.

Number of old people	Religion	Hindu in % (n=214)	Muslim in % (n=258)	Total in % (n=472)
0		6.1	5.4	5.7
1		15.0	10.5	12.5
2		20.6	14.0	16.9
3		18.2	18.2	18.2
4		22.4	18.2	20.1
5		8.9	12.8	11.0
6		5.1	9.3	7.4
7		2.3	5.4	4.0
8		0.9	3.5	2.3
9		0.5	1.2	0.8
10		0.0	1.2	0.6
13		0.0	0.4	0.2
Total		100.0	100.0	100.0

SOURCE: UNIVERSITY OF BASEL, DEPT. OF GEOGRAPHY AND ALL INDIA DISASTER MITIGATION INSTITUTE, AHMEDABAD, INDIA 2005. SOCIAL SCIENCE SURVEY IN SELECTED SLUM COMMUNITIES IN THE CITY OF BHUJ, GUJARAT, INDIA.

Table 10.20 Number of old people, by slum.

Number of old people	Slum	Bhimraonagar in % (n=129)	Jayprakashnagar in % (n=53)	Mustuffanagar in % (n=151)	Shantinagar in % (n=141)	Total in % (n=474)
0		2.3	9.4	9.9	2.8	5.7
1		16.3	20.8	7.3	11.3	12.4
2		18.6	11.3	17.2	17.7	17.1
3		20.9	18.9	17.2	17.0	18.4
4		24.8	18.9	16.6	19.9	20.0
5		10.1	11.3	11.3	11.3	11.0
6		3.9	5.7	10.6	7.8	7.4
7		1.6	3.8	3.3	7.1	4.0
8		0.8	0.0	4.0	2.8	2.3
9		0.8	0.0	1.3	0.7	0.8
10		0.0	0.0	0.7	1.4	0.6
13		0.0	0.0	0.7	0.0	0.2
Total		100.0	100.0	100.0	100.0	100.0

SOURCE: UNIVERSITY OF BASEL, DEPT. OF GEOGRAPHY AND ALL INDIA DISASTER MITIGATION INSTITUTE, AHMEDABAD, INDIA 2005. SOCIAL SCIENCE SURVEY IN SELECTED SLUM COMMUNITIES IN THE CITY OF BHUJ, GUJARAT, INDIA.

Table 10.21 Number of old people, by age of family head.

Number of old people	Age 0-19 in % (n=1)	20-29 in % (n=55)	30-39 in % (n=125)	40-49 in % (n=125)	50-59 in % (n=67)	60-69 in % (n=64)	70-79 in % (n=24)	80-89 in % (n=7)	>90 in % (n=5)	Total in % (n=473)
0	0.0	9.1	4.0	6.4	1.5	4.7	12.5	0.0	40.0	5.7
1	0.0	12.7	6.4	9.6	20.9	23.4	8.3	14.3	0.0	12.5
2	0.0	34.5	11.2	16.0	14.9	14.1	25.0	28.6	20.0	17.1
3	0.0	18.2	24.0	17.6	17.9	15.6	4.2	0.0	20.0	18.2
4	100.0	14.5	23.2	25.6	20.9	9.4	12.5	14.3	20.0	20.1
5	0.0	3.6	16.0	7.2	10.4	10.9	20.8	28.6	0.0	11.0
6	0.0	1.8	8.0	10.4	3.0	9.4	12.5	0.0	0.0	7.4
7	0.0	5.5	2.4	4.8	7.5	3.1	0.0	0.0	0.0	4.0
8	0.0	0.0	1.6	1.6	3.0	6.3	0.0	14.3	0.0	2.3
9	0.0	0.0	0.8	0.8	0.0	3.1	0.0	0.0	0.0	0.8
10	0.0	0.0	1.6	0.0	0.0	0.0	4.2	0.0	0.0	0.6
13	0.0	0.0	0.8	0.0	0.0	0.0	0.0	0.0	0.0	0.2
Total	100.0	100.0	100.0	100.0	100.0	100.0	100.0	100.0	100.0	100.0

SOURCE: UNIVERSITY OF BASEL, DEPT. OF GEOGRAPHY AND ALL INDIA DISASTER MITIGATION INSTITUTE, AHMEDABAD, INDIA 2005. SOCIAL SCIENCE SURVEY IN SELECTED SLUM COMMUNITIES IN THE CITY OF BHUJ, GUJARAT, INDIA.

By average daily wages of household members (Tab. 10.22). Whereas in nearly all income groups the percentage of those without any old person in the household is very low (1.3% to 8.1%), it is remarkably high in the category "50-130 Rs. per day", namely at 35.5% and 20.0% (Tab. 10.22). One is inclined to suppose that households with good daily wages do not necessarily follow the traditional family model with everyone living together. They might be able to support their elderly parents at a different place than their own. This income category also shows the lowest proportions of households with three or more dependant old people per household, as compared to all other groups. Indeed, the category with the highest daily wage shows one of the highest percentages of just one old person (19.4% and 20.0%), and an important proportion of two old people per household (29.0% and 20.0%) (Tab. 10.22). One can observe that with growing average daily wages, the proportions of households with just two dependant old people per household are increasing as well (0-9 Rs.: 8.1%, 50-89 Rs.: 29.0%, Tab. 10.22), and that at the same time, the percentages of four or more old people in a household are decreasing (5 people: from 10.8% down to 0.0%, Tab. 10.22). However, all average daily wage categories have rather high proportions of one to four old people per household.

Table 10.23 Number of old people, by occupation (with reference to families).

Occupation / Number of old people	textile/ industry in % (n=35)	government in % (n=13)	casual labour in % (n=76)	construction in % (n=80)	farming in % (n=12)	automotive related job in % (n=39)	vendor/ shop in % (n=41)	crafts in % (n=17)	service sector in % (n=44)	retiree/ housewife/ unemployed in % (n=97)	unclear/ indian in % (n=13)	Total in % (n=467)
0	14.3	15.4	1.3	5.0	0.0	2.6	4.9	0.0	11.4	7.2	0.0	5.8
1	5.7	0.0	14.5	12.5	0.0	5.1	14.6	11.8	20.5	14.4	7.7	12.2
2	20.0	7.7	15.8	11.3	25.0	17.9	29.3	29.4	13.6	17.5	7.7	17.1
3	22.9	15.4	15.8	15.0	25.0	30.8	17.1	29.4	20.5	13.4	23.1	18.4
4	25.7	23.1	21.1	16.3	33.3	15.4	24.4	17.6	15.9	18.6	30.8	19.9
5	0.0	15.4	10.5	17.5	0.0	15.4	7.3	5.9	9.1	10.3	23.1	10.9
6	5.7	23.1	13.2	13.8	0.0	2.6	0.0	5.9	4.5	5.2	0.0	7.5
7	0.0	0.0	2.6	6.3	16.7	7.7	2.4	0.0	2.3	4.1	7.7	4.1
8	2.9	0.0	2.6	1.3	0.0	0.0	0.0	0.0	2.3	6.2	0.0	2.4
9	0.0	0.0	1.3	1.3	0.0	0.0	0.0	0.0	0.0	2.1	0.0	0.9
10	0.0	0.0	1.3	0.0	0.0	2.6	0.0	0.0	0.0	1.0	0.0	0.6
13	2.9	0.0	0.0	0.0	0.0	0.0	0.0	0.0	0.0	0.0	0.0	0.2
Total	100	100	100	100	100	100	100	100	100	100	100	100

SOURCE: UNIVERSITY OF BASEL, DEPT. OF GEOGRAPHY AND ALL INDIA DISASTER MITIGATION INSTITUTE, AHMEDABAD, INDIA 2005. SOCIAL SCIENCE SURVEY IN SELECTED SLUM COMMUNITIES IN THE CITY OF BHUJ, GUJARAT, INDIA.

Table 10.24 Number of old people, by occupation (with reference to single persons)

Occupation / Number of old people	textile/ industry in % (n=176)	government in % (n=15)	casual labour in % (n=124)	construction in % (n=170)	farming in % (n=20)	automotive related job in % (n=72)	vendor/ shop in % (n=83)	crafts in % (n=64)	service sector in % (n=122)	retiree/ housewife/ unemployed in % (n=590)	unclear/ indian in % (n=2)	Total in % (n=1438)
0	17.6	13.3	3.2	7.1	0.0	6.9	4.8	1.6	10.7	3.6	0.0	6.5
1	6.3	0.0	12.9	11.2	5.0	6.9	8.4	15.6	13.1	8.0	0.0	9.2
2	23.3	13.3	16.9	12.4	20.0	11.1	22.9	25.0	17.2	12.9	0.0	15.9
3	21.0	20.0	14.5	13.5	15.0	22.2	16.9	20.3	18.9	16.8	50.0	17.4
4	14.8	20.0	23.4	21.2	45.0	16.7	21.7	21.9	17.2	21.7	50.0	20.7
5	9.7	13.3	8.1	13.5	0.0	12.5	13.3	7.8	10.7	13.6	0.0	11.8
6	1.7	20.0	12.9	9.4	0.0	5.6	8.4	3.1	4.1	9.2	0.0	7.6
7	1.7	0.0	4.0	6.5	15.0	6.9	1.2	3.1	2.5	6.6	0.0	5.0
8	2.3	0.0	1.6	1.2	0.0	8.3	2.4	1.6	5.7	4.6	0.0	3.5
9	0.6	0.0	0.8	1.8	0.0	1.4	0.0	0.0	0.0	1.5	0.0	1.0
10	0.0	0.0	1.6	2.4	0.0	1.4	0.0	0.0	0.0	1.7	0.0	1.2
13	1.1	0.0	0.0	0.0	0.0	0.0	0.0	0.0	0.0	0.0	0.0	0.1
Total	100.0	100.0	100.0	100.0	100.0	100.0	100.0	100.0	100.0	100.0	100.0	100.0

SOURCE: UNIVERSITY OF BASEL, DEPT. OF GEOGRAPHY AND ALL INDIA DISASTER MITIGATION INSTITUTE, AHMEDABAD, INDIA 2005. SOCIAL SCIENCE SURVEY IN SELECTED SLUM COMMUNITIES IN THE CITY OF BHUJ, GUJARAT, INDIA.

Table 10.22 Number of old people, by average daily wages of household members (in Rs.).

Number of old people	Wage 0 to 9 Rs. in % (n=37)	10 to 19 Rs. in % (n=155)	20 to 29 Rs. in % (n=136)	30 to 39 Rs. in % (n=70)	40 to 49 Rs. in % (n=26)	50 to 89 Rs. in % (n=31)	90 to 130 Rs. in % (n=5)	Total in % (n=460)
0	8.1	1.3	2.9	2.9	7.7	35.5	20.0	5.4
1	10.8	9.7	8.1	24.3	11.5	16.1	40.0	12.4
2	8.1	10.3	16.2	30.0	26.9	29.0	20.0	17.2
3	13.5	13.5	28.7	15.7	23.1	12.9	0.0	18.7
4	13.5	23.9	22.8	18.6	19.2	6.5	0.0	20.2
5	10.8	18.1	10.3	4.3	3.8	0.0	0.0	10.9
6	5.4	14.2	5.1	1.4	3.8	0.0	20.0	7.4
7	13.5	4.5	3.7	0.0	3.8	0.0	0.0	3.9
8	8.1	2.6	0.7	2.9	0.0	0.0	0.0	2.2
9	5.4	1.3	0.0	0.0	0.0	0.0	0.0	0.9
10	2.7	0.6	0.7	0.0	0.0	0.0	0.0	0.7
13	0.0	0.0	0.7	0.0	0.0	0.0	0.0	0.2
Total	100.0	100.0	100.0	100.0	100.0	100.0	100.0	100.0

SOURCE: UNIVERSITY OF BASEL, DEPT. OF GEOGRAPHY AND ALL INDIA DISASTER MITIGATION INSTITUTE, AHMEDABAD, INDIA 2005. SOCIAL SCIENCE SURVEY IN SELECTED SLUM COMMUNITIES IN THE CITY OF BHUJ, GUJARAT, INDIA.

10.4 Conclusion

This chapter addressed the relationship between the number of children and different levels of education and income. The underlying question was whether or not children are explanatory variables of poverty. The analyses showed that an increasing education level of the family head has a decreasing effect to the number of children. However, it can not be verified that families with more children are poorer than families with few children. One can assume that a higher income reduces the necessity for a high number of children as financial supporters and old-age provision. In this regard it can be mentioned that the higher the number of children between 8-17 years the higher the daily wages of a family as they may contribute to the family income. The importance of the financial contribution of children can also be seen by crosstabulating the number of children with the occupation of the family head. Households where the contributor to the family income holds a job with great health or accident risks, show a higher number of children as households were the family head holds a stable, well paying job. But in order to improve the job and with it, the income situation, a better education needs to be *the* major factor rather than an increasing number of children as one has to take into consideration that women taking care of many children cannot contribute to the family income by working outside of the house. To make people move out of poverty the focus therefore has to lie upon increasing education levels.

Demographic determinants – child bearing and age structure

Map 10.1 Households with children up to 7 years in Bhimraonagar

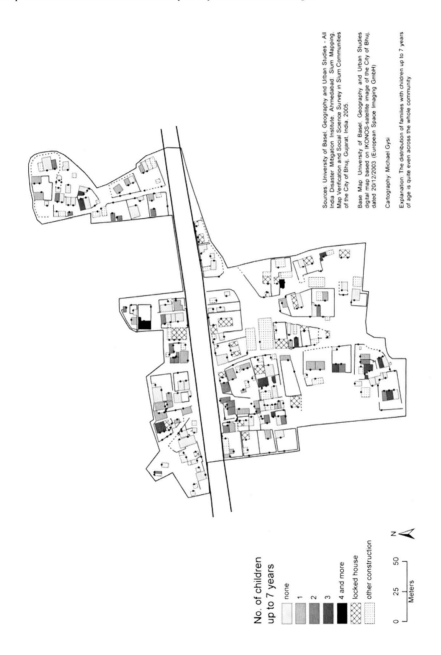

172 Demographic determinants – child bearing and age structure

Map 10.2 Households with children up to 7 years in Jayprakashnagar

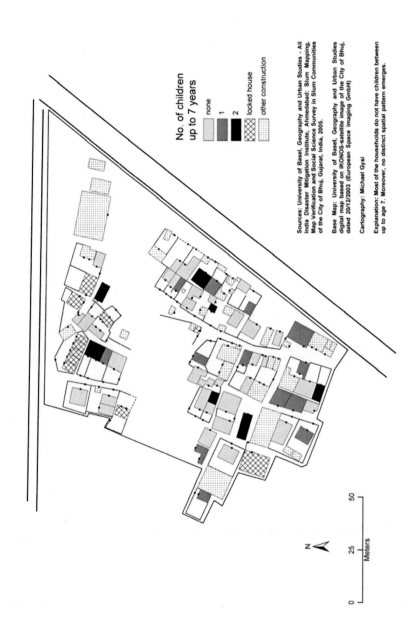

Map 10.3 Households with children up to 7 years in Mustuffanagar

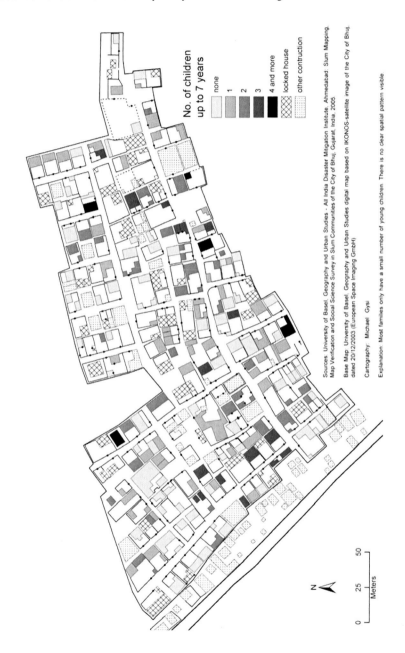

Map 10.4 Households with children up to 7 years in Shantinagar

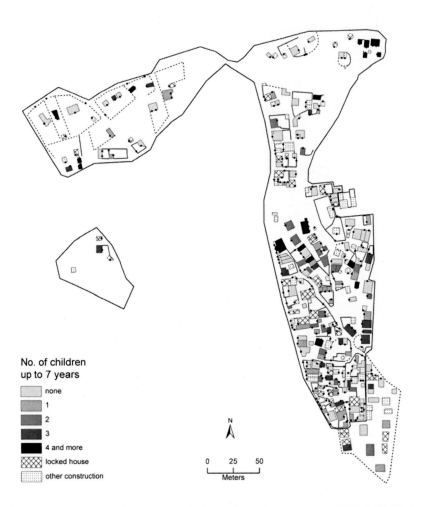

Sources: University of Basel, Geography and Urban Studies - All India Disaster Mitigation Institute, Ahmedabad: Slum Mapping, Map Verification and Social Science Survey in Slum Communities of the City of Bhuj, Gujarat, India, 2005.

Base Map: University of Basel, Geography and Urban Studies digital map based on IKONOS-satellite image of the City of Bhuj, dated 20/12/2003 (European Space Imaging GmbH)

Cartography: Michael Gysi

Explanation: Most families have fewer than 4 children between 0 and 7 years. The distribution over the slum area is quite even. However, in the central part of the community with a larger concentration of tribals, there is a cluster of large families. Only in the very northeastern part, there are a few households having more than 4 children bewteen 0 and 7 years.

Demographic determinants – child bearing and age structure 175

Map 10.5 Households with children between 8-17 years in Bhimraonagar

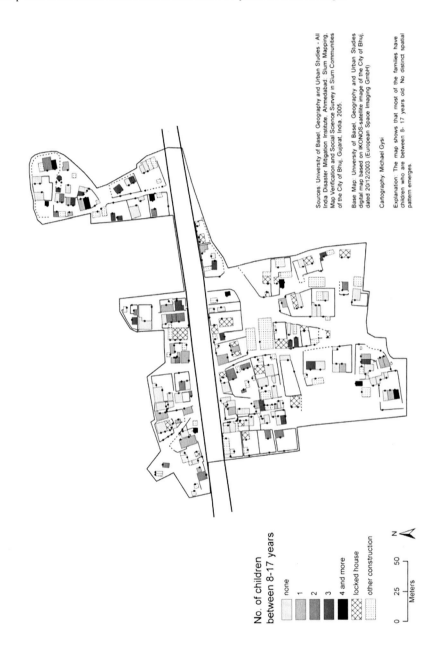

Map 10.6 Households with children between 8-17 years in Jayprakashnagar

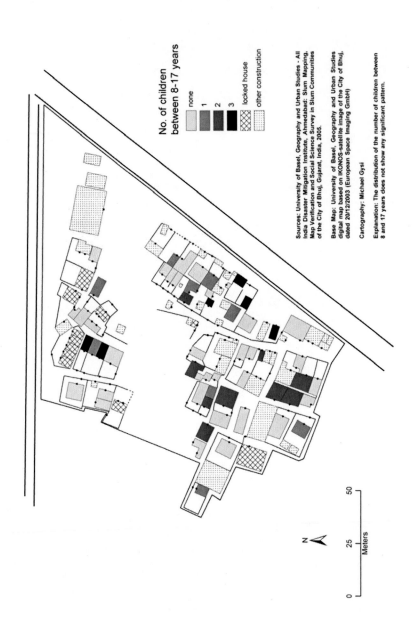

Demographic determinants – child bearing and age structure

Map 10.7 Households with children between 8-17 years in Mustuffanagar

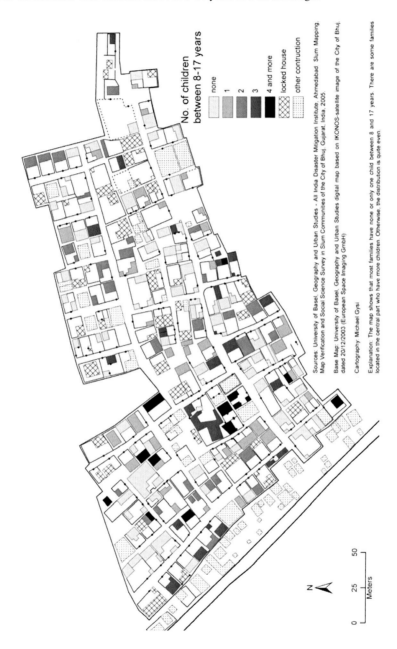

Map 10.8 Households with children between 8-17 years in Shantinagar

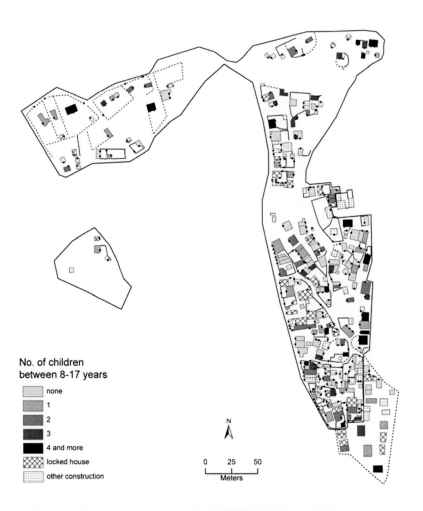

Demographic determinants – child bearing and age structure 179

Map 10.9 Households with dependent old people in Bhimraonagar

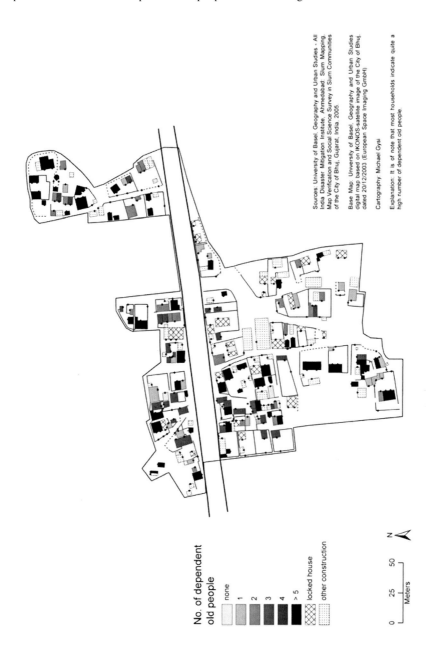

180 Demographic determinants – child bearing and age structure

Map 10.10 Households with dependent old people in Jayprakashnagar

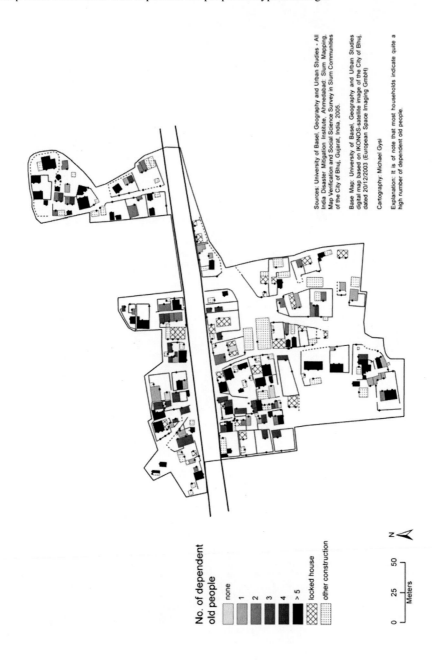

Map 10.11 Households with dependent old people in Mustuffanagar

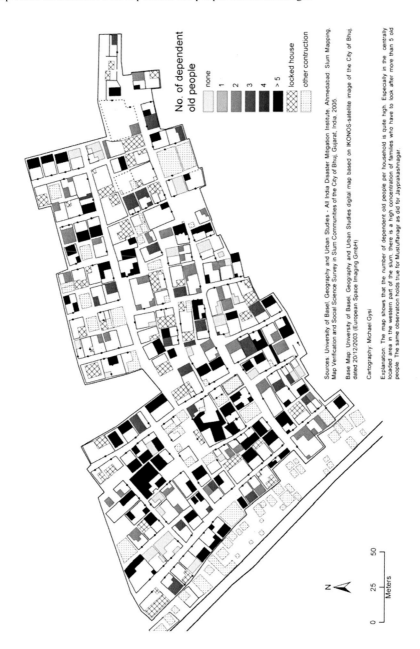

Map 10.12 Households with dependent old people in Shantinagar

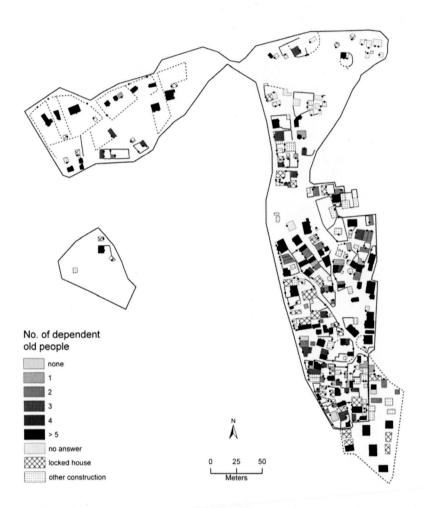

Sources: University of Basel, Geography and Urban Studies - All India Disaster Mitigation Institute, Ahmedabad: Slum Mapping. Map Verification and Social Science Survey in Slum Communities of the City of Bhuj, Gujarat, India, 2005.

Base Map: University of Basel, Geography and Urban Studies digital map based on IKONOS-satellite image of the City of Bhuj, dated 20/12/2003 (European Space Imaging GmbH)

Cartography: Michael Gysi

Explanation: Most families have elderly to look after. However, there is no distinct spatial distribution visible. There are tribal and non tribal households with dependent old people. Given the generally poor condition of Shantinagar this supports the notion that the elderly are indeed dependent and do not contribute much to the family income, if at all.

11 Educational achievements – occupational structure and political participation

A. Staub, N. Sliwa, S. Waldburger
University of Basel

11.1 Introduction

The following chapter portrays the level of education in the different slum different communities as a function of geographic context, age, sex and average daily wages. It will be outlined in what way education influences livelihood and the socioeconomic situation of people, as well as their political participation. The main questions will be the following:

- What are the education standards like in the four slum communities?
- What effect does education have on the livelihood of the slum dwellers?
- What occupations do the people in the slums follow, and how does this affect their livelihood or political participation?
- What are factors that affect the political participation?

The social science survey in some 800 households of the four slums Bhimrao-, Jayprakash-, Mustuffa- and Shantinagar illustrated strong disparities between the communities in terms of education standards and thereby, livelihood conditions.

11.2 Education

By slum (Tab. 11.1). Of all four slum communities, Jayprakashnagar shows the highest percentage of people with rather good education standards: 35.6% have finished standard 7-9, and 13.7% have completed the 12th standard. The illiteracy rate is comparatively low, at "only" 19.6%. Also, Jayprakashnagar shows the highest proportion of people with a completed graduation or a completed diploma, as compared to the other slum communities (Tab. 11.1). Whereas Bhimrao- and Mustuffanagar also have relatively high percentages of people with better education standards, Shantinagar shows an exceptionally high illiteracy rate (57.1%). Moreover, it also shows the lowest percentage of people with a completed graduation or a completed diploma. The rates for education standards 1-3, 4-6 and 7-9 in Shantinagar are between 12% and 13%, while all other slums show percentages between 13% and 35% (Tab. 11.1). The low education standards in Shantinagar – probably due to the high proportions of tribal population there – do correspond with other observations on site: Shantinagar always stood out as the least developed slum community.

Table 11.1 Education standard, by slum.

Slum Education	Bhimraonagar in % (n=535)	Jayprakashnagar in % (n=219)	Mustuffanagar in % (n=798)	Shantinagar in % (n=736)	Total in % (n=2288)
Hrs. 1-3	15.0	10.0	15.4	13.5	14.2
Hrs. 4-6	22.2	16.9	23.9	13.7	19.6
Hrs. 7-9	24.9	35.6	25.9	12.5	22.3
Hrs. 10-12	7.3	13.7	11.0	2.9	7.8
Completed Diploma	0.2	0.5	0.1	0.0	0.1
Completed Graduation	1.1	3.7	1.4	0.4	1.2
Illiterate	29.3	19.6	22.2	57.1	34.8
Total	100.0	100.0	100.0	100.0	100.0

SOURCE: UNIVERSITY OF BASEL, DEPT. OF GEOGRAPHY AND ALL INDIA DISASTER MITIGATION INSTITUTE, AHMEDABAD, INDIA 2005. SOCIAL SCIENCE SURVEY IN SELECTED SLUM COMMUNITIES IN THE CITY OF BHUJ, GUJARAT, INDIA.

By age (Tab. 11.2). Generally, the older people are, the lower their level of education is. Amongst the 60-69 year old people, the illiteracy rate is at 74%, while it is only at 18.8% among those younger than 19 years. The low rate of people with completed graduation or diploma among the people up to 19 years is due to their young age. The relation between lower education standards and age becomes evident in the age categories over 20 years. Whereas more than 14% of those between 20 and 29 years have completed their diploma, it is only at around 8% in the following age groups and at 1.8% for those between 60 and 69 years. At the same time, an increase in the illiteracy rate with age can be observed: While 25.2% of the young people between 20 and 29 years are illiterate, the percentage is between roughly 80% and 90% for people who are older than 70. One can conclude that apparently, education standards in the surveyed communities have risen during the past decades and that the government's efforts concerning education have been fruitful to some extent. However, while general figures on education standards suggest that an improvement has taken place, one should note that still a quarter of the surveyed population between 20 and 29, and even more than half of those between 40 and 49 years are illiterate. Also, general figures do not point out the disparities within poor communities, respectively the important differences in development among slum communities: some have higher education standards, others are below average. Those disparities and the question *why* there are such differences in development need to be emphasized and analysed more if one wants to improve living conditions for *all* the poor population in the different areas.

Table 11.2 Education standard, by age.

Age Education	0-19 in % (n=900)	20-29 in % (n=444)	30-39 in % (n=389)	40-49 in % (n=247)	50-59 in % (n=137)	60-69 in % (n=113)	70-79 in % (n=45)	80-89 in % (n=12)	>90 in % (n=7)	Total in % (n=2294)
Hrs. 1-3	25.2	4.7	6.9	4.5	17.5	8.8	13.3	0.0	0.0	14.2
Hrs. 4-6	26.7	18.9	18.0	11.3	8.8	10.6	4.4	8.3	14.3	19.6
Hrs. 7-9	23.2	33.3	22.4	17.8	12.4	3.5	2.2	0.0	0.0	22.2
Hrs. 10-12	5.9	14.4	8.2	8.9	3.6	1.8	0.0	0.0	0.0	7.8
Completed Diploma	0.0	0.5	0.3	0.0	0.0	0.0	0.0	0.0	0.0	0.1
Completed Graduation	0.2	2.9	1.3	2.0	1.5	0.9	0.0	0.0	0.0	1.2
Illiterate	18.8	25.2	42.9	55.5	56.2	74.3	80.0	91.7	85.7	34.8
Total	100.0	100.0	100.0	100.0	100.0	100.0	100.0	100.0	100.0	100.0

SOURCE: UNIVERSITY OF BASEL, DEPT. OF GEOGRAPHY AND ALL INDIA DISASTER MITIGATION INSTITUTE, AHMEDABAD, INDIA 2005. SOCIAL SCIENCE SURVEY IN SELECTED SLUM COMMUNITIES IN THE CITY OF BHUJ, GUJARAT, INDIA.

By sex (Tab. 11.3). The illiteracy rate of the female population is almost twice as high as the one of the male population (male: 24.7%, female: 45.3%, Tab. 11.3). Whereas male and female proportions do not differ much in the two lower education standards 1-3 and 4-6, there is a clear gap between the sexes from standards 7-9 onwards (7-9 female: 16.2%, compared to male: 28.1%). It seems that although young girls go to school, they have to leave it at a certain age, probably as soon as they are old enough to work either in the house or outside and contribute to the family income. Boys, on the other hand, seem to pursue higher education to a greater extent than girls. Two things might be of influence here: the fact that by letting their daughters go to school, the parents cannot compensate the loss of work force in the house or of income outside of it. Another aspect might be the fact that daughters leave their family's house once they get married, and that any further investment in daughters does not help the family itself in the long run – on the contrary, dowries will have to be paid for them. However, the discrimination of girls in terms of education has long-term consequences: the previous chapter (Tab. 10.1) clearly demonstrated how tightly education standards and number of children per household are related. If women are illiterate or only have low education standards, they are also likely to have more children, without being able to financially contribute to the family's situation by holding a job: the lack of education and the high number of children will prevent them from it.

By personal daily wages of household members (Tab. 11.4). While among household members with lower education standards such as 1-3 and 4-6, a general majority earns rather low average daily wages, the opposite is true for household members with higher levels of education: higher proportions of them earn better wages, too (Standard 7-9: 37.3% earn 51-70 Rs. a day, compared to 10.5% of those with standard 1-3, Tab. 11.4). Whereas in just 1.2% of the total surveyed households a family member had a completed diploma, 5.2% of them earned more than 100 Rs. a day. There is a decisive relation between a person's education standard and its income. Therefore, it must be a main concern in any development aid to focus on education. A good education is a key factor in improving a household's income situation and through income, livelihood as a whole for the family. Nevertheless, development efforts with a focus on education can only be successful if women are not neglected: if they are generally less educated than men, cannot generate income and have to take care of a large family depending on one income – the husband's – the risk of poverty is high. Without women having profited from a good education themselves and in a financially unstable situation, chances are that the children of the next generation will as well not be sent to school long enough – especially the girls – but will have to contribute to the family income by work. Not only does this circle make poverty a constant risk for the family, but it creates *a constant situation of poverty* with no way out except education.

Table 11.3 Education standard, by sex.

Sex / Education	Female in % (n=1130)	Male in % (=1163)	Total in % (n=2293)
Hrs. 1-3	13.4	15.0	14.2
Hrs. 4-6	19.0	20.2	19.6
Hrs. 7-9	16.2	28.1	22.2
Hrs. 10-12	5.0	10.3	7.7
Completed Diploma	0.0	0.3	0.1
Completed Graduation	1.1	1.4	1.2
Illiterate	45.3	24.7	34.8
Total	100.0	100.0	100.0

SOURCE: UNIVERSITY OF BASEL, DEPT. OF GEOGRAPHY AND ALL INDIA DISASTER MITIGATION INSTITUTE, AHMEDABAD, INDIA 2005. SOCIAL SCIENCE SURVEY IN SELECTED SLUM COMMUNITIES IN THE CITY OF BHUJ, GUJARAT, INDIA.

Table 11.4 Education standard, by personal daily wages (in Rs.).

Wage / Education	0-10 in % (n=501)	11-20 in % (n=71)	21-30 in % (n=50)	31-40 in % (n=53)	41-50 in % (n=142)	51-70 in % (n=153)	71-100 in % (n=228)	101+ in % (n=96)	Total in % (n=2294)
Hrs. 1-3	18.3	9.9	6.0	3.8	4.9	10.5	4.4	7.3	14.2
Hrs. 4-6	21.2	15.5	14.0	13.2	20.4	14.4	18.0	15.6	19.6
Hrs. 7-9	17.7	22.5	28.0	45.3	24.6	37.3	29.4	32.3	22.2
Hrs. 10-12	5.4	7.0	10.0	7.5	11.3	5.9	15.4	24.0	7.8
Completed Diploma	0.0	0.0	0.0	0.0	0.0	0.0	0.4	2.1	0.1
Completed Graduation	1.1	1.4	0.0	1.9	0.7	0.0	1.8	5.2	1.2
Illiterate	36.4	43.7	42.0	28.3	38.0	32.0	30.7	13.5	34.8
Total	100.0	100.0	100.0	100.0	100.0	100.0	100.0	100.0	100.0

SOURCE: UNIVERSITY OF BASEL, DEPT. OF GEOGRAPHY AND ALL INDIA DISASTER MITIGATION INSTITUTE, AHMEDABAD, INDIA 2005. SOCIAL SCIENCE SURVEY IN SELECTED SLUM COMMUNITIES IN THE CITY OF BHUJ, GUJARAT, INDIA.

By religion (Tab. 11.5). Despite the fact that Mustuffanagar, a predominantly Muslim community, is in a visibly better condition than the other slums, the comparison of education standards by religion shows that Muslims have higher illiteracy rates (39.3%) than Hindus (27.8%, Tab. 11.5). The high illiteracy rate among Muslims might be explained by the fact that in Shantinagar, the community with the highest illiteracy of all slums (Tab. 11.1), the Muslim proportion of the population is important and certainly affects the general illiteracy rate among Muslims, without necessarily being related to being a Muslim.

Since the proportions of Muslims and Hindus from the lower to the higher education standards do not differ distinctively except for the illiteracy rate – that is again extremely high with females – one might suppose that religion in itself does not determine or influence education standards. It appears that after all, whether or not people go to school, depends strongly on their surroundings, that is family and neighbourhood, as well as gender, but not on their religious background.

Table 11.5 Education standard, by religion.

Religion / Education	Hindu in % (n=889)	Muslim in % (n=1388)	Sikh in % (n=3)	Christian in % (n=6)	Total in % (n=2286)
Hrs. 1-3	13.6	14.5	66.7	0.0	14.2
Hrs. 4-6	20.4	19.2	0.0	16.7	19.6
Hrs. 7-9	27.8	18.8	0.0	33.3	22.3
Hrs. 10-12	8.5	7.3	0.0	16.7	7.8
Completed Diploma	0.2	0.1	0.0	0.0	0.1
Completed Graduation	1.7	0.9	0.0	16.7	1.2
Illiterate	27.8	39.3	33.3	16.7	34.8
Total	100.0	100.0	100.0	100.0	100.0

SOURCE: UNIVERSITY OF BASEL, DEPT. OF GEOGRAPHY AND ALL INDIA DISASTER MITIGATION INSTITUTE, AHMEDABAD, INDIA 2005. SOCIAL SCIENCE SURVEY IN SELECTED SLUM COMMUNITIES IN THE CITY OF BHUJ, GUJARAT, INDIA.

By castes (Tab. 11.6). The comparison of education standards by caste brings out some interesting and partly rather unexpected results. Scheduled Tribes (ST) showed around 41% illiteracy and the lowest proportion of people with a high education standard (Standard 10-12: 2.2%). These percentages correspond to the generally poor education of the tribal population, of whom in the surveyed communities a majority was living in Shantinagar. Also, the tribal population showed the highest proportions of people with education standard 4-6 (24.3%), as compared to the other castes, which matches with their very low percentage of those with a better education standard. Nevertheless, it is the Other Backward Caste (OBC) population, being Muslims and mostly living in Mustuffa- and Shantinagar that shows the highest illiteracy rate with more than 48%, almost half of the population. It is also the OBC that have the lowest proportions, namely between 12% and 13%, of people with education standards 1 up to 9, as compared to all other castes. One would have supposed that the Scheduled Tribes would show the poorest education level of all, but obviously, illiteracy is higher and proportions of education standards 1 up to 9 are generally lower in the OBC. However, 6.2% among the OBC have education standard 10-12, compared to only 2.2% of the Scheduled Tribes. General and Scheduled Castes (SC) do not differ much in the proportions they show for education standards 1 up to 9. General castes stand out with the highest percentage of Standard 10-12 (11.1%), completed graduation (1.8%) and at the same time, the lowest illiteracy rate (20.5%). Other than that, the differences between the two castes in terms of their education standards are rather small. The following aspects are of note:

- Rather surprisingly, it is not the ST that show the highest illiteracy rate or the lowest education standards, but the OBC. However, both castes are the ones with the highest illiteracy rate (48.4%, 40.9%, Tab. 11.6). The population of both castes is predominantly situated in Shantinagar, the community with the generally poorest education standard.
- The differences between General and Scheduled Castes in terms of education levels are small.
- All castes have the highest proportions of their population in the lower education standards 1-3, 4-6 and 7-9. Also, in all castes, only small proportions of people have higher education levels.

One can conclude that caste alone is not responsible for a certain education level, since the majority of all the four castes (SC, ST, OBC and General Castes) has rather low education standards from 1-9. The two castes with the highest illiteracy rates are mainly in Shantinagar, as if the surroundings had a stronger influence on the education level than the caste itself. However, the illiteracy rate, although spread differently throughout the slums, is high in all of the surveyed castes, and the proportions of those with higher education are very low in all castes, too. In all of the surveyed communities, it did not seem to be caste alone that was responsible for certain livelihood conditions or poverty, but education that was lacking.

Therefore, one must support any effort regarding a rise of the education level and with it, as seen before, a rise of income and an improvement of livelihood. The situation regarding education might have improved over the last decades (Tab. 11.2), but as long as women are spared from this positive development and have illiteracy rates twice as high as the male population, as long as illiteracy is still at 25% for those between 20 and 29 years – the age of founding a family and determining the next generation's lives – and as long as only few get through high school, development efforts must focus primarily on rising the level of education of the population as a whole, including women. Education is the key that helps people improve their job and income situation and that makes them move out of poverty *themselves*.

Table 11.6 Education standard, by caste.

Caste / Education	SC in % (n=368)	ST in % (n=230)	OBC in % (n=888)	General in % (n=795)	Total in % (n=2281)
Hrs. 1-3	13.9	14.8	13.6	14.8	14.2
Hrs. 4-6	21.2	24.3	15.2	22.1	19.5
Hrs. 7-9	27.2	17.0	15.3	29.4	22.3
Hrs. 10-12	7.9	2.2	6.2	11.1	7.8
Completed Diploma	0.0	0.4	0.0	0.3	0.1
Completed Graduation	0.5	0.4	1.2	1.8	1.2
Illiterate	29.3	40.9	48.4	20.5	34.9
Total	100.0	100.0	100.0	100.0	100.0

SOURCE: UNIVERSITY OF BASEL, DEPT. OF GEOGRAPHY AND ALL INDIA DISASTER MITIGATION INSTITUTE, AHMEDABAD, INDIA 2005. SOCIAL SCIENCE SURVEY IN SELECTED SLUM COMMUNITIES IN THE CITY OF BHUJ, GUJARAT, INDIA.

11.3 Occupation

By age (Tab. 11.7, 11.8). The occupation category "housewife" not only shows the highest total percentage (34.2% of the people in the slums work as housewives), but also the highest proportions through all age groups, from 0-19 up to over 90 years. Housewives are the only ones who continue working even in the age group "over 90 years" (16.7% versus 83.3% retirees) and who also show a proportion of 50% in the age group 80-89 years (Tab. 11.8). In the context of Indian urban slums, in families with many children, a housewife's work is still very hard and unpaid, too. The fact that housewives show the highest proportions in all age groups makes clear that traditional family and role models – women being housewives and taking care of children, men earning money outside of the house – still prevail. However, the potential of women contributing to the family income and thus, improving livelihood conditions, is not used. Almost a third of the people under 19 years work as a "housewife", which might prevent young girls from finishing school or making a degree.

A high share of young people up to 19 years works in jobs of the second sector such as "textile/industry" (18.6%), "casual labour" (9.9%) or "construction" (7.5%), but also in "crafts" (9.3%). The occupation categories "textile/industry" and "crafts" are the only ones that show decreasing percentages with age. Both kinds of work can be done home-based, which might explain why the category "textile/industry" shows the highest percentage for young people up to 19 years. In all other occupations, the percentages rise with age and decrease again from age 60-69, when people usually start retiring.

It is also the second sector, namely textile/industry, construction and casual labour that the highest proportions of slum inhabitants work in, regardless of their age. As a matter of fact, textile work, in particular weaving and dyeing, is traditionally done by lower castes, especially SC. However, the high proportions of people working in jobs such as construction, casual labour or textile/industry might be related to generally low education standards in the slum communities rather than to caste itself. It appears that from an early age on, most of the slum inhabitants work in these jobs – they do not necessarily require high education standards or special skills, as compared to governmental or crafts jobs. As emphasized before and in the previous chapter, low income jobs like construction or casual labour with great health risks and no social security (i.e. pension plans), increase the probability of poverty for a (usually large) family. Table 11.8 indicates that these jobs are taken from an early age on, which anticipates unstable socioeconomic situations for the next generations` families. Investing in young people's education, however, means investing in their and their children's future, therefore it is of concern that high proportions of the young people up to 19 years work in these unstable jobs. But as long as education standards remain on a low level, chances for better jobs are small.

It is striking that 12.5% of people between 80 and 89 years still work as vendors/in shops or in the service sector, since those two occupation categories only make up for 6%, respectively 8% of the Total Occupation.

Table 11.7 Occupation, by age (-59).

Age (-59) Occupation	20-29 in % (n=406)	30-39 in % (n=379)	40-49 in % (n=244)	50-59 in % (n=129)	Total in % (n=1158)
textile/industry	14.5	13.2	9.8	4.7	12.0
government	0.5	0.5	4.1	0.0	1.2
casual labour	7.1	11.1	11.9	7.8	9.5
construction	11.8	15.0	14.3	9.3	13.1
farming	1.5	1.1	1.2	4.7	1.6
automotive related job	6.9	7.7	3.3	3.9	6.0
vendor/shop	4.4	5.0	9.0	3.9	5.5
crafts	4.7	3.7	2.9	3.9	3.9
service sector	9.9	7.7	10.2	9.3	9.2
retiree	0.0	0.0	1.6	10.1	1.5
housewife	36.0	33.5	29.9	40.3	34.4
unemployed	2.7	1.6	1.6	2.3	2.1
Total	100.0	100.0	100.0	100.0	100.0

SOURCE: UNIVERSITY OF BASEL, DEPT. OF GEOGRAPHY AND ALL INDIA DISASTER MITIGATION INSTITUTE, AHMEDABAD, INDIA 2005. SOCIAL SCIENCE SURVEY IN SELECTED SLUM COMMUNITIES IN THE CITY OF BHUJ, GUJARAT, INDIA.

By education standard (Tab. 11.9). Occupation analyzed as a function of education standards outlines some notable tendencies: the proportions of people working in jobs that require a certain level of education or specific skills increase with rising education standards. By contrast, in occupation categories where school education is not necessarily needed, the proportions of illiterates or of people with low education standards are high. With rising levels of education, the proportions of people working in such jobs decrease.

No one with low education standards works in government jobs, which make up for just 1% of the total Occupation, anyway (Tab. 11.9) – again an indicator of generally low education standards in the different slum communities. However, 3.8% of those with standards 10-12 and 4.5% of those with a completed graduation hold governmental jobs. Whereas a high share of illiterates (11.7%) does casual labour, it is only around 5% of those with educations standards 10-12 and no one with a completed diploma or a completed graduation. The proportion of illiterates working in construction is around 11%, too, and here, percentages remain between 10.8% and 14% for education standards 1 up to 12. However, construction must not only refer to unskilled labour, which casual labour usually does. Only around 3% of the illiterates work as vendors, as compared to 10% of those with education standard 10-12. The percentages of those working as vendors/in a shop increasing with higher education levels are coherent when one thinks of the writing and calculation vendors need to do, which might not easily be done by illiterates, for instance. A similar picture emerges for the categories "service sector" and, to a lesser degree, for "automotive related jobs". The fact that the service sector is a multifaceted one, including unskilled labour as well as specialized work, might be reflected by the nearly 17% of those with education standard 10-12, and 27.3% of those with a completed graduation working in it. On the other hand, the proportions of those with lower education standards employed in the service sector are lower.

The rather high share of people through all education standards working in "textile/industry" might be explained by the importance of textile work in Gujarat, particularly in Kutch, a region that is known for traditional textile work.

The percentages of illiterates and of those with low education standards working as housewives are appalling: 46.2% of the illiterates and 30% to 34% of those with education standards 1-3 and 4-6 are housewives, as compared to only 18.5% of those with standard 10-12. Again, it appears that women with low or no education standards are mainly housewives. As seen in chapter 10, low education standards and a high number of children are related. With only one income (the husband's) and a large family depending on it, poverty becomes a probability. Knowing that the female illiteracy rate is twice as high the male one (Tab. 11.3), that they are likely to give birth to many children and to remain housewives with financial insecurity, development efforts must focus on the neglected potential of women improving the family's livelihood conditions through better education and good job opportunities.

Table 11.8 Occupation, by age (all ages).

Age (all ages) / Occupation	0-19 in % (n=161)	20-29 in % (n=406)	30-39 in % (n=379)	40-49 in % (n=244)	50-59 in % (n=129)	60-69 in % (n=105)	70-79 in % (n=36)	80-89 in % (n=8)	>90 in % (n=6)	Total in % (n=1474)
textile/ industry	18.6	14.5	13.2	9.8	4.7	6.7	0.0	0.0	0.0	11.9
government	0.6	0.5	0.5	4.1	0.0	0.0	0.0	0.0	0.0	1.0
casual labour	9.9	7.1	11.1	11.9	7.8	8.6	2.8	0.0	0.0	9.2
construction	7.5	11.8	15.0	14.3	9.3	7.6	2.8	0.0	0.0	11.7
farming	0.6	1.5	1.1	1.2	4.7	1.0	2.8	0.0	0.0	1.5
automotive related job	2.5	6.9	7.7	3.3	3.9	1.0	0.0	0.0	0.0	5.1
vendor/ shop	6.8	4.4	5.0	9.0	3.9	5.7	5.6	12.5	0.0	5.7
crafts	9.3	4.7	3.7	2.9	3.9	2.9	2.8	0.0	0.0	4.3
service sector	6.8	9.9	7.7	10.2	9.3	3.8	2.8	12.5	0.0	8.3
retiree	0.0	0.0	0.0	1.6	10.1	23.8	36.1	25.0	83.3	4.2
housewife	29.8	36.0	33.5	29.9	40.3	36.2	41.7	50.0	16.7	34.2
unemployed	7.5	2.7	1.6	1.6	2.3	2.9	2.8	0.0	0.0	2.7
Total	100.0	100.0	100.0	100.0	100.0	100.0	100.0	100.0	100.0	100.0

SOURCE: UNIVERSITY OF BASEL, DEPT. OF GEOGRAPHY AND ALL INDIA DISASTER MITIGATION INSTITUTE, AHMEDABAD, INDIA 2005. SOCIAL SCIENCE SURVEY IN SELECTED SLUM COMMUNITIES IN THE CITY OF BHUJ, GUJARAT, INDIA.

Table 11.9 Occupation, by education standard.

Education / Occupation	Hrs. 1-3 in % (n=102)	Hrs. 4-6 in % (n=228)	Hrs. 7-9 in % (n=349)	Hrs. 10-12 in % (n=130)	Completed Diploma in % (n=3)	Completed Graduation in % (n=22)	Illiterate in % (n=606)	Total in % (n=1440)
textile/ industry	16.7	15.8	15.5	14.6	0.0	0.0	7.6	11.9
government	0.0	0.4	2.0	3.8	0.0	4.5	0.2	1.0
casual labour	8.8	8.8	7.4	5.4	0.0	0.0	11.7	9.2
construction	11.8	11.4	14.0	10.8	33.3	4.5	10.9	11.7
farming	1.0	0.0	1.1	1.5	0.0	0.0	2.3	1.5
automotive related job	2.9	4.8	8.6	6.2	33.3	0.0	3.0	4.9
vendor/ shop	6.9	5.7	8.0	10.0	0.0	4.5	3.3	5.7
crafts	7.8	6.1	5.7	5.4	0.0	9.1	2.0	4.4
service sector	4.9	7.0	10.0	16.9	33.3	27.3	5.3	8.1
retiree	5.9	4.4	1.7	4.6	0.0	9.1	4.8	4.1
housewife	30.4	34.2	22.1	18.5	0.0	36.4	46.2	34.6
unemployed	2.9	1.3	3.7	2.3	0.0	4.5	2.8	2.8
Total	100.0	100.0	100.0	100.0	100.0	100.0	100.0	100.0

SOURCE: UNIVERSITY OF BASEL, DEPT. OF GEOGRAPHY AND ALL INDIA DISASTER MITIGATION INSTITUTE, AHMEDABAD, INDIA 2005. SOCIAL SCIENCE SURVEY IN SELECTED SLUM COMMUNITIES IN THE CITY OF BHUJ, GUJARAT, INDIA.

11.4
Home based occupation

By slum (Tab. 11.10). Only 17.3% of all the interviewed families in the surveyed slums indicated following home based occupations, but there are clear differences between the different communities. Whereas no one in Jayprakashnagar and only 8.4% in Shantinagar indicated "yes, home based occupation", the percentage is at 14.6% in Bhimraonagar and highest in Mustuffanagar with 34.2%. The different education levels in the different slum communities (Tab. 11.1) might offer some explanations, with Jayprakash- and Shantinagar representing two poles: Jayprakashnagar is the community with the lowest illiteracy rate, the highest proportion of people with good education standards and a completed graduation/diploma. One might suppose that people here do not primarily follow home based, mainly manual work. By contrast, Shantinagar is the community with the poorest education level, but for home based occupation, certain skills are needed or a stable home which a high share of the population here did not seem to have. Many of the inhabitants of Shantinagar might do casual labour or construction, jobs often held by people with little or no education, but this is not home based work. People in Bhimrao- and particularly in Mustuffanagar often had rather good education standards, although proportions here were lower and illiteracy in both communities higher than in Jayprakashnagar. However, a high proportion of families in Mustuffanagar does textile work that can be done at home. A similar picture emerges for Bhimraonagar.

Table 11.10 Home based occupation, by slum.

Slum Home based occupation	Bhimraona-gar in % (n=130)	Jayprakashna-gar in % (n=53)	Mustuffana-gar in % (n=158)	Shantina-gar in % (n=155)	Total in % (n=496)
no	83.1	94.3	65.2	87.7	80.0
yes, home based occupation	14.6	0.0	34.2	8.4	17.3
yes, storage	0.0	3.8	0.0	1.9	1.0
yes, as shop	2.3	1.9	0.6	1.9	1.6
Total	100.0	100.0	100.0	100.0	100.0

SOURCE: UNIVERSITY OF BASEL, DEPT. OF GEOGRAPHY AND ALL INDIA DISASTER MITIGATION INSTITUTE, AHMEDABAD, INDIA 2005. SOCIAL SCIENCE SURVEY IN SELECTED SLUM COMMUNITIES IN THE CITY OF BHUJ, GUJARAT, INDIA.

By education of the family head (Tab. 11.11). The family head's level of education does not necessarily equal the one of the other family members. However, the education of the family head does have an influence on the kind of work he or she is does, which might determine whether or not other family members follow home based occupations or not. Only about 12% of the families whose family head is illiterate do home based work. As table 11.9 showed, a majority of illiterates are housewives who do not earn money. Also, a high share of illiterates work in construction or do casual labour which is not home based. Home based occupation, however, would be a good way of earning extra money especially for women who mostly work in the house anyway. Women following home based occupations do not even question the traditional family model prevailing in the communities, but they could help stabilize the family income with their home based work. Obviously, there is a potential of integrating women, often illiterate, into the economic circuit and helping them improve the family's socioeconomic situation, evading poverty. The families that stated having a shop at home usually showed middle education classes (standards 4 up to 9), which indicates that some basic education (such as basic knowledge of mathematics and writing) is necessary to successfully run a shop.

Table 11.11 Home based occupation, by education of family head.

Education / Home based occupation	Hrs. 1-3 in % (n=46)	Hrs. 4-6 in % (n=82)	Hrs. 7-9 in % (n=107)	Hrs. 10-12 in % (n=36)	Completed Diploma in % (n=1)	Completed Graduation in % (n=6)	Illiterate in % (n=217)	Total in % (n=495)
no	73.9	74.4	77.6	75.0	100.0	66.7	85.7	80.0
yes, home based occupation	21.7	24.4	18.7	22.2	0.0	16.7	12.4	17.4
yes, storage	0.0	0.0	0.9	2.8	0.0	0.0	1.4	1.0
yes, as shop	4.3	1.2	2.8	0.0	0.0	16.7	0.5	1.6
Total	100.0	100.0	100.0	100.0	100.0	100.0	100.0	100.0

SOURCE: UNIVERSITY OF BASEL, DEPT. OF GEOGRAPHY AND ALL INDIA DISASTER MITIGATION INSTITUTE, AHMEDABAD, INDIA 2005. SOCIAL SCIENCE SURVEY IN SELECTED SLUM COMMUNITIES IN THE CITY OF BHUJ, GUJARAT, INDIA

By occupation of the family head (Tab. 11.12). Nearly 40% of those employed in the textile sector and 36.3% of those doing crafts work at home. These two categories are the main home based jobs. However, around 18% to 19% of the vendors and of the people employed in automotive related jobs work at home, too. Particularly textile and crafts work, the principal home based occupations, can easily be done by housewives if they have the skills or utensils they need. Training women to follow such occupations and providing the necessary tools (i.e. sewing machines) is a way of making people help themselves and improve their income situation on their own.

By daily wages of household members (Tab. 11.13). With increasing average daily wages, the percentages of households who do home based work increase as well. In other words: in families where home based work is done, the average daily wages augment because all members of the family, including housewives or the elderly, can help generate income. Thereby, average daily wages per household member rise. By contrast, in households where no one pursues a home based, income generating activity, the average daily wages per household member diminish because one main income is shared by many.

Table 11.12 Home based occupation, by occupation of family head.

Occupation / Home based occupation	textile/industry in % (n=238)	Government in % (n=71)	casual labour in % (n=458)	Construction in % (n=460)	Farming in % (n=76)	automotive related job in % (n=232)	vendor/shop in % (n=188)	Crafts in % (n=102)	service sector in % (n=232)	Retiree in % (n=301)	Housewife in % (n=141)	Unemployed in % (n=84)	Total in % (n=2583)
no	55.9	93.0	86.2	84.1	80.3	78.0	72.3	63.7	80.2	80.1	90.8	71.4	78.9
yes, home based occupation	39.5	7.0	11.4	13.3	19.7	19.8	18.6	36.3	11.6	19.9	9.2	28.6	18.2
yes, storage	0.0	0.0	2.4	1.1	0.0	0.0	3.7	0.0	2.6	0.0	0.0	0.0	1.1
yes, as shop	4.6	0.0	0.0	1.5	0.0	2.2	5.3	0.0	5.6	0.0	0.0	0.0	1.8
Total	100.0	100.0	100.0	100.0	100.0	100.0	100.0	100.0	100.0	100.0	100.0	100.0	100.0

SOURCE: UNIVERSITY OF BASEL, DEPT. OF GEOGRAPHY AND ALL INDIA DISASTER MITIGATION INSTITUTE, AHMEDABAD, INDIA 2005. SOCIAL SCIENCE SURVEY IN SELECTED SLUM COMMUNITIES IN THE CITY OF BHUJ, GUJARAT, INDIA.

Table 11.13 Home based occupation, by average daily wages of household members (in Rs.).

Wage Home based occupation	0 to 9 Rs. in % (n=39)	10 to 19 Rs. in % (n=164)	20 to 29 Rs. in % (n=140)	30 to 39 Rs. in % (n=73)	40 to 49 Rs. in % (n=27)	50 to 89 Rs. in % (n=31)	90 to 130 Rs. in % (n=5)	Total in % (n=479)
no	87.2	79.3	87.1	67.1	74.1	71.0	80.0	79.5
yes, home based occupation	12.8	18.3	12.9	27.4	22.2	19.4	0.0	17.7
yes, storage	0.0	1.8	0.0	0.0	3.7	3.2	0.0	1.0
yes, as shop	0.0	0.6	0.0	5.5	0.0	6.5	20.0	1.7
Total	100.0	100.0	100.0	100.0	100.0	100.0	100.0	100.0

SOURCE: UNIVERSITY OF BASEL, DEPT. OF GEOGRAPHY AND ALL INDIA DISASTER MITIGATION INSTITUTE, AHMEDABAD, INDIA 2005. SOCIAL SCIENCE SURVEY IN SELECTED SLUM COMMUNITIES IN THE CITY OF BHUJ, GUJARAT, INDIA.

By religion (Tab. 11.14). As table 11.14 shows, Muslims slightly exceed Hindus in terms of home based occupation: whereas 14.3% of the Hindu households follow home based occupations, it is nearly 20% of the Muslim households. Home based occupation is concentrated in the predominantly Muslim community of Mustuffanagar. This seems to be a characteristic of this particular slum community, without primarily being related to religion itself. As a matter of fact, Mustuffanagar was the community that was visibly in a much better state than some other slums. One might suppose that in Mustuffanagar, the community with the highest proportion of home based occupation, livelihood conditions are improved thereby. Home based occupation as a way of generating extra income, which obviously functions well in Mustuffanagar, could be a model for other slum communities, too.

Table 11.14 Home based occupation, by religion.

Religion Home based occupation	Hindu in % (n=217)	Muslim in % (n=277)	Total in % (n=494)
no	82.0	78.7	80.2
yes, home based occupation	14.3	19.9	17.4
yes, storage	0.9	1.1	1.0
yes, as shop	2.8	0.4	1.4
Total	100.0	100.0	100.0

SOURCE: UNIVERSITY OF BASEL, DEPT. OF GEOGRAPHY AND ALL INDIA DISASTER MITIGATION INSTITUTE, AHMEDABAD, INDIA 2005. SOCIAL SCIENCE SURVEY IN SELECTED SLUM COMMUNITIES IN THE CITY OF BHUJ, GUJARAT, INDIA.

By caste (Tab. 11.15). The analysis of home based occupation as a function of caste affiliation outlines a clear difference between the General Castes, where 31.4% do home based work, and the other three castes in the surveyed slums (SC, ST, OBC), where the percentages are between 5.3% and 11.7%. Again, it is the Scheduled Tribes that show the smallest proportion of home based occupation. This matches with other factors indicating that livelihood conditions and development in this community are at a poor level. By contrast, Muslims often belong to the OBC, where home based occupation is nearly at 12%, or to the General Castes. If home based occupation, mainly textile and crafts work, demands special skills and tools that parts of the population in different slum areas do not have, caste itself cannot be blamed for it. It is rather a lack of education and high illiteracy rates that prevent people from getting information on where to find financial or material support, governmental aid, skill training and so forth. As a consequence, they often do not know how to help themselves, i.e. how to generate extra income for the family. Since the four surveyed castes are situated geographically in areas with notable differences, one might also suppose that the geographic context – surroundings, neighbourhood and role models – influences development to a considerable degree, rather than a person's caste affiliation itself.

Table 11.15 Home based occupation, by caste.

Caste Home based occupation	SC in % (n=86)	ST in % (n=57)	OBC in % (n=180)	General in % (n=172)	Total in % (n=495)
no	84.9	91.2	86.7	66.9	80.0
yes, home based occupation	9.3	5.3	11.7	31.4	17.4
yes, storage	3.5	0.0	0.6	0.6	1.0
yes, as shop	2.3	3.5	1.1	1.2	1.6
Total	100.0	100.0	100.0	100.0	100.0

SOURCE: UNIVERSITY OF BASEL, DEPT. OF GEOGRAPHY AND ALL INDIA DISASTER MITIGATION INSTITUTE, AHMEDABAD, INDIA 2005. SOCIAL SCIENCE SURVEY IN SELECTED SLUM COMMUNITIES IN THE CITY OF BHUJ, GUJARAT, INDIA.

11.5
Election Card

By slum (Tab. 11.16). It is appalling that in general, more than 50% of the population in the surveyed slums do not possess an election card: for them, no political participation is possible. By taking a closer look, although in all four slums, the proportions of those who possess an election card are low, there are obvious differences between the communities. They confirm a picture that has already emerged for other development indicators: again, Shantinagar holds a negative record with 61.1% of the inhabitants who do not possess an election card. In Jayprakashnagar, on the other hand, this percentage is at 44%, as compared to Mustuffanagar with 50.4% and Bhimraonagar with 56.2%. However, since Shantinagar also shows the highest illiteracy rate of all the slum communities, the 61% who do not even have an election card seem to be but a consequence of it: without reading and writing abilities, how can one possibly get information on political processes or one's civil rights? If between 50% and 61% of the poor slum population do not vote or raise their voice, this also means that their concerns are not represented and heard by those in power. Besides a lack of education and generally high illiteracy rates in the slums, many people in the slums might feel that voting or participating would not make a difference in their daily lives, so that these percentages might also reflect a lack of interest in political participation as long as things have not changed and are not changing for them on a daily basis. However, this conclusion would be a fallacy, because any improvement of livelihood conditions starts with personal engagement and basic participation. One cannot help people who do not participate. Besides a major focus on improving the levels of education in the slum communities in order to help people get better jobs, awareness must be raised on how important political participation as well as participation in development efforts is in order to make a difference in people's lives.

Table 11.16 Possession of election card, by slum.

Slum / Election card	Bhimraona-gar in % (n=580)	Jayprakashna-gar in % (n=216)	Mustuffana-gar in % (n=789)	Shantina-gar in % (n=754)	Total in % (n=2339)
yes	43.8	56.0	49.6	38.9	45.3
no	56.2	44.0	50.4	61.1	54.7
Total	100.0	100.0	100.0	100.0	100.0

SOURCE: UNIVERSITY OF BASEL, DEPT. OF GEOGRAPHY AND ALL INDIA DISASTER MITIGATION INSTITUTE, AHMEDABAD, INDIA 2005. SOCIAL SCIENCE SURVEY IN SELECTED SLUM COMMUNITIES IN THE CITY OF BHUJ, GUJARAT, INDIA.

By daily personal wages of household members (Tab. 11.17). With increasing average daily wages, the percentage of those possessing an election card rises as well. Whereas only 32.4% of the households with an average daily wage of household members of 10 Rs. possess an election card, it is 78.5% of those with an average daily wage of 71-100 Rs. Since income is directly related to education standards, it appears that education or a lack of it play a key role in people's possibilities of or interest in political participation.

Table 11.17 Possession of election card, by personal daily wages (in Rs.).

Wage / Election card	0-10 in % (n=1558)	11-20 in % (n=71)	21-30 in % (n=48)	31-40 in % (n=52)	41-50 in % (n=139)	51-70 in % (n=153)	71-100 in % (n=228)	101+ in % (n=96)	Total in % (n=2345)
yes	32.4	53.5	66.7	48.1	65.5	77.8	78.5	75.0	45.2
no	67.6	46.5	33.3	51.9	34.5	22.2	21.5	25.0	54.8
Total	100.0	100.0	100.0	100.0	100.0	100.0	100.0	100.0	100.0

SOURCE: UNIVERSITY OF BASEL, DEPT. OF GEOGRAPHY AND ALL INDIA DISASTER MITIGATION INSTITUTE, AHMEDABAD, INDIA 2005. SOCIAL SCIENCE SURVEY IN SELECTED SLUM COMMUNITIES IN THE CITY OF BHUJ, GUJARAT, INDIA.

By sex and by religion (Tab. 11.18, 11.19). The possession of an election card depends neither on gender, nor on religion, as tables 11.18 and 11.19 show: the percentages are balanced in all groups. However, it is striking that nearly 55% of the total population (without differentiation of slum community) do not possess an election card.

By caste (Tab. 11.20). The possession of an election card is distributed rather evenly among the castes: between 41% and 51% of the people belonging to the ST, SC, OBC or General Castes possess an election card. Caste does not seem to be a discriminating factor in the political participation. The differences between the General Castes with 51.2%, the Scheduled Tribes with 43.5% and the Other Backward Castes with 41% are probably due to education standards and geographic contexts rather than to caste itself.

Table 11.18 Possession of election card, by sex.

Sex Election card	Female in % (n=1153)	Male in % (n=1189)	Total in % (n=2342)
yes	44.7	45.8	45.3
no	55.3	54.2	54.7
Total	100.0	100.0	100.0

SOURCE: UNIVERSITY OF BASEL, DEPT. OF GEOGRAPHY AND ALL INDIA DISASTER MITIGATION INSTITUTE, AHMEDABAD, INDIA 2005. SOCIAL SCIENCE SURVEY IN SELECTED SLUM COMMUNITIES IN THE CITY OF BHUJ, GUJARAT, INDIA.

Table 11.19 Possession of election card, by religion.

Religion Election card	Hindu in % (n=940)	Muslim in % (n=1389)	Sikh in % (n=2)	Christian in % (n=6)	Total in % (n=2337)
yes	46.4	44.6	100.0	0.0	45.2
no	53.6	55.4	0.0	100.0	54.8
Total	100.0	100.0	100.0	100.0	100.0

SOURCE: UNIVERSITY OF BASEL, DEPT. OF GEOGRAPHY AND ALL INDIA DISASTER MITIGATION INSTITUTE, AHMEDABAD, INDIA 2005. SOCIAL SCIENCE SURVEY IN SELECTED SLUM COMMUNITIES IN THE CITY OF BHUJ, GUJARAT, INDIA.

Table 11.20 Possession of election card, by caste.

Caste Election card	SC in % (n=387)	ST in % (n=237)	OBC in % (n=934)	General in % (n=777)	Total in % (n=2335)
yes	44.2	43.5	41.0	51.2	45.2
no	55.8	56.5	59.0	48.8	54.8
Total	100.0	100.0	100.0	100.0	100.0

SOURCE: UNIVERSITY OF BASEL, DEPT. OF GEOGRAPHY AND ALL INDIA DISASTER MITIGATION INSTITUTE, AHMEDABAD, INDIA 2005. SOCIAL SCIENCE SURVEY IN SELECTED SLUM COMMUNITIES IN THE CITY OF BHUJ, GUJARAT, INDIA.

11.6 Conclusion

The analysis of education, occupation and political participation proves that the level of education is one of the key factors concerning livelihood, the socioeconomic situation of families, income and job security as well as political participation. Although the efforts of the government to increase literacy levels of the population seem to have been effective to a certain degree, still a high proportion of people are illiterate, especially among the ST and SC population. This remains a problem which needs to be tackled further in the future. This is all the more important if one considers that the education influences a whole range of livelihood factors such as livelihood security, employment opportunities and also health and mental well-being of the people and their families. Generally, investments into education are of pivotal importance, and focus must be laid on the proper school enrolment of all children. During the actual field work in the slums, the number of children in school age who were not attending school was alarming, especially in Shantinagar with its high tribal population. Special attention must also be given to the schooling of girls, because if half of the population is not touched at all by development efforts, this again affects families as a whole.

Furthermore, one can conclude that home based occupation helps to significantly increase the family income, because all members of the household can be involved. Especially when old and dependent people live in the same household, they can contribute to gaining an additional income and are not a big strain on the financial situation of the family. Opportunities for home based occupation and the selling of the manufactured goods must therefore be supported.

Concerning the political participation of the slum dwellers, it is appalling that less than half of the population own an election card. This can probably be attributed to the fact that a high proportion of the slum population is illiterate and that they cannot read information of any kind, with the result that they do not participate in any way in political processes. The distribution of the election cards indicates that all people have been guaranteed the same democratic rights. However, it is the people who do not make use of their rights, either because they cannot – being illiterate – or they do not want to. However, with politics and politicians relying on the large segment of the poor, votes can be bought in exchange for basic daily goods or money that the poor do not have. The real issues and needs of the poor are thereby neither heard nor taken care of in an appropriate, long term way.

Educational achievements – occupational structure and political participation

Map 11.1 Level of education of the family head in Bhimraonagar

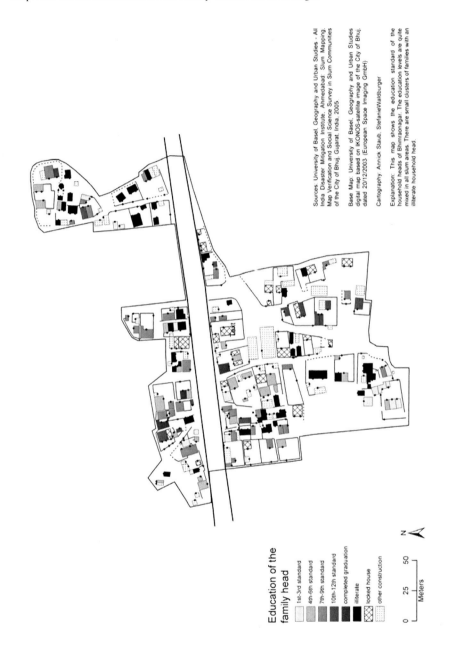

Map 11.2 Level of education of the family head in Jayprakashnagar

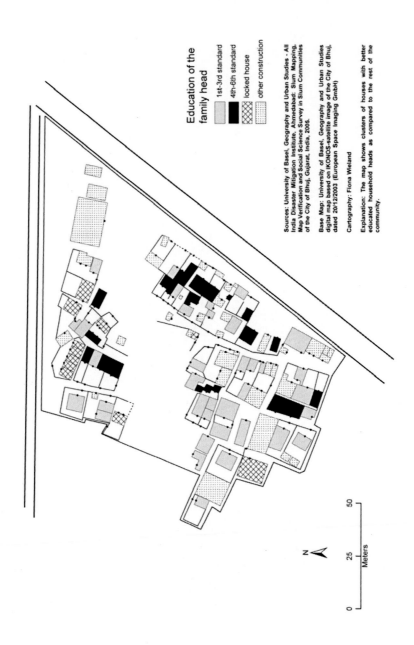

Educational achievements – occupational structure and political participation

Map 11.3 Level of education of the family head in Mustuffanagar

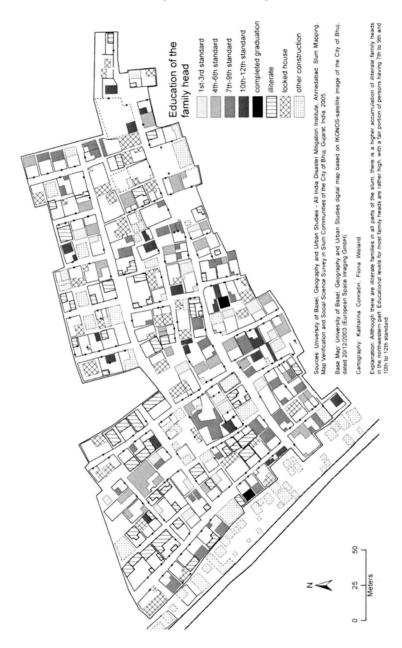

Map 11.4 Level of education of the family head in Shantinagar

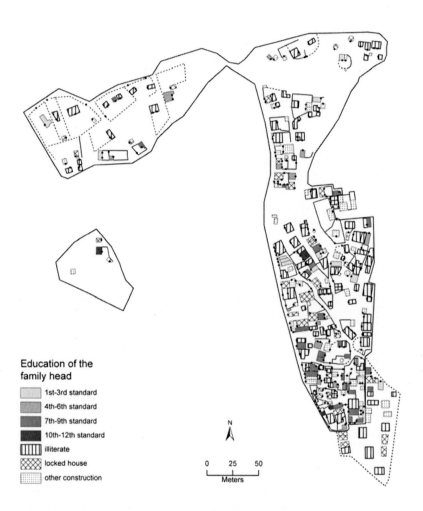

Education of the family head
- 1st-3rd standard
- 4th-6th standard
- 7th-9th standard
- 10th-12th standard
- illiterate
- locked house
- other construction

Sources: University of Basel, Geography and Urban Studies - All India Disaster Mitigation Institute, Ahmedabad: Slum Mapping, Map Verification and Social Science Survey in Slum Communities of the City of Bhuj, Gujarat, India, 2005.

Base Map: University of Basel, Geography and Urban Studies digital map based on IKONOS-satellite image of the City of Bhuj, dated 20/12/2003 (European Space Imaging GmbH)

Cartography: Katharina Conradin, Fiona Wieland

Explanation: There is no spatial pattern recognizable, due to the fact that most family heads are illiterate. Illiteracy and other variables shown on previous maps that indicated generally lower levels of development or well being in Shantinagar correspond quite well. The spatial patterns of rich indicators in Shantinagar lend credence to the notion that they may be causally related to illiteracy.

12 Problems of addiction

A. Cavelti, N. Sliwa, J. Whitebread
University of Basel

12.1
Introduction

Drug addiction is a problem with various dimensions: it affects health, livelihood and increases poverty, because money is spent on drugs and work force reduced. Often, people start taking drugs when they are desperate and without hope of improving their lives in the future. In this survey, however, addiction did not primarily seem to be a way of forgetting misery, but more a kind of luxury that people like to have, whether they can afford it or not. Although there is a clear relation between income and the kind of drugs people consume, drug addiction can be found among all income groups. Main questions that this chapter focuses on are:
- At what age do people in slums generally get addicted?
- Which are the risk groups?
- In what way does drug addiction affect livelihood and the socioeconomic situation of families?

12.2
Type of addiction

By slum (Tab. 12.1) 89.7% of the slum population are not addicted to any kind of drug. The addiction of the remaining 10.3% is distributed on alcohol, smoking bidi, tobacco and snuff. People who smoke bidi show the highest percentage of these (4.5%). Although Gujarat is a dry state, the percentage of those in the surveyed area with an alcohol addiction is at 2.8%. Alcohol addiction seems to be the severest problem in Bhimraonagar (5.1%). There is no obvious reason why alcohol seems to be a bigger problem in Bhimraonagar than in the other slums.

Table 12.1 Type of addiction, by slum.

Slum Type of addiction	Bhimraonagar in % (n=662)	Jayprakashnagar in % (n=254)	Mustuffanagar in % (n=977)	Shantinagar in % (n=902)	Total in % (n=2795)
no	87.2	93.3	90.1	90.0	89.7
alcohol	5.1	2.0	2.8	1.3	2.8
smoking bidi	5.0	3.5	3.5	5.5	4.5
tobacco	2.1	1.2	2.5	2.4	2.3
snuff	0.6	0.0	1.2	0.7	0.8
Total	100.0	100.0	100.0	100.0	100.0

SOURCE: UNIVERSITY OF BASEL, DEPT. OF GEOGRAPHY AND ALL INDIA DISASTER MITIGATION INSTITUTE, AHMEDABAD, INDIA 2005. SOCIAL SCIENCE SURVEY IN SELECTED SLUM COMMUNITIES IN THE CITY OF BHUJ, GUJARAT, INDIA.

By age (Tab. 12.2). Addiction increases continuously with age. One peak is between the age of 40 and 49 (only 66.3% are not addicted). This age group has a high percentage of people smoking bidi (17.1%) and of people addicted to alcohol (10.2%). A possible explanation is that this age group has a higher responsibility for the family and the job and consequently more to worry about. The percentage of young people between 20 and 29 years with an addiction is surprisingly low (9.8%), if one thinks of the lack of prospects for the future, but also compared to youth in western cultures, where this age group is more at risk to be addicted. Big differences are visible in comparison to the next age group (30-39 years). Here, cases of addiction increase by 10% which might mirror the increasing responsibility in families and work places.

Table 12.2 Type of addiction, by age.

Age Type of addiction	0-19 in % (n=1406)	20-29 in % (n=449)	30-39 in % (n=389)	40-49 in % (n=246)	50-59 in % (n=137)	60-69 in % (n=112)	70-79 in % (n=45)	80-89 in % (n=12)	>90 in % (n=7)	Total in % (n=2803)
no	99.6	90.2	79.2	66.3	78.8	73.2	77.8	66.7	57.1	89.7
alcohol	0.0	1.1	6.4	10.2	4.4	10.7	4.4	8.3	42.9	2.8
smoking bidi	0.1	4.0	9.3	17.1	10.2	10.7	6.7	0.0	0.0	4.5
tobacco	0.4	4.7	4.1	3.7	3.6	3.6	2.2	16.7	0.0	2.2
snuff	0.0	0.0	1.0	2.8	2.9	1.8	8.9	8.3	0.0	0.8
Total	100.0	100.0	100.0	100.0	100.0	100.0	100.0	100.0	100.0	100.0

SOURCE: UNIVERSITY OF BASEL, DEPT. OF GEOGRAPHY AND ALL INDIA DISASTER MITIGATION INSTITUTE, AHMEDABAD, INDIA 2005. SOCIAL SCIENCE SURVEY IN SELECTED SLUM COMMUNITIES IN THE CITY OF BHUJ, GUJARAT, INDIA.

By sex (Tab. 12.3). In general, it is apparent that women are less addicted than men. The differences in the addiction to alcohol and smoking bidi deserve special attention. Snuff is consumed rather by women than by men. Possible reasons could be that they have no access to money (snuffing is cheap) and that they do not have enough free time for consuming alcohol or for smoking.

Table 12.3 Type of addiction, by sex.

Sex \ Type of addiction	female in % (n=1293)	male in % (n=1345)	Total in % (n=2638)
no	95.8	82.5	89.0
alcohol	0.2	5.7	3.0
smoking bidi	0.3	9.1	4.8
tobacco	2.0	2.8	2.4
snuff	1.6	0.1	0.8
Total	100.0	100.0	100.0

SOURCE: UNIVERSITY OF BASEL, DEPT. OF GEOGRAPHY AND ALL INDIA DISASTER MITIGATION INSTITUTE, AHMEDABAD, INDIA 2005. SOCIAL SCIENCE SURVEY IN SELECTED SLUM COMMUNITIES IN THE CITY OF BHUJ, GUJARAT, INDIA.

By education (Tab. 12.4). Table 12.4 shows that illiterate persons have the highest percentage of addiction (17%) but surprisingly only 4.8% more than those with education standards 7-9 (12.2%). The people with better education (completed diploma/graduation) have the lowest percentage of addiction, perhaps because of their better prospects for the future and generally better living conditions. Snuff seems to be a problem mainly for illiterate people and for those up to standard 6. The fact that illiterate people generally have worse jobs and less income seems to be reflected by their preference for snuffing as supposed to other drugs.

Table 12.4 Type of addiction, by education standard.

Education \ Type of addiction	Hrs. 1-3 in % (n=326)	Hrs. 4-6 in % (n=450)	Hrs. 7-9 in % (n=509)	Hrs. 10-12 in % (n=178)	Completed Diploma in % (n=3)	Completed Graduation in % (n=28)	Illiterate in % (n=798)	Total in % (n=2292)
no	89.9	91.3	87.8	89.9	100.0	92.9	83.0	87.3
alcohol	3.7	1.8	3.7	3.9	0.0	3.6	4.0	3.4
smoking bidi	4.0	5.1	5.1	3.9	0.0	3.6	7.0	5.5
tobacco	1.8	1.6	3.3	2.2	0.0	0.0	3.6	2.7
snuff	0.6	0.2	0.0	0.0	0.0	0.0	2.4	1.0
Total	100.0	100.0	100.0	100.0	100.0	100.0	100.0	100.0

SOURCE: UNIVERSITY OF BASEL, DEPT. OF GEOGRAPHY AND ALL INDIA DISASTER MITIGATION INSTITUTE, AHMEDABAD, INDIA 2005. SOCIAL SCIENCE SURVEY IN SELECTED SLUM COMMUNITIES IN THE CITY OF BHUJ, GUJARAT, INDIA.

By personal daily wages (Tab. 12.5). The trend indicates that addiction increases with income. A possible conclusion could be that income plays a decisive role in this issue: spending money on drugs is luxury, and people are aware of that. The more money addicted people earn, the more they spend on alcohol which is prohibited in the state of Gujarat and can only be bought illegally for much money. The highest percentage of people smoking bidi is shown by the income group 31-40 Rs. The income group between 0-20 Rs. is more addicted to snuff than other people, probably because snuff is the cheapest of all drugs (see Tab. 12.8).

Table 12.5 Type of addiction, by personal daily wages (in Rs.).

Wage / Type of addiction	0-10 Rs. in % (n=1765)	11-20 Rs. in % (n=69)	21-30 Rs. in % (n=49)	31-40 Rs. in % (n=49)	41-50 Rs. in % (n=137)	51-70 Rs. in % (n=150)	71-100 Rs. in % (n=209)	101+ Rs. in % (n=90)	Total in % (n=2518)
no	95.6	92.8	87.8	73.5	70.8	65.3	67.5	67.8	88.5
alcohol	0.9	1.4	6.1	6.1	9.5	10.7	10.5	5.6	3.1
smoking bidi	1.2	1.4	2.0	18.4	14.6	17.3	15.3	17.8	5.0
tobacco	1.2	1.4	4.1	2.0	5.1	5.3	6.7	8.9	2.5
snuff	1.0	2.9	0.0	0.0	0.0	1.3	0.0	0.0	0.9
Total	100.0	100.0	100.0	100.0	100.0	100.0	100.0	100.0	100.0

SOURCE: UNIVERSITY OF BASEL, DEPT. OF GEOGRAPHY AND ALL INDIA DISASTER MITIGATION INSTITUTE, AHMEDABAD, INDIA 2005. SOCIAL SCIENCE SURVEY IN SELECTED SLUM COMMUNITIES IN THE CITY OF BHUJ, GUJARAT, INDIA.

By religion (Tab. 12.6). There is no difference in the behaviour of Muslims and Hindus concerning the consumption of drugs. In both religions, 89% of the slum population are not addicted to drugs. Half of the addicted people smoke bidi. Sikhs and Christians are too few to be relevant in this issue.

Table 12.6 Type of addiction, by religion.

Religion / Type of addiction	Hindu in % (n=1028)	Muslim in % (n=1598)	Sikh in % (n=3)	Christian in % (n=6)	Total in % (n=2635)
no	89.0	89.0	66.7	100.0	89.0
alcohol	3.0	2.9	0.0	0.0	3.0
smoking bidi	5.4	4.4	33.3	0.0	4.8
tobacco	2.2	2.5	0.0	0.0	2.4
snuff	0.4	1.1	0.0	0.0	0.8
Total	100.0	100.0	100.0	100.0	100.0

SOURCE: UNIVERSITY OF BASEL, DEPT. OF GEOGRAPHY AND ALL INDIA DISASTER MITIGATION INSTITUTE, AHMEDABAD, INDIA 2005. SOCIAL SCIENCE SURVEY IN SELECTED SLUM COMMUNITIES IN THE CITY OF BHUJ, GUJARAT, INDIA.

By caste (Tab. 12.7). The least addicted are the OBC (91.2%). This might be related to the strict ban on alcohol and drugs in general in Islam, the predominant religious affiliation of the OBC. Apparently, drug addiction is not only an income related issue, but might also have a cultural component. Alcohol is the biggest issue for the SC, as compared to the other castes (5.2%). Smoking bidis is the severest problem throughout all of the surveyed castes (3.2% to 5.9%).

Table 12.7 Type of addiction, by caste.

Caste \ Type of addiction	SC in % (n=427)	ST in % (n=271)	OBC in % (n=1030)	General in % (n=901)	Total in % (n=2629)
no	85.9	87.8	91.2	88.3	89.0
alcohol	5.2	4.4	2.7	1.8	3.0
smoking bidi	5.9	5.5	3.2	5.9	4.8
tobacco	2.3	2.2	2.4	2.4	2.4
snuff	0.7	0.0	0.5	1.6	0.8
Total	100.0	100.0	100.0	100.0	100.0

SOURCE: UNIVERSITY OF BASEL, DEPT. OF GEOGRAPHY AND ALL INDIA DISASTER MITIGATION INSTITUTE, AHMEDABAD, INDIA 2005. SOCIAL SCIENCE SURVEY IN SELECTED SLUM COMMUNITIES IN THE CITY OF BHUJ, GUJARAT, INDIA.

12.3
Expenses for addiction

By type of addiction (Tab. 12.8). Generally, 63% of addicted persons spend between 4-5 Rs. per day on drugs. 16.5% of the people addicted to alcohol spend 1-3 Rs. per day, and 2.5% spend 6-50 Rs. per day, but most spend 4-5 Rs. (81%). A similar picture emerges for people smoking bidi, with the exception that the percentage of people who spend 1-3 Rs. a day is a bit higher with 22.4%. Tobacco seems to be bought in all price ranges. 55.6% prefer the cheapest (1-3 Rs.), but still 11.1% spend 6-50 Rs. on it every day. Snuff is the cheapest of all drugs, which may explain the high percentage of women who are addicted to it. 86.4% spend only 1-3 Rs. daily.

Table 12.8 Daily expenses for addiction (in Rs.), by type of addiction.

Expenses \ Type of addiction	alcohol in % (n=79)	smoking bidi in % (n=125)	tobacco in % (n=63)	snuff in % (n=22)	Total in % (n=289)
1-3	16.5	22.4	55.6	86.4	32.9
4-5	81.0	76.0	33.3	9.1	63.0
6-50	2.5	1.6	11.1	4.5	4.2
Total	100.0	100.0	100.0	100.0	100.0

SOURCE: UNIVERSITY OF BASEL, DEPT. OF GEOGRAPHY AND ALL INDIA DISASTER MITIGATION INSTITUTE, AHMEDABAD, INDIA 2005. SOCIAL SCIENCE SURVEY IN SELECTED SLUM COMMUNITIES IN THE CITY OF BHUJ, GUJARAT, INDIA.

By personal daily wages (Tab. 12.9). On average, the lower income classes (0-20 Rs.) spend only 1-3 Rs. per day on drugs, whereas the higher income classes (41 and more Rs.) spend 4-5 Rs. Strikingly, the lowest income group (0 Rs.) shows nearly the highest percentage of people who spend 6-50 Rs. per day (5.2%), which means that the poorest tend to spend the most on drugs, often more than they earn, which leads to indebtedness and leaves no room for securing livelihood when disasters, job loss or health problems occur. This income group may be consuming more drugs because their situation is more desperate. However, drug addiction is a vicious circle and worsens the socioeconomic situation of families to a great deal: the high expenses on drugs lower the already low financial capacities, so poverty is being cemented and any improvement of livelihood is being impeded.

4.2% of the people who earn 81-100 and more Rs. also spend 6-50 Rs. per day on drugs. Yet, if one considers that people earning 81 Rs. a day spend up to 50 Rs. a day on drugs, only 31 Rs. are left for food, clothes, health or school expenses. This poses serious problems for the family's livelihood, income and health. These drug habits, then, consequently lead to impoverishment and immiserisation, malnutrition and ill health of the whole family.

Table 12.9 Daily expenses for addiction (in Rs.), by personal daily wages (in Rs.).

Wage / Expenses	0 Rs. in % (n=58)	1-20 Rs. in % (n=12)	21-40 Rs. in % (n=23)	41-60 Rs. in % (n=65)	61-80 Rs. in % (n=44)	81-100 Rs. in % (n=71)	101-150 Rs. in % (n=20)	151-300 Rs. in % (n=10)	Total in % (n=303)
1-3	44.8	75.0	43.5	24.6	13.6	23.9	25.0	20.0	30.0
4-5	50.0	25.0	56.5	70.8	84.1	71.8	70.0	70.0	66.0
6-50	5.2	0.0	0.0	4.6	2.3	4.2	5.0	10.0	4.0
Total	100.0	100.0	100.0	100.0	100.0	100.0	100.0	100.0	100.0

SOURCE: UNIVERSITY OF BASEL, DEPT. OF GEOGRAPHY AND ALL INDIA DISASTER MITIGATION INSTITUTE, AHMEDABAD, INDIA 2005. SOCIAL SCIENCE SURVEY IN SELECTED SLUM COMMUNITIES IN THE CITY OF BHUJ, GUJARAT, INDIA.

By education standard (Tab. 12.10). The education standard does not seem to have a direct influence on the drug expenses of people. Yet, as seen before, poorer people tend to spend more on drugs than they can afford (Tab. 12.9). The amount they earn, however, strongly depends on their level of education that is a determinant of what jobs people get and what their wages are.

Table 12.10 Daily expenses for addiction (in Rs.), by education standard.

Education / Expenses	Hrs. 1-3 in % (n=33)	Hrs. 4-6 in % (n=38)	Hrs. 7-9 in % (n=62)	Hrs. 10-12 in % (n=18)	Completed Graduation in % (n=2)	Illiterate in % (n=136)	Total in % (n=289)
1-3	33.3	21.1	33.9	27.8	0.0	36.8	32.9
4-5	60.6	76.3	59.7	66.7	100.0	60.3	63.0
6-50	6.1	2.6	6.5	5.6	0.0	2.9	4.2
Total	100.0	100.0	100.0	100.0	100.0	100.0	100.0

SOURCE: UNIVERSITY OF BASEL, DEPT. OF GEOGRAPHY AND ALL INDIA DISASTER MITIGATION INSTITUTE, AHMEDABAD, INDIA 2005. SOCIAL SCIENCE SURVEY IN SELECTED SLUM COMMUNITIES IN THE CITY OF BHUJ, GUJARAT, INDIA.

12.4
Conclusion

Returning to the research question of how to move people out of poverty, and also, why some remain in poverty and others don't, one does find clear behavioural components in the way responsibilities are understood and income is being used. Addiction remains a problem in all income strata, because generally, quite a portion of the income is spent on drug habits, with higher income groups also spending more. The effect thereof is most disastrous in those families that are most vulnerable: the very poor. Whereas high income groups deny themselves the opportunity of upward social mobility (with two thirds of the income being spent on drugs and not being used for productive investment), the extreme poor deny their families their basic levels of subsistence. At the core of both is a problem of behaviours, habits and shared responsibilities at the cost of families. Here, only one person of the family is to be held responsible for the destruction of the whole family's present and future opportunities. Addictive behaviour, while it is not as wide-spread as in Western countries, is a real and multi-facetted problem, especially in contexts of poverty. It also is a case in point that remaining in poverty cannot always be related to lack of infrastructure, jobs or governmental efforts. At the micro scale of the households, personal behaviour is a key factor. As figures clearly show, the majority of the poor are not prone to addictive habits. The other small proportion, however, does forge for themselves and their families a permanence of immiserisation.

13 Willingness to contribute towards infrastructural services

A. Cavelti, N. Sliwa, J. Whitebread
University of Basel

13.1
Introduction

In order to find out where basic household facilities such as water, electricity, toilets and sewerage systems lack or need to be improved, information is needed on the availability of such services in the slum households as well as their quality. For each household in the four slum communities, the survey has recorded which services are available at home. A ranking list of the accessibility of the services would place electricity facilities first (88.2%), then sewerage (80.8%) and toilet facilities (75.8%), and at last water facilities with 74.7%. Clearly, access to clean water is a serious problem. It is also the service that slum dwellers most urgently wish to be improved. To render such improvements possible, the surveyed people were willing to contribute.

Whereas the first part of the following chapter analyses the types of services, their accessibility and quality, a closer look at the way that people in the different slums would contribute to the infrastructural services is taken in the second part of the chapter.

13.2
Type of services available at home

Water facility in the house, by slum (Tab. 13.1). There are remarkable differences between the slums concerning the availability of services, such as water, electricity, toilet facilities and sewerage, at home. Table 13.1 shows that households generally have legal *water facilities* (68.4%). However, whereas 92% to 95% of the households in Jayprakash- and Bhimraonagar have legal water facilities in the house, the percentage is only at 49%, respectively 57% in the communities of Mustuffa- and Shantinagar. In Jayprakash- and Bhimraonagar, only 1.9% and 4.6% have no water in the house, whereas it is appalling that in Mustuffa- and Shantinagar, nearly 35% and 41% do not have any legal water facilities in the house. The reasons for the high proportions of households without legal water facilities in Shantinagar may be due to the poor financial and educational situation of the people there (see chapter 11), for Mustuffanagar, however, reasons are not that obvious. Consequences of the lack of water facilities in the households can be seen in terms of the water sources people use and in the way they treat their water.

Table 13.1 Water facility in the house, by slum.

Slum / Water	Bhimraonagar in % (n=130)	Jayprakashnagar in % (n=52)	Mustuffanagar in % (n=155)	Shantinagar in % (n=154)	Total in % (n=491)
no	4.6	1.9	34.8	40.9	25.3
yes, legal	95.4	92.3	49.0	57.1	68.4
yes, illegal	0.0	5.8	16.1	1.9	6.3
Total	100.0	100.0	100.0	100.0	100.0

SOURCE: UNIVERSITY OF BASEL, DEPT. OF GEOGRAPHY AND ALL INDIA DISASTER MITIGATION INSTITUTE, AHMEDABAD, INDIA 2005. SOCIAL SCIENCE SURVEY IN SELECTED SLUM COMMUNITIES IN THE CITY OF BHUJ, GUJARAT, INDIA.

Source of water, by slum (Tab. 13.2). The majority of people without water facilities at home purchase their water at nearby places (60.3 to 100%, Tab. 13.2). In Shantinagar, where 60.3% of the people without water facilities purchase it from nearby places, the other 39.7% of them get it from nearby wells north of the slum, without paying. Apparently, people are too poor to buy water. Yet, one might suppose that the quality of the water that people provide for themselves from nearby wells is even worse that the one of the purchased water from bullock carts (7%, Tab. 13.2).

Table 13.2 Source of water, by slum.

Slum / Source of water	Bhimraonagar in % (n=6)	Jayprakashnagar in % (n=1)	Mustuffanagar in % (n=86)	Shantinagar in % (n=63)	Total in % (n=156)
nearby well - without purchasing	0.0	0.0	2.3	39.7	17.3
purchase from nearby places (handpump / well / private tap)	100.0	100.0	90.7	60.3	78.8
purchase from bullock cart	0.0	0.0	7.0	0.0	3.8
Total	100.0	100.0	100.0	100.0	100.0

SOURCE: UNIVERSITY OF BASEL, DEPT. OF GEOGRAPHY AND ALL INDIA DISASTER MITIGATION INSTITUTE, AHMEDABAD, INDIA 2005. SOCIAL SCIENCE SURVEY IN SELECTED SLUM COMMUNITIES IN THE CITY OF BHUJ, GUJARAT, INDIA.

Water treatment, by slum (Tab. 13.3). Table 13.3 illustrates the water treatment by slum. In the two communities of Jayprakash- and Bhimraonagar, where 95.4% and 92.3% of the households have legal water facilities in the house (Tab. 13.1), it is 83.1% and 81.1% that do not treat their water at all. By contrast, in Mustuffa- and Shantinagar, where 34.8% and 40.9% have no water facilities in the house, it is a similar percentage, namely 39.6% and 37.7% that treat their water. These figures indicate that people who do not have water facilities in their houses and who have to provide it for their families from wells or hand-pumps, if they pay for it or not, are aware of the poor water quality, with nearly 40% of them treating it (Mustuffa- and Shantinagar). Still, about two thirds of the people in these two slum communities do not treat their water, the total percentage being even higher than that at 69.2%. This might be due to the lack of information on how to treat water effectively with simple means or because they do not know that water treatment might be necessary.

Table 13.3 Water treatment, by slum.

Slum / Water treatment	Bhimraonagar in % (n=130)	Jayprakashnagar in % (n=53)	Mustuffanagar in % (n=159)	Shantinagar in % (n=154)	Total in % (n=496)
yes	16.9	18.9	39.6	37.7	30.8
no	83.1	81.1	60.4	62.3	69.2
Total	100.0	100.0	100.0	100.0	100.0

SOURCE: UNIVERSITY OF BASEL, DEPT. OF GEOGRAPHY AND ALL INDIA DISASTER MITIGATION INSTITUTE, AHMEDABAD, INDIA 2005. SOCIAL SCIENCE SURVEY IN SELECTED SLUM COMMUNITIES IN THE CITY OF BHUJ, GUJARAT, INDIA.

Method of water treatment, by slum (Tab. 13.4). Between 87% and 92% of the people in all slums who treat their water do so by filtering by cloth (Tab. 13.4). Boiling is mostly used in Jayprakashnagar (8.7%), but percentages for boiling are generally very low because firewood is rare and gas expensive.

Several conclusions can be drawn from the analysis of water availability, water sources and water treatment by slum: Firstly, the availability of clean water is a serious problem in general. 25% of all households do not have water facilities and need to provide water for their families from different sources (with differing quality). Secondly, the poorest among the poor of the slums generally do not purchase water, probably because they cannot afford to buy it, which means that their water might be of even worse quality. In other words: there is a relation between the financial capacity and the water source people use, with the differing water quality affecting people's health. Thirdly, a majority of people do not treat their water at all, even if the percentage is a higher among those who get their water from wells for free.

Improving the water quality and the accessibility of clean water must therefore be a major focus in any kind of development aid. Also, it must be elaborated in further detail in what way people would and could contribute – according to their financial capacities – if the water quality was improved through their participation. As long as the water quality is generally rather bad, it is comprehensible that people are not willing to pay for it. However, awareness for the need of the people's participation in terms of water facility improvement must be raised. Also, it is coercive that people, although already aware of the water problem with a certain proportion of them treating it, learn how to improve the water quality themselves by treating it with simple means, and by changing factors that determine the poor water quality, in example (inexistent) sewerage systems.

Table 13.4 Method of water treatment, by slum

Slum / Method of treatment	Bhimraonagar in % (n=123)	Jayprakashnagar in % (n=46)	Mustuffanagar in % (n=104)	Shantinagar in % (n=110)	Total in % (n=383)
chlorine tablets	0.0	0.0	1.0	1.8	0.8
filter by cloth	93.5	87.0	93.3	92.7	92.4
boiling	2.4	8.7	1.9	0.9	2.6
filter by cloth & boiling	4.1	4.3	3.8	4.5	4.2
Total	100.0	100.0	100.0	100.0	100.0

SOURCE: UNIVERSITY OF BASEL, DEPT. OF GEOGRAPHY AND ALL INDIA DISASTER MITIGATION INSTITUTE, AHMEDABAD, INDIA 2005. SOCIAL SCIENCE SURVEY IN SELECTED SLUM COMMUNITIES IN THE CITY OF BHUJ, GUJARAT, INDIA.

Electricity facility in the house, by slum (Tab. 13.5). Most of the households (77.7%) have legal *electricity facilities* in the house, and 10.5% use illegal electricity (Tab. 13.5). Jayprakashnagar has the lowest percentage of illegal electricity facilities with only 1.9%. By contrast, Shantinagar shows the highest proportion of households with illegal electricity facilities (13.5%) and consequently has the lowest share of households with legal electricity (66.5%), as compared to all other slums, where between 77.4% and nearly 90% of the households have legal electricity facilities. At the same time, Shantinagar is the community with the highest percentage of households with no electricity at all (20%).

Table 13.5 Electricity facility in the house, by slum.

Slum / Electricity	Bhimraonagar in % (n=130)	Jayprakashnagar in % (n=53)	Mustuffanagar in % (n=159)	Shantinagar in % (n=155)	Total in % (n=497)
no	4.6	9.4	10.7	20.0	11.9
yes, legal	86.9	88.7	77.4	66.5	77.7
yes, illegal	8.5	1.9	11.9	13.5	10.5
Total	100.0	100.0	100.0	100.0	100.0

SOURCE: UNIVERSITY OF BASEL, DEPT. OF GEOGRAPHY AND ALL INDIA DISASTER MITIGATION INSTITUTE, AHMEDABAD, INDIA 2005. SOCIAL SCIENCE SURVEY IN SELECTED SLUM COMMUNITIES IN THE CITY OF BHUJ, GUJARAT, INDIA.

Toilet facility in the house, by slum (Tab. 13.6). A similar picture emerges from the analysis of the toilet facilities by slum: again, Shantinagar stands out as the least developed community. Whereas nearly 100% of the households in Jayprakash- and Mustuffanagar have toilet facilities, it is only 49% in Shantinagar, where a majority of the mainly tribal population lives according to rural principles and defecates in the open-spaces. In addition, the waste water pond between Shanti- and Jayprakashnagar and the surrounding areas invites the behaviour that is practised by the tribal population.

Table 13.6 Toilet facility in the house, by slum.

Slum Toilet	Bhimraonagar in % (n=129)	Jayprakashnagar in % (n=53)	Mustuffanagar in % (n=159)	Shantinagar in % (n=155)	Total in % (n=496)
yes	73.6	98.1	96.2	49.0	75.8
no (open spaces)	26.4	1.9	3.8	51.0	24.2
Total	100.0	100.0	100.0	100.0	100.0

SOURCE: UNIVERSITY OF BASEL, DEPT. OF GEOGRAPHY AND ALL INDIA DISASTER MITIGATION INSTITUTE, AHMEDABAD, INDIA 2005. SOCIAL SCIENCE SURVEY IN SELECTED SLUM COMMUNITIES IN THE CITY OF BHUJ, GUJARAT, INDIA.

Sewerage facility in the house, by slum (Tab. 13.7). Only 1.9% of the households in Jayprakash-, and 3.2% of the ones in Mustuffanagar have no sewerage facilities. The percentage is significantly higher in Bhimraonagar (23.8%), but particularly alarming in Shantinagar, where 40.5% of the households do not have sewerage facilities (Tab. 13.7). The large waste water pond that is used by the inhabitants of Shantinagar, of whom nearly half do not have any sewerage facilities at all, reaches incredible dimensions in the monsoon period. Lacking sewerage facilities do not only influence the immediate neighbourhood, but the hygiene standard of the slum as a whole with consequences on people's health.

A large proportion of the population in Jayprakashnagar has legal sewerage facilities (46.2%). The percentage is high in Shantinagar as well (10.7%), but most probably due to rural behaviour rather than to hygienic sewerage facilities. A majority of the slum households have sock-pits. The percentage of sock-pits is especially high in Mustuffanagar (nearly 95% of the households have them), and lowest in Shantinagar with 44.3%. In Jayprakash- and in Shantinagar, people have illegal sewerage facilities (1.9% and 4.6%), connecting their sewerage illegally to the sewer pipe. Although the rates seem low, it is again Shantinagar that shows the highest percentage (Tab. 13.6). Also, consequences for the water quality may be severe.

It is obvious that in Shantinagar in particular, awareness on the serious consequences of lacking toilet and sewerage facilities on the water quality must be raised, especially since in this community, around 41% of the households have no running water (Tab. 13.1) and get it from nearby wells, often contaminated by waste water and defecation. Attention must be called to the vicious circle of sewerage problems, lacking toilet facilities, defecation in the open space, water contamination (with high shares of households providing their water from wells) and ill health. Certainly, the level of education that varies in the different slum communities is related to varying hygienic standards. All the more, the quality and accessibility of water in the slum communities must be one of the major concerns because it has a strong impact on people's health and livelihood. It is quite evident that an improvement of the infrastructural services, particularly sewerage, toilet and water facilities, cannot take place without the active participation of the people who have to learn that it is also their behaviour that makes a difference.

Table 13.7 Sewerage facility in the house, by slum.

Slum Sewerage	Bhimraonagar in % (n=130)	Jayprakashnagar in % (n=52)	Mustuffanagar in % (n=157)	Shantinagar in % (n=131)	Total in % (n=470)
no	23.8	1.9	3.2	40.5	19.1
yes, legal	1.5	46.2	1.9	10.7	9.1
yes, illegal	0.0	1.9	0.0	4.6	1.5
yes, sock-pit	74.6	50.0	94.9	44.3	70.2
Total	100.0	100.0	100.0	100.0	100.0

SOURCE: UNIVERSITY OF BASEL, DEPT. OF GEOGRAPHY AND ALL INDIA DISASTER MITIGATION INSTITUTE, AHMEDABAD, INDIA 2005. SOCIAL SCIENCE SURVEY IN SELECTED SLUM COMMUNITIES IN THE CITY OF BHUJ, GUJARAT, INDIA.

Water facility in the house, by occupation (Tab. 13.8). Although a majority of slum households has legal *water facilities* (68.4%, Tab. 13.8), the percentage of households without any water facilities is remarkably high at 25.4%. People working in the government sector have the highest percentage of legal water facilities (92.3%) and do not use water illegally. Construction workers and farmers show the lowest proportion of households with water facilities in the house (56.8% and 53.8%) and the highest share of those without water facilities at all (around 38%).

By contrast, households with family heads working in the service sector, in crafts or as vendors have legal water facilities in the house at high percentages (between 76.1% and 85.7%), and also show the lowest rates of households with no water facilities (between 11.9 and 17.6%, Tab. 13.8).

Source of water, water treatment and method of water treatment, by occupation (Tab. 13.9, 13.10 and 13.11). Most likely, the socioeconomic situation of the family head has an impact on the access to infrastructure. Most of the households without access to water in the house purchase it from nearby places (78.4%, Tab. 13.9). Differences in the source of water people use by occupation of the family head are hard to see. Concerning the water treatment, it is noteworthy that family heads working in the government sector treat their water significantly less than the others (15.4%, Tab. 13.10). An explanation could be that the water quality is already of a higher level. Of those who treat their water, 92.3% do so by filtering it by cloth (Tab. 13.11).

Table 13.8 Water facility in the house, by occupation of family head.

Occupation / Water	textile/industry in % (n=36)	government in % (n=13)	casual labour in % (n=84)	construction in % (n=81)	farming in % (n=13)	automotive related job in % (n=42)	vendor/shop in % (n=42)	crafts in % (n=17)	service sector in % (n=46)	retiree/housewife/unemployed in % (n=97)	unclear/indian in % (n=13)	Total in % (n=484)
no	27.8	7.7	35.7	38.3	38.5	26.2	11.9	17.6	17.4	18.6	7.7	25.4
yes - legal	61.1	92.3	61.9	56.8	53.8	71.4	85.7	76.5	76.1	70.1	76.9	68.4
yes - illegal	11.1	0.0	2.4	4.9	7.7	2.4	2.4	5.9	6.5	11.3	15.4	6.2
Total	100.0	100.0	100.0	100.0	100.0	100.0	100.0	100.0	100.0	100.0	100.0	100.0

Table 13.9 Source of water, by occupation of family head.

Occupation / Source of water	textile/industry in % (n=17)	government in % (n=2)	casual labour in % (n=33)	construction in % (n=36)	farming in % (n=5)	automotive related job in % (n=12)	vendor/shop in % (n=6)	crafts in % (n=6)	service sector in % (n=14)	retiree/housewife/unemployed in % (n=21)	unclear/indian in % (n=1)	Total in % (n=153)
nearby well - without purchasing	11.8	0.0	27.3	16.7	0.0	8.3	33.3	33.3	14.3	14.3	0.0	17.6
purchase from nearby places (handpump / well / private tap)	82.4	50.0	72.7	80.6	100.0	91.7	66.7	66.7	78.6	76.2	100.0	78.4
purchase from bullock cart	5.9	50.0	0.0	2.8	0.0	0.0	0.0	0.0	7.1	9.5	0.0	3.9
Total	100.0	100.0	100.0	100.0	100.0	100.0	100.0	100.0	100.0	100.0	100.0	100.0

SOURCE: UNIVERSITY OF BASEL, DEPT. OF GEOGRAPHY AND ALL INDIA DISASTER MITIGATION INSTITUTE, AHMEDABAD, INDIA 2005. SOCIAL SCIENCE SURVEY IN SELECTED SLUM COMMUNITIES IN THE CITY OF BHUJ, GUJARAT, INDIA.

Table 13.10 Water treatment, by occupation of family head.

Occupation / Water treatment	textile/ industry in % (n=36)	government in % (n=13)	casual labour in % (n=84)	construction in % (n=84)	farming in % (n=13)	automotive related job in % (n=43)	vendor/ shop in % (n=41)	crafts in % (n=17)	service sector in % (n=47)	retiree/ housewife/ unemployed in % (n=98)	unclear/ indian in % (n=13)	Total in % (n=489)
yes	38.9	15.4	29.8	34.5	46.2	27.9	19.5	29.4	44.7	25.5	23.1	30.7
no	61.1	84.6	70.2	65.5	53.8	72.1	80.5	70.6	55.3	74.5	76.9	69.3
Total	100.0	100.0	100.0	100.0	100.0	100.0	100.0	100.0	100.0	100.0	100.0	100.0

Table 13.11 Method of water treatment, by occupation of family head.

Occupation / Method of treatment	textile/ industry in % (n=28)	government in % (n=10)	casual labour in % (n=65)	construction in % (n=65)	farming in % (n=8)	automotive related job in % (n=34)	vendor/ shop in % (n=36)	crafts in % (n=14)	service sector in % (n=33)	retiree/ housewife/ unemployed in % (n=75)	unclear/ indian in % (n=11)	Total in % (n=379)
chlorine tablets	0.0	0.0	0.0	0.0	12.5	0.0	0.0	0.0	6.1	0.0	0.0	0.8
filter by cloth	96.4	80.0	95.4	96.9	87.5	94.1	88.9	85.7	78.8	93.3	100.0	92.3
boiling	0.0	10.0	0.0	3.1	0.0	2.9	2.8	0.0	9.1	2.7	0.0	2.6
filter by cloth & boiling	3.6	10.0	4.6	0.0	0.0	2.9	8.3	14.3	6.1	4.0	0.0	4.2
Total	100.0	100.0	100.0	100.0	100.0	100.0	100.0	100.0	100.0	100.0	100.0	100.0

SOURCE: UNIVERSITY OF BASEL, DEPT. OF GEOGRAPHY AND ALL INDIA DISASTER MITIGATION INSTITUTE, AHMEDABAD, INDIA 2005. SOCIAL SCIENCE SURVEY IN SELECTED SLUM COMMUNITIES IN THE CITY OF BHUJ, GUJARAT, INDIA.

Electricity facility in the house, by occupation (Tab. 13.12). Although a majority of people, regardless of their occupation, have legal electricity facilities in the house (Tab. 13.12), certain differences can be observed: some occupation categories show lower percentages of legal electricity facilities than others. It is the farmers, those working in construction or casual labourers who dispose of legal electricity in the household at only 53.8% to 72.6%, as compared to all other occupation groups who have rates between 80% and 100% (government, Tab. 13.12).

Toilet facility in the house, by occupation (Tab. 13.13). The same differentiation among occupation categories holds true for toilet facilities in the household (Tab. 13.13). Here, the differences are even more apparent: whereas only between 10.6% and 17.6% of the households with a family head employed in the service sector, textile / industry or crafts do not have toilets in the household, it is 35.7% of those working in construction, 45.2% of those doing casual labour and even 61.5% of those working as farmers (Tab. 13.13).

Again, it appears that the socioeconomic situation of the families is a determining factor in the availability of and access to infrastructure. The fact that households with a family head employed in unstable and low-paid jobs such as construction or casual labour, have fewer legal infrastructure services in the house than other occupation categories (see Tab. 13.2 and 13.3), might be due to several factors: lower educational standards (see chapter 11) and as a consequence, worse financial capacities because of low income jobs, but also lacking knowledge on the importance of toilet and sewerage facilities and its impact on water quality and health. In families with low income, the little money is needed for food and other essentials, whereas investment in infrastructure such as water and sanitation might often be too expensive.

Sewerage facility in the house, by occupation (Tab. 13.14). Casual labourers and farmers show the lowest percentage of legal *sewerage facilities* in the house (5.7% and 0%, Tab. 13.14) and at the same time, high rates of household without any sewerage facilities at all (38.6% and 50% have none). As to the farmers, an explanation could be that they live in a traditional and rural way without setting priorities on investing in sewerage systems, or with too little money to do so. Lack of money, but also lack of knowledge on the importance of sewerage systems for water quality and health might be the main reasons for the low percentages of households with sewerage facilities in the category "casual labour" (Tab. 13.14).

To summarize: the relation between the kind of occupation people follow and the availability of basic household infrastructure such as water, sewerage systems or toilet facilities is apparent and draws a parallel to findings that previous chapters elaborated: people with lower education standards, worse job opportunities and a worse socioeconomic situation are disadvantaged in almost every aspect of livelihood conditions, be it legal access to basic infrastructure, services and their availability at home or health.

Table 13.12 Electricity facility in the house, by occupation of family head.

Occupation / Electricity	textile/ industry in % (n=36)	government in % (n=13)	casual labour in % (n=84)	construction in % (n=84)	farming in % (n=13)	automotive related job in % (n=43)	vendor/ shop in % (n=42)	crafts in % (n=17)	service sector in % (n=47)	retiree/ housewife/ unemployed in % (n=98)	unclear/ indian in % (n=13)	Total in % (n=490)
no	8.3	0.0	11.9	21.4	30.8	9.3	11.9	5.9	12.8	6.1	7.7	11.8
yes, legal	80.6	100.0	72.6	67.9	53.8	79.1	83.3	82.4	80.9	83.7	76.9	77.6
yes, illegal	11.1	0.0	15.5	10.7	15.4	11.6	4.8	11.8	6.4	10.2	15.4	10.6
Total	100.0	100.0	100.0	100.0	100.0	100.0	100.0	100.0	100.0	100.0	100.0	100.0

Table 13.13 Toilet facility in the house, by occupation of family head.

Occupation / Toilet	textile/ industry in % (n=36)	government in % (n=13)	casual labour in % (n=84)	construction in % (n=84)	farming in % (n=13)	automotive related job in % (n=43)	vendor/ shop in % (n=42)	crafts in % (n=17)	service sector in % (n=47)	retiree/ housewife/ unemployed in % (n=97)	unclear/ indian in % (n=13)	Total in % (n=489)
yes	86.1	100.0	54.8	64.3	38.5	86.0	76.2	82.4	89.4	87.6	84.6	75.7
no	13.9	0.0	45.2	35.7	61.5	14.0	23.8	17.6	10.6	12.4	15.4	24.3
Total	100.0	100.0	100.0	100.0	100.0	100.0	100.0	100.0	100.0	100.0	100.0	100.0

SOURCE: UNIVERSITY OF BASEL, DEPT. OF GEOGRAPHY AND ALL INDIA DISASTER MITIGATION INSTITUTE, AHMEDABAD, INDIA 2005. SOCIAL SCIENCE SURVEY IN SELECTED SLUM COMMUNITIES IN THE CITY OF BHUJ, GUJARAT, INDIA.

Table 13.14 Sewerage facility in the house, by occupation.

Occupation / Sewerage	textile/ industry in % (n=35)	government in % (n=13)	casual labour in % (n=70)	construction in % (n=82)	farming in % (n=10)	automotive related job in % (n=42)	vendor/ shop in % (n=40)	crafts in % (n=17)	service sector in % (n=46)	retiree/ housewife/ unemployed in % (n=95)	unclear/ indian in % (n=13)	Total in % (n=463)
no	14.3	0.0	38.6	28.0	50.0	14.3	20.0	17.6	6.5	8.4	7.7	19.2
yes, legal	2.9	30.8	5.7	6.1	0.0	11.9	17.5	5.9	13.0	8.4	15.4	9.3
yes, illegal	0.0	0.0	1.4	1.2	0.0	4.8	2.5	0.0	0.0	2.1	0.0	1.5
yes, sock-pit	82.9	69.2	54.3	64.6	50.0	69.0	60.0	76.5	80.4	81.1	76.9	70.0
Total	100.0	100.0	100.0	100.0	100.0	100.0	100.0	100.0	100.0	100.0	100.0	100.0

SOURCE: UNIVERSITY OF BASEL, DEPT. OF GEOGRAPHY AND ALL INDIA DISASTER MITIGATION INSTITUTE, AHMEDABAD, INDIA 2005. SOCIAL SCIENCE SURVEY IN SELECTED SLUM COMMUNITIES IN THE CITY OF BHUJ, GUJARAT, INDIA

Water facility in the house and source of water, by caste (Tab. 13.15, 13.16).
Scheduled Castes (SC) and Scheduled Tribes (ST) have legal water facilities at higher rates than the other two surveyed castes (81% and 85.7%, as compared to 54.4% and 71.2%, Tab. 13.15). The Other Backward Castes (OBC) show the highest percentage of households with no water facilities in the house (37.2%). The proportion of people without access to water in their house is significantly lower among the Scheduled Castes and Scheduled Tribes than among Other Backward and General Castes (11.9% and 14.3%, as compared to 37.2% and 22.9%, Tab. 13.15).

Most of the households purchase their water from nearby places. Particularly households of General Castes use this source almost exclusively (95%, Tab. 13.16). ST tend to get the water from nearby places without purchasing it. Maybe this is due to their rural background with people not being used to buying their water and mostly are too poor to do so. The option of purchasing water from bullock carts is mostly used by SC (18.2%). The interpretation of the source of water people use in relation to their caste is rather difficult. One might assume that here, local geographical conditions might influence people's answers to water-related questions more than their caste affiliation itself. Given the fact that certain castes in the surveyed area concentrate in certain communities, the differences that can be observed by caste might originate primarily from the geographical distribution and conditions in the different communities.

Table 13.15 Water facility in the house, by caste.

Caste / Water	SC in % (n=84)	ST in % (n=56)	OBC in % (n=180)	General in % (n=170)	Total in % (n=490)
no	11.9	14.3	37.2	22.9	25.3
yes - legal	81.0	85.7	54.4	71.2	68.4
yes - illegal	7.1	0.0	8.3	5.9	6.3
Total	100.0	100.0	100.0	100.0	100.0

SOURCE: UNIVERSITY OF BASEL, DEPT. OF GEOGRAPHY AND ALL INDIA DISASTER MITIGATION INSTITUTE, AHMEDABAD, INDIA 2005. SOCIAL SCIENCE SURVEY IN SELECTED SLUM COMMUNITIES IN THE CITY OF BHUJ, GUJARAT, INDIA.

Table 13.16 If no in Table 15, source of water, by caste.

Caste / Source of water	SC in % (n=11)	ST in % (n=8)	OBC in % (n=77)	General in % (n=60)	Total in % (n=156)
nearby well - without purchasing	27.3	37.5	23.4	5.0	17.3
purchase from nearby places (handpump / well / private tap)	54.5	62.5	71.4	95.0	78.8
purchase from bullock cart	18.2	0.0	5.2	0.0	3.8
Total	100.0	100.0	100.0	100.0	100.0

SOURCE: UNIVERSITY OF BASEL, DEPT. OF GEOGRAPHY AND ALL INDIA DISASTER MITIGATION INSTITUTE, AHMEDABAD, INDIA 2005. SOCIAL SCIENCE SURVEY IN SELECTED SLUM COMMUNITIES IN THE CITY OF BHUJ, GUJARAT, INDIA.

Water treatment and methods of water treatment, by caste (Tab. 13.17, 13.18). Whereas 48.3% of the OBC households treat their water, only 15.8% of the ST households do so (Tab. 13.17). The high percentage of OBC households that treat their water may be due to the fact that they generally have better education standards and thus more knowledge on healthcare than the tribal population. The methods of water treatment are the same in all of the surveyed castes: if people treat their water, more than 90% filter it by cloth (Tab. 13.18).

Table 13.17 Water treatment by caste.

Caste / Water treatment	SC in % (n=86)	ST in % (n=57)	OBC in % (n=180)	General in % (n=172)	Total in % (n=495)
yes	25.6	15.8	48.3	20.3	30.9
no	74.4	84.2	51.7	79.7	69.1
Total	100.0	100.0	100.0	100.0	100.0

SOURCE: UNIVERSITY OF BASEL, DEPT. OF GEOGRAPHY AND ALL INDIA DISASTER MITIGATION INSTITUTE, AHMEDABAD, INDIA 2005. SOCIAL SCIENCE SURVEY IN SELECTED SLUM COMMUNITIES IN THE CITY OF BHUJ, GUJARAT, INDIA.

Table 13.18 Method of water treatment, by caste.

Caste / Method of treatment	SC in % (n=73)	ST in % (n=53)	OBC in % (n=99)	General in % (n=157)	Total in % (n=382)
chlorine tablets	0.0	0.0	1.0	1.3	0.8
filter by cloth	93.2	94.3	93.9	90.4	92.4
boiling	2.7	3.8	2.0	2.5	2.6
filter by cloth & boiling	4.1	1.9	3.0	5.7	4.2
Total	100.0	100.0	100.0	100.0	100.0

SOURCE: UNIVERSITY OF BASEL, DEPT. OF GEOGRAPHY AND ALL INDIA DISASTER MITIGATION INSTITUTE, AHMEDABAD, INDIA 2005. SOCIAL SCIENCE SURVEY IN SELECTED SLUM COMMUNITIES IN THE CITY OF BHUJ, GUJARAT, INDIA.

Electricity facility in the house, by caste (Tab. 13.19). It is noteworthy that it is the Other Backward Castes that show the highest percentage of households without any electricity in the house: 17.8% have none, as compared to percentages between 6.9% and 11.9% in the other surveyed castes. Also, the Other Backward Castes have the highest proportion of households using illegal electricity (15%). Whereas all castes have electricity at rates between 81.4% and 85.5%, the Other Backward Castes only show 67.2% (Tab. 13.19). However, reasons for this differentiation are difficult to find, and as said above, local geographical conditions might play a more important role than caste itself. A large proportion of the people affiliated to Other Backward Castes lives in the community of Mustuffanagar.

Table 13.19 Electricity facility in the house, by caste.

Caste Electricity	SC in % (n=86)	ST in % (n=57)	OBC in % (n=180)	General in % (n=173)	Total in % (n=496)
no	10.5	10.5	17.8	6.9	11.9
yes, legal	81.4	82.5	67.2	85.5	77.8
yes, illegal	8.1	7.0	15.0	7.5	10.3
Total	100.0	100.0	100.0	100.0	100.0

SOURCE: UNIVERSITY OF BASEL, DEPT. OF GEOGRAPHY AND ALL INDIA DISASTER MITIGATION INSTITUTE, AHMEDABAD, INDIA 2005. SOCIAL SCIENCE SURVEY IN SELECTED SLUM COMMUNITIES IN THE CITY OF BHUJ, GUJARAT, INDIA.

Toilet and sewerage facility in the house, by caste (Tab. 13.20, 13.21). Other Backward Castes are also below average concerning toilet facilities in the house (Tab. 13.20): whereas a total of 75.8% of the surveyed households have toilet facilities, it is only 62.2% of the OBC. General Castes show the highest percentage of households with toilet facilities (92.5%). They also show the highest proportion of households with a *sewerage facility* (84.2% have a sock-pit) and at the same time, the lowest percentage of households with no sewerage facilities (5.3%, Tab. 13.21). The three categories SC, ST and OBC show a very even distribution: around 60% of their households use a sock-pit, for instance, and between 23% and 28% do not have sewerage facilities. Generally, sock-pits seem to be the main sewerage system people use, the percentages for all other categories are low (Tab. 13.21).

Table 13.20 Toilet facility in the house, by caste.

Caste Toilet	SC in % (n=86)	ST in % (n=56)	OBC in % (n=180)	General in % (n=173)	Total in % (n=495)
yes	70.9	75.0	62.2	92.5	75.8
no (open spaces)	29.1	25.0	37.8	7.5	24.2
Total	100.0	100.0	100.0	100.0	100.0

SOURCE: UNIVERSITY OF BASEL, DEPT. OF GEOGRAPHY AND ALL INDIA DISASTER MITIGATION INSTITUTE, AHMEDABAD, INDIA 2005. SOCIAL SCIENCE SURVEY IN SELECTED SLUM COMMUNITIES IN THE CITY OF BHUJ, GUJARAT, INDIA.

Table 13.21 Sewerage facility in the house, by caste.

Caste Sewerage	SC in % (n=85)	ST in % (n=56)	OBC in % (n=157)	General in % (n=171)	Total in % (n=469)
no	27.1	23.2	28.7	5.3	19.2
yes, legal	8.2	12.5	7.6	9.9	9.2
yes, illegal	1.2	3.6	1.9	0.6	1.5
yes, sock-pit	63.5	60.7	61.8	84.2	70.1
Total	100.0	100.0	100.0	100.0	100.0

SOURCE: UNIVERSITY OF BASEL, DEPT. OF GEOGRAPHY AND ALL INDIA DISASTER MITIGATION INSTITUTE, AHMEDABAD, INDIA 2005. SOCIAL SCIENCE SURVEY IN SELECTED SLUM COMMUNITIES IN THE CITY OF BHUJ, GUJARAT, INDIA.

Water facility in the house, by education standard of the family head (Tab. 13.22-13.26). The *water and electricity facilities* do not seem to depend on the education of the family head (Tab. 13.22 and 13.23; Tab. 13.24-13.26). One might assume that water and electricity are services that everyone, regardless of the educational background, considers as being essential.

Table 13.22 Water facility in the house, by education standard of family head.

Education Water	Hrs. 1-3 in % (n=45)	Hrs. 4-6 in % (n=82)	Hrs. 7-9 in % (n=107)	Hrs. 10-12 in % (n=35)	Completed Diploma in % (n=1)	Completed Graduation in % (n=6)	Illiterate in % (n=214)	Total in % (n=490)
no	13.3	19.5	19.6	28.6	0.0	0.0	33.2	25.3
yes - legal	75.6	74.4	75.7	68.6	100.0	100.0	59.8	68.4
yes - illegal	11.1	6.1	4.7	2.9	0.0	0.0	7.0	6.3
Total	100.0	100.0	100.0	100.0	100.0	100.0	100.0	100.0

SOURCE: UNIVERSITY OF BASEL, DEPT. OF GEOGRAPHY AND ALL INDIA DISASTER MITIGATION INSTITUTE, AHMEDABAD, INDIA 2005. SOCIAL SCIENCE SURVEY IN SELECTED SLUM COMMUNITIES IN THE CITY OF BHUJ, GUJARAT, INDIA.

Table 13.23 If no in Table 22, source of water, by education standard of family head.

Education Source of water	Hrs. 1-3 in % (n=13)	Hrs. 4-6 in % (n=21)	Hrs. 7-9 in % (n=32)	Hrs. 10-12 in % (n=12)	Completed Diploma in % (n=0)	Completed Graduation in % (n=0)	Illiterate in % (n=78)	Total in % (n=156)
nearby well - without purchasing	0.0	14.3	0.0	0.0	0.0	0.0	30.8	17.3
purchase from nearby places (handpump / well / private tap)	100.0	85.7	96.9	75.0	0.0	0.0	66.7	78.8
purchase from bullock cart	0.0	0.0	3.1	25.0	0.0	0.0	2.6	3.8
Total	100.0	100.0	100.0	100.0	0.0	0.0	100.0	100.0

SOURCE: UNIVERSITY OF BASEL, DEPT. OF GEOGRAPHY AND ALL INDIA DISASTER MITIGATION INSTITUTE, AHMEDABAD, INDIA 2005. SOCIAL SCIENCE SURVEY IN SELECTED SLUM COMMUNITIES IN THE CITY OF BHUJ, GUJARAT, INDIA.

Table 13.24 Water treatment, by education standard of family head.

Education / Water treatment	Hrs. 1-3 in % (n=45)	Hrs. 4-6 in % (n=82)	Hrs. 7-9 in % (n=108)	Hrs. 10-12 in % (n=36)	Completed Diploma in % (n=1)	Completed Graduation in % (n=6)	Illiterate in % (n=217)	Total in % (n=495)
yes	33.3	29.3	27.8	27.8	0.0	16.7	33.6	30.9
no	66.7	70.7	72.2	72.2	100.0	83.3	66.4	69.1
Total	100.0	100.0	100.0	100.0	100.0	100.0	100.0	100.0

SOURCE: UNIVERSITY OF BASEL, DEPT. OF GEOGRAPHY AND ALL INDIA DISASTER MITIGATION INSTITUTE, AHMEDABAD, INDIA 2005. SOCIAL SCIENCE SURVEY IN SELECTED SLUM COMMUNITIES IN THE CITY OF BHUJ, GUJARAT, INDIA.

Table 13.25 Method of water treatment, by education standard of family head.

Education / Method of treatment	Hrs. 1-3 in % (n=37)	Hrs. 4-6 in % (n=64)	Hrs. 7-9 in % (n=85)	Hrs. 10-12 in % (n=30)	Completed Diploma in % (n=1)	Completed Graduation in % (n=4)	Illiterate in % (n=161)	Total in % (n=382)
chlorine tablets	0.0	0.0	0.0	3.3	0.0	0.0	1.2	0.8
filter by cloth	91.9	92.2	92.9	90.0	100.0	50.0	93.8	92.4
boiling	2.7	1.6	2.4	6.7	0.0	25.0	1.9	2.6
filter by cloth & boiling	5.4	6.3	4.7	0.0	0.0	25.0	3.1	4.2
Total	100.0	100.0	100.0	100.0	100.0	100.0	100.0	100.0

SOURCE: UNIVERSITY OF BASEL, DEPT. OF GEOGRAPHY AND ALL INDIA DISASTER MITIGATION INSTITUTE, AHMEDABAD, INDIA 2005. SOCIAL SCIENCE SURVEY IN SELECTED SLUM COMMUNITIES IN THE CITY OF BHUJ, GUJARAT, INDIA.

Table 13.26 Electricity facility in the house, by education standard of family head.

Education / Electricity	Hrs. 1-3 in % (n=46)	Hrs. 4-6 in % (n=82)	Hrs. 7-9 in % (n=108)	Hrs. 10-12 in % (n=36)	Completed Diploma in % (n=1)	Completed Graduation in % (n=6)	Illiterate in % (n=217)	Total in % (n=496)
no	4.3	12.2	6.5	11.1	0.0	0.0	16.1	11.7
yes, legal	82.6	78.0	83.3	75.0	100.0	100.0	73.7	77.8
yes, illegal	13.0	9.8	10.2	13.9	0.0	0.0	10.1	10.5
Total	100.0	100.0	100.0	100.0	100.0	100.0	100.0	100.0

SOURCE: UNIVERSITY OF BASEL, DEPT. OF GEOGRAPHY AND ALL INDIA DISASTER MITIGATION INSTITUTE, AHMEDABAD, INDIA 2005. SOCIAL SCIENCE SURVEY IN SELECTED SLUM COMMUNITIES IN THE CITY OF BHUJ, GUJARAT, INDIA.

Toilet and sewerage facility in the house, by education standard of the family head (Tab. 13.27, 13.28). 76% of all households have *toilet facilities* in the house (Tab. 13.27). Remarkably, only 60.4% of the illiterates have toilet facilities. They mostly belong to the tribals who do not have toilets because of their rural habits and who do not have the necessary knowledge of health aspects to change their habits and use toilets.

Also, the percentage of households without *sewerage facilities* and with an illiterate family head is at 31.3% which is the highest rate of all categories (Tab. 13.28) and portrays the rural behaviour that a large proportion of the tribal population, most of whom are illiterate, still have. It also indicates that their knowledge on health and hygiene issues might be little.

Table 13.27 Toilet facility in the house, by education standard of family head.

Education Toilet	Hrs. 1-3 in % (n=46)	Hrs. 4-6 in % (n=81)	Hrs. 7-9 in % (n=108)	Hrs. 10-12 in % (n=36)	Completed Diploma in % (n=1)	Completed Graduation in % (n=6)	Illiterate in % (n=217)	Total in % (n=495)
yes	87.0	86.4	88.0	91.7	100.0	100.0	60.4	76.0
no (open spaces)	13.0	13.6	12.0	8.3	0.0	0.0	39.6	24.0
Total	100.0	100.0	100.0	100.0	100.0	100.0	100.0	100.0

SOURCE: UNIVERSITY OF BASEL, DEPT. OF GEOGRAPHY AND ALL INDIA DISASTER MITIGATION INSTITUTE, AHMEDABAD, INDIA 2005. SOCIAL SCIENCE SURVEY IN SELECTED SLUM COMMUNITIES IN THE CITY OF BHUJ, GUJARAT, INDIA.

Table 13.28 Sewerage facility in the house, by education standard of family head.

Education Sewerage	Hrs. 1-3 in % (n=44)	Hrs. 4-6 in % (n=78)	Hrs. 7-9 in % (n=106)	Hrs. 10-12 in % (n=36)	Completed Diploma in % (n=1)	Completed Graduation in % (n=6)	Illiterate in % (n=198)	Total in % (n=469)
no	11.4	14.1	9.4	2.8	0.0	0.0	31.3	19.0
yes, legal	4.5	10.3	12.3	8.3	100.0	0.0	8.1	9.2
yes, illegal	0.0	0.0	3.8	0.0	0.0	0.0	1.5	1.5
yes, sock-pit	84.1	75.6	74.5	88.9	0.0	100.0	59.1	70.4
Total	100.0	100.0	100.0	100.0	100.0	100.0	100.0	100.0

SOURCE: UNIVERSITY OF BASEL, DEPT. OF GEOGRAPHY AND ALL INDIA DISASTER MITIGATION INSTITUTE, AHMEDABAD, INDIA 2005. SOCIAL SCIENCE SURVEY IN SELECTED SLUM COMMUNITIES IN THE CITY OF BHUJ, GUJARAT, INDIA.

Water facility in the house, by average daily wages of household members (Tab. 13.29). There is a tendency that households with higher daily wages are more likely to have *water facilities* in the house (Tab. 13.29). They can afford to spend money on water infrastructure and are probably willing to invest in private water facilities. With increasing income, the percentages of households with legal water facilities increase, too, while the proportion of households using illegal water facilities decreases (Tab. 13.29).

Table 13.29 Water facility in the house, by average daily wages of household members (in Rs.)

Water facility \ Wage	0 to 9 Rs. in % (n=39)	10 to 19 Rs. in % (n=164)	20 to 29 Rs. in % (n=140)	30 to 39 Rs. in % (n=73)	40 to 49 Rs. in % (n=27)	50 to 89 Rs. in % (n=31)	90 to 130 Rs. in % (n=5)	Total in % (n=479)
yes - legal	56.4	65.9	66.4	76.7	85.2	83.9	60.0	69.1
yes - illegal	5.1	6.1	8.6	8.2	3.7	0.0	0.0	6.5
no	38.5	28.0	25.0	15.1	11.1	16.1	40.0	24.4
Total	100.0	100.0	100.0	100.0	100.0	100.0	100.0	100.0

SOURCE: UNIVERSITY OF BASEL, DEPT. OF GEOGRAPHY AND ALL INDIA DISASTER MITIGATION INSTITUTE, AHMEDABAD, INDIA 2005. SOCIAL SCIENCE SURVEY IN SELECTED SLUM COMMUNITIES IN THE CITY OF BHUJ, GUJARAT, INDIA.

Source of water, water treatment and method of water treatment, by average daily wages of household members (Tab. 13.30, 13.31 and 13.32). Where the people without water facilities at home get their water from depends on the location they live in rather than on their wages. The treatment of water does not seem to be influenced by the wages people earn (Tab. 13.31 and 13.32): On average, more than two thirds (68.9%) do not treat their water at all, but of those who do, more than 90% do so by filtering it by cloth. It seems that people who can afford to spend their money on water invest in private water facilities rather than in water treatment.

Table 13.30 If no in Tab. 29, source of water, by average daily wages of household members (in Rs.)

Source of water \ Wage	0 to 9 Rs. in % (n=16)	10 to 19 Rs. in % (n=56)	20 to 29 Rs. in % (n=43)	30 to 39 Rs. in % (n=17)	40 to 49 Rs. in % (n=7)	50 to 89 Rs. in % (n=8)	90 to 130 Rs. in % (n=2)	Total in % (n=149)
nearby well - without purchasing	18.8	26.8	16.3	5.9	0.0	0.0	0.0	17.4
purchase from nearby places (handpump / well / pravet tap)	81.3	69.6	79.1	88.2	100.0	100.0	50.0	78.5
purchase from bullock cart	0.0	3.6	4.7	5.9	0.0	0.0	50.0	4.0
Total	100.0	100.0	100.0	100.0	100.0	100.0	100.0	100.0

SOURCE: UNIVERSITY OF BASEL, DEPT. OF GEOGRAPHY AND ALL INDIA DISASTER MITIGATION INSTITUTE, AHMEDABAD, INDIA 2005. SOCIAL SCIENCE SURVEY IN SELECTED SLUM COMMUNITIES IN THE CITY OF BHUJ, GUJARAT, INDIA.

Table 13.31 Water treatment, by average daily wages of household members (in Rs.).

Wage Water treatment	0 to 9 Rs. in % (n=39)	10 to 19 Rs. in % (n=164)	20 to 29 Rs. in % (n=140)	30 to 39 Rs. in % (n=73)	40 to 49 Rs. in % (n=27)	50 to 89 Rs. in % (n=31)	90 to 130 Rs. in % (n=5)	Total in % (n=479)
yes	33.3	34.8	29.3	26.0	33.3	32.3	0.0	31.1
no	66.7	65.2	70.7	74.0	66.7	67.7	100.0	68.9
Total	100.0	100.0	100.0	100.0	100.0	100.0	100.0	100.0

SOURCE: UNIVERSITY OF BASEL, DEPT. OF GEOGRAPHY AND ALL INDIA DISASTER MITIGATION INSTITUTE, AHMEDABAD, INDIA 2005. SOCIAL SCIENCE SURVEY IN SELECTED SLUM COMMUNITIES IN THE CITY OF BHUJ, GUJARAT, INDIA.

Table 13.32 Method of water treatment, by average daily wages of household members (in Rs.).

Wage Method of treatment	0 to 9 Rs. in % (n=30)	10 to 19 Rs. in % (n=117)	20 to 29 Rs. in % (n=109)	30 to 39 Rs. in % (n=60)	40 to 49 Rs. in % (n=22)	50 to 89 Rs. in % (n=26)	90 to 130 Rs. in % (n=4)	Total in % (n=368)
chlorin tablets	0.0	0.9	.9	0.0	0.0	0.0	0.0	0.5
filter by cloth	96.7	94.9	90.8	93.3	95.5	88.5	25.0	92.4
boiling	3.3	1.7	2.8	3.3	0.0	0.0	50.0	2.7
filter by cloth & boiling	0.0	2.6	5.5	3.3	4.5	11.5	25.0	4.3
Total	100.0	100.0	100.0	100.0	100.0	100.0	100.0	100.0

SOURCE: UNIVERSITY OF BASEL, DEPT. OF GEOGRAPHY AND ALL INDIA DISASTER MITIGATION INSTITUTE, AHMEDABAD, INDIA 2005. SOCIAL SCIENCE SURVEY IN SELECTED SLUM COMMUNITIES IN THE CITY OF BHUJ, GUJARAT, INDIA.

Electricity, toilet and sewerage facility in the house, by average daily wages of household members (Tab. 13.33, 13.34 and 13.35). The lowest income group (0-9 Rs. per day) also shows the highest proportion of households with no electricity in the house (28.2%, Tab. 13.33), as compared to all other income categories. At the same time, the percentages of households with electricity in the house increase with income (Tab. 13.33). Remarkably, the same picture emerges by looking at the toilet facilities per household by average daily wages (Tab. 13.34): the higher the daily wages, the higher the percentage of households with toilets. Simultaneously, the proportions of those without toilet facilities decrease noticeably. Concerning sewerage facilities in the house, it is again the lowest income category that shows the highest proportion of households without sewerage (Tab. 13.35).

Clearly, there is strong relation between the income situation of households and their basic infrastructure, such as water, electricity, toilet and sewerage facilities. As previous chapters showed, the income situation of households clearly depends on the educational background and occupation of the family members. Income is related to the qualification and education of people, and income seems to determine to what extent households dispose of basic infrastructural services.

Table 13.33 Electricity facility in the house, by average daily wages of household members (in Rs.).

Wage Electricity	0 to 9 Rs. in % (n=39)	10 to 19 Rs. in % (n=164)	20 to 29 Rs. in % (n=140)	30 to 39 Rs. in % (n=73)	40 to 49 Rs. in % (n=27)	50 to 89 Rs. in % (n=31)	90 to 130 Rs. in % (n=5)	Total in % (n=479)
no	28.2	12.8	13.6	4.1	3.7	3.2	0.0	11.7
yes, legal	59.0	75.6	77.9	89.0	88.9	83.9	60.0	78.1
yes, illegal	12.8	11.6	8.6	6.8	7.4	12.9	40.0	10.2
Total	100.0	100.0	100.0	100.0	100.0	100.0	100.0	100.0

SOURCE: UNIVERSITY OF BASEL, DEPT. OF GEOGRAPHY AND ALL INDIA DISASTER MITIGATION INSTITUTE, AHMEDABAD, INDIA 2005. SOCIAL SCIENCE SURVEY IN SELECTED SLUM COMMUNITIES IN THE CITY OF BHUJ, GUJARAT, INDIA.

Table 13.34 Toilet facility in the house, by average daily wages of household members (in Rs.).

Wage Toilet	0 to 9 Rs. in % (n=39)	10 to 19 Rs. in % (n=164)	20 to 29 Rs. in % (n=140)	30 to 39 Rs. in % (n=73)	40 to 49 Rs. in % (n=27)	50 to 89 Rs. in % (n=31)	90 to 130 Rs. in % (n=5)	Total in % (n=479)
yes	64.1	70.7	76.4	83.6	92.6	80.6	100.0	76.0
no	35.9	29.3	23.6	16.4	7.4	19.4	0.0	24.0
Total	100.0	100.0	100.0	100.0	100.0	100.0	100.0	100.0

SOURCE: UNIVERSITY OF BASEL, DEPT. OF GEOGRAPHY AND ALL INDIA DISASTER MITIGATION INSTITUTE, AHMEDABAD, INDIA 2005. SOCIAL SCIENCE SURVEY IN SELECTED SLUM COMMUNITIES IN THE CITY OF BHUJ, GUJARAT, INDIA.

Table 13.35 Sewerage facility in the house, by average daily wages of household members (in Rs.).

Wage Sewerage	0 to 9 Rs. in % (n=35)	10 to 19 Rs. in % (n=154)	20 to 29 Rs. in % (n=132)	30 to 39 Rs. in % (n=71)	40 to 49 Rs. in % (n=27)	50 to 89 Rs. in % (n=29)	90 to 130 Rs. in % (n=5)	Total in % (n=453)
no	28.6	24.0	18.2	11.3	7.4	13.8	0.0	18.8
yes, legal	11.4	7.8	6.8	12.7	11.1	6.9	0.0	8.6
yes, illegal	2.9	0.6	2.3	0.0	0.0	3.4	0.0	1.3
yes, sock-pit	57.1	67.5	72.7	76.1	81.5	75.9	100.0	71.3
Total	100.0	100.0	100.0	100.0	100.0	100.0	100.0	100.0

SOURCE: UNIVERSITY OF BASEL, DEPT. OF GEOGRAPHY AND ALL INDIA DISASTER MITIGATION INSTITUTE, AHMEDABAD, INDIA 2005. SOCIAL SCIENCE SURVEY IN SELECTED SLUM COMMUNITIES IN THE CITY OF BHUJ, GUJARAT, INDIA.

Water facility in the house, by religion (Tab. 13.36). Since the Muslim population is concentrated in the community of Mustuffanagar, the relation between religion and services available at home contains a geographical component and must not be reduced to religious affiliation itself. Rather, it is the neighbourhood and surroundings that play an important role, which held true for the analysis of infrastructural services by caste, as well.

84.3% of the Hindu households have legal *water facilities*, as compared to only 56% of the Muslim households that have legal water facilities. Proportions of

Muslim households without water facilities are higher than in the Hindu population (34.4% as compared to only 13.9% of the Hindu households, Tab. 13.36).

Table 13.36 Water facility in the house, by religion.

Water \ Religion	Hindu in % (n=216)	Muslim in % (n=273)	Total in % (n=489)
no	13.9	34.4	25.4
yes - legal	84.3	56.0	68.5
yes - illegal	1.9	9.5	6.1
Total	100.0	100.0	100.0

SOURCE: UNIVERSITY OF BASEL, DEPT. OF GEOGRAPHY AND ALL INDIA DISASTER MITIGATION INSTITUTE, AHMEDABAD, INDIA 2005. SOCIAL SCIENCE SURVEY IN SELECTED SLUM COMMUNITIES IN THE CITY OF BHUJ, GUJARAT, INDIA.

Source of water, treatment of water and method of treatment, by religion (Tab. 13.37, 13.38 and 13.39). Where people without private water facilities get their water from does not seem to depend on their religion (Tab. 13.37), but rather on the surroundings. More Muslim than Hindu households treat their water: whereas 39.6% of the Muslim households do so, it is only 19.4% of the Hindu households (Tab. 13.38), the methods, however, are the same (mostly filtering by cloth, Tab 13.39). If a larger proportion of Muslim households does not have water facilities in the house and needs to provide it from different places, the fact that more Muslim than Hindu households treat their water might indicate their greater awareness of the poor water quality and the necessity of quality improvement by treatment.

Table 13.37 If no in Table 36, source of water, by religion.

Source of water \ Religion	Hindu in % (n=38)	Muslim in % (n=118)	Total in % (n=156)
nearby well - without purchasing	15.8	17.8	17.3
purchase from nearby places (handpump / well / private tap)	84.2	77.1	78.8
purchase from bullock cart	0.0	5.1	3.8
Total	100.0	100.0	100.0

SOURCE: UNIVERSITY OF BASEL, DEPT. OF GEOGRAPHY AND ALL INDIA DISASTER MITIGATION INSTITUTE, AHMEDABAD, INDIA 2005. SOCIAL SCIENCE SURVEY IN SELECTED SLUM COMMUNITIES IN THE CITY OF BHUJ, GUJARAT, INDIA.

Table 13.38 Water treatment, by religion

Water treatment \ Religion	Hindu in % (n=216)	Muslim in % (n=278)	Total in % (n=494)
yes	19.4	39.6	30.8
no	80.6	60.4	69.2
Total	100.0	100.0	100.0

SOURCE: UNIVERSITY OF BASEL, DEPT. OF GEOGRAPHY AND ALL INDIA DISASTER MITIGATION INSTITUTE, AHMEDABAD, INDIA 2005. SOCIAL SCIENCE SURVEY IN SELECTED SLUM COMMUNITIES IN THE CITY OF BHUJ, GUJARAT, INDIA.

Table 13.39 Method of water treatment, by religion.

Religion / Method of treatment	Hindu in % (n=197)	Muslim in % (n=185)	Total in % (n=382)
chlorine tablets	0.5	1.1	0.8
filter by cloth	91.4	93.5	92.4
boiling	3.0	2.2	2.6
filter by cloth & boiling	5.1	3.2	4.2
Total	100.0	100.0	100.0

SOURCE: UNIVERSITY OF BASEL, DEPT. OF GEOGRAPHY AND ALL INDIA DISASTER MITIGATION INSTITUTE, AHMEDABAD, INDIA 2005. SOCIAL SCIENCE SURVEY IN SELECTED SLUM COMMUNITIES IN THE CITY OF BHUJ, GUJARAT, INDIA.

Electricity, toilet and sewerage facility in the house, by religion (Tab. 13.40, 13.41 and 13.42). *Electricity* and *toilet facilities* are almost equally existent in households of both religions (Tab. 13.40, 13.41). However, Hindu households have more legal *sewerage facilities* in the house than Muslims (14.2%, as compared to 5.1%, Tab. 13.42). Muslim households, on the other hand, have more sock-pits than Hindus (75.9%, 63%).

Table 13.40 Electricity facility in the house, by religion.

Religion / Electricity	Hindu in % (n=217)	Muslim in % (n=278)	Total in % (n=495)
no	8.8	14.0	11.7
yes, legal	82.5	74.1	77.8
yes, illegal	8.8	11.9	10.5
Total	100.0	100.0	100.0

SOURCE: UNIVERSITY OF BASEL, DEPT. OF GEOGRAPHY AND ALL INDIA DISASTER MITIGATION INSTITUTE, AHMEDABAD, INDIA 2005. SOCIAL SCIENCE SURVEY IN SELECTED SLUM COMMUNITIES IN THE CITY OF BHUJ, GUJARAT, INDIA.

Table 13.41 Toilet facility in the house, by religion.

Religion / Toilet	Hindu in % (n=217)	Muslim in % (n=277)	Total in % (n=494)
yes	75.6	75.8	75.7
no (open spaces)	24.4	24.2	24.3
Total	100.0	100.0	100.0

SOURCE: UNIVERSITY OF BASEL, DEPT. OF GEOGRAPHY AND ALL INDIA DISASTER MITIGATION INSTITUTE, AHMEDABAD, INDIA 2005. SOCIAL SCIENCE SURVEY IN SELECTED SLUM COMMUNITIES IN THE CITY OF BHUJ, GUJARAT, INDIA.

Table 13.42 Sewerage facility in the house, by religion.

Sewerage / Religion	Hindu in % (n=211)	Muslim in % (n=257)	Total in % (n=468)
no	21.3	17.5	19.2
yes, legal	14.2	5.1	9.2
yes, illegal	1.4	1.6	1.5
yes, sock-pit	63.0	75.9	70.1
Total	100.0	100.0	100.0

SOURCE: UNIVERSITY OF BASEL, DEPT. OF GEOGRAPHY AND ALL INDIA DISASTER MITIGATION INSTITUTE, AHMEDABAD, INDIA 2005. SOCIAL SCIENCE SURVEY IN SELECTED SLUM COMMUNITIES IN THE CITY OF BHUJ, GUJARAT, INDIA.

13.3
Priority of improvements of services at home

By slum (Tab. 13.43). A total of 66.5% of the slum households does not view the improvement of housing substance as most necessary (Tab. 13.43). The percentages are particularly high in Jayprakashnagar and Mustuffanagar, where housing generally seemed to be fairly good.

Table 13.43 Most necessary improvement of housing substance, by slum.

Housing substance / Slum	Bhimraonagar in % (n=130)	Jayprakashnagar in % (n=52)	Mustuffanagar in % (n=154)	Shantinagar in % (n=154)	Total in % (n=490)
yes	49.2	26.9	23.4	32.5	33.5
no	50.8	73.1	76.6	67.5	66.5
Total	100.0	100.0	100.0	100.0	100.0

SOURCE: UNIVERSITY OF BASEL, DEPT. OF GEOGRAPHY AND ALL INDIA DISASTER MITIGATION INSTITUTE, AHMEDABAD, INDIA 2005. SOCIAL SCIENCE SURVEY IN SELECTED SLUM COMMUNITIES IN THE CITY OF BHUJ, GUJARAT, INDIA.

By contrast, *drinking water* supply seems to be a big issue (Tab. 13.44): 75% of the households wish improvements in that sector which points out the general awareness of the water problem. Only in Jayprakashnagar, a majority of people (63.5%) does not regard improvement of drinking water supplies as most necessary, but here, water facilities were better than in the other slums. As table 13.1 indicated, 92.3% of the households in Jayprakashnagar have legal water facilities in the house.

Table 13.44 Most necessary improvement of drinking water supplies, by slum.

Slum Drinking water	Bhimraonagar in % (n=130)	Jayprakashnagar in % (n=52)	Mustuffanagar in % (n=154)	Shantinagar in % (n=154)	Total in % (n=490)
yes	79.2	36.5	88.3	70.1	74.7
no	20.8	63.5	11.7	29.9	25.3
Total	100.0	100.0	100.0	100.0	100.0

SOURCE: UNIVERSITY OF BASEL, DEPT. OF GEOGRAPHY AND ALL INDIA DISASTER MITIGATION INSTITUTE, AHMEDABAD, INDIA 2005. SOCIAL SCIENCE SURVEY IN SELECTED SLUM COMMUNITIES IN THE CITY OF BHUJ, GUJARAT, INDIA.

Access to *medical care* does not have priority, as 91.6% answer "no" (Tab. 13.45). Different explanations are possible: either medical care is warranted or people do not have enough money to afford good medical care, and therefore have to set priorities differently.

Table 13.45 Most necessary improvement of access to medical care, by slum.

Slum Medical care	Bhimraonagar in % (n=130)	Jayprakashnagar in % (n=52)	Mustuffanagar in % (n=154)	Shantinagar in % (n=154)	Total in % (n=490)
yes	8.5	13.5	7.1	7.8	8.4
no	91.5	86.5	92.9	92.2	91.6
Total	100.0	100.0	100.0	100.0	100.0

SOURCE: UNIVERSITY OF BASEL, DEPT. OF GEOGRAPHY AND ALL INDIA DISASTER MITIGATION INSTITUTE, AHMEDABAD, INDIA 2005. SOCIAL SCIENCE SURVEY IN SELECTED SLUM COMMUNITIES IN THE CITY OF BHUJ, GUJARAT, INDIA.

The remarkably high percentages of households indicating that *food supply* was not the most necessary improvement (96.1% say "no") should be seen in relation to the ration cards people have (Tab 13.46).

Table 13.46 Most necessary improvement of food supplies, by slum.

Slum Food supplies	Bhimraonagar in % (n=130)	Jayprakashnagar in % (n=52)	Mustuffanagar in % (n=154)	Shantinagar in % (n=154)	Total in % (n=490)
yes	6.9	0.0	2.6	3.9	3.9
no	93.1	100.0	97.4	96.1	96.1
Total	100.0	100.0	100.0	100.0	100.0

SOURCE: UNIVERSITY OF BASEL, DEPT. OF GEOGRAPHY AND ALL INDIA DISASTER MITIGATION INSTITUTE, AHMEDABAD, INDIA 2005. SOCIAL SCIENCE SURVEY IN SELECTED SLUM COMMUNITIES IN THE CITY OF BHUJ, GUJARAT, INDIA.

However, the differences are striking when it comes to the necessity of improvement of sanitation facilities by slums (Tab. 13.47): Whereas in Bhimrao- and Jayprakashnagar, only 36% and 48% of the households view this improvement as most necessary, households in Mustuffa- and Shantinagar clearly express more need of improvements of their sanitation facilities (72.1% and 82.5%). This mirrors the living conditions of the slums that are particularly bad in

Shantinagar, where a majority of the population are tribals. Mustuffanagar, on the other hand, appeared to have rather good living conditions, but a striking majority of the population there used sock-pits (94.9%, Tab. 13.7) and might wish improvement of that.

Table 13.47: Most necessary improvement of sanitation facilities, by slum

Slum / Sanitation facilities	Bhimraonagar in % (n=130)	Jayprakashnagar in % (n=52)	Mustuffanagar in % (n=154)	Shantinagar in % (n=154)	Total in % (n=490)
yes	36.2	48.1	72.1	82.5	63.3
no	63.8	51.9	27.9	17.5	36.7
Total	100.0	100.0	100.0	100.0	100.0

SOURCE: UNIVERSITY OF BASEL, DEPT. OF GEOGRAPHY AND ALL INDIA DISASTER MITIGATION INSTITUTE, AHMEDABAD, INDIA 2005. SOCIAL SCIENCE SURVEY IN SELECTED SLUM COMMUNITIES IN THE CITY OF BHUJ, GUJARAT, INDIA.

74.7% of the slum households wish an improvement of *drinking water* supplies (Tab. 13.48). Since the percentages are distributed similarly in all of the occupation categories, it is difficult to draw any further conclusions.

63.4% of the slum households wish an improvement of *sanitation facilities* (Tab. 13.49). The farmers are clearly above average with 91.7% of the households saying that improvement of sanitation facilities was most necessary. This is probably due to the fact that the largest share of farmers lived in Shantinagar where sanitation facilities are at a very poor level. The three occupation categories vendors, service sector and retiree/housewife/unemployed show the lowest proportions of households indicating that improvement of sanitations facilities was most necessary (40.5% to 58.7%, Tab. 13.49). People working as casual labourers as well as those in automotive related jobs show the highest rates of answers "improvement of sanitation as most necessary improvement", next to the farmers (74.7% to 78.6%, Tab. 13.49). A high share of people working as casual labourers live in Shantinagar where sanitation and water facilities are particularly bad, and awareness of these problems is there. In the occupation category "automotive related jobs", waste water might be a problem, too. A total of 63.4% view the improvement of sanitation facilities as most necessary.

By education. Regardless of the educational background, *drinking water* supplies are equally important for everyone (rates between 70.5% and 83.3%, Tab. 13.50). Improvement of *sanitation facilities* (Tab. 13.51) seems to be a bit less important than the improvement drinking water supplies, but percentages are still between 60.9% and 66.7%.

Table 13.48 Most necessary improvement of housing substance, by occupation of family head.

Occupation / Housing substance	textile/ industry in % (n=36)	government in % (n=13)	casual labour in % (n=83)	construction in % (n=84)	farming in % (n=12)	automotive related job in % (n=42)	vendor/ shop in % (n=42)	crafts in % (n=17)	service sector in % (n=46)	retiree/ housewife/ unemployed in % (n=95)	unclear/ indian in % (n=13)	Total in % (n=483)
yes	80.6	69.2	69.9	81.0	66.7	85.7	66.7	82.4	76.1	73.7	46.2	74.7
no	19.4	30.8	30.1	19.0	33.3	14.3	33.3	17.6	23.9	26.3	53.8	25.3
Total	100.0	100.0	100.0	100.0	100.0	100.0	100.0	100.0	100.0	100.0	100.0	100.0

Table 13.49 Most necessary improvement of drinking water supplies, by occupation of family head.

Occupation / Drinking water	textile/ industry in % (n=36)	government in % (n=13)	casual labour in % (n=83)	construction in % (n=84)	farming in % (n=12)	automotive related job in % (n=42)	vendor/ shop in % (n=42)	crafts in % (n=17)	service sector in % (n=46)	retiree/ housewife/ unemployed in % (n=95)	unclear/ indian in % (n=13)	Total in % (n=483)
yes	66.7	61.5	74.7	61.9	91.7	78.6	40.5	64.7	58.7	53.7	76.9	63.4
no	33.3	38.5	25.3	38.1	8.3	21.4	59.5	35.3	41.3	46.3	23.1	36.6
Total	100.0	100.0	100.0	100.0	100.0	100.0	100.0	100.0	100.0	100.0	100.0	100.0

SOURCE: UNIVERSITY OF BASEL, DEPT. OF GEOGRAPHY AND ALL INDIA DISASTER MITIGATION INSTITUTE, AHMEDABAD, INDIA 2005. SOCIAL SCIENCE SURVEY IN SELECTED SLUM COMMUNITIES IN THE CITY OF BHUJ, GUJARAT, INDIA.

Table 13.50 Most necessary improvement of drinking water supplies, by education standard of family head.

Education / Drinking water	Hrs. 1-3 in % (n=46)	Hrs. 4-6 in % (n=82)	Hrs. 7-9 in % (n=105)	Hrs. 10-12 in % (n=35)	Completed Diploma in % (n=1)	Completed Graduation in % (n=6)	Illiterate in % (n=214)	Total in % (n=489)
yes	78.3	75.6	70.5	82.9	0.0	83.3	74.8	74.8
no	21.7	24.4	29.5	17.1	100.0	16.7	25.2	25.2
Total	100.0	100.0	100.0	100.0	100.0	100.0	100.0	100.0

Table 13.51 Most necessary improvement of sanitation facilities, by education standard of family head.

Education / Sanitation facilities	Hrs. 1-3 in % (n=46)	Hrs. 4-6 in % (n=82)	Hrs. 7-9 in % (n=105)	Hrs. 10-12 in % (n=35)	Completed Diploma in % (n=1)	Completed Graduation in % (n=6)	Illiterate in % (n=214)	Total in % (n=489)
yes	60.9	63.4	66.7	62.9	0.0	66.7	62.6	63.4
no	39.1	36.6	33.3	37.1	100.0	33.3	37.4	36.6
Total	100.0	100.0	100.0	100.0	100.0	100.0	100.0	100.0

SOURCE: UNIVERSITY OF BASEL, DEPT. OF GEOGRAPHY AND ALL INDIA DISASTER MITIGATION INSTITUTE, AHMEDABAD, INDIA 2005. SOCIAL SCIENCE SURVEY IN SELECTED SLUM COMMUNITIES IN THE CITY OF BHUJ, GUJARAT, INDIA.

13.4
Willingness to contribute for better drinking water

The improvement of water is given first priority, with a total of 74.7% of the households wishing an improvement of it. In all of the slums, except for Jayprakashnagar, water is the biggest issue (Tab. 13.44). Since water seems to be such a severe problem for the slum population, the willingness to contribute to better drinking water has been analysed.

By slum (Tab. 13.52). A stunning majority of slum households are willing to pay for a better drinking water supply (80%, Tab. 13.52). In Mustuffanagar, the percentage is even at 90.7%, which might reflect the fact that a large part of the population there – unlike the inhabitants of Shantinagar – would be able to contribute financially. The proportion of households preferring to carry out physical work instead of paying is remarkably higher in Shantinagar than in the other three slums (25.6% in Shantinagar, as compared to rates between 7.1% and 13.1% in the other communities).This is probably due to the financial background of the inhabitants of Shantinagar: given than they are poorer, they have nothing to invest but their labour. However, it is the general willingness to contribute to an improvement of water supply that is important and should invite public agencies to act upon.

Whereas in Jayprakashnagar, 10.7% of the households would participate in AIDMI / other NGO projects, the percentage is much lower in the other communities (around 2%), which possibly indicates that AIDMI`s and other NGO`s work is not known yet to a large part of the population, whereas in Jayprakashnagar, this seems to be the case. The potential of AIDMI and NGOs in general does not seem to be fully utilised.

By occupation (Tab. 13.53). Most of the households, regardless of the occupation of their family head, would be willing to pay for better drinking water supply (80.4%, Tab. 13.52). A total of only 14.7% would carry out physical work in order to improve the drinking water supplies. However, the casual labours see it as an acceptable alternative to paying (24.2%). The participation in AIDMI or NGO projects, in general, does not seem to be an option for most of the households, especially for family heads with lower social positions. One might assume that they also have the least knowledge of and information on NGO work, particularly, if one considers that NGOs work in those communities only began after the earthquake in 2001 and few people had experience with NGOs before that. By contrast, households with a family head doing crafts or employed in the government indicate at 6.3% and 9.9% that they would participate in such projects. They might, on one hand, have more knowledge on NGO projects or, in the case of people working in crafts, already have profited from NGO support or know someone who has.

Table 13.52 Willingness to do something for better drinking water supply, by slum.

Do sth. for drinking water supply	Slum Bhimraonagar in % (n=130)	Jayprakashnagar in % (n=28)	Mustuffanagar in % (n=140)	Shantinagar in % (n=117)	Total in % (n=415)
pay for it (how much, in Rs)	78.5	78.6	90.7	70.9	80.5
carry out physical work	13.1	10.7	7.1	25.6	14.5
participate in AIDMI/NGO projects	2.3	10.7	0.0	2.6	2.2
nothing	6.2	0.0	2.1	0.9	2.9
Total	100.0	100.0	100.0	100.0	100.0

Table 13.53 Willingness to do something for better drinking water supply, by occupation of family head.

Occupation / Do sth. for drinking water supply	textile/ industry in % (n=34)	government in % (n=11)	casual labour in % (n=66)	construction in % (n=75)	farming in % (n=10)	automotive related job in % (n=34)	vendor/ shop in % (n=32)	crafts in % (n=16)	service sector in % (n=36)	retired/ housewife/ unemployed in % (n=84)	unclear/ indian in % (n=11)	Total in % (n=409)
pay for it (how much, in Rs.)	91.2	81.8	69.7	80.0	90.0	88.2	84.4	87.5	91.7	71.4	90.9	80.4
carry out physical work	5.9	9.1	24.2	18.7	10.0	11.8	12.5	6.3	5.6	16.7	9.1	14.7
participate in AIDMI/NGO projects	0.0	9.1	4.5	0.0	0.0	0.0	3.1	0.0	2.8	3.6	0.0	2.2
nothing	2.9	0.0	1.5	1.3	0.0	0.0	0.0	6.3	0.0	8.3	0.0	2.7
Total	100.0	100.0	100.0	100.0	100.0	100.0	100.0	100.0	100.0	100.0	100.0	100.0

SOURCE: UNIVERSITY OF BASEL, DEPT. OF GEOGRAPHY AND ALL INDIA DISASTER MITIGATION INSTITUTE, AHMEDABAD, INDIA 2005. SOCIAL SCIENCE SURVEY IN SELECTED SLUM COMMUNITIES IN THE CITY OF BHUJ, GUJARAT, INDIA.

By caste (Tab. 13.54). A total of 80.4% of all households would pay for better drinking water, with the exception of ST: only 48.9% would pay, but 31% would carry out physical work. 11% of the ST households would not do anything. Particularly the rather high proportion of those who would do nothing for better drinking water supply might reflect the lacking comprehension of the necessity to contribute oneself in order to make a difference.

Table 13.54 Willingness to do something for better drinking water supply, by caste.

Do sth. for drinking water supply	Caste	SC in % (n=70)	ST in % (n=45)	OBC in % (n=155)	General in % (n=144)	Total in % (n=414)
pay for it (how much, in Rs.)		80.0	48.9	83.9	86.8	80.4
carry out physical work		12.9	31.1	14.8	9.7	14.5
participate in AIDMI/NGO projects		2.9	8.9	0.0	2.1	2.2
nothing		4.3	11.1	1.3	1.4	2.9
Total		100.0	100.0	100.0	100.0	100.0

SOURCE: UNIVERSITY OF BASEL, DEPT. OF GEOGRAPHY AND ALL INDIA DISASTER MITIGATION INSTITUTE, AHMEDABAD, INDIA 2005. SOCIAL SCIENCE SURVEY IN SELECTED SLUM COMMUNITIES IN THE CITY OF BHUJ, GUJARAT, INDIA.

By education (Tab. 13.55). There is a tendency that with rising education standards, the percentage of those willing to pay better services also increases. (Standard 1-3: 81.4%, Standard 10-12: 84.8%, Tab. 13.55). The illiterates show the lowest proportion of households willing to contribute financially (73.1%, as compared to rates between 81.4% and 89.2% for other categories), at the same, the have the highest share of households willing to carry out physical work. This might be due to their generally weak financial situation. They also show the highest percentage of households not willing to do anything for an improvement (4.4%), probably, because some feel simply left alone by the government that should provide certain services. However, one can see that willingness to contribute, be it financially or physically, is generally there and a potential that needs to be utilised in order to improve the living conditions.

By average daily wages (Tab. 13.56). Clearly, the more people earn, the more they prefer paying for better drinking water supply to carrying out physical work (0-9 Rs.: 58.1%, 30-39 Rs.: 86.7% of the households would pay, Tab. 13.56). The least income category shows the highest percentage of households not willing to do anything for better drinking water supply (9.7%). Awareness for the necessity of people's participation in order to improve services must be risen. Even if providing infrastructural services is part of the government's responsibility, the people themselves must participate in efforts to improve the living conditions, because their own behaviour and participation makes a difference and helps improve things. Everyone needs to contribute the way they are able to.

Table 13.55 Willingness to do something for better drinking water supply, by education standard of family head.

Education Do sth. for drinking water supply	Hrs. 1-3 in % (n=43)	Hrs. 4-6 in % (n=68)	Hrs. 7-9 in % (n=83)	Hrs. 10-12 in % (n=33)	Completed Diploma in % (n=0)	Completed Graduation in % (n=6)	Illiterate in % (n=182)	Total in % (n=415)
pay for it (how much, in Rs.)	81.4	85.3	89.2	84.8	0.0	100.0	73.1	80.5
carry out physical work	16.3	8.8	7.2	12.1	0.0	0.0	20.3	14.5
participate in AIDMI/NGO projects	0.0	2.9	2.4	3.0	0.0	0.0	2.2	2.2
nothing	2.3	2.9	1.2	0.0	0.0	0.0	4.4	2.9
Total	100.0	100.0	100.0	100.0	0.0	100.0	100.0	100.0

SOURCE: UNIVERSITY OF BASEL, DEPT. OF GEOGRAPHY AND ALL INDIA DISASTER MITIGATION INSTITUTE, AHMEDABAD, INDIA 2005. SOCIAL SCIENCE SURVEY IN SELECTED SLUM COMMUNITIES IN THE CITY OF BHUJ, GUJARAT, INDIA.

Table 13.56 Willingness to do something for better drinking water supply, by average daily wages of household members (in Rs.).

Wage Do sth. for drinking water supply	0 to 9 Rs. in % (n=31)	10 to 19 Rs. in % (n=142)	20 to 29 Rs. in % (n=116)	30 to 39 Rs. in % (n=60)	40 to 49 Rs. in % (n=22)	50 to 89 Rs. in % (n=24)	90 to 130 Rs. in % (n=5)	Total in % (n=400)
pay for it	58.1	76.1	83.6	86.7	100.0	95.8	80.0	81.0
carry out physical work	32.3	17.6	13.8	10.0	0.0	0.0	0.0	14.3
participate in DMI/NGO projects	0.0	4.2	0.9	0.0	0.0	4.2	20.0	2.3
nothing	9.7	2.1	1.7	3.3	0.0	0.0	0.0	2.5
Total	100.0	100.0	100.0	100.0	100.0	100.0	100.0	100.0

SOURCE: UNIVERSITY OF BASEL, DEPT. OF GEOGRAPHY AND ALL INDIA DISASTER MITIGATION INSTITUTE, AHMEDABAD, INDIA 2005. SOCIAL SCIENCE SURVEY IN SELECTED SLUM COMMUNITIES IN THE CITY OF BHUJ, GUJARAT, INDIA.

By religion (Tab. 13.57). It seems that the willingness to contribute is not related to religion in any way.

Table 13.57 Willingness to do something for better drinking water supply, by religion.

Religion Do sth. for drinking water supply	Hindu in % (n=172)	Muslim in % (n=241)	Total in % (n=413)
pay for it (how much, in Rs.)	79.7	81.3	80.6
carry out physical work	12.8	15.4	14.3
participate in AIDMI/NGO projects	4.1	0.8	2.2
nothing	3.5	2.5	2.9
Total	100.0	100.0	100.0

SOURCE: UNIVERSITY OF BASEL, DEPT. OF GEOGRAPHY AND ALL INDIA DISASTER MITIGATION INSTITUTE, AHMEDABAD, INDIA 2005. SOCIAL SCIENCE SURVEY IN SELECTED SLUM COMMUNITIES IN THE CITY OF BHUJ, GUJARAT, INDIA.

13.5 Conclusion

The slum households generally prefer to pay for better drinking water. To carry out physical work is only an option for poorer people who do not have money but can work. The people who had significantly high percentages in this category were illiterates, scheduled tribes, casual labourers and in general people with a low income. To improve the services it is important to take these differences into account and to insure that everyone who wants improvements can take part in the contribution, be it with financial or physical strength. It is also conceivable, that people are more willing to invest in a service which they will have at home than in a service which would serve the whole community, like clearing up the waste water and rubbish.

Map 13.1 Water facilities in Bhimraonagar

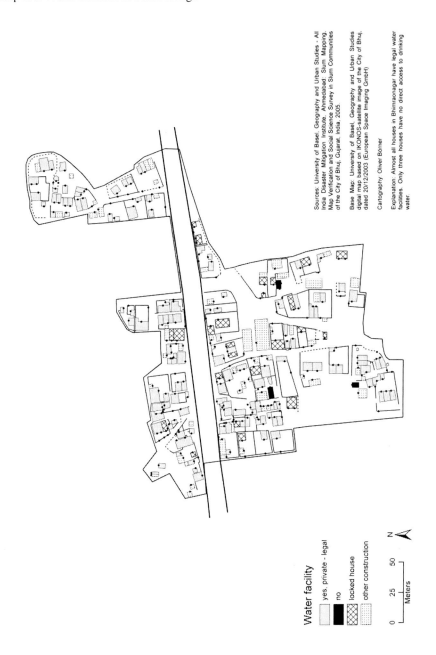

Map 13.2 Water facilities in Jayprakashnagar

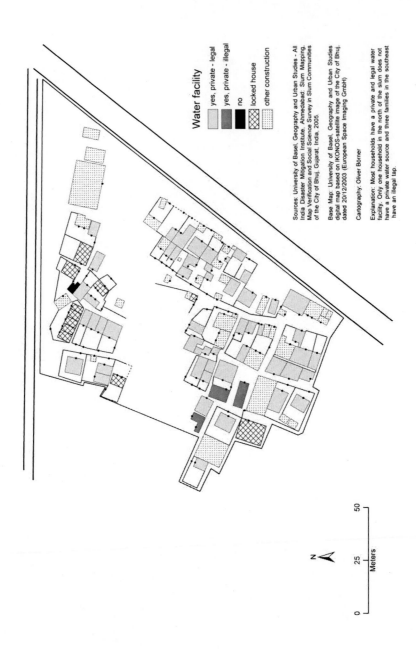

Map 13.3 Water facilities in Mustuffanagar

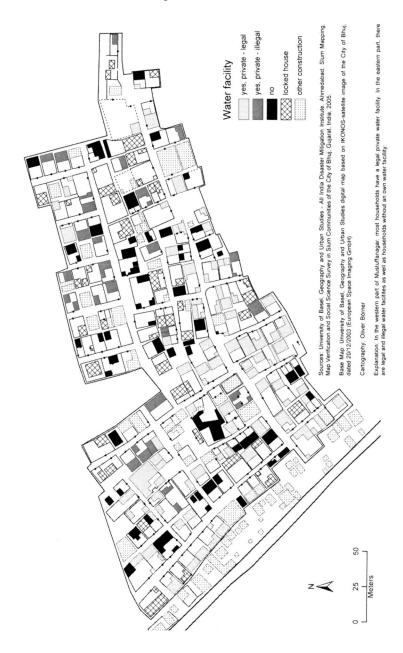

248   Willingness to contribute towards infrastructural services

Map 13.4 Water facilities in Shantinagar

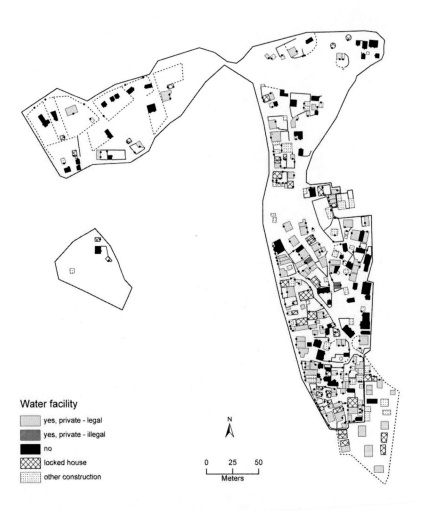

Sources: University of Basel, Geography and Urban Studies - All India Disaster Mitigation Institute, Ahmedabad: Slum Mapping, Map Verification and Social Science Survey in Slum Communities of the City of Bhuj, Gujarat, India, 2005.

Base Map: University of Basel, Geography and Urban Studies digital map based on IKONOS-satellite image of the City of Bhuj, dated 20/12/2003 (European Space Imaging GmbH)

Cartography: Oliver Börner

Explanation: It is striking that still quite a few houses do not have an own water facility. Clusters are visible in the northern and central parts, particularly in the area where tribal people reside.

Map 13.5 Water sources in Bhimraonagar

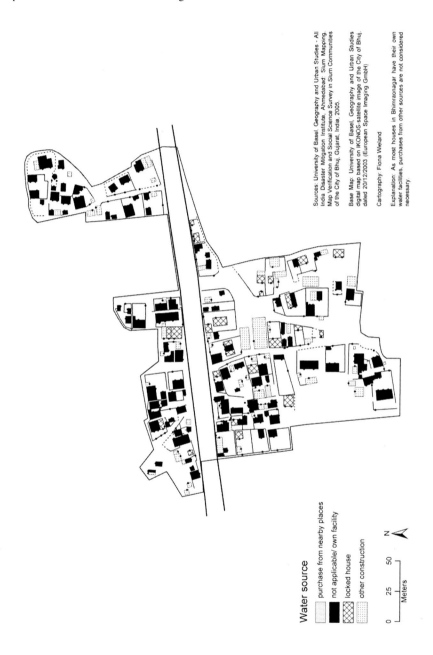

250 Willingness to contribute towards infrastructural services

Map 13.6 Water sources in Jayprakashnagar

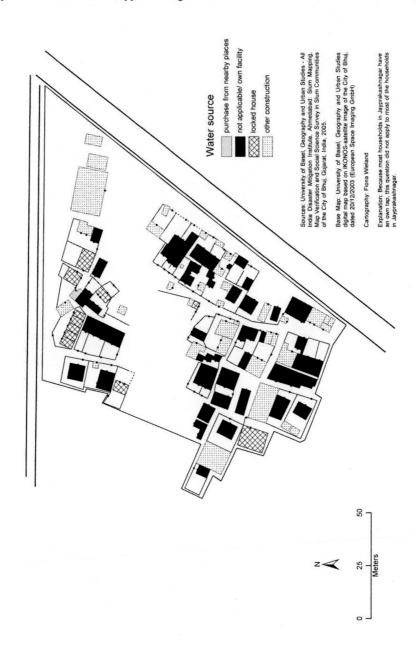

Willingness to contribute towards infrastructural services 251

Map 13.7 Water sources in Mustuffanagar

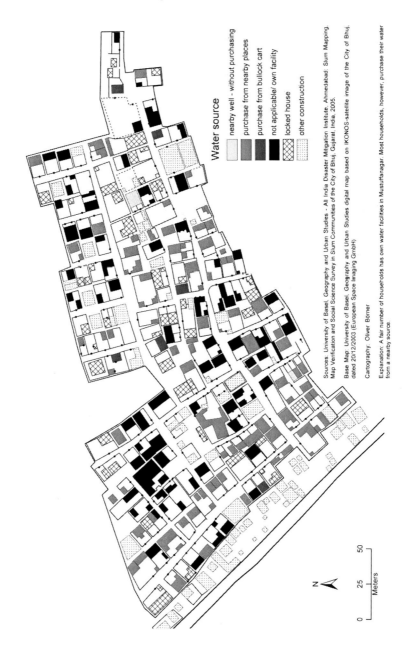

Map 13.8 Water sources in Shantinagar

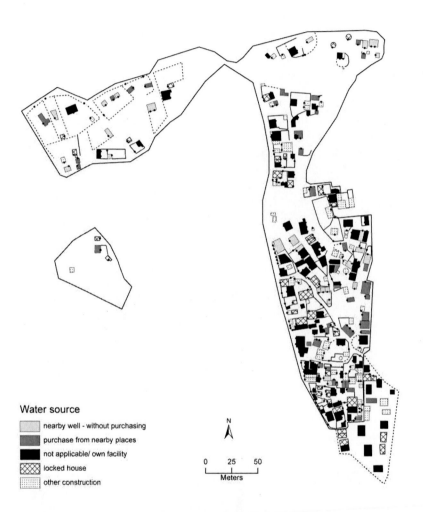

Map 13.9 Households using water treatment, Bhimraonagar

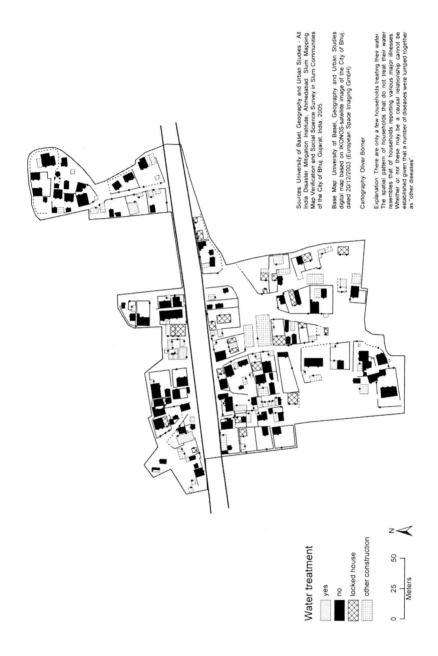

254 Willingness to contribute towards infrastructural services

Map 13.10 Households using water treatment, Jayprakashnagar

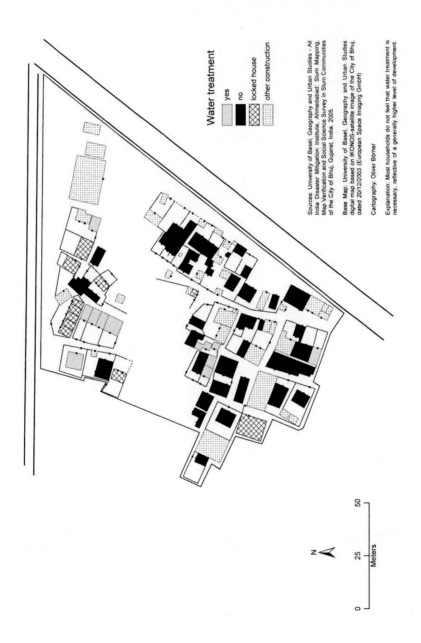

Willingness to contribute towards infrastructural services 255

Map 13.11 Households using water treatment, Mustuffanagar

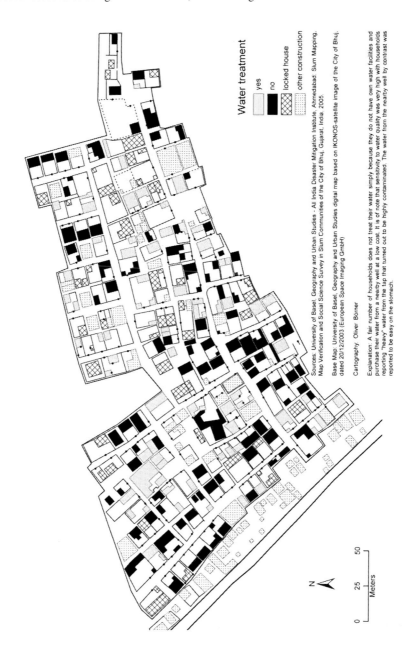

256 Willingness to contribute towards infrastructural services

Map 13.12 Households using water treatment, Shantinagar

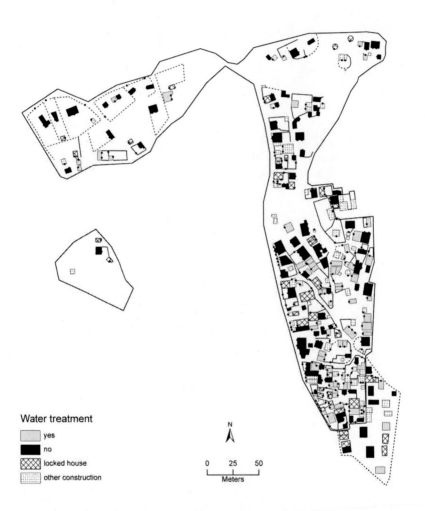

Sources: University of Basel, Geography and Urban Studies - All India Disaster Mitigation Institute, Ahmedabad: Slum Mapping, Map Verification and Social Science Survey in Slum Communities of the City of Bhuj, Gujarat, India, 2005.

Base Map: University of Basel, Geography and Urban Studies digital map based on IKONOS-satellite image of the City of Bhuj, dated 20/12/2003 (European Space Imaging GmbH)

Cartography: Oliver Börner

Explanation: A rather large number of households, primarily tribals, does not treat their water.

Map 13.13 Households with electricity, Bhimraonagar

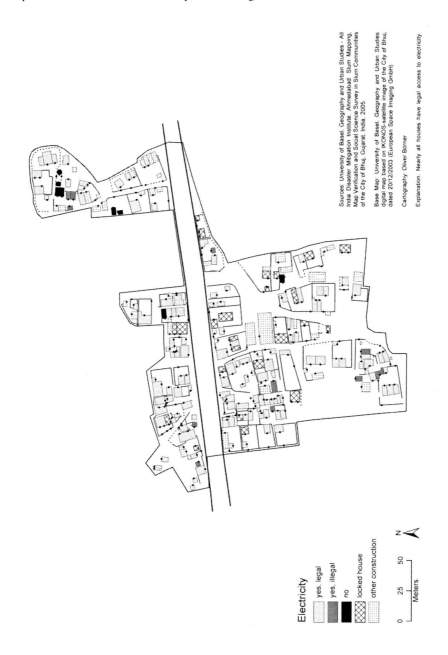

Map 13.14 Households with electricity, Jayprakashnagar

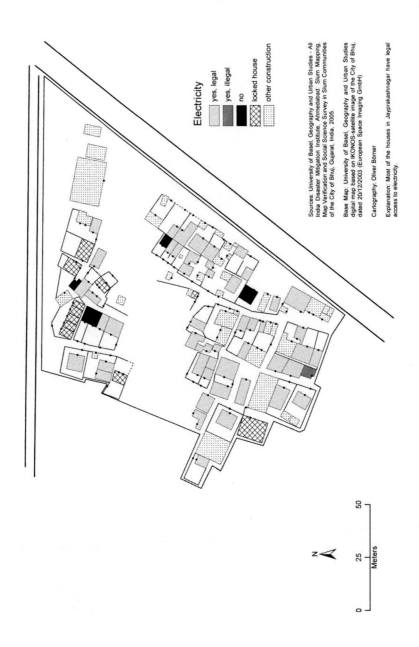

Map 13.15 Households with electricity, Mustuffanagar

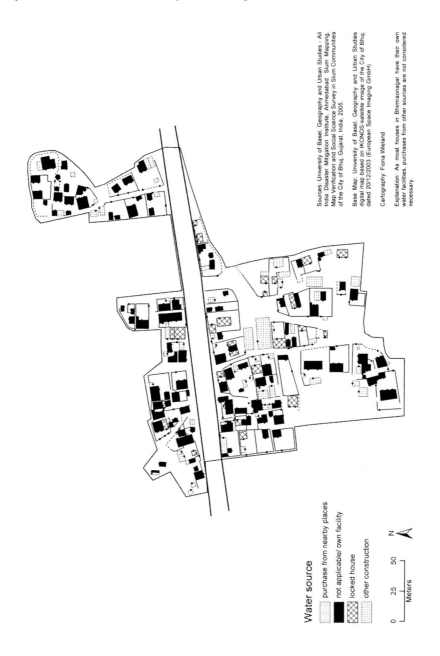

Map 13.16 Households with electricity, Shantinagar

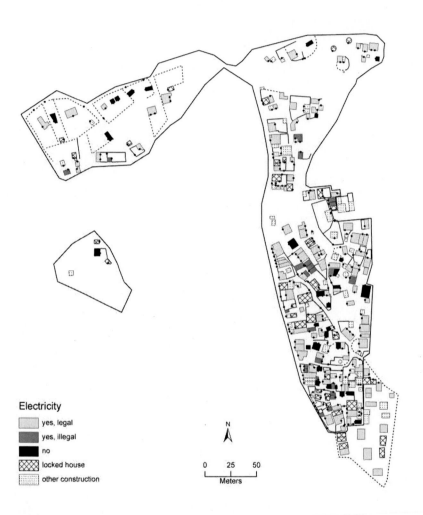

Map 13.17 Households with toilets, Bhimraonagar

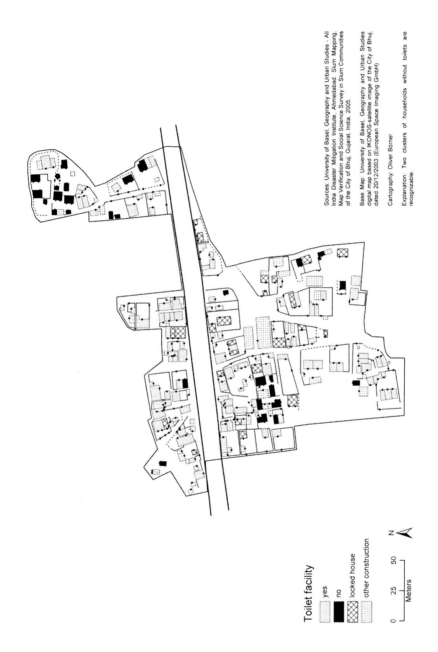

Map 13.18 Households with toilets, Jayprakashnagar

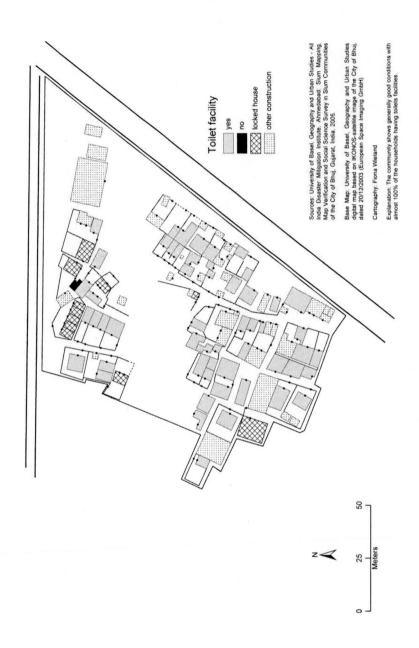

Map 13.19 Households with toilets, Mustuffanagar

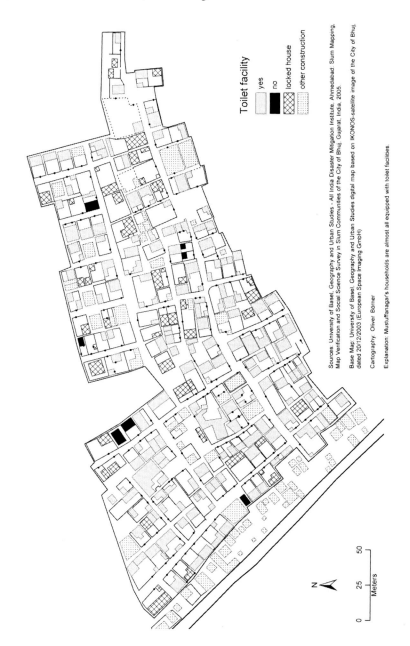

Map 13.20 Households with toilets, Shantinagar

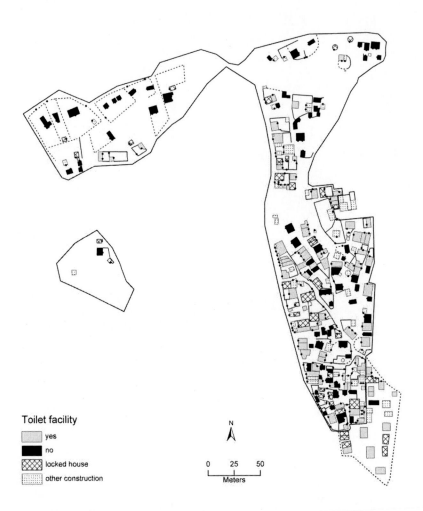

Sources: University of Basel, Geography and Urban Studies - All India Disaster Mitigation Institute, Ahmedabad: Slum Mapping, Map Verification and Social Science Survey in Slum Communities of the City of Bhuj, Gujarat, India, 2005.

Base Map: University of Basel, Geography and Urban Studies digital map based on IKONOS-satellite image of the City of Bhuj, dated 20/12/2003 (European Space Imaging GmbH)

Cartography: Oliver Börner

Explanation: A large number of households have no toilet facilities. The spatial pattern identifies tribal, but also non-tribal households.

Map 13.21 Households with access to the sewerage system, Bhimraonagar

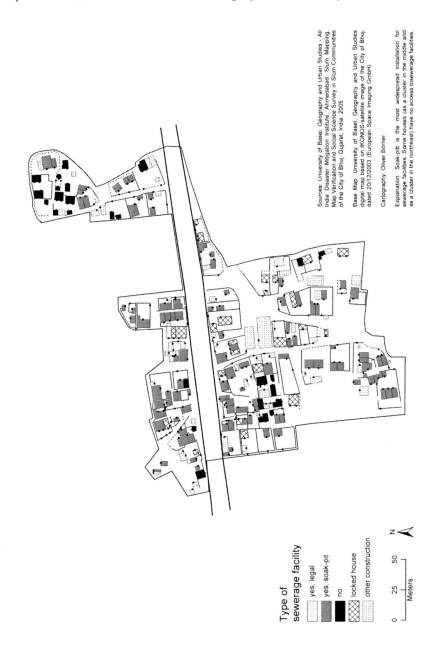

Map 13.22 Households with access to the sewerage system, Jayprakashnagar

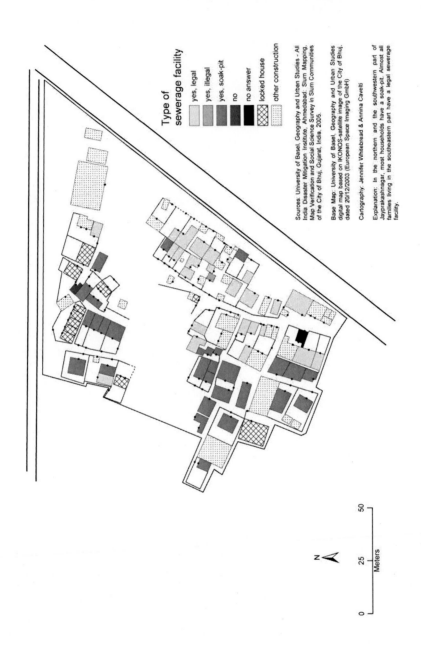

Map 13.23 Households with access to the sewerage system, Mustuffanagar

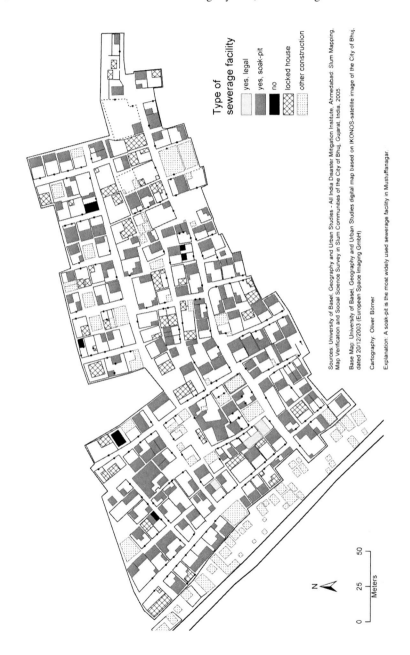

Map 13.24 Households with access to the sewerage system, Shantinagar

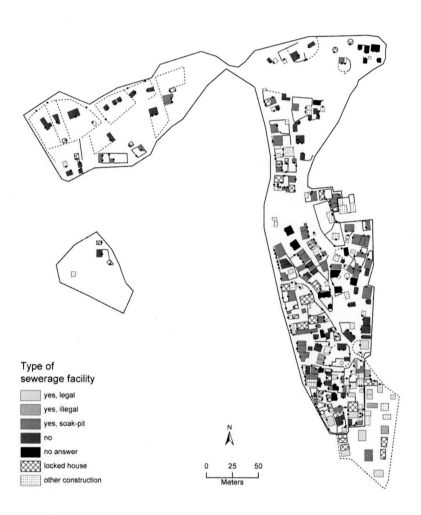

Sources: University of Basel, Geography and Urban Studies - All India Disaster Mitigation Institute, Ahmedabad: Slum Mapping, Map Verification and Social Science Survey in Slum Communities of the City of Bhuj, Gujarat, India, 2005.

Base Map: University of Basel, Geography and Urban Studies digital map based on IKONOS-satellite image of the City of Bhuj, dated 20/12/2003 (European Space Imaging GmbH)

Cartography: Oliver Börner

Explanation: While a soak-pit is the most common form of sewerage facility in Shantinagar, there are still many tribal and non-tribal households without a legal facility at all.

Map 13.25 Felt need for the improvement of the housing substance, Bhimraonagar

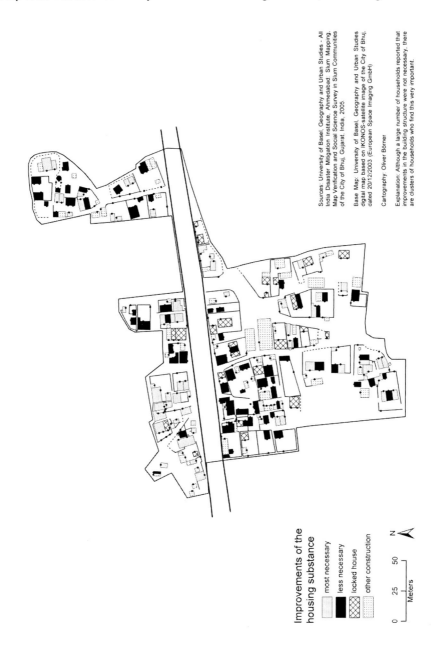

Map 13.26 Felt need for the improvement of the housing substance, Jayprakashnagar

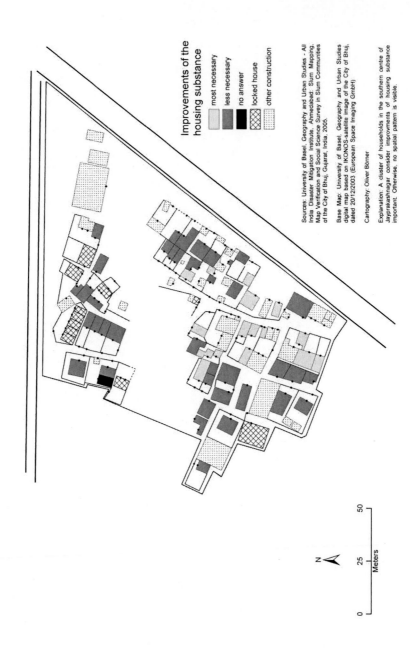

Willingness to contribute towards infrastructural services 271

Map 13.27 Felt need for the improvement of the housing substance, Mustuffanagar

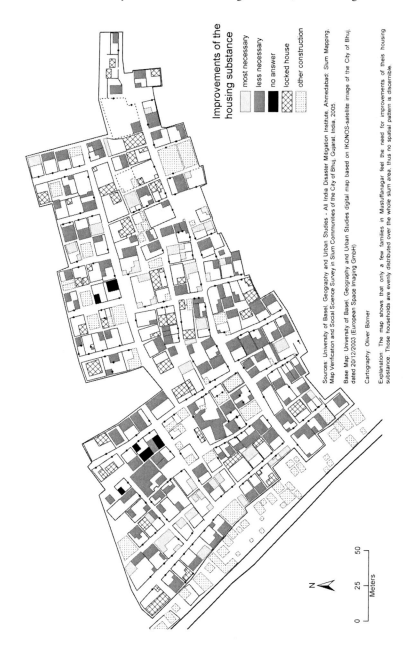

Map 13.28 Felt need for the improvement of the housing substance, Shantinagar

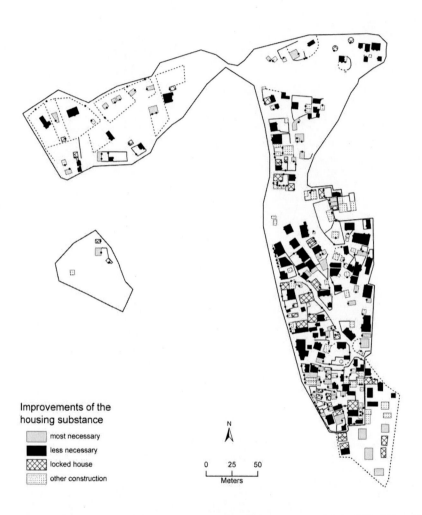

Map 13.29 Felt need for the improvement of drinking water supplies, Bhimraonagar

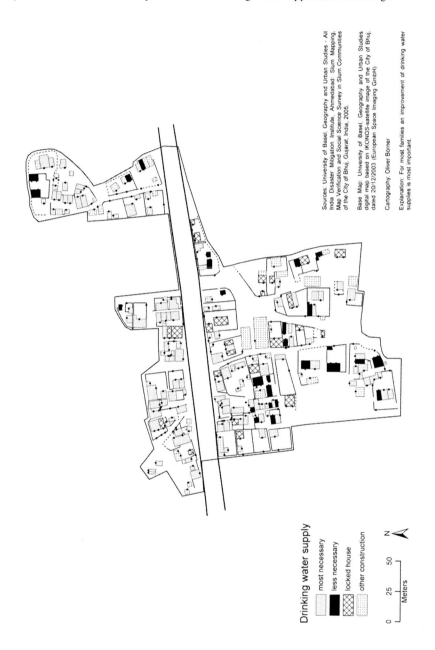

Map 13.30 Felt need for the improvement of drinking water supplies, Jayprakashnagar

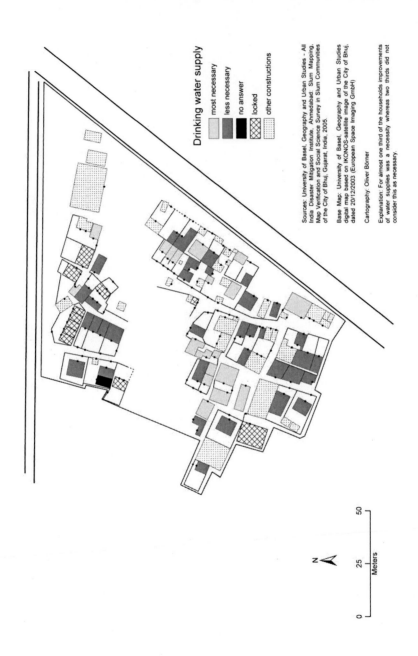

Map 13.31 Felt need for the improvement of drinking water supplies, Mustuffanagar

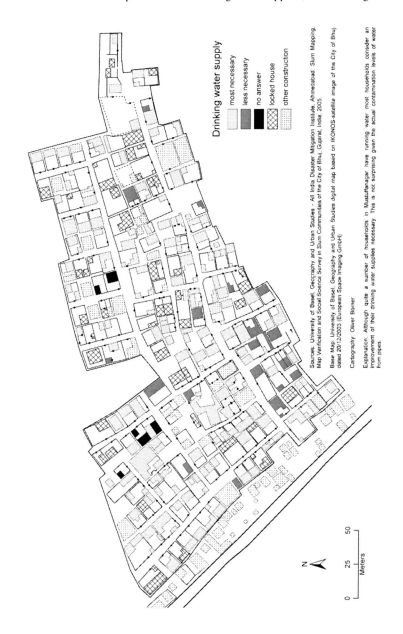

276   Willingness to contribute towards infrastructural services

Map 13.32 Felt need for the improvement of drinking water supplies, Shantinagar

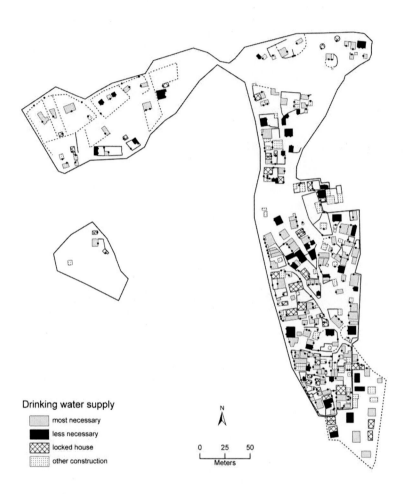

Sources: University of Basel, Geography and Urban Studies - All India Disaster Mitigation Institute, Ahmedabad: Slum Mapping, Map Verification and Social Science Survey in Slum Communities of the City of Bhuj, Gujarat, India, 2005.

Base Map: University of Basel, Geography and Urban Studies digital map based on IKONOS-satellite image of the City of Bhuj, dated 20/12/2003 (European Space Imaging GmbH)

Cartography: Oliver Börner

Explanation: For most families the improvement of their drinking water supplies was most important.

Map 13.33 Felt need for the improvement of sanitation facilities, Bhimraonagar

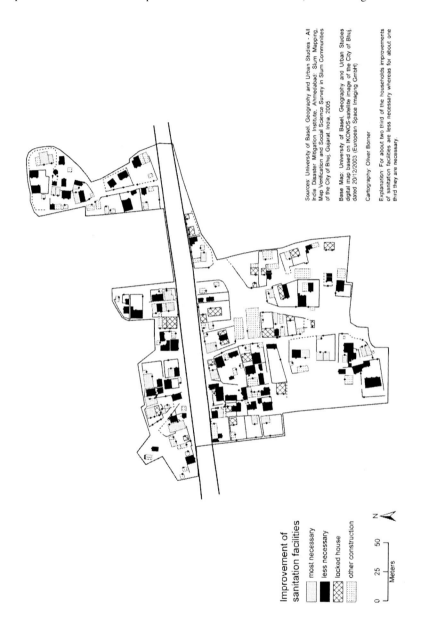

Map 13.34 Felt need for the improvement of sanitation facilities, Jayprakashnagar

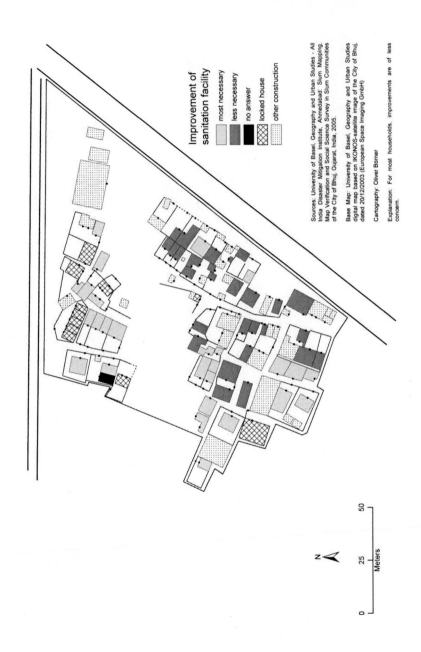

Map 13.35 Felt need for the improvement of sanitation facilities, Mustuffanagar

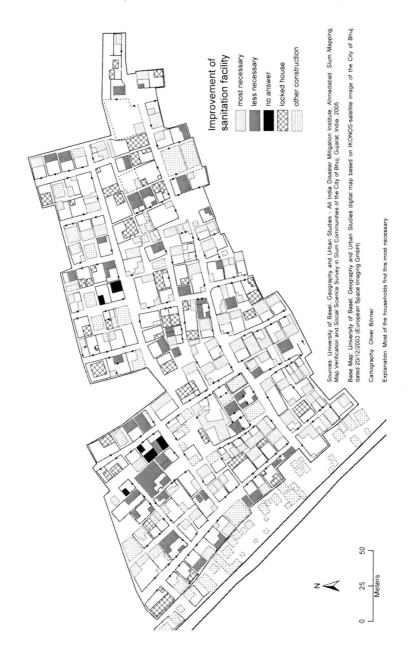

Map 13.36 Felt need for the improvement of sanitation facilities, Shantinagar

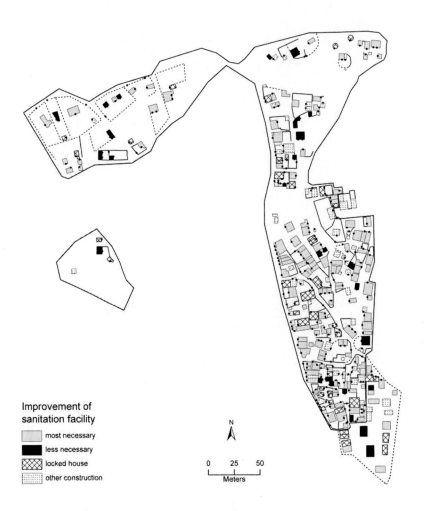

Sources: University of Basel, Geography and Urban Studies - All India Disaster Mitigation Institute, Ahmedabad: Slum Mapping, Map Verification and Social Science Survey in Slum Communities of the City of Bhuj, Gujarat, India, 2005.

Base Map: University of Basel, Geography and Urban Studies digital map based on IKONOS-satellite image of the City of Bhuj, dated 20/12/2003 (European Space Imaging GmbH)

Cartography: Oliver Börner

Explanation: For almost all households of the community improvement of sanitation facilities was a major concern.

Willingness to contribute towards infrastructural services 281

Map 13.37 Willingness to contribute towards better drinking water supplies, Bhimraonagar

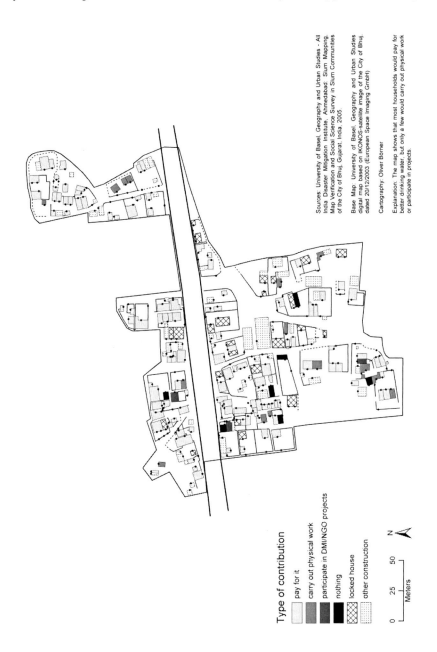

Map 13.38 Willingness to contribute towards better drinking water supplies, Jayprakashnagar

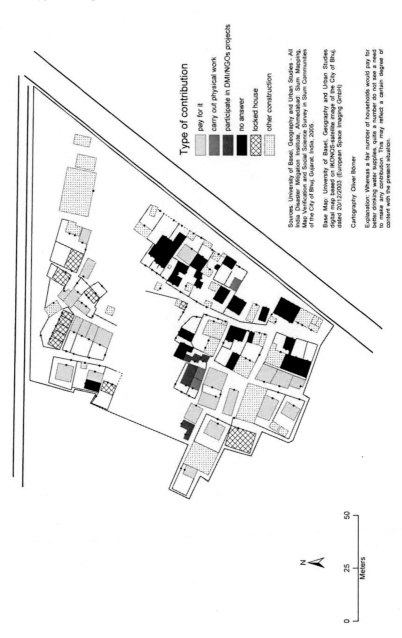

Map 13.39 Willingness to contribute towards better drinking water supplies, Mustuffanagar

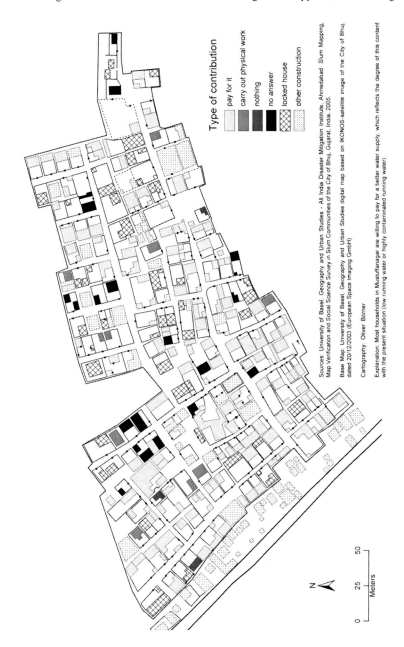

Map 13.40 Willingness to contribute towards better drinking water supplies, Shantinagar

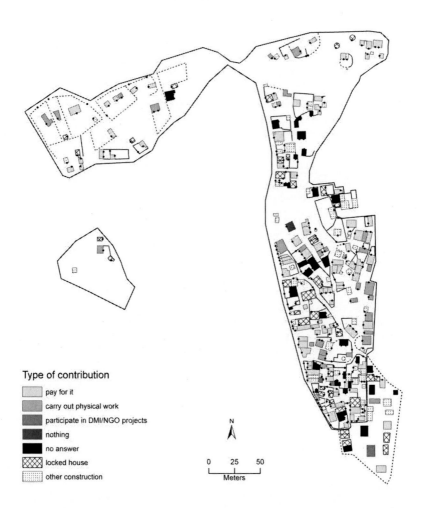

Sources: University of Basel, Geography and Urban Studies - All India Disaster Mitigation Institute, Ahmedabad: Slum Mapping, Map Verification and Social Science Survey in Slum Communities of the City of Bhuj, Gujarat, India, 2005.

Base Map: University of Basel, Geography and Urban Studies digital map based on IKONOS-satellite image of the City of Bhuj, dated 20/12/2003 (European Space Imaging GmbH)

Cartography: Oliver Börner

Explanation: Better water is of major concern in Shantinagar. Since most households are rather poor many are willing to carry out physical work for a better drinking water supply.

14 Willingness to pay for the legalization of land

M. Barmettler, R. Schneider-Sliwa, P. Thum
University of Basel

14.1
Introduction

This chapter investigates the readiness of the households to contribute to providing infrastructural services at home. The main infrastructural services included in the survey were: provision of drinking water, drainage and sanitation as well as solid waste removal. The main points of interest were:

- Which types of households are willing to pay for such services?
- What influences the households in their respective willingness to pay?
- Can the willingness to pay be raised if there is a shared financial responsibility?
- How much and to what extent are people willing to pay for the legalization of their property?
- Are the households willing to pay taxes?
- In the view of the slum households, what are the most urgent governmental benefit schemes?

The data for this chapter was collected in a household based survey, in which the statement of the family head reflected the opinion of the whole family. The most important factors concerning the above questions were livelihood factors such as income and occupation. Others, such as sex, age, caste and religion have also been tested, but have not found to be explanatory.

14.2
Good drinking water, drainage/sanitation, solid waste removal

By average daily wages of household members in Rs. (Tab. 14.1, 14.2 and 14.3).
Wealthier families are less willing to spend large amounts for good drinking water than poorer ones. They probably already have access to good water or can purchase it easily. Thus, they might not see the need to spend additional amounts.

In Mustuffanagar, for example, there is a hand pump near the main road where one can buy drinking water. This water is of much better quality than the one people get from their own hand pump within their compound wall (Tab. 14.1). Low income households show a comparatively strong interest to invest in drainage and sanitation. The readiness to do so varies among the households that are in a better situation (daily wages of 50 to 89 Rs.): More than 30% of them are willing to invest more than 500 Rs., but at the same time, more than 20% are not willing to pay more than 50 Rs. per month (Tab. 14.2). Solid waste removal is seen as a real problem, with 80% of all households being ready to pay up to 170 Rs. per month. However, neither the wealthier nor the poor families do not seem to be willing to spend high amounts on solid waste removal. Only 10% would pay up to 400 Rs. per month (Tab. 14.3). This is an important problem, as – probably due to their illegal status – slum areas are often neglected by the municipal cleaning agencies, and the litter gravely influences the living conditions of the slum dwellers. Yet, it seems that people`s awareness on how they can influence the waste problem through their financial participation must be raised.

Table 14.1 Willingness to pay for good drinking water (per month in Rs.), by average daily wages of household members(in Rs.).

Wage / Pay for good drinking water	0 to 9 Rs. in % (n=24)	10 to 19 Rs. in % (n=147)	20 to 29 Rs. in % (n=123)	30 to 39 Rs. in % (n=60)	40 to 49 Rs. in % (n=24)	50 to 89 Rs. in % (n=23)	90 to 130 Rs. in % (n=5)	Total in % (n=406)
1 to 60	12.5	15.0	13.8	13.3	20.8	17.4	20.0	14.8
61 to 200	50.0	22.4	16.3	20.0	8.3	17.4	20.0	20.7
201 to 400	12.5	28.6	16.3	18.3	29.2	17.4	60.0	22.2
401 to 600	12.5	22.4	29.3	16.7	8.3	21.7	0.0	21.9
› 601	12.5	11.6	24.4	31.7	33.3	26.1	0.0	20.4
Total	100.0	100.0	100.0	100.0	100.0	100.0	100.0	100.0

SOURCE: UNIVERSITY OF BASEL, DEPT. OF GEOGRAPHY AND ALL INDIA DISASTER MITIGATION INSTITUTE, AHMEDABAD, INDIA 2005. SOCIAL SCIENCE SURVEY IN SELECTED SLUM COMMUNITIES IN THE CITY OF BHUJ, GUJARAT, INDIA.

Table 14.2 Willingness to pay for drainage and sanitation (per month in Rs.), by average daily wages of household members(in Rs.).

Wage Pay for drainage and sanitation	0 to 9 Rs. in % (n=30)	10 to 19 Rs. in % (n=154)	20 to 29 Rs. in % (n=127)	30 to 39 Rs. in % (n=62)	40 to 49 Rs. in % (n=24)	50 to 89 Rs. in % (n=29)	90 to 130 Rs. in % (n=5)	Total in % (n=431)
1 to 50	26.7	25.3	22.0	16.1	33.3	20.7	20.0	23.2
51 to 100	20.0	5.8	3.1	11.3	4.2	3.4	0.0	6.5
101 to 200	23.3	24.7	14.2	21.0	8.3	13.8	20.0	19.3
201 to 300	0.0	11.7	8.7	3.2	0.0	10.3	20.0	8.1
301 to 500	20.0	20.1	28.3	24.2	20.8	17.2	40.0	23.2
› 501	10.0	12.3	23.6	24.2	33.3	34.5	0.0	19.7
Total	100.0	100.0	100.0	100.0	100.0	100.0	100.0	100.0

SOURCE: UNIVERSITY OF BASEL, DEPT. OF GEOGRAPHY AND ALL INDIA DISASTER MITIGATION INSTITUTE, AHMEDABAD, INDIA 2005. SOCIAL SCIENCE SURVEY IN SELECTED SLUM COMMUNITIES IN THE CITY OF BHUJ, GUJARAT, INDIA.

Table 14.3 Willingness to pay for solid waste removal (per month in Rs.), by average daily wages of household members(in Rs.)

Wage Pay for solid waste removal	0 to 9 Rs. in % (n=21)	10 to 19 Rs. in % (n=124)	20 to 29 Rs. in % (n=103)	30 to 39 Rs. in % (n=51)	40 to 49 Rs. in % (n=21)	50 to 89 Rs. in % (n=28)	90 to 130 Rs. in % (n=5)	Total in % (n=353)
1 to 9	28.6	22.6	18.4	13.7	28.6	10.7	20.0	19.8
10 to 15	28.6	22.6	21.4	11.8	0.0	7.1	40.0	18.7
16 to 40	0.0	8.9	18.4	19.6	0.0	21.4	0.0	13.0
41 to 170	28.6	23.4	28.2	27.5	33.3	46.4	0.0	27.8
171 to 400	4.8	12.9	5.8	15.7	19.0	0.0	40.0	10.5
401 to 700	9.5	5.6	2.9	9.8	9.5	14.3	0.0	6.5
› 701	0.0	4.0	4.9	2.0	9.5	0.0	0.0	3.7
Total	100.0	100.0	100.0	100.0	100.0	100.0	100.0	100.0

SOURCE: UNIVERSITY OF BASEL, DEPT. OF GEOGRAPHY AND ALL INDIA DISASTER MITIGATION INSTITUTE, AHMEDABAD, INDIA 2005. SOCIAL SCIENCE SURVEY IN SELECTED SLUM COMMUNITIES IN THE CITY OF BHUJ, GUJARAT, INDIA.

By slum (Tab. 14.4, 14.5 and 14.6). In Bhimraonagar, only a small percentage of the households affirm the willingness to pay low amounts (1 to 60 Rs.) for good drinking water, for drainage and sanitation, as well as for solid waste removal. By contrast, a large proportion of families (26.1%) is willing to spend high amounts. It is possible that the living conditions in this slum are very bad, which corresponds to the impression on site: the solid waste problem in Bhimraonagar seemed to be worse than in other slum areas.

The findings for Jayprakashnagar are exactly contrary to Bhimraonagar. 80% are willing to invest only between 1 and 60 Rs. This is explained by the fact that there seemed to be some responsible persons for the removal of solid waste – the slum was wiped clean every morning. Whether this was an own initiative by the inhabitants of Jayprakashnagar, or whether it was due to the fact that some houses are legal and this particular community is economically comparably well off, can not be said for sure.

In Mustuffanagar und Shantinagar, the percentages indicating the willingness to invest in good drinking water and drainage and sanitation systems are similarly distributed (Tab. 14.4 and 14.5). However, in Mustuffanagar, as compared to Shantinagar, higher proportions of people would pay amounts from 171 to over 600 Rupees a month in order to have solid waste removal (Tab. 14.6). On one hand, waste seemed to be a serious issue in Mustuffanagar, which might explain why high shares of households are willing to pay much for a solution of this problem, but on the other hand, although waste removal is a severe problem in Shantinagar, people there could not afford to spend high amounts on an improvement of the situation. The problems seem to be the same in all four communities (drinking water, drainage and sanitation as well as waste), but the amounts people are willing or able to invest mirror the different economic situation of the slums.

Table 14.4 Willingness to pay for good drinking water (per month in Rs.), by slum

Slum / Pay For good drinking water	Bhimraonagar in % (n=124)	Jayprakashnagar in % (n=30)	Mustuffanagar in % (n=145)	Shantinagar in % (n=122)	Total in % (n=421)
1 to 60	0.8	80.0	12.4	17.2	15.2
61 to 200	22.6	0.0	20.7	26.2	21.4
201 to 400	16.9	10.0	24.8	25.4	21.6
401 to 600	26.6	6.7	22.1	19.7	21.6
› 601	33.1	3.3	20.0	11.5	20.2
Total	100.0	100.0	100.0	100.0	100.0

SOURCE: UNIVERSITY OF BASEL, DEPT. OF GEOGRAPHY AND ALL INDIA DISASTER MITIGATION INSTITUTE, AHMEDABAD, INDIA 2005. SOCIAL SCIENCE SURVEY IN SELECTED SLUM COMMUNITIES IN THE CITY OF BHUJ, GUJARAT, INDIA.

Table 14.5 Willingness to pay for drainage and sanitation (per month in Rs.), by slum

Slum / Pay for drainage and sanitation	Bhimraona-gar in % (n=122)	Jayprakashna-gar in % (n=31)	Mustuffana-gar in % (n=147)	Shantina-gar in % (n=147)	Total in % (n=447)
1 to 50	4.1	87.1	22.4	26.5	23.3
51 to 100	6.6	0.0	7.5	8.8	7.2
101 to 200	18.0	3.2	20.4	22.4	19.2
201 to 300	11.5	0.0	8.8	6.1	8.1
301 to 500	35.2	6.5	20.4	18.4	22.8
› 501	24.6	3.2	20.4	17.7	19.5
Total	100.0	100.0	100.0	100.0	100.0

SOURCE: UNIVERSITY OF BASEL, DEPT. OF GEOGRAPHY AND ALL INDIA DISASTER MITIGATION INSTITUTE, AHMEDABAD, INDIA 2005. SOCIAL SCIENCE SURVEY IN SELECTED SLUM COMMUNITIES IN THE CITY OF BHUJ, GUJARAT, INDIA.

Table 14.6 Willingness to pay for solid waste removal (per month in Rs.), by slum.

Slum Pay for solid waste removal	Bhimraonagar in % (n=96)	Jayprakashnagar in % (n=30)	Mustuffanagar in % (n=128)	Shantinagar in % (n=112)	Total in % (n=366)
1 to 9	3.1	73.3	14.1	27.7	20.2
10 to 15	15.6	6.7	20.3	25.0	19.4
16 to 40	20.8	3.3	7.0	15.2	12.8
41 to 170	26.0	13.3	33.6	24.1	27.0
› 171	34.4	3.3	25.0	8.0	20.5
Total	100.0	100.0	100.0	100.0	100.0

SOURCE: UNIVERSITY OF BASEL, DEPT. OF GEOGRAPHY AND ALL INDIA DISASTER MITIGATION INSTITUTE, AHMEDABAD, INDIA 2005. SOCIAL SCIENCE SURVEY IN SELECTED SLUM COMMUNITIES IN THE CITY OF BHUJ, GUJARAT, INDIA.

14.3
Affordable amount of money to legalize the land (in Rs.)

By average daily wage of household members in Rs. (Tab. 14.7). The households are generally interested in legalizing the land they occupy. There is a general tendency that those who earn more are also willing – or rather able – to pay more than those with lower incomes. While in the lowest income category, 55.6% will pay less than 1.000 Rs, and only 27.8% are willing to pay more than 2.000 Rs., the situation is different in the higher income groups. In the 50 to 89 Rs. category, a total of 77.0% is willing to pay more than 2.000 Rs., of which 16.7% alone are willing to pay between 10.000 and 100.000 Rs. Only about 10% are ready to invest more than 10.000 Rs. for the legalization of the land. The figures indicate that people are generally willing to pay, but always within the limits of their respective financial situation.

Table 14.7 Affordable amount of money to legalize the land (in Rs.), by average daily wages of household members (in Rs.).

Waste Affordable amount	0 to 9 Rs. in % (n=36)	10 to 19 Rs. in % (n=160)	20 to 29 Rs. in % (n=138)	30 to 39 Rs. in % (n=71)	40 to 49 Rs. in % (n=27)	50 to 89 Rs. in % (n=30)	90 to 130 Rs. in % (n=5)	Total in % (n=467)
1 to 1000	55.6	30.0	20.3	12.7	22.2	23.3	20.0	25.5
1001 to 2000	27.8	21.9	18.8	14.1	7.4	0.0	20.0	18.0
2001 to 5000	11.1	26.3	34.1	38.0	22.2	43.3	20.0	30.0
5001 to 10000	5.6	15.0	18.1	21.1	22.2	16.7	0.0	16.5
10001 to 100000	0.0	6.9	8.7	14.1	25.9	16.7	40.0	10.1
Total	100.0	100.0	100.0	100.0	100.0	100.0	100.0	100.0

SOURCE: UNIVERSITY OF BASEL, DEPT. OF GEOGRAPHY AND ALL INDIA DISASTER MITIGATION INSTITUTE, AHMEDABAD, INDIA 2005. SOCIAL SCIENCE SURVEY IN SELECTED SLUM COMMUNITIES IN THE CITY OF BHUJ, GUJARAT, INDIA.

By slum (Tab. 14.8). In all four slums, the highest proportion of people would invest 2.001 to 5.000 Rs. in the legalization of their land. Again – due to the generally higher economical standard in Jayprakashnagar – the amount people are willing to invest is slightly higher in Jayprakashnagar, where 22% of the people are would invest 10.001 up to 100.000 Rs. to legalise their land. The share of people willing to invest that much is clearly lower in the other three slum areas, (generally around 9%). It appears again that a large majority of people are willing to pay according to their financial capacities. This is a potential that should be focussed upon in order to make people participate in the improvement of their livelihood.

Table 14.8 Affordable amount of money to legalize the land (in Rs.), by slum.

Affordable amount	Bhimraonagar in % (n=124)	Jayprakashnagar in % (n=50)	Mustuffanagar in % (n=158)	Shantinagar in % (n=153)	Total in % (n=485)
1 to 1000 Rs.	29.0	20.0	29.1	21.6	25.8
1001 to 2000 Rs.	21.0	4.0	15.2	22.2	17.7
2001 to 5000 Rs.	30.6	26.0	26.6	34.0	29.9
5001 to 10000 Rs.	11.3	28.0	19.6	13.1	16.3
10001 to 100000 Rs.	8.1	22.0	9.5	9.2	10.3
Total	100.0	100.0	100.0	100.0	100.0

SOURCE: UNIVERSITY OF BASEL, DEPT. OF GEOGRAPHY AND ALL INDIA DISASTER MITIGATION INSTITUTE, AHMEDABAD, INDIA 2005. SOCIAL SCIENCE SURVEY IN SELECTED SLUM COMMUNITIES IN THE CITY OF BHUJ, GUJARAT, INDIA.

14.4
Willingness to pay property tax

By average daily wages of household members in Rs. (Tab. 14.9). Households of all income categories agree to pay property tax at rates between 94.4% and 100%. Only in the lowest income class, the percentage of those willing to pay income taxes is significantly lower (84.6%). In the income categories above 40 Rs. per person, 100% agree to pay property tax. However, one must keep in mind that the number of households belonging to these income groups is smaller. The generally high percentages are probably due to the fact that people hope for legalization of their housing status if they pay property tax.

Table 14.9 Willingness to pay property tax (per month in Rs.), by average daily wages of household members (in Rs.).

Wage Willingness to pay property tax	0 to 9 Rs. in % (n=39)	10 to 19 Rs. in % (n=160)	20 to 29 Rs. in % (n=133)	30 to 39 Rs. in % (n=71)	40 to 49 Rs. in % (n=25)	50 to 89 Rs. in % (n=28)	90 to 130 Rs. in % (n=5)	Total in % (n=461)
yes	84.6	94.4	97.7	95.8	100.0	100.0	100.0	95.4
no	15.4	5.6	2.3	4.2	0.0	0.0	0.0	4.6
Total	100.0	100.0	100.0	100.0	100.0	100.0	100.0	100.0

SOURCE: UNIVERSITY OF BASEL, DEPT. OF GEOGRAPHY AND ALL INDIA DISASTER MITIGATION INSTITUTE, AHMEDABAD, INDIA 2005. SOCIAL SCIENCE SURVEY IN SELECTED SLUM COMMUNITIES IN THE CITY OF BHUJ, GUJARAT, INDIA.

By slum (Tab. 14.10). The acceptance to pay property tax is very high in all four slums, with rates of around 97% for Jayprakashnagar, Mustuffanagar and Shantinagar, but slightly lower in Bhimraonagar (90.6%). Reasons for the lower percentage in Bhimraonagar are difficult to find. The high acceptance in all slum communities to pay property tax underlines how important legalization of the property is and to what extent people would be willing to contribute in order to improve their living conditions. However, the amounts people would invest are limited, as table 14.12 shows.

Table 14.10 Willingness to pay property tax (per month in Rs.), by slum.

Slum Willingness to pay property tax	Bhimraonagar in % (n=127)	Jayprakashnagar in % (n=47)	Mustuffanagar in % (n=152)	Shantinagar in % (n=151)	Total in % (n=477)
yes	90.6	97.9	96.7	97.4	95.4
no	9.4	2.1	3.3	2.6	4.6
Total	100.0	100.0	100.0	100.0	100.0

SOURCE: UNIVERSITY OF BASEL, DEPT. OF GEOGRAPHY AND ALL INDIA DISASTER MITIGATION INSTITUTE, AHMEDABAD, INDIA 2005. SOCIAL SCIENCE SURVEY IN SELECTED SLUM COMMUNITIES IN THE CITY OF BHUJ, GUJARAT, INDIA.

By education (Tab. 14.11). There is a slight connection between the education and the willingness to pay property tax. With better education, the proportion of households willing to pay property tax also rises, although it is high already throughout all income groups. 93% of the illiterates are willing to pay property tax, but 100% of the people with education standard 10-12 or more would pay property tax. This might be due to the relation of income and education - better education usually leads to a higher income.

Table 14.11 Willingness to pay property tax (per month in Rs.), by education standard.

Education / Willingness to pay property tax	Hrs. 1-3 in % (n=46)	Hrs. 4-6 in % (n=79)	Hrs. 7-9 in % (n=98)	Hrs. 10-12 in % (n=33)	Completed Diploma in % (n=1)	Completed Graduation in % (n=6)	Illiterate in % (n=213)	Total in % (n=476)
yes	93.5	97.5	98.0	100.0	100.0	100.0	93.0	95.4
no	6.5	2.5	2.0	0.0	0.0	0.0	7.0	4.6
Total	100.0	100.0	100.0	100.0	100.0	100.0	100.0	100.0

SOURCE: UNIVERSITY OF BASEL, DEPT. OF GEOGRAPHY AND ALL INDIA DISASTER MITIGATION INSTITUTE, AHMEDABAD, INDIA 2005. SOCIAL SCIENCE SURVEY IN SELECTED SLUM COMMUNITIES IN THE CITY OF BHUJ, GUJARAT, INDIA.

14.5
Willingness to pay property tax (in Rs. per month)

By average daily wage of household members in Rs. (Tab. 14.12). The monthly amount people are willing to spend on property tax is limited; this is true for all income categories. Roughly a third of all households would spend 1 to 10, respectively 11 to 20 Rs. per month on property tax, which are the highest percentages: for monthly amounts higher than that, the share of households willing to invest that is significantly lower. Only between up to 10% are willing to pay more than 100 Rs. per month. An exception are households where people have a daily income of between 40 and 49 Rs., of whom roughly 40% are ready to pay 51 to 100 Rs. per month. Those households are, in terms of their income, by far better off than others. This might explain why they would also invest more in property tax: they could more easily afford it. One can therefore conclude that although the willingness to spend money on property tax is high, people are not able to pay much.

Table 14.12 Willingness to pay property tax (per month in Rs.), by average daily wages of household members (in Rs.).

Wage / Willingness to pay property tax	0 to 9 Rs. in % (n=33)	10 to 19 Rs. in % (n=148)	20 to 29 Rs. in % (n=129)	30 to 39 Rs. in % (n=67)	40 to 49 Rs. in % (n=25)	50 to 89 Rs. in % (n=28)	90 to 130 Rs. in % (n=5)	Total in % (n=435)
1-10 Rs.	36.4	31.8	30.2	28.4	20.0	7.1	20.0	28.7
11-20 Rs.	30.3	30.4	34.1	26.9	28.0	46.4	0.0	31.5
21-30 Rs.	9.1	13.5	14.7	7.5	4.0	17.9	0.0	12.2
31-50 Rs.	12.1	3.4	6.2	11.9	4.0	17.9	20.0	7.4
51-100 Rs.	12.1	18.9	12.4	14.9	40.0	3.6	40.0	16.3
101-1000 Rs.	0.0	2.0	2.3	10.4	4.0	7.1	20.0	3.9
Total	100.0	100.0	100.0	100.0	100.0	100.0	100.0	100.0

SOURCE: UNIVERSITY OF BASEL, DEPT. OF GEOGRAPHY AND ALL INDIA DISASTER MITIGATION INSTITUTE, AHMEDABAD, INDIA 2005. SOCIAL SCIENCE SURVEY IN SELECTED SLUM COMMUNITIES IN THE CITY OF BHUJ, GUJARAT, INDIA.

By slum (Tab. 14.13). The willingness to pay property tax varies among the slums. While the proportions of households that can afford 1 to 20 Rs. per month is similar in Bhimraonagar (54.5%), Jayprakashnagar (57.4%) and Mustuffanagar (56.8%), almost 70% of the people in Shantinagar would up to 20 Rs. a month, which is explained by the fact that in this particular community, people are generally poorer. The amount people are willing (and able) to invest in property tax is rather low anyway: the highest total share of households would invest between 21 and 30 Rs. a month (31.9%, Tab. 14.13).

Table 14.13 Willingness to pay property tax (per month in Rs.), by slum.

Slum / Willingness to pay property tax	Bhimraonagar in % (n=110)	Jayprakashnagar in % (n=47)	Mustuffanagar in % (n=148)	Shantinagar in % (n=146)	Total in % (n=451)
1-10 Rs.	41.8	34.0	28.4	17.1	28.6
11-20 Rs.	12.7	23.4	28.4	52.7	31.9
21-30 Rs.	5.5	12.8	9.5	19.2	12.0
31-50 Rs.	6.4	12.8	8.1	5.5	7.3
51-100 Rs.	30.9	12.8	17.6	4.8	16.2
101-1000 Rs.	2.7	4.3	8.1	0.7	4.0
Total	100.0	100.0	100.0	100.0	100.0

SOURCE: UNIVERSITY OF BASEL, DEPT. OF GEOGRAPHY AND ALL INDIA DISASTER MITIGATION INSTITUTE, AHMEDABAD, INDIA 2005. SOCIAL SCIENCE SURVEY IN SELECTED SLUM COMMUNITIES IN THE CITY OF BHUJ, GUJARAT, INDIA.

14.6
Willingness to pay water tax (in Rs. per month)

By average daily wage of household members in Rs. (Tab. 14.14). Throughout all income categories, the willingness to pay for water is striking. However, a total majority of the households (87.2%) would not pay up to 30 Rs. a month for water. This holds true for households with higher daily wages, too.

By slum (Tab. 14.15). The differences between the slums are remarkable. While in Bhimraonagar, the highest proportion of households would pay 1 to 10 Rs. a month for water (54.8%), only 4.8% of those in Jayprakashnagar would spend this little amount. By contrast, it is 85.7% of the households in Jayprakashnagar that are willing to pay a monthly water tax of between 21 and 30 Rs. These figures indicate the varying economic situation in the different slums. A total of 86.5% of the households in all of the four slums are not willing or able to pay more than 30 Rs. a month for water. A total of only 9.3% could pay between 31 and 50 Rs. a month. However, there are some noteworthy points: Although the community of Shantinagar is generally by far poorer than the others, 43.8% of the households here are willing to pay a monthly water tax of 21 to 30 Rs., which is the second highest proportion after Jayprakashnagar with 85.7% The strikingly high share of households in Shantinagar willing to invest amounts that one might assume they can hardly afford, portrays to what extent clean water is a problem in this community.

Table 14.14 Willingness to pay water tax (per month in Rs.), by average daily wages of household members (in Rs.).

Wage Willingness to pay water tax	0 to 9 Rs. in % (n=36)	10 to 19 Rs. in % (n=155)	20 to 29 Rs. in % (n=128)	30 to 39 Rs. in % (n=68)	40 to 49 Rs. in % (n=23)	50 to 89 Rs. in % (n=28)	90 to 130 Rs. in % (n=5)	Total in % (n=443)
1-10 Rs.	38.9	33.5	36.7	25.0	13.0	21.4	0.0	31.4
11-20 Rs.	19.4	22.6	18.0	19.1	13.0	25.0	40.0	20.3
21-30 Rs.	38.9	32.3	32.8	39.7	52.2	35.7	40.0	35.4
31-50 Rs.	0.0	11.0	10.9	8.8	8.7	10.7	0.0	9.5
51-100 Rs.	2.8	0.0	0.8	4.4	8.7	0.0	20.0	1.8
101-400 Rs.	0.0	0.6	0.8	2.9	4.3	7.1	0.0	1.6
Total	100.0	100.0	100.0	100.0	100.0	100.0	100.0	100.0

SOURCE: UNIVERSITY OF BASEL, DEPT. OF GEOGRAPHY AND ALL INDIA DISASTER MITIGATION INSTITUTE, AHMEDABAD, INDIA 2005. SOCIAL SCIENCE SURVEY IN SELECTED SLUM COMMUNITIES IN THE CITY OF BHUJ, GUJARAT, INDIA.

Table 14.15 Willingness to pay water tax (per month in Rs.), by slum.

Slum Willingness to pay water tax	Bhimraonagar in % (n=124)	Jayprakashnagar in % (n=42)	Mustuffanagar in % (n=150)	Shantinagar in % (n=144)	Total in % (n=460)
1 - 10 Rs.	54.8	4.8	31.3	18.1	31.1
11 - 20 Rs.	7.3	7.1	25.3	31.3	20.7
21 - 30 Rs.	21.0	85.7	25.3	43.8	35.4
31 - 50 Rs.	13.7	2.4	10.7	6.3	9.3
51 - 100 Rs.	3.2	0.0	2.0	0.7	1.7
101 - 400 Rs.	0.0	0.0	5.3	0.0	1.7
Total	100.0	100.0	100.0	100.0	100.0

SOURCE: UNIVERSITY OF BASEL, DEPT. OF GEOGRAPHY AND ALL INDIA DISASTER MITIGATION INSTITUTE, AHMEDABAD, INDIA 2005. SOCIAL SCIENCE SURVEY IN SELECTED SLUM COMMUNITIES IN THE CITY OF BHUJ, GUJARAT, INDIA.

14.7
Willingness to invest in house when land is legalized

By average daily wage of household members in Rs. (Tab. 14.16). There is a relationship between the average daily wages household members earn and the amount that they would invest in the house within one or two years, if the government transferred the land into the house owner's name. Of the households with average daily wages of 0 to 9 Rs., almost a third (32.3%) can only afford to invest up to 1.000 Rs. With increasing income, the amount people want to invest is rising, too. One third of the inhabitants that earn more than 50 Rs. a day would invest more than 20.000 Rs. in their houses.

Table 14.16 Willingness to invest in house when land is legalized, by average daily wages of household members (in Rs.).

Wage Willingness to invest in own house	0 to 9 Rs. in % (n=31)	10 to 19 Rs. in % (n=150)	20 to 29 Rs. in % (n=129)	30 to 39 Rs. in % (n=63)	40 to 49 Rs. in % (n=23)	50 to 89 Rs. in % (n=25)	90 to 130 Rs. in % (n=5)	Total in % (n=426)
1-1000	32.3	8.7	9.3	4.8	0.0	8.0	0.0	9.4
1001-2000	22.6	20.0	10.1	9.5	0.0	8.0	0.0	13.6
2001-3000	0.0	10.7	13.2	6.3	0.0	0.0	20.0	8.9
3001-5000	22.6	20.7	14.7	27.0	8.7	12.0	20.0	18.8
5001-10000	16.1	18.7	24.0	22.2	17.4	28.0	0.0	20.9
10001-20000	0.0	11.3	14.7	11.1	47.8	16.0	20.0	13.8
20001-200000	6.5	10.0	14.0	19.0	26.1	28.0	40.0	14.6
Total	100.0	100.0	100.0	100.0	100.0	100.0	100.0	100.0

SOURCE: UNIVERSITY OF BASEL, DEPT. OF GEOGRAPHY AND ALL INDIA DISASTER MITIGATION INSTITUTE, AHMEDABAD, INDIA 2005. SOCIAL SCIENCE SURVEY IN SELECTED SLUM COMMUNITIES IN THE CITY OF BHUJ, GUJARAT, INDIA.

By slum (Tab. 14.17). The amounts people are willing to invest in their houses if the land is legalised vary in all four slums. While in Bhimraonagar, high proportions of people would invest up to 5.000 Rs. (71.1%), the percentages in Jayprakashnagar are particularly high in the investment categories of 5001 up to over 20 000 Rs. In this community, a significant share of 31% would invest 10 001 to 20 000 Rs. In Mustuffanagar, the largest proportion would invest between 3.001 and 20.000 Rs (42.9%). By contrast, in Shantinagar, higher proportions of people would invest rather lower amounts, as compared to the other communities: 12% and 15.5% would spend 1 to 1000 and 1001 up to 2000 Rs. Most people here are not able to invest much because of their poverty. However, still 18.3% and 22.5% would spend 3001 to 5000 and 5001 to 10 000 Rs., which illustrates the importance of the legalization of land particularly in the slum community of Shantinagar, where large parts of the population live in illegal squatter settlements. The amounts of money people would spend on the legalization of their land, analyzed by slum reflect the differing economic situation in the communities. Yet, the willingness to contribute whatever is possible is evident in all of the slum communities.

14.8
Priority benefit in new government scheme – compensations for loss of earnings

By average daily wage of household members in Rs. (Tab. 14.18). For households with a daily income of less than 20 Rs., the compensation of daily wage loss due to wage earners' illnesses is judged as the most favourable in a new scheme of benefits. Those families live on the verge of, or already in extreme poverty and are highly vulnerable already. A daily wage loss is more serious for them than in families who have of some savings. The percentages of those who prioritise such a scheme vary strongly across the different income classes, but a trend or a tendency is not perceivable. In the income categories of 20 to 29 and 30 to 39 Rs. a day, high shares of households (61.2% and 72.6%) do not attribute a high priority to this scheme. This could be a sign that this family has more than one or two earning members, hence, if one is ill, the others one can make up for the loss temporarily so that the family's livelihood is secured to some extent. Moreover, each family sets different priorities.

Table 14.17 Willingness to invest in house when land is legalized, by slum.

Slum Willingness to invest in your house	Bhimraonagar in % (n=124)	Jayprakashnagar in % (n=42)	Mustuffanagar in % (n=133)	Shantinagar in % (n=142)	Total in % (n=441)
1-1000	8.9	4.8	9.0	12.0	9.5
1001-2000	19.4	4.8	8.3	15.5	13.4
2001-3000	19.4	0.0	6.0	4.9	8.8
3001-5000	23.4	4.8	20.3	18.3	19.0
5001-10000	14.5	28.6	22.6	22.5	20.9
10001-20000	9.7	31.0	17.3	7.7	13.4
20001-200000	4.8	26.2	16.5	19.0	15.0
Total	100.0	100.0	100.0	100.0	100.0

SOURCE: UNIVERSITY OF BASEL, DEPT. OF GEOGRAPHY AND ALL INDIA DISASTER MITIGATION INSTITUTE, AHMEDABAD, INDIA 2005. SOCIAL SCIENCE SURVEY IN SELECTED SLUM COMMUNITIES IN THE CITY OF BHUJ, GUJARAT, INDIA.

Table 14.18 Priority benefit in new government scheme, compensation of daily wage loss, by average daily wages of household members

Waste Wage earner's illness	0 to 9 Rs. in % (n=39)	10 to 19 Rs. in % (n=163)	20 to 29 Rs. in % (n=139)	30 to 39 Rs. in % (n=73)	40 to 49 Rs. in % (n=25)	50 to 89 Rs. in % (n=31)	90 to 130 Rs. in % (n=5)	Total in % (n=475)
yes	48.7	47.9	38.8	27.4	64.0	48.4	0.0	42.5
no	51.3	52.1	61.2	72.6	36.0	51.6	100.0	57.5
Total	100.0	100.0	100.0	100.0	100.0	100.0	100.0	100.0

SOURCE: UNIVERSITY OF BASEL, DEPT. OF GEOGRAPHY AND ALL INDIA DISASTER MITIGATION INSTITUTE, AHMEDABAD, INDIA 2005. SOCIAL SCIENCE SURVEY IN SELECTED SLUM COMMUNITIES IN THE CITY OF BHUJ, GUJARAT, INDIA.

By slum (Tab. 14.19). The need for a new scheme of benefits that would cover daily wage loss due to wage earner's illness seems to be the most important in every slum. A total of 43.2% of the households agree on this question. But remarkable differences between the individual slums remain: In Jayprakashnagar, 75% advocate these benefits. By contrast, only 16.2% agree in Bhimraonagar. This highly significant result may be due to the fact that a larger percentage of construction workers live in Bhimraonagar. Because of the boom in construction since the earthquake and the road construction under the new Bhuj Collectorate, the likelihood to lose a job due to illness is lower and temporary losses of income can be made up for because the chances in the job market are now generally good. The high share of households in Shantinagar who prioritise this scheme over others (59.7%) might be due to the fact that a high number of people there is very poor and cannot compensate the losses very well.

Table 14.19 Priority benefit in new government scheme, compensation of daily wage loss, by slum.

Slum Wage earner's illness	Bhimraonagar in % (n=130)	Jayprakashnagar in % (n=52)	Mustuffanagar in % (n=157)	Shantinagar in % (n=154)	Total in % (n=493)
yes	16.2	75.0	38.9	59.7	43.2
no	83.8	25.0	61.1	40.3	56.8
Total	100.0	100.0	100.0	100.0	100.0

SOURCE: UNIVERSITY OF BASEL, DEPT. OF GEOGRAPHY AND ALL INDIA DISASTER MITIGATION INSTITUTE, AHMEDABAD, INDIA 2005. SOCIAL SCIENCE SURVEY IN SELECTED SLUM COMMUNITIES IN THE CITY OF BHUJ, GUJARAT, INDIA.

14.9
Priority benefit in new government scheme – improving housing conditions

By slum (Tab. 14.20). For more than one third of the total population (36.2%) in the four slums, improving housing condition is only second priority. In Jayprakashnagar, the necessity of these benefits is less urgent (19.2%) then in all other communities. This is due to the generally good housing substance on one hand, but it might as well reflect some kind of disillusion with housing issues after the demolition of houses for the new highway in that community. The high percentage of people in Bhimraonagar (42.3%) who consider this scheme as very important suggests that in this community, still a large number of houses is in a bad condition after the 2001 earthquake.

Table 14.20 Priority benefit in new government scheme: Improve housing condition, by slum.

Slum Improve Housing condition	Bhimraonagar in % (n=130)	Jayprakashnagar in % (n=52)	Mustuffanagar in % (n=157)	Shantinagar in % (n=154)	Total in % (n=493)
yes	42.3	19.2	38.9	34.4	36.3
no	57.7	80.8	61.1	65.6	63.7
Total	100.0	100.0	100.0	100.0	100.0

SOURCE: UNIVERSITY OF BASEL, DEPT. OF GEOGRAPHY AND ALL INDIA DISASTER MITIGATION INSTITUTE, AHMEDABAD, INDIA 2005. SOCIAL SCIENCE SURVEY IN SELECTED SLUM COMMUNITIES IN THE CITY OF BHUJ, GUJARAT, INDIA.

14.10
Conclusion

The analysis of the question whether or not slum households can and want to contribute to infrastructural improvements – in particular access to good drinking water, drainage/sanitation and solid waste removal – clearly shows that people are very much willing to pay. The same holds true for the willingness to pay their fair share towards legalising their land, and people are also willing to invest in their houses. It is their illegal housing status that seems to be an issue of grave concern. This leads to the conclusion that these are the severest problems people have to face and that they are motivated to contribute financially the way they can if problems could be solved by their participation.

Most of the households indicate a high acceptance for shared financial responsibilities in order to improve their living conditions. However, the amounts they are willing to invest depend to a large extent on their income levels. With income being the critical determinant and poverty being a fact of life for the majority of the households, it is of no surprise that the greatest priority is given to compensation for wage loss due to earner's illness, if the government was to create a new scheme of benefits.

Map 14.1 Willingness to pay towards good drinking water supply, Bhimraonagar

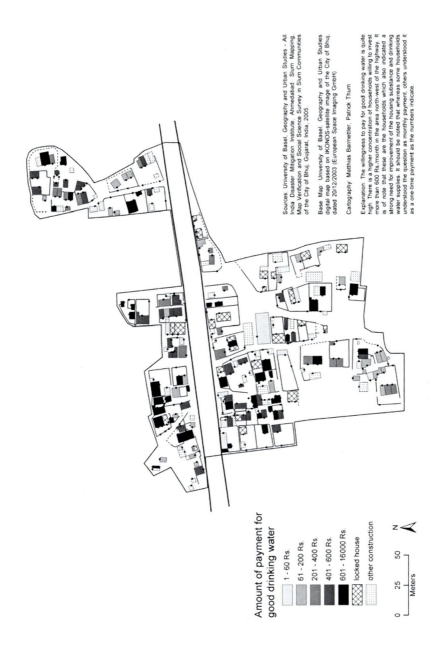

Map 14.2 Willingness to pay towards good drinking water supply, Jayprakashnagar

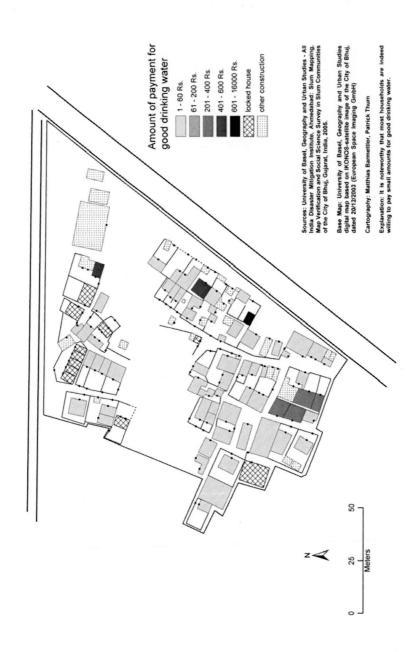

Willingness to pay for the legalization of land 301

Map 14.3 Willingness to pay towards good drinking water supply, Mustuffanagar

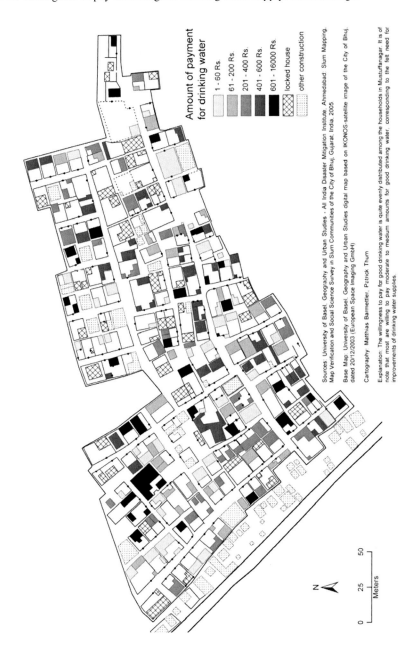

302   Willingness to pay for the legalization of land

Map 14.4 Willingness to pay towards good drinking water supply, Shantinagar

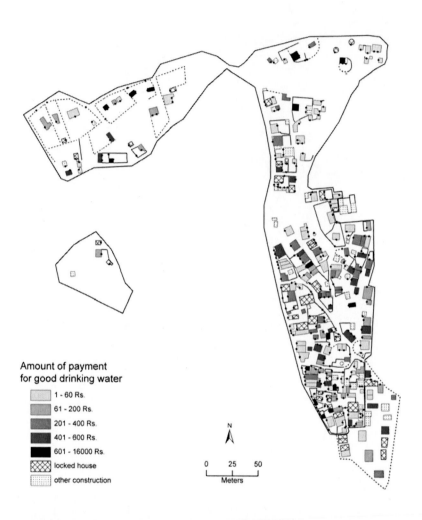

Willingness to pay for the legalization of land 303

Map 14.5 Willingness to pay for drainage/sanitation, Bhimraonagar

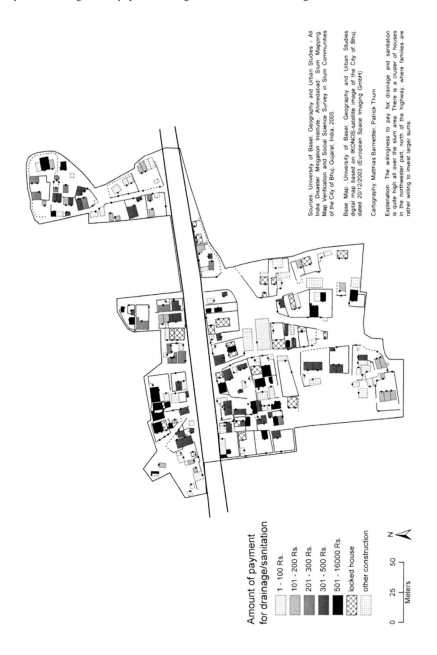

Map 14.6 Willingness to pay for drainage/sanitation, Jayprakashnagar

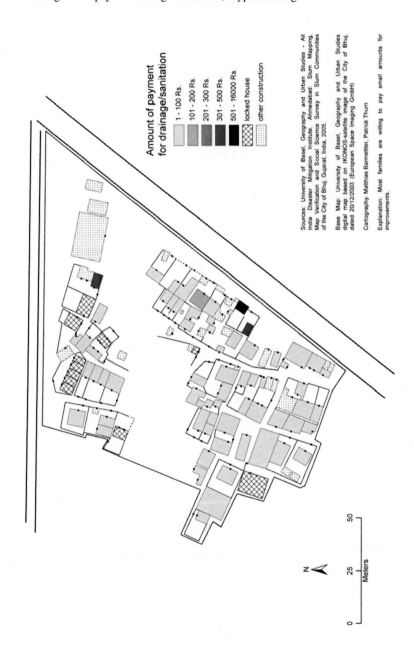

Map 14.7 Willingness to pay for drainage/sanitation, Mustuffanagar

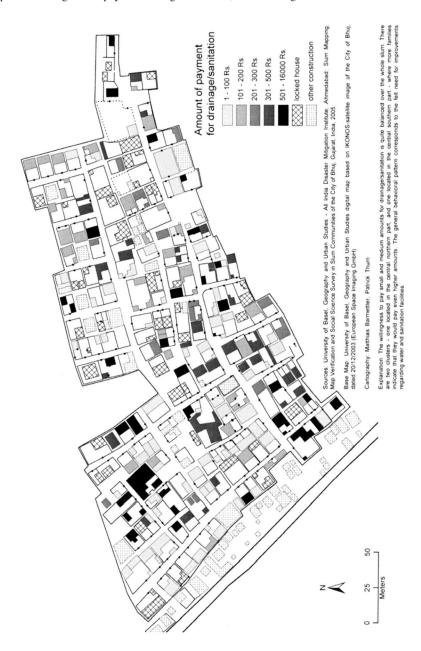

Map 14.8 Willingness to pay for drainage/sanitation, Shantinagar

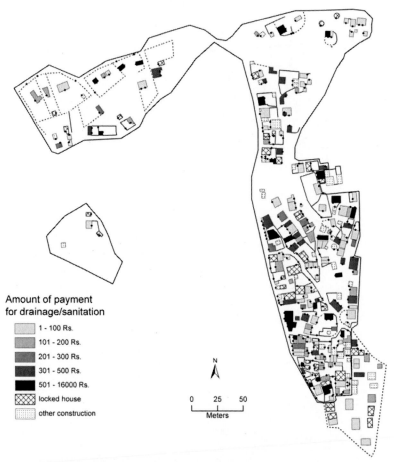

Map 14.9 Willingness to pay for solid waste removal, Bhimraonagar

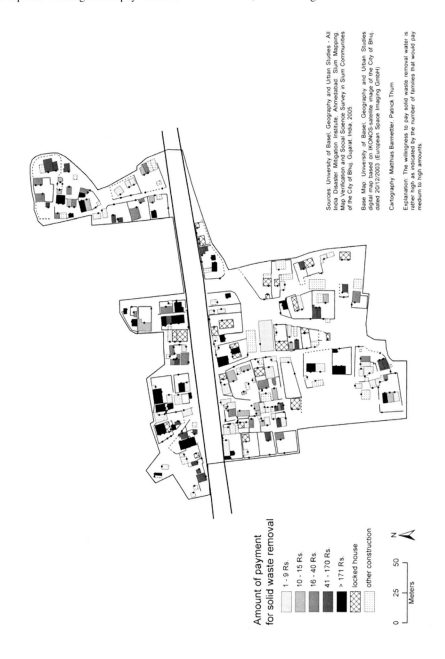

308   Willingness to pay for the legalization of land

Map 14.10 Willingness to pay for solid waste removal, Jayprakashnagar

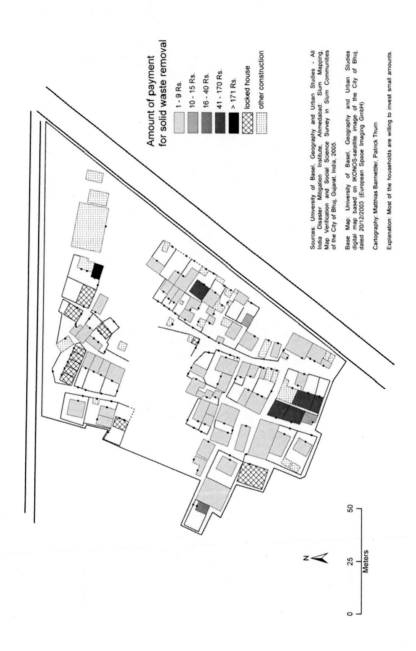

Willingness to pay for the legalization of land 309

Map 14.11 Willingness to pay for solid waste removal, Mustuffanagar

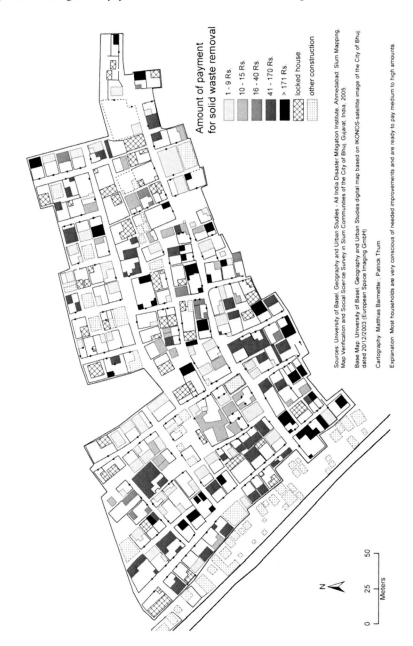

Map 14.12 Willingness to pay for solid waste removal, Shantinagar

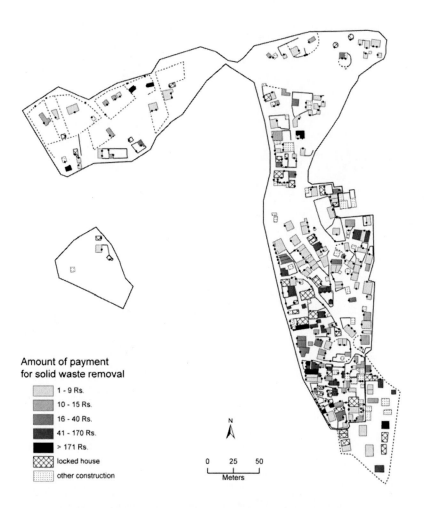

Map 14.13 Amount households would pay for the legalization of the land, Bhimraonagar

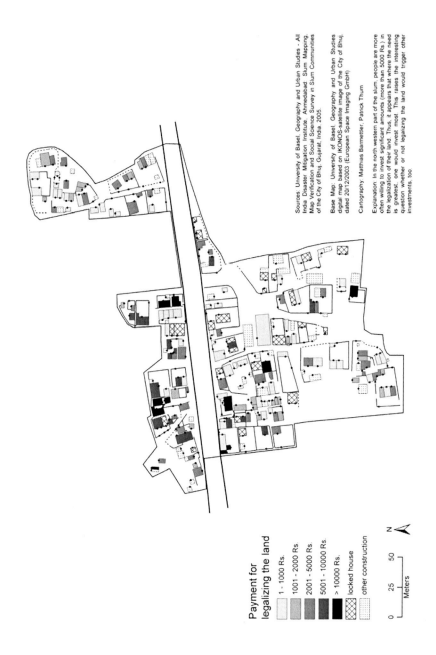

312   Willingness to pay for the legalization of land

Map 14.14 Amount households would pay for the legalization of the land, Jayprakashnagar

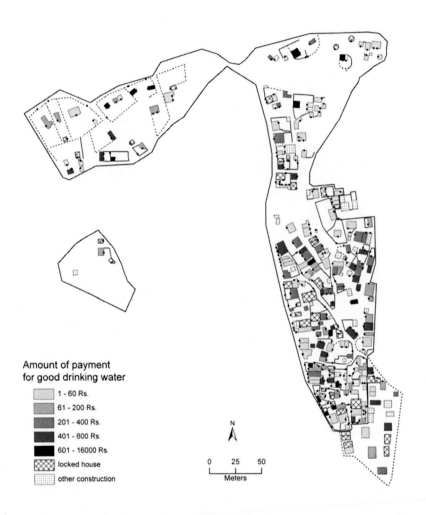

Willingness to pay for the legalization of land 313

Map 14.15 Amount households would pay for the legalization of the land, Mustuffanagar

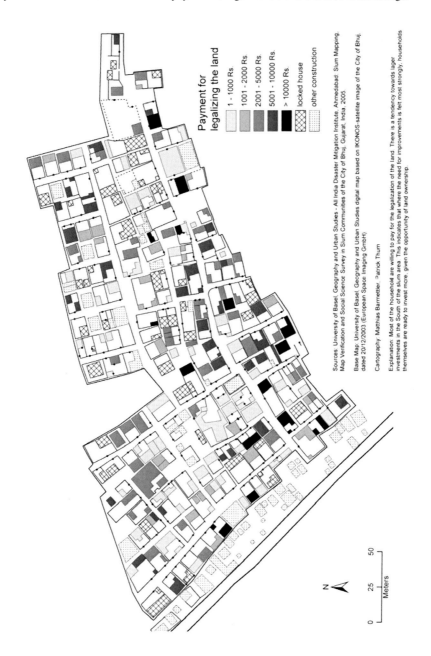

314   Willingness to pay for the legalization of land

Map 14.16 Amount households would pay for the legalization of the land, Shantinagar

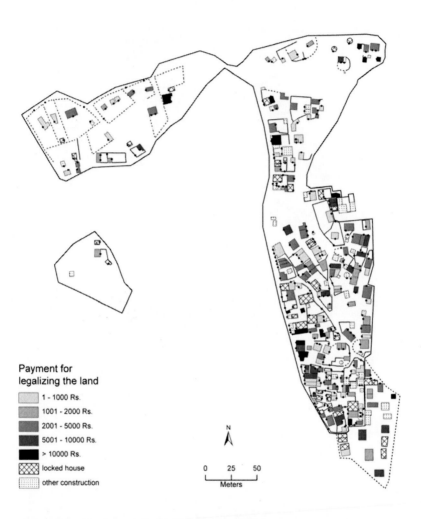

Willingness to pay for the legalization of land 315

Map 14.17 Amount households would invest into their houses after the legalization of land, Bhimraonagar

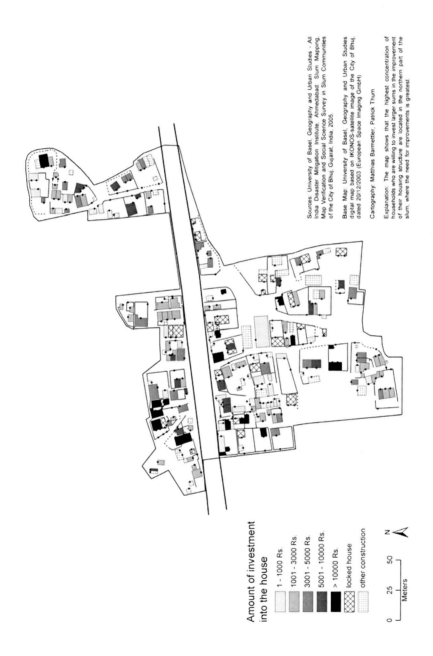

Map 14.18 Amount households would invest into their houses after the legalization of land, Jayprakashnagar

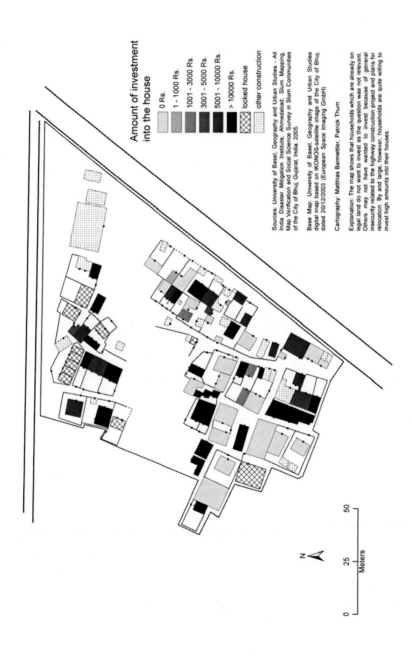

Map 14.19 Amount households would invest into their houses after the legalization of land, Mustuffanagar

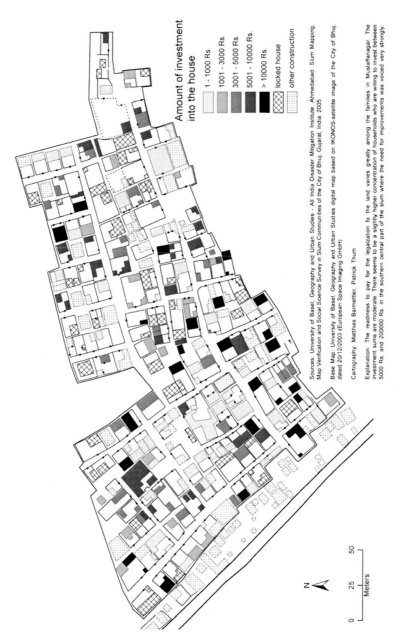

318 Willingness to pay for the legalization of land

Map 14.20 Amount households would invest into their houses after the legalization of land, Shantinagar

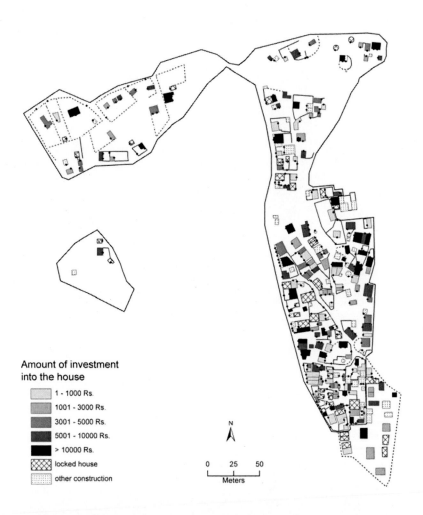

15 Willingness to relocate

B. Lietzke, D. Michel
University of Basel

15.1
Introduction

For the betterment of slum conditions, public agencies often take to relocation schemes. Relocation settlements are thought, on the one hand, to take pressure from overcrowded slum conditions. On the other hand, relocation sites allow public planning to "get things right" from the very beginning and to prevent slum conditions to emerge. Relocation is costly for the government and not always well accepted by the target group of beneficiaries. Whereas it is certainly legitimate to ask slum households to contribute towards the betterment of their living conditions it is not at all clear that this needs to be done through relocation. The question as to the willingness to relocate is therefore very relevant to prevent costly mistakes and the disruption of the social fabric.

15.2
Acceptance for relocation with land and services

The overall distribution of the requirement of relocation shows clearly that 2/3 of all interviewed slum dwellers do not want to relocate and that those people who would want to relocate prefer land, services and built-up houses (approximately 23%).

By slum name (Tab. 15.1). Bhimraonagar is the only area where only approximately one half of the households does *not* want to relocate. In Jayprakashnagar one third and in Mustuffa- and Shantinagar over 70% of the slum households state that they do not want to relocate. The majority of all households that do want to relocate state that they want land, services and built-up.

Table 15.1 Relocation, by slum.

Relocation \ Slum	Bhimraonagar in % (n=127)	Jayprakashnagar in % (n=51)	Mustuffanagar in % (n=152)	Shantinagar in % (n=147)	Total in % (n=477)
do not want to relocate	51.2	66.7	72.4	71.4	65.8
yes, with land & cash	0.8	13.7	0.7	6.1	3.8
yes, with land & service	16.5	5.9	3.3	3.4	7.1
yes, land & services & built-up	31.5	13.7	23.7	19.0	23.3
Total	100.0	100.0	100.0	100.0	100.0

SOURCE: UNIVERSITY OF BASEL, DEPT. OF GEOGRAPHY AND ALL INDIA DISASTER MITIGATION INSTITUTE, AHMEDABAD, INDIA 2005. SOCIAL SCIENCE SURVEY IN SELECTED SLUM COMMUNITIES IN THE CITY OF BHUJ, GUJARAT, INDIA.

By religion (Tab. 15.2). Concerning the requirement of relocation, there is a remarkable difference between Hindu and Muslim households whereas 56.9% of the Hindus do not want to relocate, 72.9% of the Muslims do not either. There may be a relation between the latter and the distribution of ownership documents among Muslims. An explanation could be the generally better infrastructure in Mustuffanagar which makes this a preferred location. It is possible that the 2/3 of all Hindu households, mostly located in Jayprakashnagar, who would relocate with land, services and built up shows the disillusionment and fear after town planning tore down 26 houses for the highway.

Table 15.2 Relocation, by religion.

Relocation \ Religion	Hindu in % (n=209)	Muslim in % (n=266)	Total in % (n=475)
do not want to relocate	56.9	72.9	65.9
yes, with land & cash	2.4	4.9	3.8
yes, with land & service	10.0	4.5	6.9
yes, land & services & built-up	30.6	17.7	23.4
Total	100.0	100.0	100.0

SOURCE: UNIVERSITY OF BASEL, DEPT. OF GEOGRAPHY AND ALL INDIA DISASTER MITIGATION INSTITUTE, AHMEDABAD, INDIA 2005. SOCIAL SCIENCE SURVEY IN SELECTED SLUM COMMUNITIES IN THE CITY OF BHUJ, GUJARAT, INDIA.

By caste (Tab. 15.3). The relation to the caste reflects more or less the overall distribution. Approximately 2/3 of the members of every caste do not want to relocate with the exception of the members of the other backward castes (OBC) where 79.7% state that they do not want to relocate. On the whole it is clear then that willingness to relocate is not caste specific.

Table 15.3 Relocation, by caste.

Caste / Relocation	SC in % (n=83)	ST in % (n=56)	OBC in % (n=172)	General in % (n=165)	Total in % (n=476)
do not want to relocate	60.2	60.7	79.7	56.4	66.0
yes, with land & cash	0.0	3.6	6.4	3.0	3.8
yes, with land & service	8.4	17.9	1.7	7.9	6.9
yes, land & services & built-up	31.3	17.9	12.2	32.7	23.3
Total	100.0	100.0	100.0	100.0	100.0

SOURCE: UNIVERSITY OF BASEL, DEPT. OF GEOGRAPHY AND ALL INDIA DISASTER MITIGATION INSTITUTE, AHMEDABAD, INDIA 2005. SOCIAL SCIENCE SURVEY IN SELECTED SLUM COMMUNITIES IN THE CITY OF BHUJ, GUJARAT, INDIA.

By average daily income of household members (Tab. 15.4). It is remarkable that the percentage of people who do not want to relocate is highest (100.0%) among those of the lowest income category (0-9 Rs.). It is possible that people in the category of those earning 0–9 Rs. cannot afford moving or are afraid of doing so because an imminent loss of money. It is interesting to note that government relocation schemes are mostly oriented towards these poorest and that these targeted beneficiaries are the least willing to accept the benefit of relocation.

Table 15.4 Relocation, by average daily wage of household members (in Rs.).

Wage / Relocation	0 to 9 Rs. in % (n=39)	10 to 19 Rs. in % (n=161)	20 to 29 Rs. in % (n=134)	30 to 39 Rs. in % (n=69)	40 to 49 Rs. in % (n=25)	50 to 89 Rs. in % (n=29)	90 to 130 Rs. in % (n=5)	Total in % (n=462)
do not want to relocate	76.9	64.6	61.2	69.6	36.0	65.5	100.0	64.3
yes, with land & cash	0.0	5.0	4.5	0.0	20.0	0.0	0.0	4.1
yes, with land & service	2.6	10.6	6.7	4.3	12.0	3.4	0.0	7.4
yes, land & services & built-up	20.5	19.9	27.6	26.1	32.0	31.0	0.0	24.2
Total	100.0	100.0	100.0	100.0	100.0	100.0	100.0	100.0

SOURCE: UNIVERSITY OF BASEL, DEPT. OF GEOGRAPHY AND ALL INDIA DISASTER MITIGATION INSTITUTE, AHMEDABAD, INDIA 2005. SOCIAL SCIENCE SURVEY IN SELECTED SLUM COMMUNITIES IN THE CITY OF BHUJ, GUJARAT, INDIA.

By education standard (Tab. 15.5). There is no relation between the requirement of relocation and the education standard. The distribution reflects the overall distribution of 2/3 who do *not* want to relocate. The benefits of relocation then are not understood no matter what educational level was achieved. Stated in other words, the disadvantage of relocation is well understood among all educational levels, even among the illiterates.

Table 15.5 Relocation, by education standard.

Education Relocation	Hrs. 1-3 in % (n=46)	Hrs. 4-6 in % (n=80)	Hrs. 7-9 in % (n=101)	Hrs. 10-12 in % (n=33)	completed Diploma in % (n=1)	completed Graduation in % (n=6)	Illiterate in % (n=209)	Total in % (n=476)
do not want to relocate	71.7	58.8	68.3	51.5	100.0	33.3	68.9	65.8
yes, with land & cash	2.2	3.8	5.0	0.0	0.0	0.0	4.3	3.8
yes, with land & service	10.9	11.3	4.0	9.1	0.0	16.7	5.7	7.1
yes, land & services & built-up	15.2	26.3	22.8	39.4	0.0	50.0	21.1	23.3
Total	100.0	100.0	100.0	100.0	100.0	100.0	100.0	100.0

SOURCE: UNIVERSITY OF BASEL, DEPT. OF GEOGRAPHY AND ALL INDIA DISASTER MITIGATION INSTITUTE, AHMEDABAD, INDIA 2005. SOCIAL SCIENCE SURVEY IN SELECTED SLUM COMMUNITIES IN THE CITY OF BHUJ, GUJARAT, INDIA.

By age and occupation of the family head (Tab. 15.6, 15.7). There is no noticeable difference between the distribution of the requirement of relocation by age of the interviewed. It is of note that not even younger people show an above average intention to relocate nor do older people want to relocate. Occupational characteristics are not important.

Table 15.6 Relocation, by age of family head.

Age Relocation	20-29 in % (n=55)	30-39 in % (n=131)	40-49 in % (n=126)	50-59 in % (n=64)	60-69 in % (n=65)	70-79 in % (n=23)	80-89 in % (n=7)	>90 in % (n=5)	Total in % (n=476)
do not want to relocate	60.0	66.4	62.7	71.9	64.6	82.6	71.4	40.0	65.8
yes, with land & cash	1.8	6.9	3.2	4.7	1.5	0.0	0.0	0.0	3.8
yes, with land & service	10.9	6.9	7.1	9.4	4.6	0.0	0.0	20.0	7.1
yes, land & services & built-up	27.3	19.8	27.0	14.1	29.2	17.4	28.6	40.0	23.3
Total	100.0	100.0	100.0	100.0	100.0	100.0	100.0	100.0	100.0

SOURCE: UNIVERSITY OF BASEL, DEPT. OF GEOGRAPHY AND ALL INDIA DISASTER MITIGATION INSTITUTE, AHMEDABAD, INDIA 2005. SOCIAL SCIENCE SURVEY IN SELECTED SLUM COMMUNITIES IN THE CITY OF BHUJ, GUJARAT, INDIA.

Table 15.7 Relocation, by occupation of family head.

Occupation Relocation	textile/industry in % (n=35)	government in % (n=13)	casual labour in % (n=81)	construction in % (n=83)	farming in % (n=12)	automotive related job in % (n=42)	vendor/shop in % (n=41)	crafts in % (n=15)	service sector in % (n=44)	retiree/housewife/unemployed in % (n=91)	unclear/indian in % (n=13)	Total in % (n=470)
do not want to relocate	74.3	84.6	67.9	63.9	75.0	54.8	65.9	60.0	63.6	63.7	69.2	65.5
yes, with land & cash	2.9	0.0	3.7	6.0	16.7	7.1	4.9	0.0	0.0	2.2	0.0	3.8
yes, with land & service	2.9	7.7	7.4	10.8	0.0	4.8	7.3	6.7	6.8	5.5	23.1	7.2
yes, land & services & built-up	20.0	7.7	21.0	19.3	8.3	33.3	22.0	33.3	29.5	28.6	7.7	23.4
Total	100.0	100.0	100.0	100.0	100.0	100.0	100.0	100.0	100.0	100.0	100.0	100.0

SOURCE: UNIVERSITY OF BASEL, DEPT. OF GEOGRAPHY AND ALL INDIA DISASTER MITIGATION INSTITUTE, AHMEDABAD, INDIA 2005. SOCIAL SCIENCE SURVEY IN SELECTED SLUM COMMUNITIES IN THE CITY OF BHUJ, GUJARAT, INDIA.

15.3
Willingness to move with own family and other families

About two thirds of the people who state that they want to relocate say that they want to take their families with them. The other third would only relocate if other families came with them, which implies a clear acceptance of relocation only if some part of the old neighbourhood gets transferred too.

By slum name (Tab. 15.8). In Bhimrao- and Shantinagar, the distribution reflects the overall distribution. ¾ of the people that want to relocate in Mustuffanagar and 81.3% of the people that want to relocate in Jayprakashnagar want to move with their families. It is obvious that for most families it is more important that the family stays together than to move with other families.

Table 15.8 Willingness to move with the family, by slum.

Slum Willingness to relocate	Bhimraona- gar in % (n=61)	Jayprakashna -gar in % (n=16)	Mustuffana- gar in % (n=37)	Shantina- gar in % (n=40)	Total in % (n=154)
yes, with my family	60.7	81.3	75.7	62.5	66.9
no, only with other families	39.3	18.8	24.3	37.5	33.1
Total	100.0	100.0	100.0	100.0	100.0

SOURCE: UNIVERSITY OF BASEL, DEPT. OF GEOGRAPHY AND ALL INDIA DISASTER MITIGATION INSTITUTE, AHMEDABAD, INDIA 2005. SOCIAL SCIENCE SURVEY IN SELECTED SLUM COMMUNITIES IN THE CITY OF BHUJ, GUJARAT, INDIA.

By religion (Tab. 15.9). It seems that Hindu households have stronger ties with other families than Muslim households because 43.7% of the Hindus who want to relocate want to do this with other families, as compared to only 19.7% of the Muslim families.

Table 15.9 Willingness to move with the family, by religion.

Religion Willingness to relocate	Hindu in % (n=87)	Muslim in % (n=66)	Total in % (n=153)
yes, with my family	56.3	80.3	66.7
no, only with other families	43.7	19.7	33.3
Total	100.0	100.0	100.0

SOURCE: UNIVERSITY OF BASEL, DEPT. OF GEOGRAPHY AND ALL INDIA DISASTER MITIGATION INSTITUTE, AHMEDABAD, INDIA 2005. SOCIAL SCIENCE SURVEY IN SELECTED SLUM COMMUNITIES IN THE CITY OF BHUJ, GUJARAT, INDIA.

By caste (Tab. 15.10). In the other backward castes (OBC) more households (42.9%) than in all other categories (~30%) state that they only want to relocate with other families. This shows that a strong feeling of security is derived from collective relocation, if one has to relocate.

Table 15.10 Willingness to move with the family, by caste.

Caste Willingness to relocate	SC in % (n=32)	ST in % (n=22)	OBC in % (n=35)	General in % (n=64)	Total in % (n=153)
yes, with my family	68.8	72.7	57.1	68.8	66.7
no, only with other families	31.3	27.3	42.9	31.3	33.3
Total	100.0	100.0	100.0	100.0	100.0

SOURCE: UNIVERSITY OF BASEL, DEPT. OF GEOGRAPHY AND ALL INDIA DISASTER MITIGATION INSTITUTE, AHMEDABAD, INDIA 2005. SOCIAL SCIENCE SURVEY IN SELECTED SLUM COMMUNITIES IN THE CITY OF BHUJ, GUJARAT, INDIA.

By average daily income of household members, education and occupation (Tab. 15.11, 15.12 and 15.13). There is no relation between the two categories of relocation and the family income, education or occupation. The results reflect the overall distribution of roughly two thirds who want to relocate with their families.

Table 15.11 Willingness to move with the family, by average daily wage of household members (in Rs.).

Wage Willingness to relocate	0 to 9 Rs. in % (n=8)	10 to 19 Rs. in % (n=54)	20 to 29 Rs. in % (n=51)	30 to 39 Rs. in % (n=21)	40 to 49 Rs. in % (n=13)	50 to 89 Rs. in % (n=10)	Total in % (n=157)
yes, with my family	75.0	61.1	70.6	61.9	76.9	60.0	66.2
no, only with other families	25.0	38.9	29.4	38.1	23.1	40.0	33.8
Total	100.0	100.0	100.0	100.0	100.0	100.0	100.0

SOURCE: UNIVERSITY OF BASEL, DEPT. OF GEOGRAPHY AND ALL INDIA DISASTER MITIGATION INSTITUTE, AHMEDABAD, INDIA 2005. SOCIAL SCIENCE SURVEY IN SELECTED SLUM COMMUNITIES IN THE CITY OF BHUJ, GUJARAT, INDIA.

Table 15.12 Willingness to move with the family, by education standard.

Education Willingness to relocate	Hrs. 1-3 in % (n=13)	Hrs. 4-6 in % (n=31)	Hrs. 7-9 in % (n=28)	Hrs. 10-12 in % (n=16)	Completed Graduation in % (n=4)	Illiterate in % (n=62)	Total in % (n=154)
yes, with my family	76.9	67.7	78.6	56.3	100.0	59.7	66.9
no, only with other families	23.1	32.3	21.4	43.8	0.0	40.3	33.1
Total	100.0	100.0	100.0	100.0	100.0	100.0	100.0

SOURCE: UNIVERSITY OF BASEL, DEPT. OF GEOGRAPHY AND ALL INDIA DISASTER MITIGATION INSTITUTE, AHMEDABAD, INDIA 2005. SOCIAL SCIENCE SURVEY IN SELECTED SLUM COMMUNITIES IN THE CITY OF BHUJ, GUJARAT, INDIA.

By sex of family head (Tab. 15.14). The percentage of female family heads that want to move with their family (78.3%) is higher than the percentage of male family heads (64.9%). There is a gender-specific aspect in the understanding of responsibility for a family and related priorities.

Table 15.13 Willingness to move with the family, by occupation of family head.

Occupation Willingness to relocate	textile/industry in % (n=8)	government in % (n=2)	casual labour in % (n=25)	construction in % (n=28)	farming in % (n=3)	automotive related job in % (n=16)	vendor/shop in % (n=14)	crafts in % (n=6)	service sector in % (n=16)	retiree/housewife/unemployed in % (n=31)	unclear/indian in % (n=4)	Total in % (n=153)
yes, with my family	62.5	100.0	64.0	60.7	100.0	68.8	71.4	50.0	87.5	64.5	25.0	66.7
no, only with other families	37.5	0.0	36.0	39.3	0.0	31.3	28.6	50.0	12.5	35.5	75.0	33.3
Total	100.0	100.0	100.0	100.0	100.0	100.0	100.0	100.0	100.0	100.0	100.0	100.0

SOURCE: UNIVERSITY OF BASEL, DEPT. OF GEOGRAPHY AND ALL INDIA DISASTER MITIGATION INSTITUTE, AHMEDABAD, INDIA 2005. SOCIAL SCIENCE SURVEY IN SELECTED SLUM COMMUNITIES IN THE CITY OF BHUJ, GUJARAT, INDIA.

Table 15.14 Willingness to move with the family, by sex of family head.

Sex Willingness to relocate	female in % (n=23)	male in % (n=131)	Total in % (n=154)
yes, with my family	78.3	64.9	66.9
no, only with other families	21.7	35.1	33.1
Total	100.0	100.0	100.0

SOURCE: UNIVERSITY OF BASEL, DEPT. OF GEOGRAPHY AND ALL INDIA DISASTER MITIGATION INSTITUTE, AHMEDABAD, INDIA 2005. SOCIAL SCIENCE SURVEY IN SELECTED SLUM COMMUNITIES IN THE CITY OF BHUJ, GUJARAT, INDIA.

Maximum relocation distance (in km)

By slum (Tab. 15.15). It is remarkable that most of those few (n=155) people who would want to relocate are not inclined to move farther than within the same region or area they are already staying in. The majority (~45%) wants to move only 1.1 - 2 km. ¼ of all interviewed households are willing to move 2.1 - 3 km. It is not unlikely that those willing to relocate more than 4 km think about moving to certain official relocation sites in the Bhuj area which were established within that distance. One third of the people in Shantinagar who would relocate only want to move 1km or less, whereas in Bhimraonagar this is only 3.2%. Half of the inhabitants of Bhimrao- and Mustuffanagar who want to relocate want to move not more than 1.1 – 2 km.

Table 15.15 Maximum relocation distance (in km), by slum.

Slum Maximum distance	Bhimraonagar in % (n=62)	Jayprakashnagar in % (n=17)	Mustuffanagar in % (n=38)	Shantinagar in % (n=42)	Total in % (n=159)
0.1-1	3.2	23.5	13.2	31.0	15.1
1.1-2	50.0	29.4	52.6	38.1	45.3
2.1-3	30.6	35.3	15.8	23.8	25.8
3.1-4	1.6	0.0	0.0	0.0	0.6
>4.1	14.5	11.8	18.4	7.1	13.2
Total	100.0	100.0	100.0	100.0	100.0

SOURCE: UNIVERSITY OF BASEL, DEPT. OF GEOGRAPHY AND ALL INDIA DISASTER MITIGATION INSTITUTE, AHMEDABAD, INDIA 2005. SOCIAL SCIENCE SURVEY IN SELECTED SLUM COMMUNITIES IN THE CITY OF BHUJ, GUJARAT, INDIA.

By religion (Tab. 15.16). 27.5 % of the interviewed Muslims who state that they are willing to relocate want to move only less than 1.1 km away, while only 4.5 % of the Hindu households want this.

Table 15.16 Maximum relocation distance (in km), by religion.

Religion Maximum distance	Hindu in % (n=88)	Muslim in % (n=69)	Total in % (n=157)
0.1-1	4.5	27.5	14.6
1.1-2	50.0	40.6	45.9
2.1-3	30.7	20.3	26.1
3.1-4	1.1	0.0	0.6
>4.1	13.6	11.6	12.7
Total	100.0	100.0	100.0

SOURCE: UNIVERSITY OF BASEL, DEPT. OF GEOGRAPHY AND ALL INDIA DISASTER MITIGATION INSTITUTE, AHMEDABAD, INDIA 2005. SOCIAL SCIENCE SURVEY IN SELECTED SLUM COMMUNITIES IN THE CITY OF BHUJ, GUJARAT, INDIA.

By caste (Tab. 15.17). More than 1/3 of the other backward castes (OBC) (37.8%) who state that they want to relocate do not want to move more than 1 km, whereas in the other castes this value is less than 10%. The maximum in the general and ST caste lies in the category of 1.1 – 2 km. Almost 1/5 of the ST and SC caste want to move more than 4 km.

Table 15.17 Maximum relocation distance (in km), by caste.

Caste Maximum distance	SC in % (n=34)	ST in % (n=22)	OBC in % (n=37)	General in % (n=65)	Total in % (n=158)
0.1-1	5.9	9.1	37.8	9.2	15.2
1.1-2	29.4	59.1	29.7	56.9	44.9
2.1-3	47.1	13.6	24.3	20.0	25.9
3.1-4	0.0	0.0	0.0	1.5	0.6
>4.1	17.6	18.2	8.1	12.3	13.3
Total	100.0	100.0	100.0	100.0	100.0

SOURCE: UNIVERSITY OF BASEL, DEPT. OF GEOGRAPHY AND ALL INDIA DISASTER MITIGATION INSTITUTE, AHMEDABAD, INDIA 2005. SOCIAL SCIENCE SURVEY IN SELECTED SLUM COMMUNITIES IN THE CITY OF BHUJ, GUJARAT, INDIA.

By average daily income of household members, education, sex, occupation (Tab. 15.18, 15.19, 15.20 and 15.21). There is no significant relation with the daily income of household members, education, sex, or occupation.

By age of the family head (Tab. 15.22). In general the distribution reflects the overall distribution, except in the group of the 50-59 years old, where there is an almost homogeneous distribution of 23% to 29% in the categories of 0.1 – 1 km, 1.1 – 2 km and 2.1 – 3 km.

Table 15.18 Maximum relocation distance (in km), by average daily wage of household members (in Rs.).

Wage Maximum distance	0 to 9 Rs. in % (n=8)	10 to 19 Rs. in % (n=52)	20 to 29 Rs. in % (n=53)	30 to 39 Rs. in % (n=22)	40 to 49 Rs. in % (n=14)	50 to 89 Rs. in % (n=10)	Total in % (n=159)
0.1-1	0.0	19.2	17.0	4.5	14.3	20.0	15.1
1.1-2	62.5	55.8	37.7	45.5	35.7	30.0	45.3
2.1-3	25.0	13.5	32.1	36.4	21.4	40.0	25.8
3.1-4	0.0	1.9	0.0	0.0	0.0	0.0	0.6
>4.1	12.5	9.6	13.2	13.6	28.6	10.0	13.2
Total	100.0	100.0	100.0	100.0	100.0	100.0	100.0

SOURCE: UNIVERSITY OF BASEL, DEPT. OF GEOGRAPHY AND ALL INDIA DISASTER MITIGATION INSTITUTE, AHMEDABAD, INDIA 2005. SOCIAL SCIENCE SURVEY IN SELECTED SLUM COMMUNITIES IN THE CITY OF BHUJ, GUJARAT, INDIA.

Table 15.19 Maximum relocation distance (in km), by education standard.

Education Maximum distance	Hrs. 1-3 in % (n=13)	Hrs. 4-6 in % (n=31)	Hrs. 7-9 in % (n=31)	Hrs. 10-12 in % (n=16)	Completed Graduation in % (n=4)	Illiterate in % (n=64)	Total in % (n=159)
0.1-1	23.1	16.1	19.4	0.0	0.0	15.6	15.1
1.1-2	53.8	54.8	29.0	43.8	25.0	48.4	45.3
2.1-3	7.7	16.1	32.3	43.8	50.0	25.0	25.8
3.1-4	0.0	3.2	0.0	0.0	0.0	0.0	0.6
>4.1	15.4	9.7	19.4	12.5	25.0	10.9	13.2
Total	100.0	100.0	100.0	100.0	100.0	100.0	100.0

SOURCE: UNIVERSITY OF BASEL, DEPT. OF GEOGRAPHY AND ALL INDIA DISASTER MITIGATION INSTITUTE, AHMEDABAD, INDIA 2005. SOCIAL SCIENCE SURVEY IN SELECTED SLUM COMMUNITIES IN THE CITY OF BHUJ, GUJARAT, INDIA.

Table 15.20 Maximum relocation distance (in km), by sex of family head.

Sex Maximum distance	female in % (n=23)	male in % (n=136)	Total in % (n=159)
0.1-1	17.4	14.7	15.1
1.1-2	39.1	46.3	45.3
2.1-3	26.1	25.7	25.8
3.1-4	0.0	0.7	0.6
>4.1	17.4	12.5	13.2
Total	100.0	100.0	100.0

SOURCE: UNIVERSITY OF BASEL, DEPT. OF GEOGRAPHY AND ALL INDIA DISASTER MITIGATION INSTITUTE, AHMEDABAD, INDIA 2005. SOCIAL SCIENCE SURVEY IN SELECTED SLUM COMMUNITIES IN THE CITY OF BHUJ, GUJARAT, INDIA.

Table 15.21 Maximum relocation distance (in km), by occupation of family head.

Occupation Maximum distance	textile/ industry in % (n=9)	govern- ment in % (n=2)	casual labour in % (n=24)	construction in % (n=28)	farming in % (n=4)	automotive related job in % (n=19)	vendor/ shop in % (n=14)	crafts in % (n=7)	service sector in % (n=16)	retiree/ housewife/ unemployed in % (n=31)	unclear/ indian in % (n=4)	Total in % (n=158)
0.1-1	33.3	0.0	8.3	10.7	25.0	15.8	14.3	57.1	12.5	12.9	0.0	15.2
1.1-2	22.2	0.0	66.7	42.9	50.0	52.6	14.3	28.6	50.0	45.2	100.0	45.6
2.1-3	33.3	0.0	20.8	28.6	0.0	10.5	50.0	14.3	31.3	29.0	0.0	25.3
3.1-4	0.0	0.0	0.0	0.0	0.0	0.0	0.0	0.0	0.0	3.2	0.0	0.6
>4.1	11.1	100.0	4.2	17.9	25.0	21.1	21.4	0.0	6.3	9.7	0.0	13.3
Total	100.0	100.0	100.0	100.0	100.0	100.0	100.0	100.0	100.0	100.0	100.0	100.0

SOURCE: UNIVERSITY OF BASEL, DEPT. OF GEOGRAPHY AND ALL INDIA DISASTER MITIGATION INSTITUTE, AHMEDABAD, INDIA 2005. SOCIAL SCIENCE SURVEY IN SELECTED SLUM COMMUNITIES IN THE CITY OF BHUJ, GUJARAT, INDIA.

Table 15.22 Maximum relocation distance (in km), by age of family head.

Age Maximum distance	20-29 in % (n=22)	30-39 in % (n=42)	40-49 in % (n=44)	50-59 in % (n=21)	60-69 in % (n=21)	70-79 in % (n=4)	80-89 in % (n=2)	>90 in % (n=3)	Total in % (n=159)
0.1-1	9.1	19.0	9.1	28.6	19.0	0.0	0.0	0.0	15.1
1.1-2	63.6	40.5	50.0	23.8	42.9	50.0	50.0	66.7	45.3
2.1-3	22.7	23.8	25.0	28.6	28.6	50.0	50.0	0.0	25.8
3.1-4	0.0	0.0	0.0	0.0	0.0	0.0	0.0	33.3	0.6
>4.1	4.5	16.7	15.9	19.0	9.5	0.0	0.0	0.0	13.2
Total	100.0	100.0	100.0	100.0	100.0	100.0	100.0	100.0	100.0

SOURCE: UNIVERSITY OF BASEL, DEPT. OF GEOGRAPHY AND ALL INDIA DISASTER MITIGATION INSTITUTE, AHMEDABAD, INDIA 2005. SOCIAL SCIENCE SURVEY IN SELECTED SLUM COMMUNITIES IN THE CITY OF BHUJ, GUJARAT, INDIA.

15.4 Conclusion

It is very clear that for only one third of the households, relocation for the sake of bettering their housing conditions is a viable option – for almost two thirds, it is not because it uproots people and destroys the social fabric of neighbourhoods and communities. Even for those willing to relocate the trend to move over very short distances is obvious. It appears that relocation as such is not a prime choice for improving personal living conditions and that a strong emphasis is placed upon living in familiar surroundings or family and neighbourhood contexts. In other words, any measures that assist in upgrading existing slum communities are preferred to relocating.

332 Willingness to relocate

Map 15.1 Households willing to relocate, Bhimraonagar

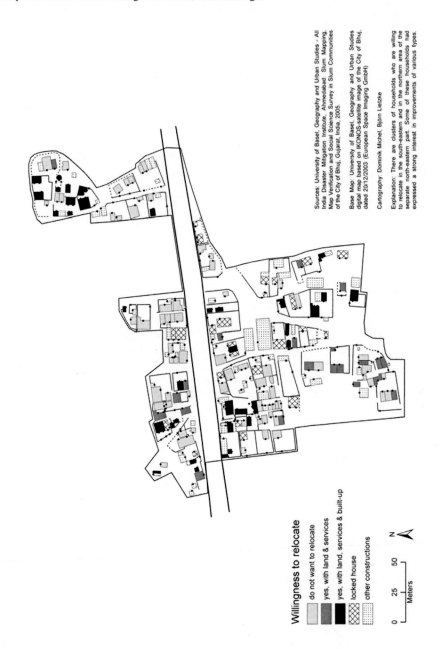

Willingness to relocate 333

Map 15.2 Households willing to relocate, Jayprakashnagar

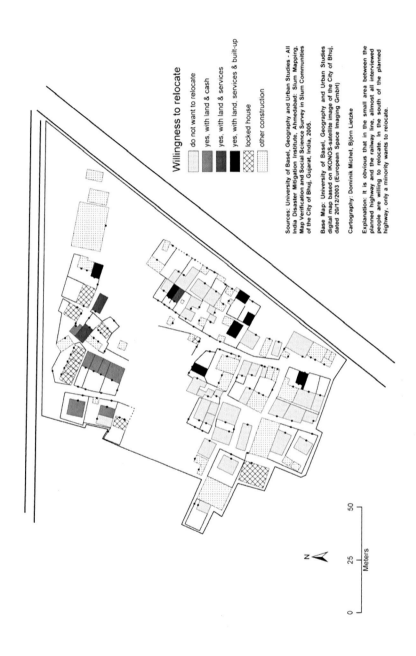

334   Willingness to relocate

Map 15.3 Households willing to relocate, Mustuffanagar

Map 15.4 Households willing to relocate, Shantinagar

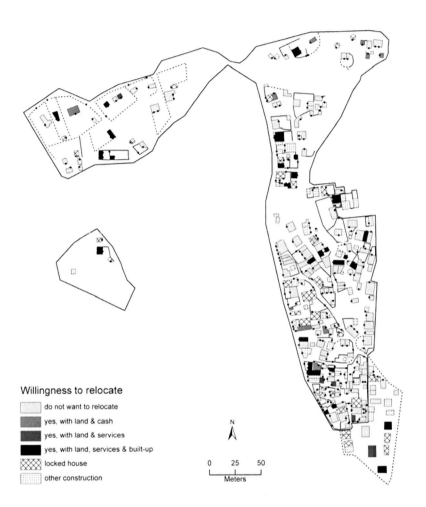

336 Willingness to relocate

Map 15.5 Households willing to relocate with parts of the community only, Bhimraonagar

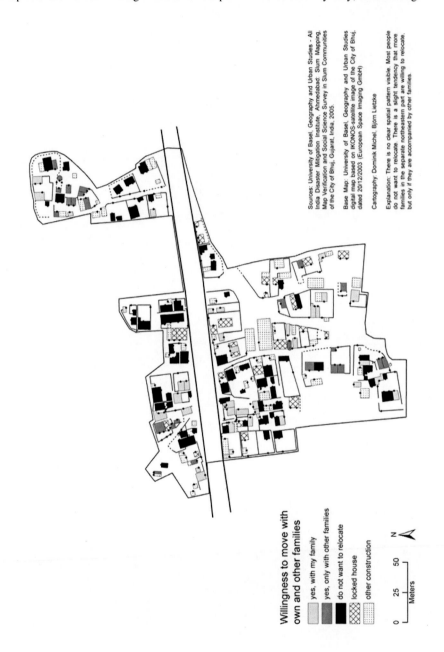

Map 15.6 Households willing to relocate with parts of the community only, Jayprakashnagar

338 Willingness to relocate

Map 15.7 Households willing to relocate with parts of the community only, Mustuffanagar

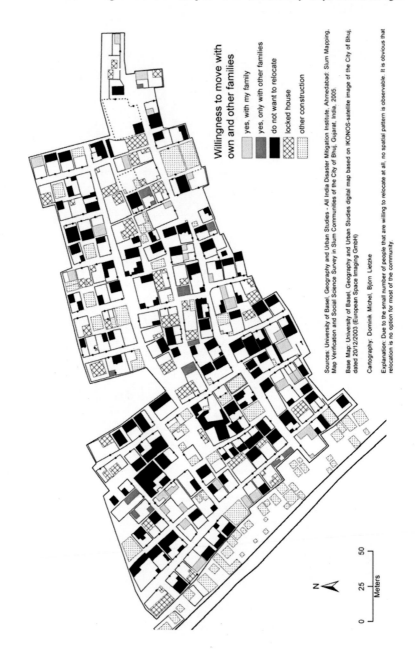

Map 15.8 Households willing to relocate with parts of the community only, Shantinagar

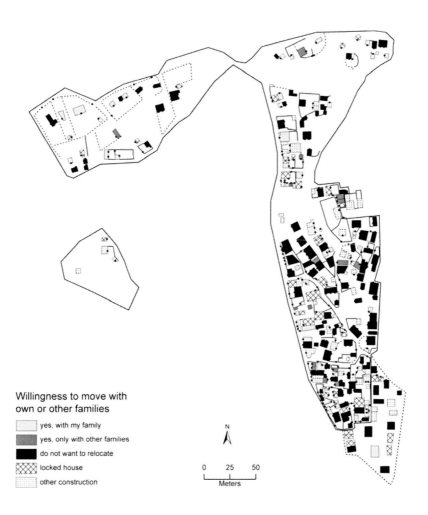

Willingness to move with own or other families
- yes, with my family
- yes, only with other families
- do not want to relocate
- locked house
- other construction

N

0 25 50
Meters

Sources: University of Basel, Geography and Urban Studies - All India Disaster Mitigation Institute, Ahmedabad: Slum Mapping, Map Verification and Social Science Survey in Slum Communities of the City of Bhuj, Gujarat, India, 2005.

Base Map: University of Basel, Geography and Urban Studies digital map based on IKONOS-satellite image of the City of Bhuj, dated 20/12/2003 (European Space Imaging GmbH)

Cartography: Dominik Michel, Björn Lietzke

Explanation: According to the small number of people that are willing to relocate at all, no spatial pattern is visible. It is of note that even if parts of the community were also relocated, this is not an option for the community. It is rather in situ improvements that one wants, as previous maps and survey findings indicate.

340 Willingness to relocate

Map 15.9 Maximum distance willing to relocate, Bhimraonagar

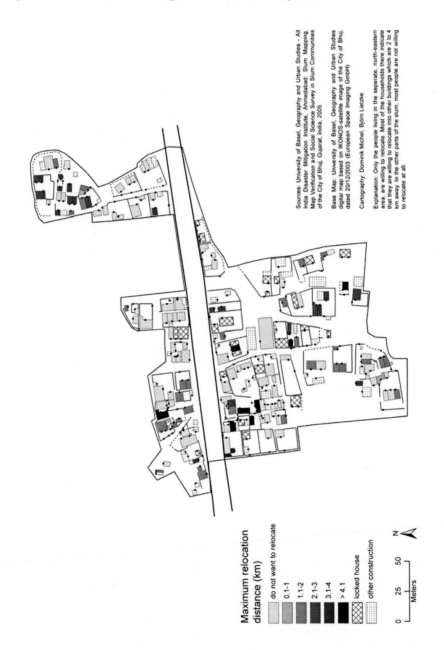

Willingness to relocate 341

Map 15.10 Maximum distance willing to relocate, Jayprakashnagar

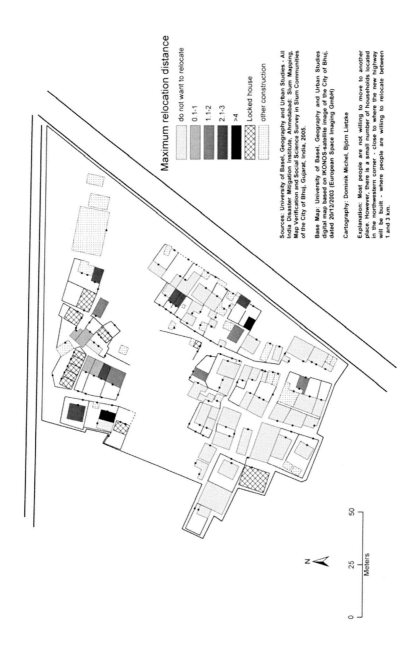

Map 15.11 Maximum distance willing to relocate, Mustuffanagar

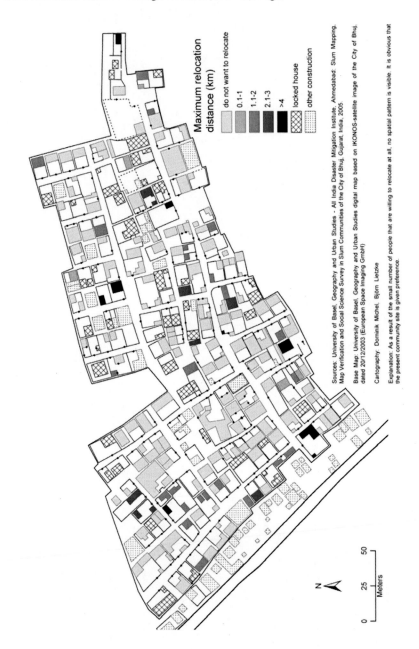

Willingness to relocate 343

Map 15.12 Maximum distance willing to relocate, Shantinagar

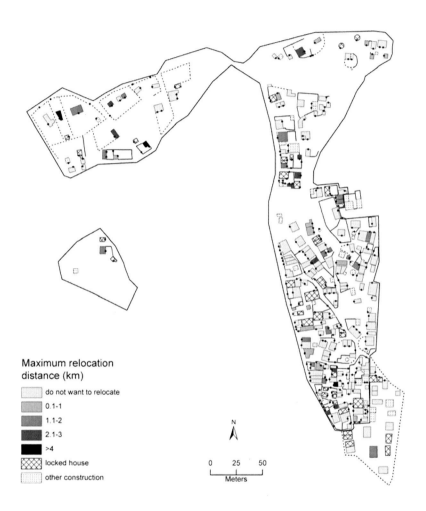

Sources: University of Basel, Geography and Urban Studies - All India Disaster Mitigation Institute, Ahmedabad: Slum Mapping, Map Verification and Social Science Survey in Slum Communities of the City of Bhuj, Gujarat, India, 2005.

Base Map: University of Basel, Geography and Urban Studies digital map based on IKONOS-satellite image of the City of Bhuj, dated 20/12/2003 (European Space Imaging GmbH)

Cartography: Dominik Michel, Björn Lietzke

Explanation: There are hardly any households who are willing to relocate.

16 Help received – help perceived

N. Sliwa, S. Wehrli
University of Basel

16.1
Introduction

The basic idea of this chapter is to elaborate upon the question whether or not and to what degree outside help, be it from the government or from non-governmental sources, as cash or in kind, was received and important in the betterment of slum conditions. The question centers around the particular forms of relief given after the earthquake of 2001 which impacted all communities and made their vulnerability and need for external assistance apparent. Because of this event, the role of relief assistance can be especially well documented because the disaster and the challenge to the livelihood security as well as the efforts necessary still figure prominently in people`s minds. With respect to relief the question whether this was given on an as needed basis or whether this was given preferentially, is of relevance because this is a concern with development aid in general.

16.2
Receiving some form of relief

By slum (Tab. 16.1). In Jayprakashnagar, a greater proportion of the households received some form of relief (51.4%) as compared to Mustaffanagar (38.3%), Shantinagar (35.7%) and Bhimraonagar, where only 19% of the households received help. This might be the result of NGO involvement: AIDMI has been working for a long time in this slum and has also been providing information on how to access governmental funds. Since education and literacy in Jayprakashnagar are relatively good and the ways of accessing information and relief might therefore be a part of people's common knowledge, this finding is not surprising.

Although Shantinagar is generally a very poorly developed and vulnerable community with housing structures and living conditions at a low level, the fact that a higher percentage of the households has received relief as compared to Bhimraonagar, for example, could be an indicator of the needs being recognized and acted upon. The community of Shantinagar did and does have a fairly large proportion of poor housing. Due to the community people's generally lower level of education, information and knowledge, one might have expected a lower percentage of households having received relief. This might portray the consciousness the officials have gained for the particularly bad livelihood of the tribal population that is mainly concentrated in Shantinagar.

Table 16.1 Receiving relief, by slum.

Slum Relief	Bhimraonagar in % (n=126)	Jayprakashnagar in % (n=35)	Mustuffanagar in % (n=128)	Shantinagar in % (n=112)	Total in % (n=401)
yes	19.0	51.4	38.3	35.7	32.7
no	81.0	48.6	61.7	64.3	67.3
Total	100	100	100	100	100

SOURCE: UNIVERSITY OF BASEL, DEPT. OF GEOGRAPHY AND ALL INDIA DISASTER MITIGATION INSTITUTE, AHMEDABAD, INDIA 2005. SOCIAL SCIENCE SURVEY IN SELECTED SLUM COMMUNITIES IN THE CITY OF BHUJ, GUJARAT, INDIA.

By religion (Tab. 16.2). The proportion of Hindu households indicating to have received help (25.6%) is significantly smaller than the proportion of the Muslim households (38.6%). This may be the result of the government supporting minorities such as the Muslims more intensively. On the other hand, this may include relief from sources from within the Muslim communities. The charity among the Muslims themselves might be higher than in other groups, due to the fact that donating to the needy is one of the five pillars of Islam, and due also to the fact that a large proportion of the Indian Muslim communities work abroad in wealthy countries like Saudi-Arabia, Oman, Bahrain, Kuwait etc. They tend to send parts of their high income from the gulf region back home to their poorer relatives or to Muslim communities in general (Personal communication with Yunus Khatri, February 2005).

Table 16.2 Received relief, by religion.

Religion Relief	Hindu in % (n=176)	Muslim in % (n=223)	Total in % (n=399)
yes	25.6	38.6	32.8
no	74.4	61.4	67.2
Total	100	100	100

SOURCE: UNIVERSITY OF BASEL, DEPT. OF GEOGRAPHY AND ALL INDIA DISASTER MITIGATION INSTITUTE, AHMEDABAD, INDIA 2005. SOCIAL SCIENCE SURVEY IN SELECTED SLUM COMMUNITIES IN THE CITY OF BHUJ, GUJARAT, INDIA.

By NGOs, by caste and slum (Tab. 16.3, 16.4). The share of households claiming not to have received any help from NGOs is generally high in all of the surveyed castes. Only 22.8% of the General Castes said they actually did get some kind of non-governmental aid. Over all, 13% of the total households got help from AIDMI or a similar kind of non-governmental organisation. This rather small percentage indicates that NGOs cannot replace governmental efforts needed, yet it does emphasize the importance of NGO engagement.

The survey showed that in Bhimraonagar, however, the percentage of households having received help from NGOs is clearly higher (21.4%) than in the other communities (ranging around 10%). This may result from the fact that AIDMI projects in Bhimraonagar are well-developed and have been on-going for quite a long time already, while projects in Shantinagar and other communities have only started.

Table 16.3 Received relief from other NGOs or similar, by caste.

Caste / Relief from NGOs	SC in % (n=69)	ST in % (n=47)	OBC in % (n=148)	General in % (n=136)	Total in % (n=400)
yes	10.1	10.6	6.1	22.8	13
no	89.9	89.4	93.9	77.2	87
Total	100	100	100	100	100

SOURCE: UNIVERSITY OF BASEL, DEPT. OF GEOGRAPHY AND ALL INDIA DISASTER MITIGATION INSTITUTE, AHMEDABAD, INDIA 2005. SOCIAL SCIENCE SURVEY IN SELECTED SLUM COMMUNITIES IN THE CITY OF BHUJ, GUJARAT, INDIA.

Table 16.4 Received relief from other NGOs or similar, by slum.

Slum / Relief from NGOs	Bhimraonagar in % (n=126)	Jayprakashnagar in % (n=35)	Mustuffanagar in % (n=128)	Shantinagar in % (n=112)	Total in % (n=401)
yes	21.4	0.0	10.9	9.8	13.0
no	78.6	100.0	89.1	90.2	87.0
Total	100	100	100	100	100

SOURCE: UNIVERSITY OF BASEL, DEPT. OF GEOGRAPHY AND ALL INDIA DISASTER MITIGATION INSTITUTE, AHMEDABAD, INDIA 2005. SOCIAL SCIENCE SURVEY IN SELECTED SLUM COMMUNITIES IN THE CITY OF BHUJ, GUJARAT, INDIA.

By NGOs, by religion (Tab. 16.5). 20.5% of all Hindu households said they had been aided by NGOs, as compared to only 6.7% of the Muslim households. Stated differently, the NGOs help did not reach 93.3% of Muslim households and 79.5% of Hindus. NGOs usually target only the poorest and might not have the capacities to help the communities at large the way governmental programs can.

Table 16.5 Received relief from other NGOs or similar, by religion.

Religion / Relief from NGOs	Hindu in % (n=176)	Muslim in % (n=223)	Total in % (n=399)
yes	20.5	6.7	12.8
no	79.5	93.3	87.2
Total	100	100	100

SOURCE: UNIVERSITY OF BASEL, DEPT. OF GEOGRAPHY AND ALL INDIA DISASTER MITIGATION INSTITUTE, AHMEDABAD, INDIA 2005. SOCIAL SCIENCE SURVEY IN SELECTED SLUM COMMUNITIES IN THE CITY OF BHUJ, GUJARAT, INDIA.

16.3
Receiving help with the reconstruction of the house

By slums (Tab. 16.6). A large proportion of the households in the four slums claims not to have received help at all to reconstruct the houses after the earthquake in 2001. Their percentage is highest in Bhimraonagar with 56.3%, followed by Mustaffanagar (49.2%), Shantinagar (43.7%) and Jayprakashnagar with the lowest percentage (30.3%). 12.1% of the households in Japrakashnagar stated that AIDMI helped in the reconstruction of their houses, in Shantinagar 8.6%, in Bhimraonagar 4.0% and in Mustaffanagar 1.5%. The finding may well reflect the fact that help had not been necessary. As to the housing structures and conditions, they are and have been surprisingly good in Mustaffanagar following the earthquake, in parts also in Bhimraonagar and Jayprakashnagar which might explain why such a high proportion did not need to get help for the reconstruction. On the other hand, housing as well as living conditions are rather poor in Shantinagar, so help from the NGO`s sides is urgent and people are very needy of their help.

The fact, however, that 12.1% percent of the households in Jayprakashnagar stated to have been helped to reconstruct their houses although their community has relatively good housing conditions can be seen in relation with the generally higher education level, as compared to Shantinagar. Due to their higher education level and better reading capacities that come with it, Jayprakashnagar`s households might have had more information on where to ask for help.

Table 16.6 Received help to reconstruct house, by slums.

Slum / Help to reconstruct	Bhimraonagar in % (n=126)	Jayprakashnagar in % (n=33)	Mustuffanagar in % (n=130)	Shantinagar in % (n=151)	Total in % (n=440)
help not required	4.0	18.2	8.5	5.3	6.8
did not get help	56.3	30.3	49.2	43.7	48.0
yes, AIDMI	4.0	12.1	1.5	8.6	5.5
yes, other NGO	3.2	6.1	2.3	4.0	3.4
yes, government	13.5	24.2	24.6	29.1	23.0
yes, friends and relatives	4.8	9.1	5.4	4.6	5.2
NGOs & government	13.5	0.0	8.5	4.6	8.0
Total	100.0	100.0	100.0	100.0	100.0

SOURCE: UNIVERSITY OF BASEL, DEPT. OF GEOGRAPHY AND ALL INDIA DISASTER MITIGATION INSTITUTE, AHMEDABAD, INDIA 2005. SOCIAL SCIENCE SURVEY IN SELECTED SLUM COMMUNITIES IN THE CITY OF BHUJ, GUJARAT, INDIA.

By caste (Tab. 16.7). Throughout all of the four surveyed castes (the Scheduled Castes (SC), Scheduled Tribes (ST), Other Backward Castes (OBC) and General Castes), the percentage of the interviewed households stating not to require help is low and at a similar level (6.5%, 4.1%, 6.0% and 8.9%). The fairly even low percentages may indicate that relief was not dependant on caste. The proportion of the households in all castes stating that the government had helped them to reconstruct their houses is generally high with 32.5% as a maximum for the OBC, 18.5% for the General Castes, 18.2% for the SC and 12.2% for the ST. This might be seen in relation with the government's mandate to support the low castes in particular. Nevertheless, the proportion of the Scheduled Tribes households (a caste that has been severely neglected in the past) indicating that the government had helped them with the reconstruction of their houses, is the smallest (12.2%). Since literacy and education among the Tribals are especially low and therefore, information levels as high, it might be difficult for them to efficiently reach for help. This finding, then, supports the notion that in a non discriminatory procedure of relief giving, it is education and information that make the difference as to whether or not households themselves access relief.

Table 16.7 Received help to reconstruct house, by caste.

Caste Help to reconstruct	SC in % (n=77)	ST in % (n=49)	OBC in % (n=166)	General in % (n=146)	Total in % (n=439)
help not required	6.5	4.1	6.0	8.9	6.8
did not get help	55.8	67.3	44.6	41.1	48.1
yes, AIDMI	3.9	8.2	6.6	4.1	5.5
yes, other NGO	1.3	6.1	4.2	2.7	3.4
yes, government	18.2	12.2	32.5	18.5	23.0
yes, friends and relatives	9.1		3.0	7.5	5.2
NGOs & government	5.2	2.0	3.0	17.1	8.0
Total	100	100	100	100	100

SOURCE: UNIVERSITY OF BASEL, DEPT. OF GEOGRAPHY AND ALL INDIA DISASTER MITIGATION INSTITUTE, AHMEDABAD, INDIA 2005. SOCIAL SCIENCE SURVEY IN SELECTED SLUM COMMUNITIES IN THE CITY OF BHUJ, GUJARAT, INDIA.

By religion (Tab. 16.8). Generally, the percentage of Hindus stating not to have received help to reconstruct their homes (43.7%) is lower than the percentage of Muslims (51.6%). Almost 8% of the Hindu households said to have been helped by AIDMI to reconstruct their homes, as compared to only 3.6% among the interviewed Muslim households that said so.

Although one could suppose that Muslims might have been neglected as compared to Hindus, a notion that is supported by Muslim proponents and some Western clichés, a different explanation emerges: the almost exclusively Muslim community Mustaffanagar is by far the slum with the best housing and living conditions. The literacy rate here is particularly high, too (AIDMI estimates 80-90%), and so people might generally have a good access to necessary information regarding help. If nevertheless a smaller proportion of Muslim households claims to have received relief, this may reflect the fact that less help was necessary which is also supported by the slum profiles. Clearly, the needs in this Muslim area are less urgent than, for example in Shantinagar, a mostly Hindu community with major problems not only in terms of housing, and where NGOs like AIDMI have started working only recently.

Interestingly, the proportion of Muslim households indicating "Yes, help from government" is larger than the percentage of the Hindu majority saying so. This differing perception among Hindus and Muslims could be the result of positive discrimination towards the Muslim minority from the official side (Hindu households claim "Yes, help from the government to reconstruct the house" at 18.4%, Muslims state that at 26.2%).

Table 16.8 Received help to reconstruct house, by religion.

Religion / Help to reconstruct	Hindu in % (n=190)	Muslim in % (n=248)	Total in % (n=438)
help not required	7.4	6.5	6.8
did not get help	43.7	51.6	48.2
yes, AIDMI	7.9	3.6	5.5
yes, other NGO	4.2	2.8	3.4
yes, government	18.4	26.2	22.8
yes, friends and relatives	6.3	4.4	5.3
NGOs & government	12.1	4.8	8.0
Total	100	100	100

SOURCE: UNIVERSITY OF BASEL, DEPT. OF GEOGRAPHY AND ALL INDIA DISASTER MITIGATION INSTITUTE, AHMEDABAD, INDIA 2005. SOCIAL SCIENCE SURVEY IN SELECTED SLUM COMMUNITIES IN THE CITY OF BHUJ, GUJARAT, INDIA.

By occupation (Tab. 16.9). The findings support the notion that governmental help was well spread and did not depend on socio-economic conditions of the households. Generally, the proportions of those stating to have been helped by the government to reconstruct the houses are high throughout all professions. The exceptions in terms of specific professions are those who hold government jobs: the share that perceives that "help is not required" is highest in this occupation category (9.1%). Their situation might be more stable due to the safe jobs they have, so help might be less needed compared to people working in the informal sector without any social security.

Table 16.9 Received help to reconstruct house, by occupation of family head.

Occupation Help to reconstruct	textile/ industry in % (n=31)	government in % (n=11)	casual labour in % (n=79)	construction in % (n=78)	farming in % (n=12)	automotive related job in % (n=40)	vendor/ shop in % (n=36)	crafts in % (n=14)	service sector in % (n=38)	retiree/ housewife/ unemployed in % (n=82)	unclear/ indian in % (n=12)	Total in % (n=433)
help not required	6.5	9.1	5.1	1.3	0.0	5.0	8.3	14.3	15.8	7.3	16.7	6.7
did not get help	48.4	36.4	41.8	47.4	50.0	60.0	47.2	35.7	55.3	53.7	25.0	48.3
yes, AIDMI	0.0	0.0	7.6	7.7	0.0	5.0	8.3	0.0	7.9	3.7	8.3	5.5
yes, other NGO	3.2	0.0	3.8	2.6	8.3	2.5	2.8	0.0	2.6	4.9	8.3	3.5
yes, government	22.6	36.4	27.8	28.2	25.0	17.5	19.4	28.6	7.9	22.0	25.0	23.1
yes, friends and relatives	9.7	18.2	10.1	0.0	0.0	0.0	8.3	14.3	2.6	2.4	8.3	5.1
NGOs & government	9.7	0.0	3.8	12.8	16.7	10.0	5.6	7.1	7.9	6.1	8.3	7.9
Total	100	100	100	100	100	100	100	100	100	100	100	100

SOURCE: UNIVERSITY OF BASEL, DEPT. OF GEOGRAPHY AND ALL INDIA DISASTER MITIGATION INSTITUTE, AHMEDABAD, INDIA 2005. SOCIAL SCIENCE SURVEY IN SELECTED SLUM COMMUNITIES IN THE CITY OF BHUJ, GUJARAT, INDIA

16.4
Receiving different types of help

16.4.1
Material

By caste (Tab. 16.10). A high proportion of the Scheduled Tribes households indicated to have received material relief, as compared to households of the Scheduled Castes (53.3%) or Other Backward Castes (34.2%). Since the Scheduled Tribes usually live in tents or non stable housing made up of stones and rocks put on top of each other, they are more vulnerable to earthquakes and their need for material help is greater. The fact that they did receive material relief to a high degree might be an indicator of their particular needs being recognized and being acted upon.

Table 16.10 Type of relief received: material, by caste.

Caste / Material	SC in % (n=22)	ST in % (n=30)	OBC in % (n=73)	General in % (n=55)	Total in % (n=180)
yes	31.8	53.3	34.2	69.1	47.8
no	68.2	46.7	65.8	30.9	52.2
Total	100	100	100	100	100

SOURCE: UNIVERSITY OF BASEL, DEPT. OF GEOGRAPHY AND ALL INDIA DISASTER MITIGATION INSTITUTE, AHMEDABAD, INDIA 2005. SOCIAL SCIENCE SURVEY IN SELECTED SLUM COMMUNITIES IN THE CITY OF BHUJ, GUJARAT, INDIA.

By religion (Tab. 16.11). A smaller proportion of Muslim households (36.1%) than Hindu ones (61.0%) stated to have received material relief. This could be expected taking into consideration that the Muslim community of Mustaffanagar generally has a remarkably good housing situation with stable buildings and large compounds, whereas other, mainly Hindu communities, have a major need of development concerning the living and housing conditions. As such, both religion and caste do not make a difference. Rather it is the need that arises from the particular local conditions.

Table 16.11 Type of relief received: material, by religion.

Religion / Material	Hindu in % (n=82)	Muslim in % (n=97)	Total in % (n=179)
yes	61.0	36.1	47.5
no	39.0	63.9	52.5
Total	100	100	100

SOURCE: UNIVERSITY OF BASEL, DEPT. OF GEOGRAPHY AND ALL INDIA DISASTER MITIGATION INSTITUTE, AHMEDABAD, INDIA 2005. SOCIAL SCIENCE SURVEY IN SELECTED SLUM COMMUNITIES IN THE CITY OF BHUJ, GUJARAT, INDIA.

16.4.2
Cash

By caste (Tab. 16.12). A total of 66.1% of the interviewed people have been given financial support either by the government or by non-governmental organisations. 73.3% of the Scheduled Tribes, 69.9% of the Other Backward Castes and 68.2% of the Scheduled Castes did get governmental cash assistance. It seems that the people most affected by poverty and most vulnerable to natural and other disasters actually do get most of governmental and other aid. Still, a third of the total households (33.9%) did not get any financial aid at all. This may reflect the fact that they did not get cash assistance because their houses were not affected and livelihood not worsened, or that they received material relief because this was the most appropriate type of assistance.

Table 16.12 Type of relief received: cash, by caste.

Cash	Caste	SC in % (n=22)	ST in % (n=30)	OBC in % (n=73)	General in % (n=55)	Total in % (n=180)
yes		68.2	73.3	69.9	56.4	66.1
no		31.8	26.7	30.1	43.6	33.9
Total		100	100	100	100	100

SOURCE: UNIVERSITY OF BASEL, DEPT. OF GEOGRAPHY AND ALL INDIA DISASTER MITIGATION INSTITUTE, AHMEDABAD, INDIA 2005. SOCIAL SCIENCE SURVEY IN SELECTED SLUM COMMUNITIES IN THE CITY OF BHUJ, GUJARAT, INDIA.

By religion (Tab. 16.13). As table 16.13 shows, the Muslim households clearly got more financial aid than the Hindus (77.3% vs. 53.7%). Reasons for this might be the ones elaborated before: many Muslim households have family members working abroad in wealthy Arab countries, supporting their families financially from abroad.

Table 16.13 Type of relief received: cash, by religion.

Cash	Religion	Hindu in % (n=82)	Muslim in % (n=97)	Total in % (n=179)
yes		53.7	77.3	66.5
no		46.3	22.7	33.5
Total		100	100	100

SOURCE: UNIVERSITY OF BASEL, DEPT. OF GEOGRAPHY AND ALL INDIA DISASTER MITIGATION INSTITUTE, AHMEDABAD, INDIA 2005. SOCIAL SCIENCE SURVEY IN SELECTED SLUM COMMUNITIES IN THE CITY OF BHUJ, GUJARAT, INDIA.

By slum (Tab. 16.14). Table 16.14 shows that the Muslim community of Mustuffanagar got more financial aid per capita (82.8%) than any other of the slum communities in question, second is Bhimraonagar with 65.6%. However, only 52.7 % of the visibly poorer population of Shantinagar got financial support after the earthquake. This is probably related to the fact that the many Tribals and illiterates living in this slum do not have the same access to governmental or other help. There is a high degree of illiteracy and therefore these people do not have the knowledge on how to get governmental assistance. Also, they cannot make themselves heard as other communities do. Also, the low percentage of households having received financial aid by non-governmental organisations like AIDMI might be explained by the fact that they have started working in this community very recently only.

Table 16.14 Type of relief received: cash, by slum.

Cash \ Slum	Bhimraonagar in % (n=64)	Jayprakashnagar in % (n=3)	Mustuffanagar in % (n=58)	Shantinagar in % (n=55)	Total in % (n=180)
yes	65.6	0.0	82.8	52.7	66.1
no	34.4	100.0	17.2	47.3	33.9
Total	100	100	100	100	100

SOURCE: UNIVERSITY OF BASEL, DEPT. OF GEOGRAPHY AND ALL INDIA DISASTER MITIGATION INSTITUTE, AHMEDABAD, INDIA 2005. SOCIAL SCIENCE SURVEY IN SELECTED SLUM COMMUNITIES IN THE CITY OF BHUJ, GUJARAT, INDIA.

16.4.3 Information

By caste (Tab. 16.15). Obviously, there is still a severe lack of information concerning earthquake-proof building, damage prevention and disaster mitigation in all of the surveyed slums. 98.9% of the households stated not having received any information, be it from the governmental or another side. 96.7% of the Scheduled Tribes and even 100% of the Scheduled and Other Backward Castes stated not having been informed. The high percentages underline to what extent the dissemination of information is still difficult and inefficient. It is not mandatory to attend information meetings and possibly, considerable parts of the slum population never met with people from AIDMI or other NGOs, let alone government agencies.

Moreover, the dissemination of information cannot easily be coordinated. It entirely depends on the local individuals (NGO-volunteers and their work, but also the community inhabitants themselves), if people talk to each other about prevention measures, if they are willing to learn from each other and to participate actively in learning programs.

Table 16.15 Type of relief received: information, by caste.

Information \ Caste	SC in % (n=22)	ST in % (n=30)	OBC in % (n=73)	General in % (n=55)	Total in % (n=180)
yes	0.0	3.3	1.4	0.0	1.1
no	100.0	96.7	98.6	100.0	98.9
Total	100	100	100	100	100

SOURCE: UNIVERSITY OF BASEL, DEPT. OF GEOGRAPHY AND ALL INDIA DISASTER MITIGATION INSTITUTE, AHMEDABAD, INDIA 2005. SOCIAL SCIENCE SURVEY IN SELECTED SLUM COMMUNITIES IN THE CITY OF BHUJ, GUJARAT, INDIA.

By religion (Tab. 16.16). Muslim and Hindu households show a similar lack of knowledge of disaster mitigation possibilities. A total of only 2.4% of the Hindu households actually did receive knowledge and information training of some kind. The Muslims state not to have received any informal aid at all.

Table 16.16 Type of relief received: information, by religion.

Religion / Information	Hindu in % (n=82)	Muslim in % (n=97)	Total in % (n=179)
yes	2.4	0.0	1.1
no	97.6	100.0	98.9
Total	100	100	100

SOURCE: UNIVERSITY OF BASEL, DEPT. OF GEOGRAPHY AND ALL INDIA DISASTER MITIGATION INSTITUTE, AHMEDABAD, INDIA 2005. SOCIAL SCIENCE SURVEY IN SELECTED SLUM COMMUNITIES IN THE CITY OF BHUJ, GUJARAT, INDIA.

By slum (Tab. 16.17). Table 16.17 confirms the general lack of information on earthquake-proof building and disaster mitigation possibilities in the slums. Whereas in Shantinagar, 98.4% of the households claim not to have received information, this value reaches 100% in Jayprakash- and Mustuffanagar. This is all the more alarming if one considers that the Bhuj earthquake killed nearly 50 000 people and that the region is a risk zone. Yet, people have not learned how to protect their families from such natural disasters and how to build earthquake-proof housing.

Table 16.17 Type of relief received: information, by slum.

Slum / Information	Bhimraonagar in % (n=64)	Jayprakashnagar in % (n=3)	Mustuffanagar in % (n=58)	Shantinagar in % (n=55)	Total in % (n=180)
yes	1.6	0.0	0.0	1.8	1.1
no	98.4	100.0	100.0	98.2	98.9
Total	100	100	100	100	100

SOURCE: UNIVERSITY OF BASEL, DEPT. OF GEOGRAPHY AND ALL INDIA DISASTER MITIGATION INSTITUTE, AHMEDABAD, INDIA 2005. SOCIAL SCIENCE SURVEY IN SELECTED SLUM COMMUNITIES IN THE CITY OF BHUJ, GUJARAT, INDIA.

16.5
Receiving relief from the government

By slum (Tab. 16.18). In all four slum communities, high proportions of households confirmed government assistance. A very high share of relief from the government was received in Bhimraonagar (70.1%) and in Mustaffanagar (52.34%), the Muslim area that might be supported by the government in particular due to its inhabitants` minority status, but also a community of fairly good educational levels and hence, options for getting the necessary information more easily.

The percentage of those stating to have received relief from the government is high in Shantinagar as well (41.7%). Relief here is and will be very necessary since the community is ill-developed. Many inhabitants belong to the Scheduled Tribes that have particularly bad living conditions and high illiteracy rates. The fact that higher percentages of households from this community received governmental relief might reflect the new priorities from the official side to help the least developed communities in particular. It might also reflect the fact that due to the poor housing substance, disaster impact was greatest and therefore also the need of relief.

Table 16.18 Received relief from government, by slum.

Slum Relief from Government	Bhimraonagar in % (n=126)	Jayprakashnagar in % (n=35)	Mustuffanagar in % (n=128)	Shantinagar in % (n=112)	Total in % (n=401)
yes	70.6	34.3	52.3	41.1	53.4
no	29.4	65.7	47.7	58.9	46.6
Total	100	100	100	100	100

SOURCE: UNIVERSITY OF BASEL, DEPT. OF GEOGRAPHY AND ALL INDIA DISASTER MITIGATION INSTITUTE, AHMEDABAD, INDIA 2005. SOCIAL SCIENCE SURVEY IN SELECTED SLUM COMMUNITIES IN THE CITY OF BHUJ, GUJARAT, INDIA.

By sex of family head (Tab. 16.19). Family heads of both sexes stated to have received relief from the government, yet the percentage of female family heads saying so is remarkably higher than the male headed households` percentage (female: 67.3% compared to 51.2% of the male). This could indicate that females have different ways of accessing information on relief and of taking action when it comes to needs of the family. Also, the female perception of what relief is might differ from the male points of view. As to the interviewed women, they apparently are more able to access relief for their families from the government. Possibly their communication with the officials is different and more effective than that of male persons. However, this must be seen as a tendency only since the numbers of female headed households are by far smaller than those of male headed households, making it difficult to establish statistical significance.

Table 16.19 Received relief from government, by sex of family head.

Sex Relief from Government	Female in % (n=55)	Male in % (n=346)	Total in % (n=401)
yes	67.3	51.2	53.4
no	32.7	48.8	46.6
Total	100	100	100

SOURCE: UNIVERSITY OF BASEL, DEPT. OF GEOGRAPHY AND ALL INDIA DISASTER MITIGATION INSTITUTE, AHMEDABAD, INDIA 2005. SOCIAL SCIENCE SURVEY IN SELECTED SLUM COMMUNITIES IN THE CITY OF BHUJ, GUJARAT, INDIA.

By religion, by caste, by education and by age (Tab. 16.20, 16.21, 16.22 and 16.23). In general, government relief does not seem to have been influenced whatsoever by people's religion, caste membership, education or age. The fact that these cross-tabulations were in no case statistically significant indicates that governmental relief is distributed in an egalitarian way, based on need only.

Table 16.20 Received relief from government, by religion.

Religion Relief from Government	Hindu in % (n=176)	Muslim in % (n=223)	Total in % (n=399)
yes	55.1	52.0	53.4
no	44.9	48.0	46.6
Total	100	100	100

SOURCE: UNIVERSITY OF BASEL, DEPT. OF GEOGRAPHY AND ALL INDIA DISASTER MITIGATION INSTITUTE, AHMEDABAD, INDIA 2005. SOCIAL SCIENCE SURVEY IN SELECTED SLUM COMMUNITIES IN THE CITY OF BHUJ, GUJARAT, INDIA.

Table 16.21 Received relief from government, by caste.

Caste Relief from Government	SC in % (n=69)	ST in % (n=47)	OBC in % (n=148)	General in % (n=136)	Total in % (n=400)
yes	60.9	57.4	50.0	52.2	53.5
no	39.1	42.6	50.0	47.8	46.5
Total	100	100	100	100	100

SOURCE: UNIVERSITY OF BASEL, DEPT. OF GEOGRAPHY AND ALL INDIA DISASTER MITIGATION INSTITUTE, AHMEDABAD, INDIA 2005. SOCIAL SCIENCE SURVEY IN SELECTED SLUM COMMUNITIES IN THE CITY OF BHUJ, GUJARAT, INDIA.

Table 16.22 Received relief from government, by education standard of family head.

Education Relief from Government	Hrs. 1-3 in % (n=40)	Hrs. 4-6 in % (n=63)	Hrs. 7-9 in % (n=84)	Hrs. 10-12 in % (n=30)	Completed graduation in % (n=5)	Illiterate in % (n=179)	Total in % (n=401)
yes	62.5	44.4	51.2	53.3	80.0	54.7	53.4
no	37.5	55.6	48.8	46.7	20.0	45.3	46.6
Total	100.0	100.0	100.0	100.0	100.0	100.0	100.0

SOURCE: UNIVERSITY OF BASEL, DEPT. OF GEOGRAPHY AND ALL INDIA DISASTER MITIGATION INSTITUTE, AHMEDABAD, INDIA 2005. SOCIAL SCIENCE SURVEY IN SELECTED SLUM COMMUNITIES IN THE CITY OF BHUJ, GUJARAT, INDIA.

Table 16.23 Received relief from government, by age of family head.

Age Relief from Government	0-19 in % (n=1)	20-29 in % (n=44)	30-39 in % (n=102)	40-49 in % (n=106)	50-59 in % (n=59)	60-69 in % (n=55)	70-79 in % (n=22)	80-89 in % (n=7)	>90 in % (n=5)	Total in % (n=401)
yes	100	27.3	52.0	56.6	61.0	56.4	59.1	71.4	60.0	53.4
no	0.0	72.7	48.0	43.4	39.0	43.6	40.9	28.6	40.0	46.6
Total	100	100	100	100	100	100	100	100	100	100

SOURCE: UNIVERSITY OF BASEL, DEPT. OF GEOGRAPHY AND ALL INDIA DISASTER MITIGATION INSTITUTE, AHMEDABAD, INDIA 2005. SOCIAL SCIENCE SURVEY IN SELECTED SLUM COMMUNITIES IN THE CITY OF BHUJ, GUJARAT, INDIA.

16.6
Receiving relief from AIDMI

By slum (Tab. 16.24). The highest proportions of relief received from AIDMI were observed in the communities of Shantinagar and Jayprakashnagar (24.1% and 14.3%). This is not surprising, as AIDMI has been working in Jayprakashnagar intensively for a longer period and since the relief work in Shantinagar, the poorest among the four slum communities, has been a major priority of AIDMI`s.

As Mustaffanagar has the best living and housing conditions among all of the slums and AIDMI has been involved here for a long time, the current perception of relief received from AIDMI might have changed due to the fact that the needs are not as urgent and basic anymore – a lot of work from the non governmental side has obviously been done here already.

Table 16.24 Received relief from AIDMI, by slum.

Slum Relief from AIDMI	Bhimraonagar in % (n=126)	Jayprakashnagar in % n=35)	Mustuffanagar in % (n=128)	Shantinagar in % (n=112)	Total in % (n=401)
yes	11.1	14.3	7.8	24.1	14.0
no	88.9	85.7	92.2	75.9	86.0
Total	100	100	100	100	100

SOURCE: UNIVERSITY OF BASEL, DEPT. OF GEOGRAPHY AND ALL INDIA DISASTER MITIGATION INSTITUTE, AHMEDABAD, INDIA 2005. SOCIAL SCIENCE SURVEY IN SELECTED SLUM COMMUNITIES IN THE CITY OF BHUJ, GUJARAT, INDIA.

By caste (Tab. 16.25). A higher percentage of households of the Scheduled Tribes (ST) stated to have received relief from AIDMI (23.4%), followed by the OBC households (16.9%), households belonging to SC (10.1%) and General Castes (9.6%). Since AIDMI has intensified its work in the community of Shantinagar, where a large part of the households belongs to the Scheduled Tribes, it is not surprising that they state to have received relief from this organisation at the highest percentage. One of AIDMI `s priorities is to help the poorest and most vulnerable segments of the population first - the Tribals (ST) generally belong to the most vulnerable, and therefore, their perception of having received relief from AIDMI at a high percentage corresponds to AIDMI`s efforts.

Table 16.25 Received relief from AIDMI, by caste.

Caste Relief from AIDMI	SC in % (n=69)	ST in % (n=47)	OBC in % (n=148)	General in % (n=136)	Total in % (n=401)
yes	10.1	23.4	16.9	9.6	14.0
no	89.9	76.6	83.1	90.4	86.0
Total	100	100	100	100	100

SOURCE: UNIVERSITY OF BASEL, DEPT. OF GEOGRAPHY AND ALL INDIA DISASTER MITIGATION INSTITUTE, AHMEDABAD, INDIA 2005. SOCIAL SCIENCE SURVEY IN SELECTED SLUM COMMUNITIES IN THE CITY OF BHUJ, GUJARAT, INDIA.

16.7
General linkages with AIDMI

By slum, religion, caste and sex of family head (Tab. 16.26 to 16.29). The most common linkage people have with AIDMI is that they are residents of AIDMI's working slum area (82.7% in total). All the other linkages are comparably rare and range between 1.6% for having Afatvimo (Micro insurance) and 6.9% of the households being shelter relief beneficiaries. On the whole, this picture does not change considerably between male- and female-headed households, castes and slums. Mustuffanagar shows the highest percentage of residents of an AIDMI working slum area (85.4%), Bhimraonagar the lowest, with a percentage that is still fairly high (78.5%). There are more Muslim than Hindu households (87%, 77.7%) in AIDMI's working slum area. The statistics reflect the efforts made by AIDMI that, contrary to other organisations and institutions, focuses its aid on the poorest and most vulnerable parts of the society and thus extends aid and support also in Muslim communities that have minority status and oftentimes are deemed to be poorer.

Table 16.26 Linkages with AIDMI, by slum.

Slum Linkages with AIDMI	Bhimraona-gar in % (n=130)	Jayprakashna-gar in % (n=54)	Mustuffana-gar in % (n=130)	Shantina-gar in % (n=138)	Total in % (n=452)
having afatvimo	3.8	0.0	0.8	2.9	2.2
member of CCISB	2.3	0.0	3.8	1.4	2.2
livelihood relief beneficiary	8.5	0.0	6.2	8.7	6.9
shelter relief beneficiary	1.5	1.9	0.0	2.2	1.3
resident of AIDMI's Working Slum Area	78.5	85.2	85.4	83.3	82.7
having afatvimo & livelihood relief beneficiary	5.4	0.0	3.8	1.4	3.1
Total	100	100	100	100	100

SOURCE: UNIVERSITY OF BASEL, DEPT. OF GEOGRAPHY AND ALL INDIA DISASTER MITIGATION INSTITUTE, AHMEDABAD, INDIA 2005. SOCIAL SCIENCE SURVEY IN SELECTED SLUM COMMUNITIES IN THE CITY OF BHUJ, GUJARAT, INDIA.

Table 16.27 Linkages with AIDMI, by religion.

Linkages with AIDMI	Religion	Hindu in % (n=202)	Muslim in % (n=247)	Total in % (n=449)
member of CCISB		2.0	2.0	2.0
livelihood relief beneficiary		5.9	7.7	6.9
shelter relief beneficiary		2.5	0.4	1.3
resident of AIDMI's Working Slum Area		77.7	87.0	82.9
having afatvimo & livelihood relief beneficiary		5.0	1.6	3.1
Total		100	100	100

SOURCE: UNIVERSITY OF BASEL, DEPT. OF GEOGRAPHY AND ALL INDIA DISASTER MITIGATION INSTITUTE, AHMEDABAD, INDIA 2005. SOCIAL SCIENCE SURVEY IN SELECTED SLUM COMMUNITIES IN THE CITY OF BHUJ, GUJARAT, INDIA.

Table 16.28 Linkages with AIDMI, by caste.

Linkages with AIDMI	Caste	SC in % (n=86)	ST n % (n=55)	OBC in % (n=171)	General in % (n=138)	Total in % (n=451)
having afatvimo		2.3	5.5	0.6	2.9	2.2
member of CCISB		3.5	3.6	1.8	1.4	2.2
livelihood relief beneficiary		5.8	12.7	8.2	3.6	6.9
shelter relief beneficiary		2.3	3.6	0.6	0.7	1.3
resident of AIDMI's Working Slum Area		77.9	65.5	87.7	86.2	82.7
having afatvimo & livelihood relief beneficiary		5.8	3.6	1.2	3.6	3.1
Total		100	100	100	100	100

SOURCE: UNIVERSITY OF BASEL, DEPT. OF GEOGRAPHY AND ALL INDIA DISASTER MITIGATION INSTITUTE, AHMEDABAD, INDIA 2005. SOCIAL SCIENCE SURVEY IN SELECTED SLUM COMMUNITIES IN THE CITY OF BHUJ, GUJARAT, INDIA.

Table 16.29 Linkages with AIDMI, by sex of family head.

Linkages with AIDMI	Sex	female in % (n=63)	male n % (n=387)	Total in % (n=450)
having afatvimo		3.2	2.1	2.2
member of CCISB		1.6	2.3	2.2
livelihood relief beneficiary		11.1	6.2	6.9
shelter relief beneficiary		0.0	1.6	1.3
resident of AIDMI's Working Slum Area		81.0	82.9	82.7
having afatvimo & livelihood relief beneficiary		1.6	3.4	3.1
Total		100	100	100

SOURCE: UNIVERSITY OF BASEL, DEPT. OF GEOGRAPHY AND ALL INDIA DISASTER MITIGATION INSTITUTE, AHMEDABAD, INDIA 2005. SOCIAL SCIENCE SURVEY IN SELECTED SLUM COMMUNITIES IN THE CITY OF BHUJ, GUJARAT, INDIA.

16.8
Evaluation: role of relief donors

By sex of family head (Tab. 16.30). With 65%, the government is the most important contributor of disaster relief in the slum communities, followed by AIDMI (17.5%) and other NGOs (11.7%). Slightly more women than men (69.2%, as compared to 64.2%) claimed to have received some kind of governmental aid. The difference is even more evident when focussing on AIDMI`s aid which supports female-headed households in 25.6% of all cases, and households with a male head of family in 16.1% of the cases. In clear contrast to this, aid by other NGOs was mainly given to male heads of families (12.8% vs. 5.1%) and their households. Also, help by families and friends seems is more likely to be given to male heads of families than to female ones. It is clear that the government is the most important agent of change, furthermore, that NGOs address the particularly vulnerable segments of society. In this particular case, however, they do this differently than AIDMI that sets the prime role in helping poor women as society's most neglected segment.

Table 16.30 Who helped the most, by sex of family head.

Helped most	Sex / female in % (n=65)	male in % (n=431)	Total in % (n=496)
government	41.5	32.5	33.7
AIDMI	15.4	8.1	9.1
other NGOs	3.1	6.5	6.0
families and friends	0.0	3.5	3.0
Total	100	100	100

SOURCE: UNIVERSITY OF BASEL, DEPT. OF GEOGRAPHY AND ALL INDIA DISASTER MITIGATION INSTITUTE, AHMEDABAD, INDIA 2005. SOCIAL SCIENCE SURVEY IN SELECTED SLUM COMMUNITIES IN THE CITY OF BHUJ, GUJARAT, INDIA.

By religion (Tab. 16.31). Governmental aid was considered most important in Muslim communities (70.8%), while help by AIDMI (20%) and other NGOs (15.2%) was considered especially important in Hindu communities. The latter could be accidental or requires further explanations. The importance of help by family and by friends was considered nearly equally high (Hindus: 5.6%, Muslims: 6.2%). Interestingly, government aid was considered slightly more important in Muslim households, maybe because they are particularly aware of their minority status and of the role of the government therein.

Table 16.31 Who helped the most, by religion.

Helped most / Religion	Hindu in % (n=125)	Muslim in % (n=130)	Total in % (n=255)
government	59.2	70.8	65.1
AIDMI	20	15.4	17.6
other NGOs	15.2	7.7	11.4
families and friends	5.6	6.2	5.9
Total	100	100	100

SOURCE: UNIVERSITY OF BASEL, DEPT. OF GEOGRAPHY AND ALL INDIA DISASTER MITIGATION INSTITUTE, AHMEDABAD, INDIA 2005. SOCIAL SCIENCE SURVEY IN SELECTED SLUM COMMUNITIES IN THE CITY OF BHUJ, GUJARAT, INDIA.

By slum (Tab. 16.32). Governmental aid was perceived as more important in Mustuffanagar (71.2%) and Jayprakashnagar (70.6%), whereas AIDMI's help is focused on Shantinagar (33.3%). This seems to be the logic consequence of Shantinagar being the poorest of all communities. On the whole, all slums are more or less equally considered either by government or by NGOs. Why AIDMI assistance is not considered very important in a Muslim environment might be explained by the fact that Mustaffanagar, the predominantly Muslim community, is by far better off than the other surveyed areas. Also, it was not as much impacted by the disaster and therefore did not seek AIDMI assistance that intensively.

Table 16.32 Who helped the most, by slum.

Helped most / Slum	Bhimraonagar in % (n=102)	Jayprakashnagar in % (n=17)	Mustuffanagar in % (n=66)	Shantinagar in % (n=72)	Total in % (n=257)
government	65.7	70.6	71.2	56.9	65
AIDMI	10.8	23.5	9.1	33.3	17.5
other NGOs	18.6	0.0	12.1	4.2	11.7
families and friends	4.9	5.9	7.6	5.6	5.8
Total	100	100	100	100	100

SOURCE: UNIVERSITY OF BASEL, DEPT. OF GEOGRAPHY AND ALL INDIA DISASTER MITIGATION INSTITUTE, AHMEDABAD, INDIA 2005. SOCIAL SCIENCE SURVEY IN SELECTED SLUM COMMUNITIES IN THE CITY OF BHUJ, GUJARAT, INDIA.

16.9 Conclusion

Several conclusions can be drawn from the analysis of help received and its perception. Generally, the importance of NGO work in communities that government programs have not reached or where they have not been efficient became evident: while government relief was named first, it was NGO work that came directly after (Tab. 16.30). This portrays the importance of NGO relief and development work. However, it is noteworthy that AIDMI, contrary to other

NGOs, particularly focuses on women, being the most vulnerable and neglected part of society. Knowing that among women, illiteracy is higher and education generally lower, as compared to men (see previous chapters), this is exactly the kind of effort needed to help the slum communities and the families as a whole.

In communities where development projects of AIDMI had been on-going for some time, the situation was clearly better than in those where development had just started (Tab. 16.3 and 16.4, Tab. 16.24). Yet, it is also obvious that non-governmental organisations do not dispose of the means and the capacities that governmental efforts can show, and that they cannot replace the latter (only 13% of the total households profited from NGO relief, Tab. 16.3). Rather, NGOs can, through their work *in situ* and their knowledge of the most urgent necessities, help the government improve the efficiency of their relief programs and development efforts.

The analysis of the help received and perceived in the four slum communities also brought out to what extent lacking education prevents people from receiving relief and improving their lives: if they are not able to read, they cannot access information on where to receive help, which consequently leaves them with the perception of being left alone. This might explain why quite a proportion of the community inhabitants does not attend meetings that NGOs organise and do not participate actively in programs.

Natural disasters not only illustrate that the poorest are the most vulnerable. Furthermore, they show that it is not only poverty, but lacking knowledge on protection, i.e. earthquake-proof housing, that can literally be deadly. It is striking that even one of the severest earthquakes in recent Indian history has not been, for a large share of the population, the initiation of active participation in order to improve their living conditions and shelter from future disasters.

The fact that active participation is a major key in the improvement of livelihood, but also in the security from disasters, must be focussed upon more strongly: one cannot help if people do not make an effort themselves. Again, it all comes down to high illiteracy and lacking education of people that prevent them from accessing information they would need to make a difference in their lives. As seen before, women are more likely to be illiterate or less educated than men, which is why efforts to help them in particular are essential. Any long-term development aid must stress education that enables people to help themselves and their families in the future.

Map 16.1 Households having received relief, Bhimraonagar

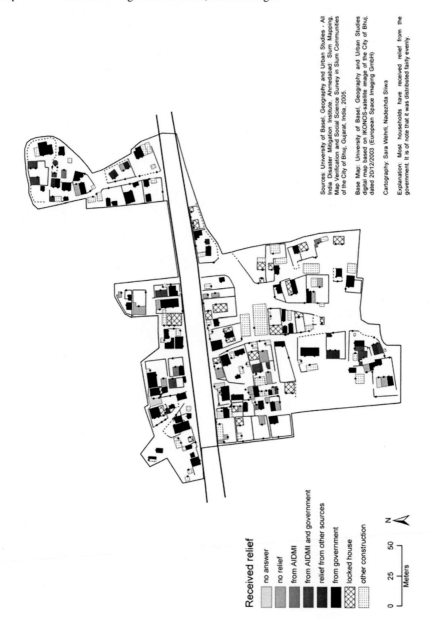

Map 16.2 Households having received relief, Jayprakashnagar

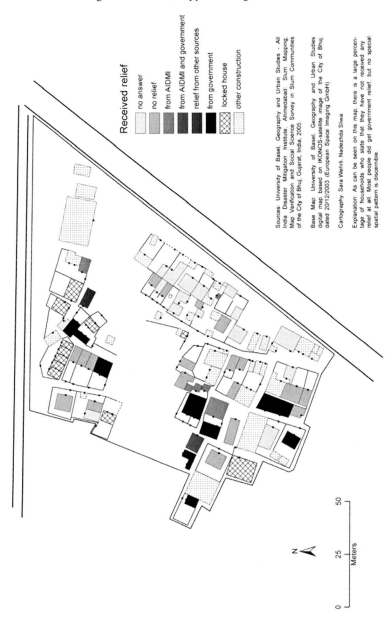

366   Help received - help perceived

Map 16.3 Households having received relief, Mustuffanagar

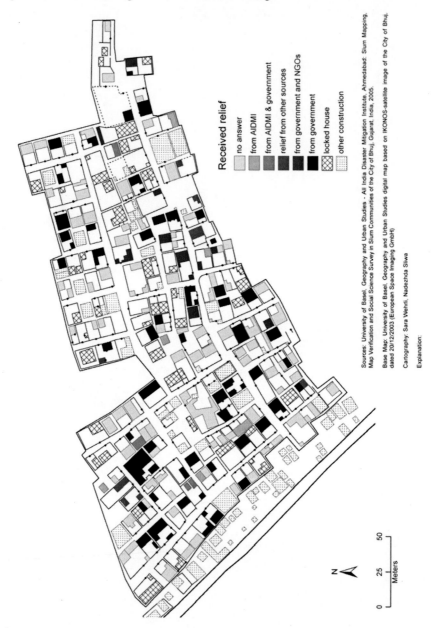

Map 16.4 Households having received relief, Shantinagar

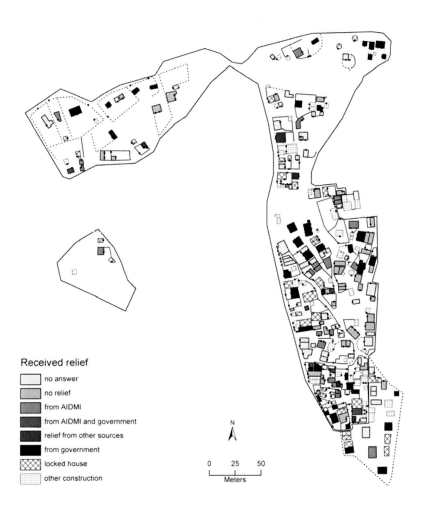

Map 16.5 Help for reconstructing the house, Bhimraonagar

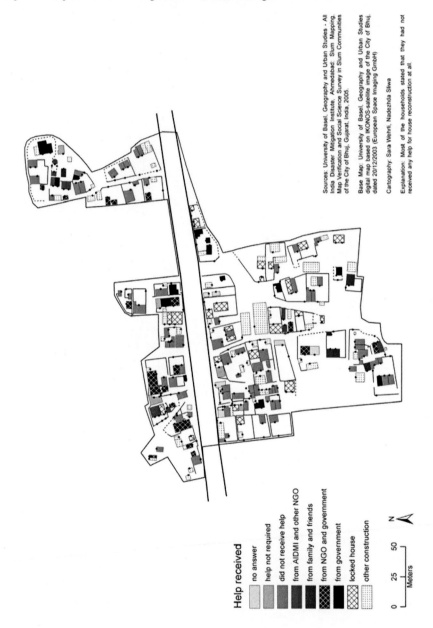

Map 16.6 Help for reconstructing the house, Jayprakashnagar

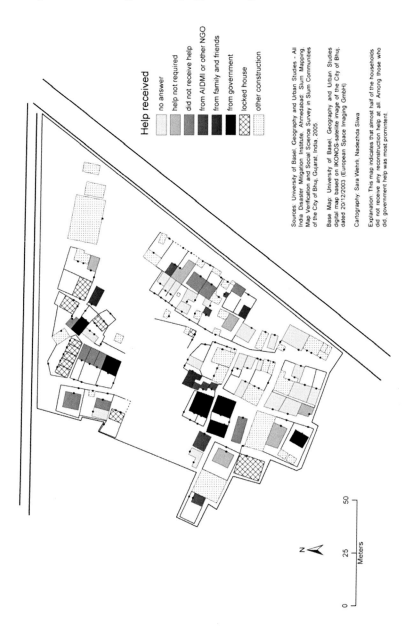

370 Help received - help perceived

Map 16.7 Help for reconstructing the house, Mustuffanagar

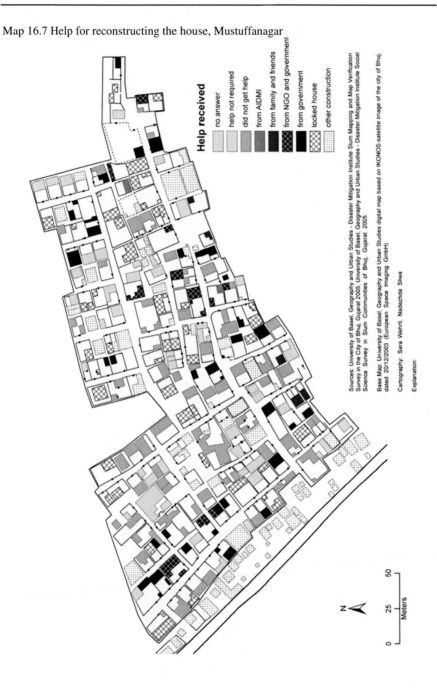

Help received - help perceived 371

Map 16.8 Help for reconstructing the house, Shantinagar

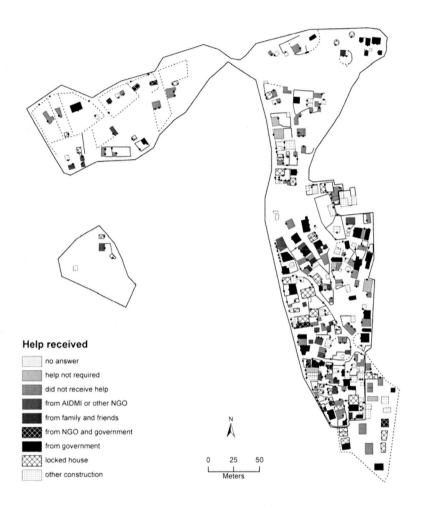

Map 16.9 Type of relief received, Bhimraonagar

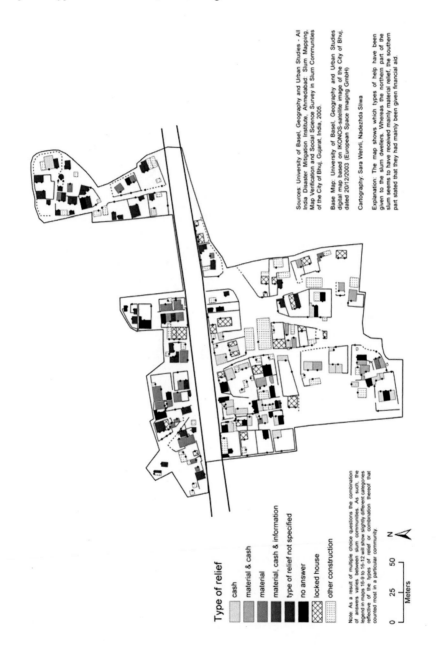

Map 16.10 Type of relief received, Jayprakashnagar

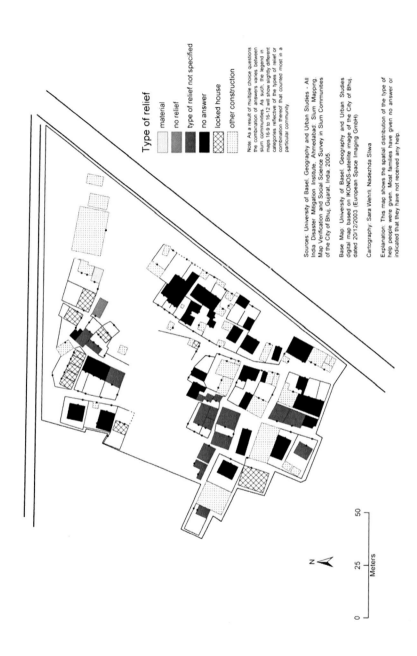

Map 16.11 Type of relief received, Mustuffanagar

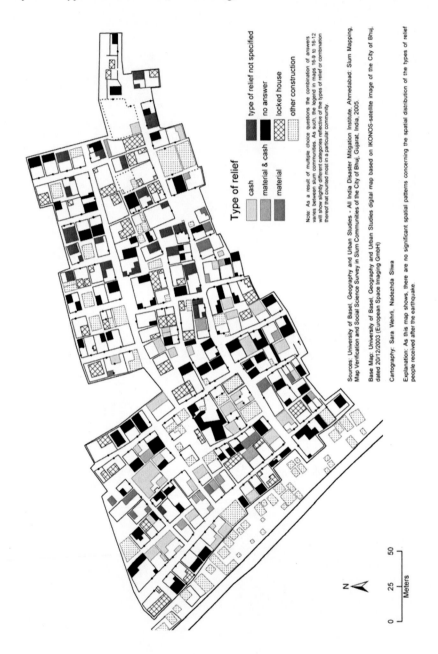

Map 16.12 Type of relief received, Shantinagar

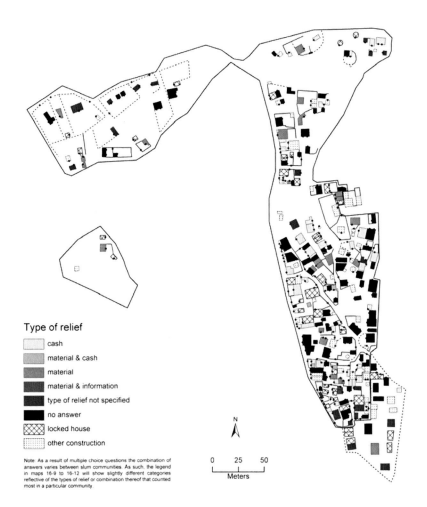

Map 16.13 Households with linkages with AIDMI, Bhimraonagar

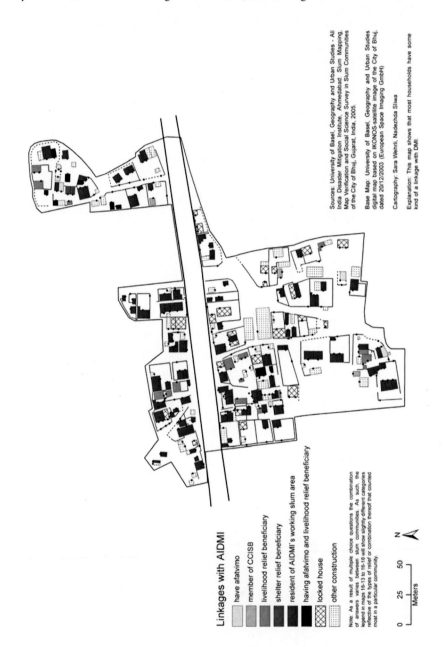

Map 16.14 Households with linkages with AIDMI, Jayprakashnagar

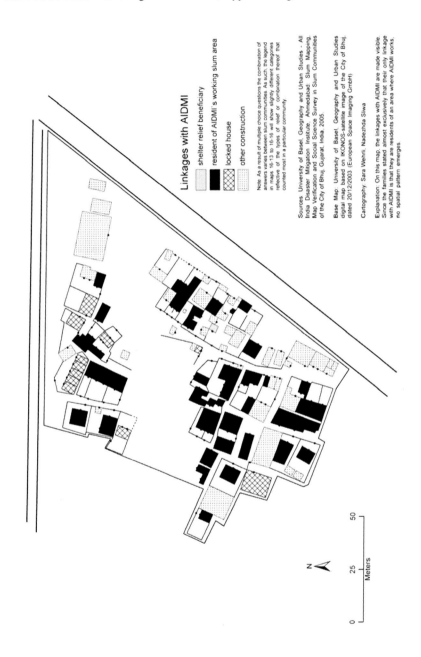

378 Help received - help perceived

Map 16.15 Households with linkages with AIDMI, Mustuffanagar

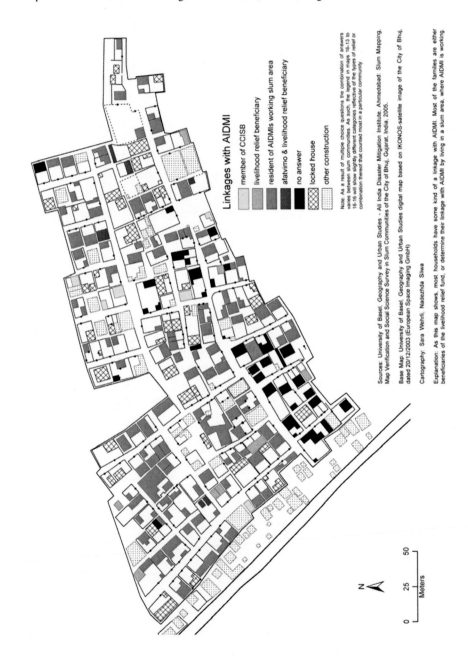

Map 16.16 Households with linkages with AIDMI, Shantinagar

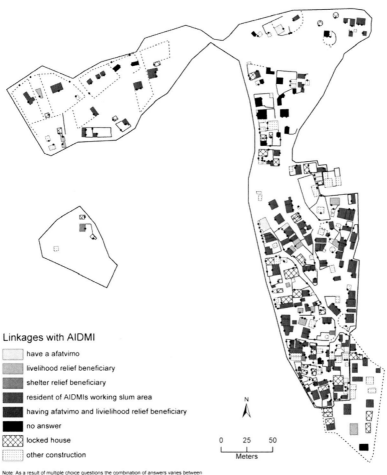

380   Help received - help perceived

Map 16.17 Most important source of help, Bhimraonagar

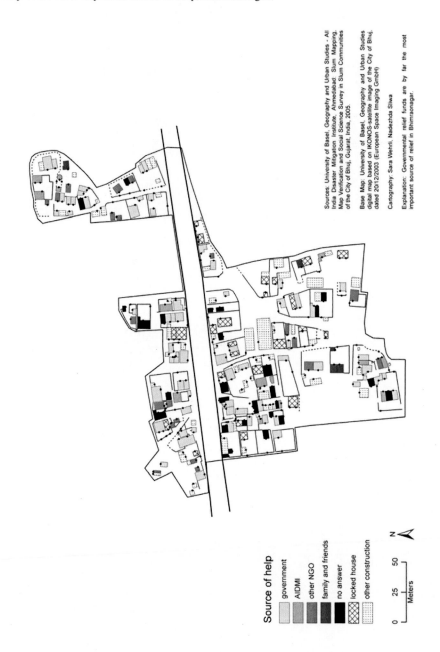

Help received - help perceived 381

Map 16.18 Most important source of help, Jayprakashnagar

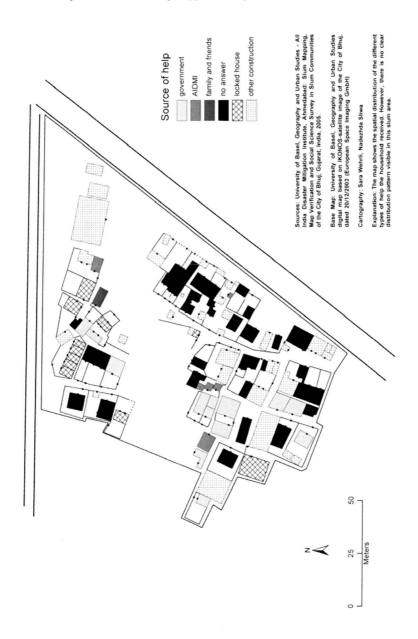

Map 16.19 Most important source of help, Mustuffanagar

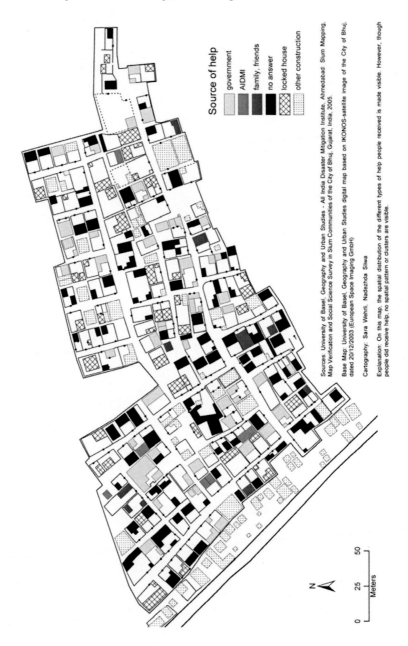

Map 16.20 Most important source of help, Shantinagar

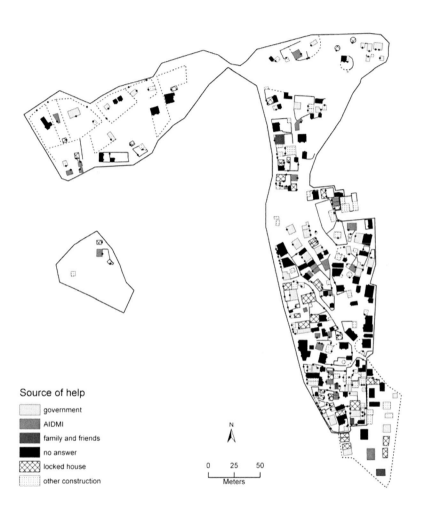

17 Basic infrastructure – basic problems – the case of drinking water supplies

F. Wieland
University of Basel

17.1
Introduction

The most important environmental health risks in slum communities of developing countries are insufficient and unsafe water as well as the inadequate disposal of excrements. The different risks related to water and sanitation may account for most cases of sickness and death among poorer communities such as the ones in urban slum areas in India.

A water body can contribute to the transmission of disease in two ways: firstly, the existence of a water body is a precondition for water borne vectors like mosquitoes or worms, which can transmit Malaria or Dracunculiasis. Secondly, (drinking) water is also an important transmitter of germs contained in human faeces of infected people.

Human faeces may contain a range of disease-causing organisms, including viruses, bacteria and eggs or larvae of parasites. Containment and safe disposal of human excreta is therefore a primary barrier for the transmission of excreta-related disease (Fig. 17.1).

The micro organisms contained in human faeces may enter the body through contaminated hands, food, water, eating and cooking utensils or soil. Diarrhoea, cholera and typhoid are spread in this way and are major causes of illness and death among slum dwellers. Because the consumption of contaminated drinking water is the most common way to get infected by such micro organisms, the analysis of the drinking water used by the surveyed households builds the subject of this chapter, which summarizes the author's diploma thesis.

Figure 17.1 Water and sanitation related diseases

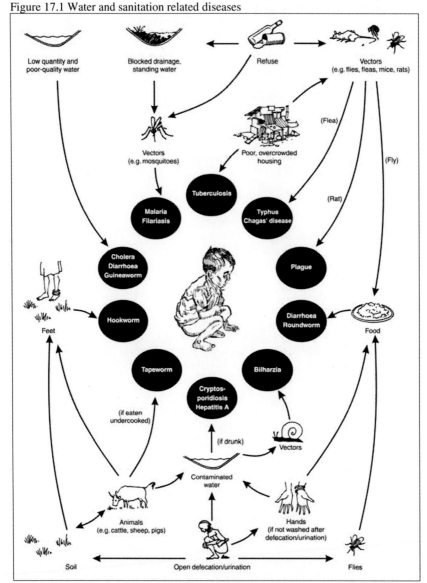

Source: Water engineering development centre (WEDC) Running water (1999): 74.

17.2
Used methodology

This chapter deals with the water quality found in the four slums studied. In order to determine key variables which represent the water quality of the surveyed households, it will be examined whether the water quality in a household and hygienic infrastructure, demographic, social or financial factors are correlated. The objective of the study is to get an overview of the prevailing drinking water situation in the four slums and the factors related to differences in drinking water quality. This can help to identify.

- indicator variables for the quality of water
- areas with urgent drinking water problems
- the need for action.

For the testing of drinking water, many methods have been developed which analyse all kinds of pathogens and chemicals in the water. For this study, the analysis has been limited to pathogens. Many waterborne pathogens can be detected directly, but require complicated and expensive analytical methods. Instead of directly measuring pathogens, it is easier to use indicator organisms indicating faecal pollution in the water. A faecal indictor organism has to meet the following criteria:

- it is present in human faeces in a high number
- it is detected by simple methods
- it does not grow in natural waters
- its persistence in water and it's removal by the water treatment method is similar to the water-borne pathogens.

Many of these criteria are fulfilled by Escherichia coli (E.coli, which is faecal coliform). E.coli is therefore a good indicator organism to assess faecal contamination of drinking water. The use of this indicator is particularly important if the resources for microbiological examination are limited. Testing the E.coli is also possible under difficult field conditions in a developing country by using the portable DelAgua field test kit from Oxfam which uses the membrane filtration (more information on this drinking water test kit can be found at: http://robenscentres.com/delagua/) [Sandec 2002: 13].

In this method, a minimum volume of 10ml of the sample is introduced aseptically into a sterile or properly disinfected filtration assembly containing a sterile membrane filter with a nominal pore size of 0.2 or 0.45 µm. The volume which has to be filtered depends strongly on the degree of pollution of the water which has to be examined. The World Health Organization (WHO) recommends a standard volume of 100ml in its guidelines for safe drinking water. But if, for example, water of a river is examined, then a dilution of the sample is meaningful. With a high degree of pollution that can be expected in such kind of surface water, bacteria colonies would no longer be countable.

By vacuum, the sample is drawn through the membrane filter. All indicator organisms are retained on or within the filter. The filter is then transferred to a suitable selective culture medium in a Petri dish. The Petri dish is then transferred to an incubator at an appropriate selective temperature. There, it is incubated for a determined time to allow the replication of the indicator organisms. Visually identifiable and countable colonies are formed. The result is expressed in number of "colonies forming units" (CFU) per 100ml of original sample.

Weaknesses of this method are related to the turbidity of the waters and the financial circumstances. This technique is inappropriate for waters with a high level of turbidity that would cause the filter to become blocked before an adequate volume of water could pass through. Also, the required membrane filters may be very expensive in some countries.

For this study the membrane-filter method was chosen for its advantages and adequacy in this study. Since the analysis of the water samples had to take place in the field, other methods where not adapted. The equipment, a water testing kid from Qxfam, could be borrowed from the Swiss Federal Institute of Environmental Science and Technology (EAWAG), Department of Water and Sanitation in Developing Countries (Sandec), so that there was no need of expensive consumables.

The water quality tests by membrane filtration were carried out for around 100 household drinking water samples which covers one fifth of all surveyed households in the four slums. Because of the different sizes of the four slums, the number of water samples taken in the four communities differs, too. In Mustuffanagar, 30 water samples have been taken, in Bhimraonagar 26 and in Shantinagar 24 water samples, while in Jayprakashnagar, only 13 water samples could be taken.

In addition to the water sampling on household level, important wells and hand pumps have also been sampled and some treatment methods have been tested. This second part of the analysis makes a contribution to the development of adequate treatment methods respectively tries to give some advice as to the application to the end-user, the slum dweller.

17.3
Religion

The analysis of the water qualities found in the four surveyed slums by religion does not show a clear pattern. While 16.3% of all Muslim households have a very high water quality (0 E.coli/100ml) and 14.0% of them have only 1-10 E.coli/100ml, there are also 27.9% of the households using drinking water with more than 450 E.coli/100ml. The Hindu households also show a high variation of drinking water quality, but their water is, on the whole, better than that of Muslim families. Although about 23.5% of the Hindu households show a water quality between 200 and 400 E.coli/100ml, there are no households with drinking water quality worse than that.

Regarding the rather well-off slum community of Mustuffanagar being mostly Muslim, these results are a bit surprising. One would have assumed to find better drinking water quality among the better off households than among the poorer ones. However, Mustuffanagar is not the only slum with a high fraction of Muslim families. Shantinagar shows a high density of Muslim households, too. It is also the poorest of the four slums. The fact that Muslim households are found in the poorest as well as in the best-off slum community could explain the high variation in the quality of their drinking water. The Hindu families predominantly living in Jayprakashnagar and Bhimraonagar have an acceptable water quality by the majority, even if most of them do not have very good drinking water anyway.

This means that it is rather the affiliation to a certain slum community that affects the quality of a family's drinking water than the religious affiliation. This notion will be approved in subchapter 17.17, where the drinking water quality is analysed by slum community.

Table 17.1 Water quality (E.coli), by religion

Religion E.coli bacteria	Hindu in % (n=34)	Muslim in % (n=43)	Total in % (n=77)
0	14.7	16.3	15.6
1 - 10	20.6	14.0	16.9
10 - 70	17.6	18.6	18.2
70 - 100	8.8	11.6	10.4
100 - 200	8.8	9.3	9.1
200 - 400	23.5	2.3	11.7
450 - 1000	0.0	11.6	6.5
1000 - 2000	5.9	9.3	7.8
> 2000	0.0	7.0	3.9
Total	100.0	100.0	100.0

SOURCE: UNIVERSITY OF BASEL, DEPT. OF GEOGRAPHY AND ALL INDIA DISASTER MITIGATION INSTITUTE, AHMEDABAD, INDIA 2005. SOCIAL SCIENCE SURVEY IN SELECTED SLUM COMMUNITIES IN THE CITY OF BHUJ, GUJARAT, INDIA.

17.4 Caste

The analysis of water quality by caste affiliation shows a remarkably high variation. The Other Backwards Castes (OBC), a term mostly used for the social stratification of the Muslim households, show a comparable pattern of their water quality as already seen in Tab. 17.1. The Scheduled Castes (SC) show a high percentage of households with a water quality of 1-10 E.coli/100ml or 200-400 E.coli/100ml. There is only one household with worse drinking water quality (1000-2000 E.coli/100ml). Among Scheduled Tribes (ST), around 75% of all sampled households have drinking water with less than 100 E.coli/100ml. The General Castes show the highest percentage of households with a very high water quality of 0 E.coli/100ml (17.9%), and there are almost no families with a drinking water quality of over 500 E.coli/100ml. This implies that, concerning the water quality, there are no great differences among the castes. Caste affiliation does not seem to be decisive for the water quality of a household.

Table 17.2 Water quality (E.coli), by caste

Caste / E.coli bacteria	SC in % (n=14)	ST in % (n=8)	OBC in % (n=27)	General in % (n=28)	Total in % (n=77)
0	14.3	12.5	14.8	17.9	15.6
1 - 10	28.6	25.0	18.5	7.1	16.9
10 - 70	7.1	12.5	14.8	28.6	18.2
70 - 100	0.0	25.0	7.4	14.3	10.4
100 - 200	14.3	0.0	3.7	14.3	9.1
200 - 400	28.6	12.5	0.0	14.3	11.7
450 - 1000	0.0	0.0	18.5	0.0	6.5
1000 - 2000	7.1	12.5	11.1	3.6	7.8
> 2000	0.0	0.0	11.1	0.0	3.9
Total	100.0	100.0	100.0	100.0	100.0

SOURCE: UNIVERSITY OF BASEL, DEPT. OF GEOGRAPHY AND ALL INDIA DISASTER MITIGATION INSTITUTE, AHMEDABAD, INDIA 2005. SOCIAL SCIENCE SURVEY IN SELECTED SLUM COMMUNITIES IN THE CITY OF BHUJ, GUJARAT, INDIA.

The water results for the General and the Scheduled Castes might partially be explained by the structure of their monthly income. Regarding the monthly income and the differences between the various castes, these two castes show the highest incomes (Tab. 17.3). This could be the reason for the better water quality of their drinking water, as compared to the water from the other castes. But the allocation of the water quality values among the Scheduled Tribes and the OBC can not directly be associated with the monthly income of the families. As the OBC have a higher average income, their water should be better than the water of the worse earning households of the Scheduled Tribes. But the water samples taken from Scheduled Tribe families show a higher water quality. As these discrepancies can also be seen between the monthly income and the water quality of the family, the thesis that a higher income allows for a better water quality can therefore not be confirmed completely.

Table 17.3 Monthly income, by caste (only water sampled households)

Caste / Monthly income	SC in % (n=14)	ST in % (n=8)	OBC in % (n=27)	General in % (n=28)	Total in % (n=77)
< 1500	7.1	25.0	18.5	7.1	13.0
1500-3000	35.7	37.5	33.3	53.6	41.6
3000-5000	35.7	37.5	29.6	21.4	28.6
5000-42000	21.4	0.0	18.5	17.9	16.9
Total	100.0	100.0	100.0	100.0	100.0

SOURCE: UNIVERSITY OF BASEL, DEPT. OF GEOGRAPHY AND ALL INDIA DISASTER MITIGATION INSTITUTE, AHMEDABAD, INDIA 2005. SOCIAL SCIENCE SURVEY IN SELECTED SLUM COMMUNITIES IN THE CITY OF BHUJ, GUJARAT, INDIA.

17.5
Number of family members

An obvious trend is apparent in all categories except in families with 3 or less and families with 4 members. Whereas in families with 5 members, 52.6% have less than 10 E.coli/100ml in their drinking water, in families with 7 members, it is 54.6%. In families with more than 8 members, only 27.3% of the households show the same water quality. This group also shows the highest percentage (45.5%) of households with more than 400 E.coli/100ml. This means that the distribution of the water qualities among families with 7 members or less does not show great variations. However, in families with 8 or more members, the water quality worsens significantly.

A slight trend that families with more members have a poorer water quality than smaller families can therefore be concluded. It seems that the water quality does not depend on a difference of one or two family members, but when a certain number is overstepped the water quality gets poorer. An explanation could be that the more people live in a household, the more of them are either dependent old people or young children, both of whom cannot contribute to the family income, but who lower the average wage per person and with it, the possibility of investments in better water supply. The family head may not earn enough money to feed his family well *and* pay for improvements in their water supply.

Another important fact is that the more people live in a household, the higher is the potential of (re-)contaminating the drinking water through lack of hygiene.

Table 17.4 Water quality (E.coli), by number of family member

Number of family members / E.coli bacteria	3 or less in % (n=10)	4 in % (n=10)	5 in % (n=19)	6 in % (n=12)	7 in % (n=11)	8 or more in % (n=11)	Total in % (n=74)
0	0.0	0.0	26.3	8.3	36.4	9.1	15.1
1 - 10	10.0	0.0	26.3	16.7	18.2	18.2	16.4
10 - 70	30.0	10.0	26.3	25.0	0.0	9.1	17.8
70 - 100	10.0	20.0	5.3	8.3	27.3	0.0	11.0
100 - 200	10.0	20.0	0.0	25.0	0.0	9.1	9.6
200 - 400	10.0	20.0	10.5	16.7	9.1	9.1	12.3
450 - 1000	10.0	10.0	0.0	0.0	0.0	18.2	5.5
1000 - 2000	20.0	10.0	5.3	0.0	9.1	9.1	8.2
>2000	0.0	10.0	0.0	0.0	0.0	18.2	4.1
Total	100.0	100.0	100.0	100.0	100.0	100.0	100.0

SOURCE: UNIVERSITY OF BASEL, DEPT. OF GEOGRAPHY AND ALL INDIA DISASTER MITIGATION INSTITUTE, AHMEDABAD, INDIA 2005. SOCIAL SCIENCE SURVEY IN SELECTED SLUM COMMUNITIES IN THE CITY OF BHUJ, GUJARAT, INDIA.

17.6
Case of illness or death in the last year

There is no significant relation between the water quality of a household and the occurrence of illness or death in the last year (Tab. 17.5). The fact that most households sampled (n=58) stated that there was no illness in the family in the last year makes it even more difficult to see a trend. The households without any illness or death show a high range of water qualities, while the households with death or illness show a high accumulation (41.6%) of water with less than 70 E.coli/100ml. Another high share of 23.1% of the households have water with around 200-400 E.coli/100ml.

Table 17.5 Water quality (E.coli), by illness or death

Illness or death / E.coli bacteria	no, nobody in % (n=58)	serious illness or death in % (n=13)	Total in % (n=71)
0	13.8	15.4	14.1
1 - 10	15.5	23.1	16.9
10 - 70	13.8	23.1	15.5
70 - 100	12.1	7.7	11.3
100 - 200	12.1	0.0	9.9
200 - 400	10.3	23.1	12.7
450 - 1000	8.6	0.0	7.0
1000 - 2000	8.6	7.7	8.5
>2000	5.2	0.0	4.2
Total	100.0	100.0	100.0

SOURCE: UNIVERSITY OF BASEL, DEPT. OF GEOGRAPHY AND ALL INDIA DISASTER MITIGATION INSTITUTE, AHMEDABAD, INDIA 2005. SOCIAL SCIENCE SURVEY IN SELECTED SLUM COMMUNITIES IN THE CITY OF BHUJ, GUJARAT, INDIA.

This means that it is rather difficult to explain the cases of illness or death in a family by the quality of their drinking water. Tab. 17.6 shows a correlation of the families in which illness and death occurred in the last year and their food. While among the households getting their food from the ration shop, 20% had a seriously ill family member or a case of death in the last year, only 12.5% of those getting their food from a different place reported a seriously ill or dead family member. These results can not fully explain the occurrence of illness or death among certain families, but they underline at the importance of an adequate food supply for personal health.

Table 17.6 Illness or death, by food supply (ration shop)

Food from ration shop / Illness or death	Yes in % (n=230)	No in % (n=137)	Total in % (n=367)
no, nobody	81.3	87.6	83.7
serious illness or death	18.7	12.4	16.3
Total	100.0	100.0	100.0

SOURCE: UNIVERSITY OF BASEL, DEPT. OF GEOGRAPHY AND ALL INDIA DISASTER MITIGATION INSTITUTE, AHMEDABAD, INDIA 2005. SOCIAL SCIENCE SURVEY IN SELECTED SLUM COMMUNITIES IN THE CITY OF BHUJ, GUJARAT, INDIA.

At this point, it seems to be necessary to add some thoughts on the slum dwellers` perception of illness. While working in the slums, it was obvious that there was a high rate of respiratory and intestinal illness, especially among the children. Coryza, cough and diarrhoea seemed to belong to people's common health condition. These observances and the mostly low education level of the people could explain why most households declared that there was and is no illness in their family. Diseases, like those named above, which are caused by bad living conditions, are felt to be absolutely normal, and they will therefore not be stated. Children growing up with such complaints will never become acquainted with a different, better health condition. As adults, they will not be alarmed when their children show the same symptoms. The analysis of this question is therefore very difficult and must be handled carefully.

17.7
Place for health check-up

Comparing the water quality of households that visit government hospitals and those visiting private hospitals for health check-ups, a remarkable trend was detected (Tab. 17.7). Households visiting private hospitals for their health check-up have slightly better drinking water than the other households. 40% of the private hospital visitors have access to drinking water with less than 10 E.coli/100ml, while only 31.4% of the households visiting government hospitals have drinking water of the same quality. Moreover, 14.6% of those households show a drinking water quality of more than 1000 E.coli/100ml. Among the households which frequent private hospitals, only 4% have the same E.coli concentration. The number of households that visit private practitioners, ayurvedic centres and other places for health check-ups is very low and therefore not relevant for this evaluation.

Regarding the dependency between the drinking water quality and the households` places for health check-ups, this evaluation can also be an indicator for the relation between the drinking water quality and the income of a family. Tab. 17.8 shows that the places for health check-ups are highly related with the monthly income of a household. Families with a low income have no money left for an expensive visit in a private hospital and have to go to the cheaper government hospitals, which perhaps even grant price-reduction for below poverty card owners (BPL). Better off families have a free choice between the individual health institutions and probably visit a better and uncongested place. To sum up the results, we may have both an income and information effect that accounts for the better quality of water and the place of a health check up.

Table 17.7 Water quality (E.coli), by place for health check up

Place for health check up / E.coli bacteria	government hospital in % (n=48)	private hospital in % (n=25)	other in % (n=4)	Total in % (n=77)
0	14.6	20.0	0.0	15.6
1 - 10	16.7	20.0	0.0	16.9
10 - 70	18.8	16.0	25.0	18.2
70 - 100	8.3	8.0	50.0	10.4
100 - 200	8.3	12.0	0.0	9.1
200 - 400	12.5	12.0	0.0	11.7
450 - 1000	6.3	8.0	0.0	6.5
1000 - 2000	10.4	0.0	25.0	7.8
>2000	4.2	4.0	0.0	3.9
Total	100.0	100.0	100.0	100.0

SOURCE: UNIVERSITY OF BASEL, DEPT. OF GEOGRAPHY AND ALL INDIA DISASTER MITIGATION INSTITUTE, AHMEDABAD, INDIA 2005. SOCIAL SCIENCE SURVEY IN SELECTED SLUM COMMUNITIES IN THE CITY OF BHUJ, GUJARAT, INDIA.

Table 17.8 Monthly income, by place for health check-up (only water sampled households)

Monthly income / Place for health check up	< 1500 in % (n=10)	1500-3000 in % (n=32)	3000-5000 in % (n=22)	5000-42000 in % (n=13)	Total in % (n=77)
government hospital	80.0	65.6	59.1	46.2	62.3
private hospital	10.0	31.3	40.9	38.5	32.5
other	10.0	3.1	0.0	15.4	5.2
Total	100.0	100.0	100.0	100.0	100.0

SOURCE: UNIVERSITY OF BASEL, DEPT. OF GEOGRAPHY AND ALL INDIA DISASTER MITIGATION INSTITUTE, AHMEDABAD, INDIA 2005. SOCIAL SCIENCE SURVEY IN SELECTED SLUM COMMUNITIES IN THE CITY OF BHUJ, GUJARAT, INDIA.

17.8
Monthly expenses for medicine

To confirm the hypothesis of the previous subchapter, the dependency of the water quality and the monthly expenses for medicine was tested (Tab. 17.9). The best water qualities are reached in the category with the lowest monthly expenses (<50 Rs.). This category shows a percentage of 75.1% of the households which have less than 70 E.coli/100ml and 25% of the households without any E.coli bacteria. The highest income category (500-5000Rs.) has both the highest percentage (20.0%) of clean drinking water (0 E.coli/100ml) and the highest percentage (20.0%) of very bad water with more than 2000 E.coli/100ml.

Although only 5 households are taken into account for this statement, it allows us to set up two further theses. On one hand, good drinking water quality can lead to lower monthly expenses for medicine, on the other hand, the monthly expenses for medicine could be seen as an indicator for the income of a family and therefore implicate a better water quality. These theses are underlined by the fact that the category with average expenses for medicine of 100-200 Rs. shows the worst water quality of all categories. 83.3% of all households in this category have a drinking water quality of 70-1000 E.coli/100ml. Their monthly expenses could be that high due to bad water quality, but it could also be seen as an indicator for an ordinary monthly income which would not allow further investments in their water supply.

Table 17.9 Water quality (E.coli), by monthly expenses for medicine

Monthly expenses for medicine / E.coli bacteria	1 - 50 in % (n=16)	51 - 100 in % (n=9)	101 - 200 in % (n=6)	201 - 500 in % (n=13)	501 - 5000 in % (n=5)	Total in % (n=49)
0	25.0	11.1	0.0	7.7	20.0	14.3
1 - 10	31.3	22.2	16.7	23.1	0.0	22.4
10 - 70	18.8	33.3	0.0	30.8	40.0	24.5
70 - 100	12.5	11.1	16.7	7.7	0.0	10.2
100 - 200	0.0	11.1	16.7	7.7	0.0	6.1
200 - 400	6.3	0.0	33.3	23.1	20.0	14.3
450 - 1000	6.3	0.0	16.7	0.0	0.0	4.1
>2000	0.0	11.1	0.0	0.0	20.0	4.1
Total	100.0	100.0	100.0	100.0	100.0	100.0

SOURCE: UNIVERSITY OF BASEL, DEPT. OF GEOGRAPHY AND ALL INDIA DISASTER MITIGATION INSTITUTE, AHMEDABAD, INDIA 2005. SOCIAL SCIENCE SURVEY IN SELECTED SLUM COMMUNITIES IN THE CITY OF BHUJ, GUJARAT, INDIA.

17.9
Monthly income of the family

Comparing only the water quality of the lowest income households (< 1500 Rs.) with the water quality of those with the highest income (5000-42000 Rs.), a definite trend can be observed (Tab. 17.10). The percentage of households with clean water (0 E.coli/100ml) rises from 10% in the lowest income category to 30.8% in the highest category. The proportion of households with a water quality of over 450 E.coli/100ml falls from 40% in the lowest to 15.4% in the highest income class. Yet, taking a look over all four income classes, a high fluctuation is apparent. The 2nd category (1500-3000 Rs.), for instance, shows a better water quality than the 3rd category (3000-5000 Rs.). If the quality of the drinking water depends on the monthly income of a family, this should be related inversely. The high significance (Chi= 0.018) of the correlation between these two parameters indicates that 78% of the water quality can be associated with the different income classes to which the households belong.

A highly important conclusion can be drawn, in spite of the high fluctuation: the households with the lowest monthly incomes also have the worst water quality. The fluctuation in the upper income classes may indicate that above all, a somewhat good water quality is related to a specific minimum income. It is then no longer important how high that income exactly is, if the household is above this threshold.

Table 17.10 Water quality (E.coli), by monthly income of the family

Monthly income E.coli bacteria	<1500 in % (n=10)	1500-3000 in % (n=32)	3000-5000 in % (n=22)	5000-42000 in % (n=13)	Total in % (n=77)
0	10.0	15.6	9.1	30.8	15.6
1 - 10	0.0	18.8	18.2	23.1	16.9
10 - 70	10.0	31.3	9.1	7.7	18.2
70 - 100	30.0	9.4	4.5	7.7	10.4
100 - 200	0.0	15.6	4.5	7.7	9.1
200 - 400	10.0	0.0	31.8	7.7	11.7
450 - 1000	20.0	6.3	4.5	0.0	6.5
1000 - 2000	20.0	0.0	9.1	15.4	7.8
>2000	0.0	3.1	9.1	0.0	3.9
Total	100.0	100.0	100.0	100.0	100.0

SOURCE: UNIVERSITY OF BASEL, DEPT. OF GEOGRAPHY AND ALL INDIA DISASTER MITIGATION INSTITUTE, AHMEDABAD, INDIA 2005. SOCIAL SCIENCE SURVEY IN SELECTED SLUM COMMUNITIES IN THE CITY OF BHUJ, GUJARAT, INDIA.

17.10
Knowledge of the relation between hygiene and health

Tab. 17.11 brings out the definite trend of a correlation between water quality and knowledge. 61.2% of the households stating that there is a relation between hygiene and health have less than 70 E.coli/100ml in their drinking water. Among the households saying that they do not know about such a dependency, only 30.8% had the same water quality. Moreover, 34.6% of the households which do not know about the relation between hygiene and health showed a drinking water quality of over 450 E.coli/100ml, while only 10.2% of the households knowing about that relation had comparably bad drinking water. This implies that households that know about the relation between hygiene and health generally show a better water quality than households without that knowledge. It cannot be said that households which know about that relation have better water supply. It is more likely that based on their knowledge, they handle their drinking water more carefully than the other households. Hygiene behaviour within the family prevents recontamination of the water through dirty hands, dippers and so on. The heads of those families probably have a higher education level and have been taught in school or university to behave hygienically.

Table 17.11 Water quality (E.coli), by knowledge about relation between hygiene and health

Knowledge / E.coli bacteria	yes in % (n=49)	no in % (n=26)	Total in % (n=75)
0	18.4	7.7	14.7
1 - 10	22.4	7.7	17.3
10 - 70	20.4	15.4	18.7
70 - 100	6.1	15.4	9.3
100 - 200	10.2	7.7	9.3
200 - 400	12.2	11.5	12.0
450 - 1000	4.1	11.5	6.7
1000 - 2000	4.1	15.4	8.0
> 2000	2.0	7.7	4.0
Total	100.0	100.0	100.0

SOURCE: UNIVERSITY OF BASEL, DEPT. OF GEOGRAPHY AND ALL INDIA DISASTER MITIGATION INSTITUTE, AHMEDABAD, INDIA 2005. SOCIAL SCIENCE SURVEY IN SELECTED SLUM COMMUNITIES IN THE CITY OF BHUJ, GUJARAT, INDIA.

Therefore, it is also relevant to correlate the people's knowledge of hygiene with their degree of education, in order to find out if there is a higher awareness of hygiene problems among people with a higher education level than among the illiterate or poorly educated people (Tab. 17.12). The lowest percentage of people that stated to know about a relation between hygiene and health can be found among the illiterate family heads (60.0%), while around 67-70% of the family heads belonging to a different education category stated to know about this dependency. In spite of these differences between the illiterate family heads and those having an education degree, the rate of knowledge is generally very high. However, with such kind of questions, we must involve the possibility of subconscious answer manipulation. If the respondent is asked: "Do you know about the relation between hygiene and health?" he will in most cases agree, even if he did not know. It is therefore important to find a more precise question or to include the possibility of answer manipulation in the analysis.

Table 17.12 Knowledge about the relation between hygiene and health, by education of family head (only water sampled households)

Education of family head / Knowledge	Hrs. 1-4 in % (n=10)	Hrs. 5-7 in % (n=15)	Hrs. 8-10 in % (n=12)	complete graduation in % (n=3)	Illiterate in % (n=35)	Total in % (n=75)
yes	70.0	73.3	66.7	66.7	60.0	65.3
no	30.0	26.7	33.3	33.3	40.0	34.7
Total	100.0	100.0	100.0	100.0	100.0	100.0

SOURCE: UNIVERSITY OF BASEL, DEPT. OF GEOGRAPHY AND ALL INDIA DISASTER MITIGATION INSTITUTE, AHMEDABAD, INDIA 2005. SOCIAL SCIENCE SURVEY IN SELECTED SLUM COMMUNITIES IN THE CITY OF BHUJ, GUJARAT, INDIA.

17.11
Improvement of drinking water supply: most urgent need

Given a choice of improvements they would consider most important, households could name "drinking water", "sanitation facilities", "housing substance", or "medical care". Tab. 17.13 shows the relation between households choosing better drinking water and their drinking water quality. It was expected that households with poor water quality would indicate that drinking water improvements were most important. However, the reverse was found to be true. Households which ranked the drinking water improvements highest have a remarkably better water quality than the others: 60.4% of them have drinking water with less than 70 E.coli/100ml and 17.0% have no E.coli bacteria at all in their drinking water. 49.9% of households stating other improvements to be more necessary than drinking water have a worse water quality ranging from 70-400 E.coli/100ml. These results are rather unusual at a first sight. A possible explanation for these results could be the education of the family head. A higher educational degree could be an indicator for a better perception of problems related to the quality of the drinking water. This might be the reason why households with a higher education level perceive that drinking water is the major problem, even if there is much better water than the one other families use. It is obvious that the illiterates show one of the highest percentages of "no" answers which means that they find other problems to be more important than the drinking water supply.

Table 17.13 Water quality (E.coli), by drinking water supplies as most important improvement

Better water / E.coli bacteria	yes in % (n=53)	no in % (n=22)	Total in % (n=75)
0	17.0	9.1	14.7
1 - 10	20.8	9.1	17.3
10 - 70	22.6	9.1	18.7
70 - 100	5.7	22.7	10.7
100 - 200	7.5	13.6	9.3
200 - 400	11.3	13.6	12.0
450 - 1000	5.7	9.1	6.7
1000 - 2000	5.7	9.1	6.7
> 2000	3.8	4.5	4.0
Total	100.0	100.0	100.0

SOURCE: UNIVERSITY OF BASEL, DEPT. OF GEOGRAPHY AND ALL INDIA DISASTER MITIGATION INSTITUTE, AHMEDABAD, INDIA 2005. SOCIAL SCIENCE SURVEY IN SELECTED SLUM COMMUNITIES IN THE CITY OF BHUJ, GUJARAT, INDIA.

This notion is furthermore supported by the results of Tab. 17.14: The higher the educational degree of the family head, the better is the drinking water quality. It is therefore crucial to draw the linkage between education and the answers given to questions concerning water quality, water related problems and the pereceived necessity of improvement (Tab. 17.15).

Table 17.14 Water quality (E.coli), by education of the family head

E.coli bacteria \ Education of family head	Hrs. 1-4 in % (n=10)	Hrs. 5-7 in % (n=15)	Hrs. 8-10 in % (n=12)	complete graduation in % (n=3)	Illiterate in % (n=37)	Total in % (n=77)
0	30.0	13.3	8.3	0.0	16.2	15.6
1 - 10	0.0	26.7	33.3	33.3	10.8	16.9
10 - 70	10.0	26.7	33.3	33.3	10.8	18.2
70 - 100	10.0	0.0	16.7	0.0	13.5	10.4
100 - 200	10.0	6.7	8.3	0.0	10.8	9.1
200 - 400	20.0	13.3	0.0	33.3	10.8	11.7
450 - 1000	20.0	0.0	0.0	0.0	8.1	6.5
1000 - 2000	0.0	6.7	0.0	0.0	13.5	7.8
> 2000	0.0	6.7	0.0	0.0	5.4	3.9
Total	100.0	100.0	100.0	100.0	100.0	100.0

SOURCE: UNIVERSITY OF BASEL, DEPT. OF GEOGRAPHY AND ALL INDIA DISASTER MITIGATION INSTITUTE, AHMEDABAD, INDIA 2005. SOCIAL SCIENCE SURVEY IN SELECTED SLUM COMMUNITIES IN THE CITY OF BHUJ, GUJARAT, INDIA.

Table 17.15 Education, by drinking water supplies as most important improvement (only water sampled households)

Drinking water improvements \ Education of family head	Hrs. 1-4 in % (n=10)	Hrs. 5-7 in % (n=15)	Hrs. 8-10 in % (n=12)	complete graduation in % (n=3)	Illiterate in % (n=35)	Total in % (n=75)
yes	70.0	86.7	58.3	100.0	65.7	70.7
no	30.0	13.3	41.7	0.0	34.3	29.3
Total	100.0	100.0	100.0	100.0	100.0	100.0

SOURCE: UNIVERSITY OF BASEL, DEPT. OF GEOGRAPHY AND ALL INDIA DISASTER MITIGATION INSTITUTE, AHMEDABAD, INDIA 2005. SOCIAL SCIENCE SURVEY IN SELECTED SLUM COMMUNITIES IN THE CITY OF BHUJ, GUJARAT, INDIA.

17.12
Water facilities in the house

There is a remarkable trend concerning the relation between the water quality and the existence of an own water facility in the house (Tab. 17.16). Households with an own water facility in the house seem to have a better drinking water quality than households that must get their water from a public place: 40.0% of those households show a water quality of 450-2000 E.coli/100ml. The water quality of households with an own tap ranges more around 0-100 E.coli/100ml, while legal or illegal water facilities make little difference. Households with illegal water facilities show an even better drinking water quality, but it should be noted that there is a comparably small number (n=8) of households with illegal facilities that is not representative.

Table 17.16 Water quality (E.coli), by water facility in the house

Water facility in the house E.coli bacteria	no in % (n=15)	yes – legal in % (n=52)	yes – illegal in % (n=8)	Total in % (n=75)
0	0.0	15.4	25.0	13.3
1 - 10	6.7	17.3	37.5	17.3
10 - 70	20.0	17.3	25.0	18.7
70 - 100	13.3	11.5	0.0	10.7
100 - 200	6.7	9.6	12.5	9.3
200 - 400	6.7	15.4	0.0	12.0
450 - 1000	20.0	3.8	0.0	6.7
1000 - 2000	20.0	5.8	0.0	8.0
>2000	6.7	3.8	0.0	4.0
Total	100.0	100.0	100.0	100.0

SOURCE: UNIVERSITY OF BASEL, DEPT. OF GEOGRAPHY AND ALL INDIA DISASTER MITIGATION INSTITUTE, AHMEDABAD, INDIA 2005. SOCIAL SCIENCE SURVEY IN SELECTED SLUM COMMUNITIES IN THE CITY OF BHUJ, GUJARAT, INDIA.

These results indicate that basically, private water facilities show a higher water quality than public facilities. Water contamination, therefore, plays an important role. Public water facilities like a well or surface water can be contaminated much more easily than a private tap or hand pump. Open defecation, for example, is a major source of contamination which especially affects surface water sources. These results are therefore not surprising, but they do point to the role of public authorities in providing access to safe individual water pipes.

17.13
Willingness to get involved towards achieving better drinking water

In the cross tabulation of the households' drinking water quality and their willingness to contribute, the number of cases is too small to be representative (Tab. 17.17). It appears, however, that households that would offer physical work tend to have a worse water quality than households that are willing to pay for better drinking water. One might assume that households offering physical work for better drinking water do not have enough money to pay for it. This would implement a low monthly income, less education and this in turn would explain the bad water quality of these households.

Table 17.17 Water quality (E.coli), by willingness to get involved towards achieving better drinking water

Activity E.coli bacteria	pay for it in % (n=53)	carry out physical work in % (n=5)	nothing in % (n=1)	Total in % (n=59)
0	17.0	0.0	0.0	15.3
1 - 10	17.0	20.0	0.0	16.9
10 - 70	22.6	0.0	0.0	20.3
70 - 100	7.5	0.0	100.0	8.5
100 - 200	11.3	20.0	0.0	11.9
200 - 400	11.3	40.0	0.0	13.6
450 - 1000	3.8	20.0	0.0	5.1
1000 - 2000	5.7	0.0	0.0	5.1
>2000	3.8	0.0	0.0	3.4
Total	100.0	100.0	100.0	100.0

SOURCE: UNIVERSITY OF BASEL, DEPT. OF GEOGRAPHY AND ALL INDIA DISASTER MITIGATION INSTITUTE, AHMEDABAD, INDIA 2005. SOCIAL SCIENCE SURVEY IN SELECTED SLUM COMMUNITIES IN THE CITY OF BHUJ, GUJARAT, INDIA.

Concerning the amount of rupees the individual households are willing to pay, interesting trends emerge (17.18). The more households are willing to pay for better drinking water per month, the better the quality of their drinking water already is. The water quality of 0-10 E.coli/100ml increases from 25% in the category "< 100 Rs." to 35.1% in the category "100-500 Rs." to 44.4% in the highest income category (1000-16000 Rs.). Accordingly, the percentage of water samples with a quality of more than 450 E.coli/100ml decreases from 29.1% in the lowest category (<100 Rs.), to 16.2% in the category "100-500 E.coli/100ml", to 0% in the category "1000-16000 Rs." This result deserves special attention. Why should households that already have better drinking water than other families be willing to pay more for an improvement of their drinking water supply? Actually, one would have expected the opposite. By keeping an eye on the relationship between drinking water quality and education, we find answers. Tab. 17.19 shows that the better the education of the family head, the higher the monthly income of the family is. The proportion of families earning more than 5000 Rs. per month increases from 10.8% in families with an illiterate family head to 66.7% in families having a family head with a complete graduation. By implication, then, families with a better water quality also have a higher income. It is therefore not astounding that these families are willing to pay more for good drinking water than families with a lower income, even if those households would need an improvement of their drinking water supply even more urgently.

Table 17.18 Water quality (E.coli), by willingness to pay for good water

E.coli bacteria \ Willingness to pay for good water	< 100 in % (n=24)	100 – 500 in % (n=37)	500 – 1000 in % (n=7)	1000 – 16000 in % (n=9)	Total in % (n=77)
0	16.7	13.5	0.0	33.3	15.6
1 - 10	8.3	21.6	28.6	11.1	16.9
10 - 70	8.3	16.2	28.6	44.4	18.2
70 - 100	20.8	2.7	14.3	11.1	10.4
100 - 200	12.5	10.8	0.0	0.0	9.1
200 - 400	4.2	18.9	14.3	0.0	11.7
450 - 1000	8.3	8.1	0.0	0.0	6.5
1000 - 2000	12.5	8.1	0.0	0.0	7.8
>2000	8.3	0.0	14.3	0.0	3.9
Total	100.0	100.0	100.0	100.0	100.0

SOURCE: UNIVERSITY OF BASEL, DEPT. OF GEOGRAPHY AND ALL INDIA DISASTER MITIGATION INSTITUTE, AHMEDABAD, INDIA 2005. SOCIAL SCIENCE SURVEY IN SELECTED SLUM COMMUNITIES IN THE CITY OF BHUJ, GUJARAT, INDIA.

Table 17.19 Monthly income, by education of family head (only water sampled households)

Monthly income \ Education of family head	Hrs. 1-4 in % (n=10)	Hrs. 5-7 in % (n=15)	Hrs. 8-10 in % (n=12)	complete graduation in % (n=3)	Illiterate in % (n=37)	Total in % (n=77)
< 1500	30.0	0.0	0.0	0.0	18.9	13.0
1500-3000	50.0	60.0	50.0	0.0	32.4	41.6
3000-5000	10.0	20.0	25.0	33.3	37.8	28.6
5000-42000	10.0	20.0	25.0	66.7	10.8	16.9
Total	100.0	100.0	100.0	100.0	100.0	100.0

SOURCE: UNIVERSITY OF BASEL, DEPT. OF GEOGRAPHY AND ALL INDIA DISASTER MITIGATION INSTITUTE, AHMEDABAD, INDIA 2005. SOCIAL SCIENCE SURVEY IN SELECTED SLUM COMMUNITIES IN THE CITY OF BHUJ, GUJARAT, INDIA.

17.14
Water treatment

A majority of around 74% of the water sampled households stated to treat their drinking water. Only 26% indicated to have not treated their drinking water before consumption (Tab. 17.20).

Table 17.20 Simple frequency of treatment methods

Treatment	frequency	valid percentage
Filtration by cloth	52	67.5%
Boiling	1	1.3%
Filtration by cloth and boiling	4	5.2%
No treatment	20	26.0%
Total	77	100.0%

SOURCE: UNIVERSITY OF BASEL, DEPT. OF GEOGRAPHY AND ALL INDIA DISASTER MITIGATION INSTITUTE, AHMEDABAD, INDIA 2005. SOCIAL SCIENCE SURVEY IN SELECTED SLUM COMMUNITIES IN THE CITY OF BHUJ, GUJARAT, INDIA.

The fact that water samples which have been treated show such different water qualities may implicate that the treatment methods used are either not efficient or the application is inadequate because of re-pollution from unwashed hands or dirty dippers. But still, one can say that the proportion of households having a drinking water quality of less than 100 E.coli/100ml is somewhat higher among households treating their water (68.1%) than among households that do not (58.3%, Tab. 17.21).

Table 17.21 Water quality (E.coli), by water treatment

Water treatment E.coli bacteria	yes in % (n=22)	no in % (n=55)	Total in % (n=77)
0	9.1	18.2	15.6
1 - 10	13.6	18.2	16.9
10 - 70	22.7	16.4	18.2
70 - 100	22.7	5.5	10.4
100 - 200	9.1	9.1	9.1
200 - 400	4.5	14.5	11.7
450 - 1000	0.0	9.1	6.5
1000 - 2000	13.6	5.5	7.8
> 2000	4.5	3.6	3.9
Total	100.0	100.0	100.0

SOURCE: UNIVERSITY OF BASEL, DEPT. OF GEOGRAPHY AND ALL INDIA DISASTER MITIGATION INSTITUTE, AHMEDABAD, INDIA 2005. SOCIAL SCIENCE SURVEY IN SELECTED SLUM COMMUNITIES IN THE CITY OF BHUJ, GUJARAT, INDIA.

Because of the wide-ranging water qualities among the water treating households, it will be interesting to see firstly, what kind of treatment methods are used and secondly, how the water quality varies among these methods. Unfortunately, 91.2% of all sampled households treat their drinking water by the same method, which is filtration through clothes. Only one household is boiling its drinking water before use. Tab. 17.22 shows that among the filtered water samples, the water quality differs to a great extent. This indicates that this method is not very efficient to get bacteria out of the water. However, it is very cheap and can get the suspend matter, thus the visible "dirt", out of the water. For people living in slums, the eye is the only instrument to control the quality of the drinking water.

Mainly illiterate and uneducated people do not know about an invisible bacteriological pollution of their drinking water. But even if everyone knew about that kind of pollution, they would not know how to treat their water more efficiently to get these bacteria out, if they have not been taught to.

Table 17.22 Water quality (E.coli), by method of water treatment

Treatment E.coli bacteria	filter by cloth in % (n=52)	boiling in % (n=1)	filter by cloth & boiling in % (n=4)	Total in % (n=57)
0	17.3	0.0	25.0	17.5
1 - 10	19.2	0.0	0.0	17.5
10 - 70	17.3	0.0	25.0	17.5
70 - 100	5.8	0.0	25.0	7.0
100 - 200	11.5	0.0	0.0	10.5
200 - 400	13.5	100.0	25.0	15.8
450 - 1000	7.7	0.0	0.0	7.0
1000 - 2000	5.8	0.0	0.0	5.3
> 2000	1.9	0.0	0.0	1.8
Total	100.0	100.0	100.0	100.0

SOURCE: UNIVERSITY OF BASEL, DEPT. OF GEOGRAPHY AND ALL INDIA DISASTER MITIGATION INSTITUTE, AHMEDABAD, INDIA 2005. SOCIAL SCIENCE SURVEY IN SELECTED SLUM COMMUNITIES IN THE CITY OF BHUJ, GUJARAT, INDIA.

17.15
Toilet facilities in the house

Water quality and the kind of toilet facilities the household uses are significantly related. Families with an own toilet in the house seem to have much better drinking water than those without such a facility (Tab. 17.23). 85.2% of the households with a private toilet have water with less than 100 E.coli/100ml, 18.0% even have clear drinking water without any E.coli bacteria. The drinking water of households without a toilet facility is much worse. Only 18.9% of these households have drinking water with less than 100 E.coli/100ml, and just 6.3% have clean water. The majority of these households have drinking water with a quality of 100-2000 E.coli/100ml (75%). These results lead to the following hypotheses: a reason for the great differences of the water quality between households with and without a private toilet facility could be the use of a different water source. As Tab. 17.24 shows, there is a high dependency between the availability of a toilet facility and the availability of a water facility in the house. 40.0% of the households without a private toilet also do not have an own water facility in the house, either. 82.7%, respectively 100.0% of the households with a legal or illegal private water facility in the house also have a private toilet.

Table 17.23 Water quality (E.coli), by toilet facility in the house

Toilet facility in house / E.coli bacteria	yes in % (n=61)	no in % (n=16)	Total in % (n=77)
0	18.0	6.3	15.6
1 - 10	19.7	6.3	16.9
10 - 70	21.3	6.3	18.2
70 - 100	13.1	0.0	10.4
100 - 200	8.2	12.5	9.1
200 - 400	8.2	25.0	11.7
450 - 1000	1.6	25.0	6.5
1000 - 2000	6.6	12.5	7.8
> 2000	3.3	6.3	3.9
Total	100.0	100.0	100.0

SOURCE: UNIVERSITY OF BASEL, DEPT. OF GEOGRAPHY AND ALL INDIA DISASTER MITIGATION INSTITUTE, AHMEDABAD, INDIA 2005. SOCIAL SCIENCE SURVEY IN SELECTED SLUM COMMUNITIES IN THE CITY OF BHUJ, GUJARAT, INDIA.

Table 17.24 Toilet facility, by water facility in the house (only water sampled households)

Water facility / Toilet facility	no in % (n=15)	yes – legal in % (n=52)	yes – illegal in % (n=8)	Total in % (n=75)
yes	60.0	82.7	100.0	80.0
no	40.0	17.3	0.0	20.0
Total	100.0	100.0	100.0	100.0

SOURCE: UNIVERSITY OF BASEL, DEPT. OF GEOGRAPHY AND ALL INDIA DISASTER MITIGATION INSTITUTE, AHMEDABAD, INDIA 2005. SOCIAL SCIENCE SURVEY IN SELECTED SLUM COMMUNITIES IN THE CITY OF BHUJ, GUJARAT, INDIA.

As discussed in Tab. 17.16, the households with a private water facility show an overall better drinking water quality. These facts could explain the better water quality among the households with a private toilet facility. A second thesis gives even better reasons for the results: 100% of the households without a private toilet indicated to defecate in the open space. Though it is common in India to take along a can filled with water for anal cleansing, the defecation in the open space is nevertheless not as hygienic as the use of a private toilet. Even if people also use water for anal cleansing by using a private toilet, the possibility of hand washing with soap after defecation exists, while this is not the case in the open space. It is therefore possible that households whose family members defecate in the open space increase the risk of recontamination of their drinking water through unhygienic handling. The poor quality of their drinking water could then be explained independently of the water source.

17.16
Sewerage facility in the house

The thesis of the previous subchapter is supported by the results of the relation between the water quality and the sewerage facility in a household. Households with a sewerage facility in the house have remarkably better water qualities than households without (Tab. 17.25). The majority of households with a soak-pit (72.2%) or another legal sewerage facility (66.7%) have a water quality of less than 100 E.coli/100ml. Among the households without a sewerage facility in the house, only 21.3% show the same water quality. The majority (64.3%) of those households have a water quality of 200-2000 E.coli/100ml.

Table 17.25 Water quality (E.coli), by sewerage facility in the house

Sewerage facility / E.coli bacteria	no in % (n=14)	yes, legal in % (n=6)	yes, soak-pit in % (n=54)	Total in % (n=74)
0	7.1	0.0	18.5	14.9
1 - 10	7.1	16.7	20.4	17.6
10 - 70	7.1	16.7	22.2	18.9
70 - 100	0.0	33.3	11.1	10.8
100 - 200	7.1	0.0	9.3	8.1
200 - 400	28.6	16.7	7.4	12.2
450 - 1000	21.4	0.0	1.9	5.4
1000 - 2000	14.3	16.7	5.6	8.1
>2000	7.1	0.0	3.7	4.1
Total	100.0	100.0	100.0	100.0

SOURCE: UNIVERSITY OF BASEL, DEPT. OF GEOGRAPHY AND ALL INDIA DISASTER MITIGATION INSTITUTE, AHMEDABAD, INDIA 2005. SOCIAL SCIENCE SURVEY IN SELECTED SLUM COMMUNITIES IN THE CITY OF BHUJ, GUJARAT, INDIA.

These results can again be explained by the fact that the households with a sewerage facility in the house probably show a more hygienic handling of their drinking water. In addition, Tab. 17.26 shows the relation between the availability of sewerage and toilet facilities in the house. As expected, 84.6% of the households without a toilet facility do not have a sewerage facility in the house, either. Most households with a sewerage facility in the house (95.0%) also have a private toilet. The thesis that households without a toilet and a sewerage facility in the house show a worse water quality because of unhygienic handling of the water can thereby be supported.

Table 17.26 Toilet facility, by sewerage facility in the house (only water sampled households)

Toilet facility / Sewerage facility	yes in % (n=13)	no in % (n=61)	Total in % (n=74)
no	4.9	84.6	18.9
yes, legal	9.8	0.0	8.1
yes, sock-pit	85.2	15.4	73.0
Total	100.0	100.0	100.0

SOURCE: UNIVERSITY OF BASEL, DEPT. OF GEOGRAPHY AND ALL INDIA DISASTER MITIGATION INSTITUTE, AHMEDABAD, INDIA 2005. SOCIAL SCIENCE SURVEY IN SELECTED SLUM COMMUNITIES IN THE CITY OF BHUJ, GUJARAT, INDIA.

17.17
Slum

Comparing the water quality in the four different slums which were surveyed and sampled, some significant trends emerge (Tab. 17.27). The best water quality can be found in Mustuffanagar: 90% of all sampled households have drinking water with less than 100 E.coli/100ml, and 23.3% have even clean water without any E.coli bacteria. Shantinagar is at the lowest end of the water quality scale with 60.8% of all sampled households having water with more than 450 E.coli/100ml, and more than a third of the households (39.1%) showing a water quality of even more than 1000 E.coli/100ml. The other two slums have quite similar water qualities in the sampled households, even if Bhimraonagar shows a little better drinking water quality. 40.9% of the tested households in Bhimraonagar have drinking water with less than 10 E.coli/100ml, while in Jayprakashnagar, only 23.1% of the households show the same quality. Moreover, none of the sampled households in Bhimraonagar had drinking water with more than 400 E.coli/100ml, whereas in Jayprakashnagar, still 15.4% of all sampled households had a water quality of 1000-2000 E.coli/100ml.

In order to explain this distribution of water quality among the slums, one can focus on the availability of toilets and sewerage facilities in the house. As Tab. 17.28 indicate, 92.3 % of the households in Mustuffanagar have a toilet facility, and 96.0% have a sewerage facility (Tab. 17.29). In Bhimraonagar, the share of households with a toilet facility respectively a sewerage facility is not that high, but still, 78.9% have a private toilet and 73.7% of the households have access to a sewerage facility. This high proportion of households with a toilet and a sewerage facility could explain the better water quality of these two slum communities, as compared to Jayprakashnagar and Shantinagar. However, it is surprising that although 100.0% of the samples households in Jayprakashnagar have a private toilet and sewerage facility, their water quality is not as good as in Mustuffanagar. Probably, the people there do not use or maintain their facilities adequately, or there is another source of contamination present in this slum. In Shantinagar, only 52.4% of the households have a private toilet facility, and 57.9% have access to a sewerage facility. This low proportion of households with access to these facilities could be the reason for the bad water quality found in Shantinagar.

Table 17.27 Water quality (E.coli), by slum

Slum E.coli bacteria	Bhimraonagar in % (n=22)	Jayprakashnagar in % (n=13)	Mustuffanagar in % (n=30)	Shantinagar in % (n=23)	Total in % (n=88)
0	13.6	15.4	23.3	0.0	13.6
1 - 10	27.3	7.7	26.7	4.3	18.2
10 - 70	13.6	15.4	23.3	13.0	17.0
70 - 100	4.5	23.1	16.7	4.3	11.4
100 - 200	13.6	15.4	0.0	13.0	9.1
200 - 400	27.3	7.7	6.7	4.3	11.4
450 - 1000	0.0	0.0	3.3	21.7	6.8
1000 - 2000	0.0	15.4	0.0	21.7	8.0
>2000	0.0	0.0	0.0	17.4	4.5
Total	100.0	100.0	100.0	100.0	100.0

SOURCE: UNIVERSITY OF BASEL, DEPT. OF GEOGRAPHY AND ALL INDIA DISASTER MITIGATION INSTITUTE, AHMEDABAD, INDIA 2005. SOCIAL SCIENCE SURVEY IN SELECTED SLUM COMMUNITIES IN THE CITY OF BHUJ, GUJARAT, INDIA.

Table 17.28 Toilet facility in the house, by slum (only water sampled households)

Slum Toilet facility	Bhimraonagar in % (n=19)	Jayprakashnagar in % (n=11)	Mustuffanagar in % (n=26)	Shantinagar in % (n=21)	Total in % (n=77)
yes	78.9	100.0	92.3	52.4	79.2
no	21.1	0.0	7.7	47.6	20.8
Total	100.0	100.0	100.0	100.0	100.0

SOURCE: UNIVERSITY OF BASEL, DEPT. OF GEOGRAPHY AND ALL INDIA DISASTER MITIGATION INSTITUTE, AHMEDABAD, INDIA 2005. SOCIAL SCIENCE SURVEY IN SELECTED SLUM COMMUNITIES IN THE CITY OF BHUJ, GUJARAT, INDIA.

Table 17.29 Sewerage facility, by slum (only water sampled households)

Slum Sewerage facility	Bhimraonagar in % (n=19)	Jayprakashnagar in % (n=11)	Mustuffanagar in % (n=25)	Shantinagar in % (n=19)	Total in % (n=74)
no	26.3	0.0	4.0	42.1	18.9
yes, legal	0.0	54.5	0.0	0.0	8.1
yes, sock-pit	73.7	45.5	96.0	57.9	73.0
Total	100.0	100.0	100.0	100.0	100.0

SOURCE: UNIVERSITY OF BASEL, DEPT. OF GEOGRAPHY AND ALL INDIA DISASTER MITIGATION INSTITUTE, AHMEDABAD, INDIA 2005. SOCIAL SCIENCE SURVEY IN SELECTED SLUM COMMUNITIES IN THE CITY OF BHUJ, GUJARAT, INDIA.

These results imply that the existence of toilet and sewerage facilities may affect the quality of the drinking water. Yet, as the example of Jayprakashnagar shows, these facilities are no guarantee for good drinking water: they can help to protect the drinking water sources, but to do so, they have to be well used and maintained. And if the people do not act hygienically with their drinking water the probability of contamination is very high.

17.18
Type of house

The analysis of the water quality by the different types of houses can tie up to the thesis made in the previous subchapter. The type of house a family lives in can be seen as an indicator for the financial situation of the family. Unfortunately, there is no balance between the different types of houses among the tested households. Seven families live in a kachcha house, a traditional round hut without concrete walls, and 21 families live in a Pucca house, a modern concrete house with two floors of which one is a walkable roof-deck. But most families (n=49) live in a semi-pucca house which is a concrete house with only one floor. Because of this unbalance, the results are not quite representative. However, it is noteworthy that against all speculations, the poorest type of house, the kachcha house, seems to have a rather good water quality (Tab. 17.30). 57.2% of the families living in such houses have a water quality of less than 10 E.coli/100ml, while only 28.6% of the sampled households in pucca houses, and 30.6% of those in semi-pucca houses show the same water quality. By comparing only the pucca and the semi-pucca houses, we can see that the families living in pucca houses mainly show a water quality of less than 100 E.coli/100ml (71.5%), while only 53.0% of the families living in semi-pucca houses have the same drinking water quality.

Table 17.30 Water quality (E.coli), by type of house

Type of house / E.coli bacteria	Kachcha house in % (n=7)	Pucca house in % (n=21)	Semi-Pucca house in % (n=49)	Total in % (n=77)
0	14.3	14.3	16.3	15.6
1 - 10	42.9	14.3	14.3	16.9
10 - 70	0.0	28.6	16.3	18.2
70 - 100	28.6	14.3	6.1	10.4
100 - 200	0.0	4.8	12.2	9.1
200 - 400	0.0	19.0	10.2	11.7
450 - 1000	14.3	4.8	6.1	6.5
1000 - 2000	0.0	0.0	12.2	7.8
>2000	0.0	0.0	6.1	3.9
Total	100.0	100.0	100.0	100.0

SOURCE: UNIVERSITY OF BASEL, DEPT. OF GEOGRAPHY AND ALL INDIA DISASTER MITIGATION INSTITUTE, AHMEDABAD, INDIA 2005. SOCIAL SCIENCE SURVEY IN SELECTED SLUM COMMUNITIES IN THE CITY OF BHUJ, GUJARAT, INDIA.

In order to analyse if the type of house can actually be taken as an indicator for the financial situation of a family the types of houses have been correlated with the monthly income of the families. For this analysis not only the water sampled households, but all 496 households were used (Tab. 17.31). The highest percentage of families living in kachcha houses (21.3%) can be found among those earning less than 1500 Rs. a month. The percentage of families living in pucca houses increases from 12.5% among the families earning less than 1500 Rs. a month to 31.5% among those earning more than 5000 Rs. a month. But in all income categories, most families live in a semi-pucca house (around 59.6-69.5%). This implies that the higher the income class is, the more pucca houses are built. Contrary, the lower the income class, the more kachcha houses are built. These results underline the thesis that the type of house can be seen as an indicator for the financial situation of a family, with very few exceptions.

Table 17.31 Type of house, by slum

Monthly income Type of house	<1500 in % (n=80)	1500-3000 in % (n=210)	3000-5000 in % (n=114)	5000-42000 in % (n=92)	Total in % (n=496)
Kachcha house	21.3	14.8	15.8	7.6	14.7
Pucca house	12.5	15.7	24.6	31.5	20.2
Semi-Pucca house	66.3	69.5	59.6	60.9	65.1
Total	100.0	100.0	100.0	100.0	100.0

SOURCE: UNIVERSITY OF BASEL, DEPT. OF GEOGRAPHY AND ALL INDIA DISASTER MITIGATION INSTITUTE, AHMEDABAD, INDIA 2005. SOCIAL SCIENCE SURVEY IN SELECTED SLUM COMMUNITIES IN THE CITY OF BHUJ, GUJARAT, INDIA.

17.19
Analysis of water treatment methods

The most common methods of water treatment used in developing countries are:

- Filtration (by cloth or sand)
- Chlorination
- Boiling
- Solar disinfection (SODIS)

Besides the fact that each treatment method has its advantages and limitations, the efficiency of the different methods also depends on conditions such as water turbidity, average daily insolation or other environmental factors. It is therefore important to carry out some field tests before giving recommendations to slum dwellers. In the following subchapters, the water samples taken in the four slums will be divided into the different treatment methods they have passed through. Accordingly, the results of the special water samples taken from community wells and hand pumps will be showed. The water of these additional samples has been treated with chlorine and has been exposed to sunlight (SODIS).

Tab. 17.32 shows the simple frequency of the used water treatment methods among the tested households. 67.5% of them (n=52) consume their drinking water after filtering it through a piece of cloth, and only five households (6.5%) boil their water before drinking it. 26% of the households do not treat their water at all.

Table 17.32 Simple frequency of treatment methods

Treatment	frequency	valid percentage
Filtration by cloth	52	67.5%
Boiling	1	1.3%
Filtration by cloth and boiling	4	5.2%
No treatment	20	26.0%
Total	77	100.0%

SOURCE: UNIVERSITY OF BASEL, DEPT. OF GEOGRAPHY AND ALL INDIA DISASTER MITIGATION INSTITUTE, AHMEDABAD, INDIA 2005. SOCIAL SCIENCE SURVEY IN SELECTED SLUM COMMUNITIES IN THE CITY OF BHUJ, GUJARAT, INDIA.

17.20 Filtration

As most of the households stated to filter their water by cloth, the water quality could predicate the efficiency of that method.

The number of E.coli bacteria found in the tested water samples which have been treated by cloth shows a wide spectrum (Tab. 17.33). Even if 17.3% of the water samples have no E.coli bacteria, and 59.6% of them have less than 100 E.coli bacteria per 100ml, still 40.4% of the filtered water samples show more than 100 E.coli bacteria per 100ml. Also, 15.4% of the water samples have very bad water quality ranging from about 450 to over 2000 E.coli bacteria per 100ml.

Table 17.33 Simple frequency of water quality when filtered by cloth

E.coli bacteria	frequency	valid percentage
0	9	17.3%
1 - 10	10	19.2%
10 - 70	9	17.3%
70 - 100	3	5.8%
100 - 200	6	11.5%
200 - 400	7	13.5%
450 - 1000	4	7.7%
1000 - 2000	3	5.8%
>2000	1	1.9%
Total	52	100.0%

SOURCE: UNIVERSITY OF BASEL, DEPT. OF GEOGRAPHY AND ALL INDIA DISASTER MITIGATION INSTITUTE, AHMEDABAD, INDIA 2005. SOCIAL SCIENCE SURVEY IN SELECTED SLUM COMMUNITIES IN THE CITY OF BHUJ, GUJARAT, INDIA.

This high variation of the quality of the sampled drinking water shows that the filtration by cloth can not be regarded as a safe water treatment method. A family using this method to "clean" its drinking water cannot be sure that after the treatment, the water is safe to drink. It appears that the method of filtering water by cloth is not a reliable way of getting the germs out of the water.

Another explanation of the poor water quality even after treatment could be given by the possibility of a recontamination afterwards. But this fact would only explain some of the contaminated water samples; it cannot be taken for granted that 82.7% of the E.coli bacteria pollution come from recontamination by the users. Furthermore, this would implicate that all the other treatment methods show a similar water quality spectrum, because a recontamination would be possible after all different methods of water treatment.

17.21
Clorination

For the chlorination of the water samples, a product of the Swiss company *Katadyn Produkte AG* has been used. It is called *Micropur Forte*.

Micropur forte combines the strong disinfection effect from chlorine with the long-time effect of silver ions. It kills the harmful pathogens (bacteria and viruses) which can also be present in clear water. However, it does not affect worm eggs, amoebas and bilharzias. One pill is used for one litre of clear water and has to be given to the water 30 minutes before drinking it. Micropur Forte can preserve the water germfree for 6 month [Katadyn Produkte AG (2005)].

After application, the water tastes different because of the chlorine. This taste could be neutralised with another product called *Antichlor*, but because of its costs, the use of this product does not seem reasonable in developing countries like India.

To test the efficiency of a chlorination product on the locally consumed drinking water, samples from two community wells nearby Shantinagar and from a hand pump nearby Mustuffanagar had been taken. The water from the wells nearby Shantinagar is free, the water from the hand pump nearby Mustuffanagar costs about 12 Rs. for 10 litres.

Figure 17.2 Well No. 1 (Shantinagar)

Photo: F. Wieland [Shantinagar 23.02.05]

Figure 17.3 Hand pump (Mustuffanagar)

Photo: F. Wieland [Shantinagar 23.02.05]

Figure 17.4 Well No. 2 (Shantinagar)

Photo: F. Wieland [Shantinagar 23.02.05]

From each of these sources, three water samples had been taken. One was tested without having been treated, the second sample had been treated with Micropur Forte, and the last sample had been exposed to sunlight.

Well No. 1 (Shantinagar).
Figure 17.5 Water quality of well No1.

a) without treatment   b) with chlorination

 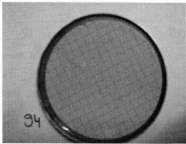

Photo: F. Wieland [Shantinagar 24.02.05]

The water sample of well No. 1 without treatment (Figure 17.5a) shows more than 1'500 E.coli bacteria per 100ml and is therefore highly contaminated with faeces. It is not advisable for the local people to drink this water without an efficient treatment. As figure 17.5b shows, there are no E.coli bacteria anymore after a treatment of the water with Micropur Forte. The chlorine residual, the free chlorine left in the water after the treatment to prevent a recontamination of the water, was found to be about 0.8 mg/l. This value is a bit higher than the norm of 0.3-0.5 mg/l, but the water can still be consumed without a doubt.

Well No. 2 (Shantinagar)
Figure 17.6 Water quality of well No. 2.

a) without treatment   b) with chlorination

Photo: F. Wieland [Shantinagar 24.02.05]

Well No. 2 nearby Shantinagar was also found to have very bad water quality with more than 1'500 E.coli bacteria per 100ml. Therefore, drinking this water without efficient treatment is also very dangerous, because such highly contaminated water can transmit many severe diseases. After treating the water with Micropur Forte, there were no living E.coli bacteria in the water anymore.

The water could now be consumed without endangering one's health. The measured chlorine residual was 0.1mg/l which is even less than the indicated norm values. However, this also means that there would not be enough free chlorine left in the water that could prevent a possible recontamination.

Hand pump (Mustuffanagar)
Figure 17.7 Water quality of handpump.
  a) without treatment   b) with chlorination

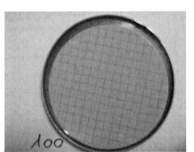

Photo: F. Wieland [Mustuffanagar 24.02.05]

As figure 17.7a illustrates, the water from the hand pump in Madihanagar nearby Mustuffanagar shows a very good water quality. Only 2 E.coli bacteria could be found in 100ml. Most people stated that they indeed had an own water source, but that they used the water only for cleaning and cooking. They get their drinking water from this hand pump, although they must pay for it. The surveyed households indicated that the water from this hand pump was lighter than the water from their own hand pumps. This might be because of some soiling in the water, yet, this guess could not be verified.

While there are only few E.coli bacteria in the water anyway, none are left after chlorination. Regarding the high water quality, it is not surprising that the chlorine residual measured is very high: 4.0mg/l of free chlorine is left in the water. The extremely high value can be explained by the fact that when more chlorine is added to the water than would be needed to kill the bacteria, it remains as free chlorine in the water. This high value of chlorine residual will prevent the water from any recontamination after this treatment, but is also harmful to the human health. Under such circumstances, the amount of chlorine added must be minimised to the needed level.

17.22
Solar disinfection (SODIS)

SODIS, solar disinfection, is a method developed by EAWAG (Swiss Federal Institute of Environmental Science and Technology). This method uses two components of the sunlight to which the pathogens are vulnerable to: radiation in the spectrum of UV-A light (which has a wavelength of 320-400μm) and heat (increased water temperature due to infrared radiation). The first component, UV-A radiation, has a germicidal effect. The second component raises the water temperature and is known as solar pasteurisation when the water temperature is raised to 70° C - 75°C.

The water samples taken from the three sources in Shantinagar and Mustuffanagar had been filled up in 1.5l PET bottles and exposed to sunlight. The two bottles from Shantinagar were placed on a roof top in the slum around 10 a.m. and had been left there until 6 p.m.

The bottle from Mustuffanagar was put on a roof in the slum (Figure 17.8) around midday and had been left there until 6 p.m.

The sun was shining during the whole day in full strength. Given such conditions, an exposure of only 2 hours would be sufficient to kill all bacteria in the water.

Figure 17.8 Bottle on the roof top.

Photo: F. Wieland [Shantinagar 23.02.05]

Well No. 1 (Shantinagar)
Figure 17.9 Water quality of well No 1.

a) without treatment   b) with SODIS

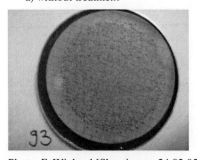 

Photo: F. Wieland [Shantinagar 24.02.05]

Although the water from well No. 1in Shantinagar had very bad water quality of over 1'500 E.coli bacteria per 100ml, there were no living bacteria anymore after the exposure of the water to sunlight for about 8 hours. All bacteria had been killed.

Well No. 2 (Shantinagar)
Figure 17.10 Water quality of well No. 2.
    a) without treatment   b) with SODIS

Photo: F. Wieland [Shantinagar 24.02.05]

Well No. 2 showed a similarly bad water quality as well No. 1. As before, all bacteria in the sample had been killed, too, after exposing the water to sunlight. We can therefore conclude that the method of exposing water contaminated with E.coli bacteria to sunlight proves to be reliable and that the possibility of a unique occurrence can be excluded.

Hand pump (Mustuffanagar)
Figure 17.11 Water quality of handpump.
    a) without treatment   b) with SODIS

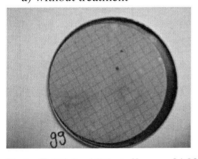

Photo: F. Wieland [Mustuffanagar 24.02.05]

The almost clean water from the hand pump in Madihanagar had been exposed to sunlight as well. After about 6 hours, the water was absolutely free of E.coli bacteria. It is worth exposing even water with only few bacteria to sunlight for some hours to ensure that there are no germs at all in it anymore.

17.23
Conclusion

The drinking water quality in households of the four slums was analysed by demographic, social and financial factors as well as by hygienic infrastructure. Demographic and social factors like religion, caste or number of family members proved to have little or no influence on the quality of a household's drinking water. By contrast, financial determinants clearly correlated with the quality of the drinking water. Especially the monthly income of a family seemed to be a factor that partly explains the drinking water quality of a household. The places for health check-ups, an indicator of the financial situation of a family, showed a high correlation with the drinking water quality, too. This means that the financial situation of a household greatly affects the quality of its drinking water. A higher monthly income may probably increase the drinking water quality of many households in the four surveyed slums. Yet, the existence of hygienic infrastructure seems to be an even more important determinant of the quality of drinking water: households with access to a private water, toilet and sewerage facility show a remarkably better drinking water quality than households without access to such facilities. The availability of toilet and sewerage facilities is found to be even more important for safe drinking water than the water supply itself. This is probably due to the fact that the absence of a toilet and sewerage facility leads to contamination both of clean or dirty water.

Another important factor influencing the quality of a household's drinking water is the level of education of its family members. Households with a highly educated family head showed better drinking water than families with an illiterate or poorly educated head. Highly educated families also stated to know about a relation between hygiene and health and showed more interest in improving their drinking water supply.

These last two factors, the existence of hygienic infrastructure and the level of education, are the main indicator for the distribution of water quality among the sampled households. The hygienic infrastructure helps to protect the drinking water sources from contamination, and a certain level of education is important in order to use and maintain such infrastructure correctly. Well educated people know the importance of hygienic behaviour and handle their drinking water more carefully. It is therefore not only crucial to make such facilities available for all households, but to also teach the families how to use and maintain these facilities. Hygienic promotion and adequate sanitation facilities seem to be the key to sustainable good drinking water in slum communities in general.

The result of the household samples showed that the quality of filtered water highly diverges. This water treatment method can therefore not be advised in the preparation of drinking water.

The chlorination with Micropur Forte killed the existing germs in all tested water samples with an efficiency of 100%. Although this method is easy to apply, there are some limitations with regard to its use in households of slums communities. Such chlorination products are quite expensive, and most households would not be able to afford them. Also, the chlorine leaves a bad aftertaste which could keep the people from drinking the cleaned water, and the amount of added chlorine must be adapted to the degree of water contamination. This would imply a regular control of the drinking water supply by the slum dwellers and the adaptation of the product to the prevailing situation. These actions would again cost money and time.

The analyses of the solar disinfection showed convincing results. All germs in the exposed water were killed, no matter how bad the water quality had been. The efficiency of this method proved to be 100%. Moreover, this method does not need any expensive material. Locally available PET bottles can be used. There is no need of any other product or additional fuel.

The solar disinfection can therefore be identified as the most applicable method for the cleaning of drinking water in slum areas. The only precondition to be fulfilled in order to make the method work is sufficient insolation during the day. In the study areas of Bhuj, Gujarat, this precondition seemed to be fulfilled even in winter time (the analyses and the tests were done in February 2005).

We conclude that in contexts of slums in hot countries like India, solar disinfection would be the easiest, cheapest and most efficient way to clear the drinking water of all bacteria. Given to what extent contaminated drinking water is responsible for illness and death in developing countries, it should be a major focus in the coming years to promote this kind of natural and easy technology throughout the developing world.

Map 17.1 Water quality, Bhimraonagar

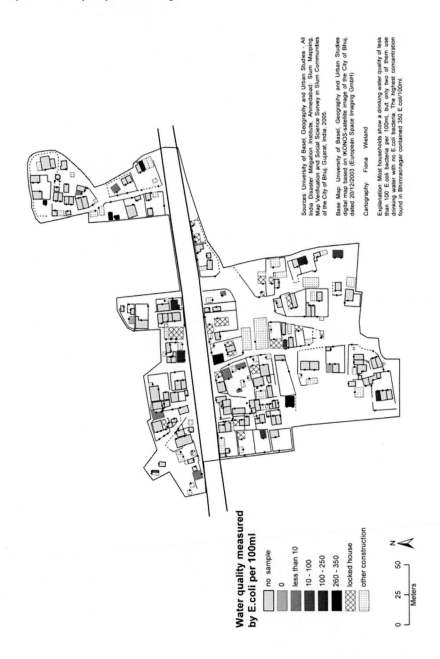

Basic infrastructure – basic problems – the case of drinking water supplies 421

Map 17.2 Water quality, Jayprakashnagar

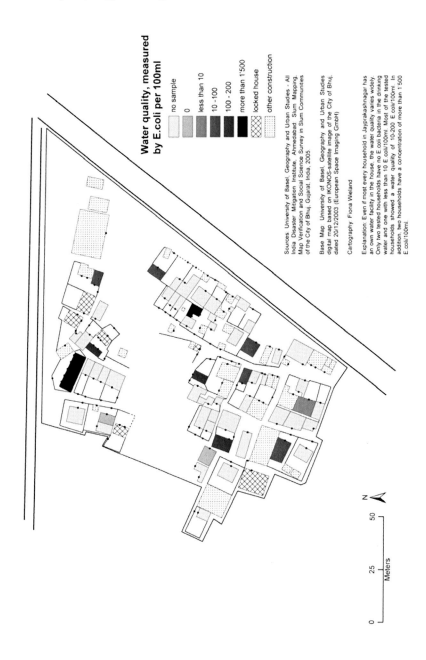

Map 17.3 Water quality, Mustuffanagar

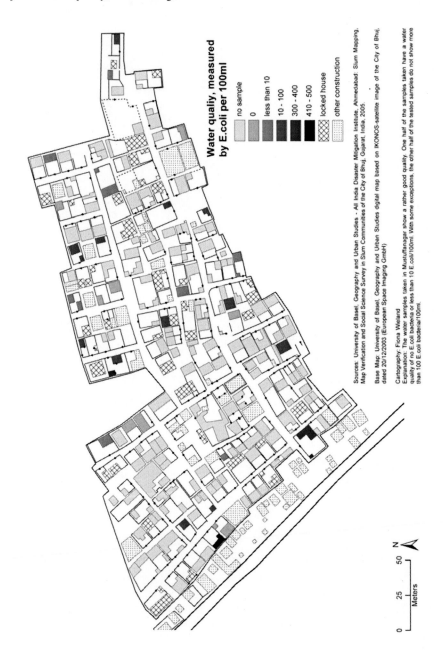

Map 17.4 Water quality, Shantinagar

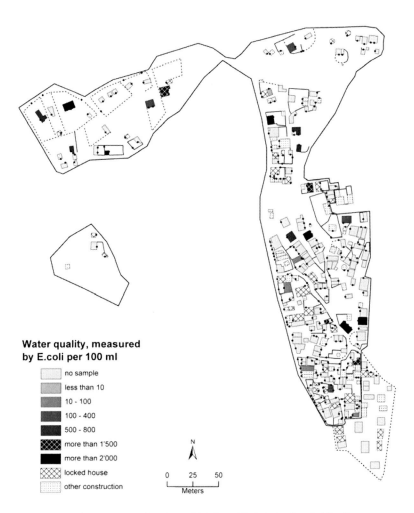

Sources: University of Basel, Geography and Urban Studies - All India Disaster Mitigation Institute, Ahmedabad: Slum Mapping, Map Verification and Social Science Survey in Slum Communities of the City of Bhuj, Gujarat, India, 2005.

Base Map: University of Basel, Geography and Urban Studies digital map based on IKONOS-satellite image of the City of Bhuj, dated 20/12/2003 (European Space Imaging GmbH)

Cartography: Fiona Wieland

Explanation: The water quality found in Shantinagar is very alarming. There was no single household with clean drinking water (without any E.coli bacteria) in the whole slum. Shantinagar is the slum with the highest concentration of E.coli bacteria found among all taken water samples. Four households showed more than 1'500 E.coli/100ml and five households had actually more than 2'000 E.coli bacteria in their drinking water (per 100ml).

18 GIS applications as tools in urban poverty reduction – methodological aspects

J. Wendel
University of Basel

18.1 Methodology

How to create useable maps at the household level? As a result of significant developments in remote sensing technologies, especially in terms of spatial resolution, different types of high-resolution satellite images are available and can be used as base for GIS maps. The images taken by QUICKBIRD, IKONOS or the Indian Remote Sensing satellites (IRS) provide very detailed images with an approximate one meter resolution. Thus, these images are suitable to do large scale mapping using the images as spatial data base.

Some general remarks. It is worth noting that mapping, whether using satellite images, GIS and GPS, should not be confused with surveying methods, using Total Stations (TPS) and Theodolites. Even if the satellite images are of an impressive resolution, the accuracy of maps based on remote sensing is less than that of maps based on surveying methods, since the one meter resolution is only given at the centre of the image. Most of the high-resolution satellites, in particular IKONOS and QUICKBIRD, take their images with an inclined view; hence the ground pixel size of the images depends upon the satellites' nadir angle. Consequently, the pixel size of certain image sections might grow up to twice of those taken at the nadir position (Jacobsen 2002:110). Furthermore, the geomorphology of the scene causes a distortion of the image. Even after correcting and georeferencing the satellite image, there remains a difference between the satellite image and the control points used for their georeferencing (RMS difference).
Indeed, this small imperfection is acceptable for most purposes, as long as the maps are not used as the only base for engineering or civil works. For that purpose, an additional survey is advised.

Demands of the project. The main challenge of the *GIS-applications in Urban Poverty Areas - Slum and risk mapping (India)* project was the problem of scale, since the objective of the pilot study was the mapping of urban slums at the household level, that is of all residential and business buildings, property borders and lots (compound walls and fences), and of selective elements like temples and mosques, wells, large trees, road lighting or health-endangering places.

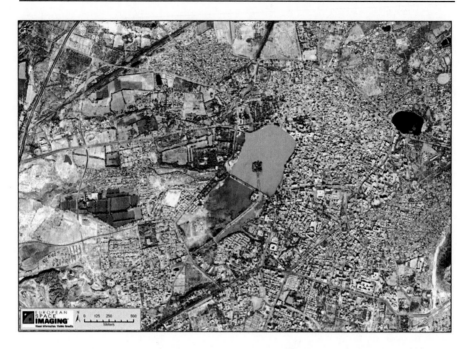

Figure 18.1 IKONOS image of Bhuj, dated December 20th 2003 (European Space Imaging)

For this pilot study, an IKONOS image with a one meter resolution was chosen as a suitable database (colour, 4 bands / 4 separate files, pan-sharpened, 11bit, DRA on, dated Dec. 20th, 2003). DRA is a processing algorithm that attempts to improve the distribution of data in an image and effectively brightens the image. However, DRA does slightly affect the distribution of radiometric values within a scene. DRA products are recommended for better visual representation of images, while a non-DRA product is recommended for applications that require the best available radiometric accuracy. Advantageously, the image is free of clouds and the area of interest (Bhuj) is in a more or less central position of the total image (figure 18.1), thus the deformation of pixels offside of the images' centre was not to rate as very problematic. IKONOS is characterized by its sharpness, enabling to digitize features of the landscape, roads and railways, buildings as well as single trees or even vehicles.

According to other studies with remote sensing based mapping, the one meter resolution of IKONOS is suitable for applications like cadastral surveys, also at the village level, or for generating thematic maps up to 1:2'500 scale, using GPS and other measurements for precision control (Raju et al. 2002:128f). The imagery is said to have a two meter horizontal and a three meter vertical accuracy, which is equivalent to a 1:2'500 scale map standard (Banerjee et al. 2002:276). As evidence for the sufficient accuracy of this technical approach, the E-governance tools, developed and promoted by the BANGALORE EGOVERNANCE FOUNDATION, should be mentioned. This E-governance project was initiated in Bangalore in 2003 by NANDAN NILEKANI, the CEO of India's most important software company INFOSYS TECHNOLOGIES LTD., and SRIKANTH NADHAMUNI. The E-governance Foundation also uses high-resolution satellite imagery to digitize cadastral plans of Bangalore and other municipalities for property tax evaluation, urban development and planning objectives.

Working steps. As a first step, the satellite image was georeferenced (datum, WGS 84). Due to the lack of recent and exact topographical maps for that purpose, twenty reference points within the city limits of Bhuj were measured locally using a GPS system. This also served to delimit four study areas (September/October 2004).The next step was the visual interpretation of the IKONOS image (single channels and RGB composite) and the onscreen digitization using ESRI ArcGIS. At this time, only buildings and compound walls, as well as major roads were digitized in polygon and poly-line layers (October/November 2004). This preliminary data was checked, corrected and supplemented in the course of a fieldtrip in February of 2005, applying the probably most simple but well-tried mapping and measuring method, namely doing triangulation using a tape measure, a compass, a drawing board and a pencil. Since the satellite image was about a year old at the time of onscreen digitizing, one could expect to see new construction. All corrections and supplementary data were sketched on hardcopies of the preliminary GIS maps and were immediately integrated into the GIS-system. Thus, in the course of the field trip, a second check of the updated GIS maps was possible. During this measurement, additional geographic information such as wells, trees and streetlights (point features) or open sewerage (line features) was mapped to complete the maps of the slums.

Simultaneously with the ground checks, the residential buildings were numbered and the social science survey on household level was carried out in co-operation with AIDMI. The complete and exact numbering of all of the residential buildings was imperative to facilitate the joining of the updated GIS layers and the results of the survey. Therefore, the correct numbering of the buildings and of the GIS features was crucial for the subsequent preparation of thematic maps. It is to state that in India, even for legal residential areas, the existence of a postal address is not necessarily customary, particularly not in slum communities. Addresses like "close to Tony's Pizza" or "opposite the cinema" are common, since the buildings, in the majority of cases, are not numbered and the streets do not have names.

Back in Switzerland, the results of the social science survey were analysed and interpreted using special statistical software (SPSS). From this data a socio-economic database was created and joint with the final geometric GIS files, using the house numbers as key variables. After all, a myriad of thematic maps was produced for the four study areas, providing information on spatial patterns of demographic and socio-economic parameters.

18.2 Problems and solutions

Accuracy of images. Several problems emerge when using satellite assisted GIS-maps of slums. Satellite images and the digitizing of slums may be done anywhere in the world. Whereas the method itself has a high degree of accuracy, local conditions dictate in every context that extensive ground checks of the onscreen digitized features be made. In this pilot project, it was necessary to get an impression about the accuracy and the error rate of this new technical approach. For objects of larger scales, like urban districts, major roads or land utilisation, the method has also been improved, as well as for cadastral surveys of legally built up areas, where the average object size is more than twice or even triple of that at the slums. Regarding the onscreen digitizing, several problems need mentioning. Some of them are to minimize by training, others are only amendable by a ground check.

The resolution of the raster images. The delimitation of the feature's edges (slum community boundaries) contains certain errors, since they can not be detected definitely. In contrast to vector graphics like shape-files used in ArcGIS, a raster image, such as the IKONOS image, is a continuity of information and is generated from single pixels containing this information. A "mixed pixel" results from the fact that individual areas, consisting of different features or classes may be below (smaller than) the resolution of the sensor. Thus, mixed pixels contain information about all the features located at its area.

Considering the pixel-size of 1x1 metres, an error of 30 to 70 centimetres is hardly avoidable. Even if one zooms into the image to a scale of 1:1, one cannot obtain more details. Since mapping is a priori not the same as a surveying map, but rather, serves a different purpose, this error is to be accepted. The most serious errors can easily be corrected by ground checks (see figure 18.2).

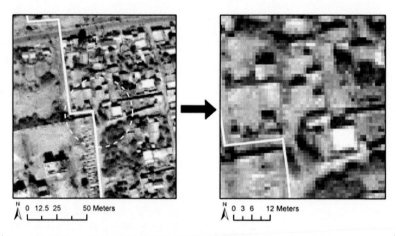

Figure 18.2 The problem of "mixed pixels" and the blurring effect in the delimitation of boundaries

Whereas the buildings in the slum community of Bhimraonagar seem to be easily limitable in the left image, it is more difficult to detect them in the right one (European Space Imaging).

Distinction of closely neighbouring features. For buildings standing closely together or for row houses it is very difficult – even impossible – to distinguish between single objects. This is, one the one hand, due to the mixed pixels but, on the other hand, due to the construction process itself. For example, uninterrupted roofs give no hints as to how the buildings are partitioned. These errors can only be corrected by a ground check (see figures 18.3 and 18.4).

Since the slums chosen for this pilot project are not very densely built up areas, the problem of inseparability of objects was not of such an importance. But for metropolitan slums, like those in Ahmedabad, where every square centimetre is used, this might become a problem of prime importance. In the context of the slum communities in Bhuj, the vegetation turned out to be an additional problem. Large trees overtopping the buildings overlay the roofs like umbrellas and thus, they also lead to misinterpretations and a wrong digitalization of the buildings` shape and size.

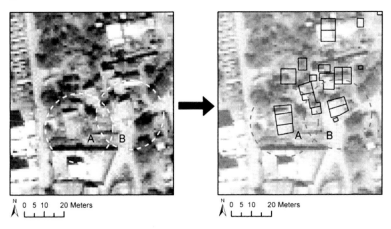

Figure 18.3 Area A and Area B
Area A exemplifies the problem of "row houses" which are not distinguishable even with a high resolution satellite image. Area B shows the problem of the transition between buildings and the adjacent surrounding area. It is impossible to distinguish between the buildings and the alley. Both areas are a part of the slum community of Bhimraonagar (European Space Imaging).

Architecture and construction materials The type of construction has implications for the digitizing of buildings. Due to the climatic conditions, flat roofs are very popular, since they can also be used as living or bed room and for doing house work. However, the flat roofs are more difficult to identify from the satellite image than pitched roofs. Moreover, many flat roofs jut out between 50 and 100 centimetres, in order to increase living space and to shade the floors below. Therefore, a house might be digitized with the outlines of the roof and not with the outlines of its walls (see figure 18.4). In addition, most houses own large non roofed terraces that are sometimes several times larger than the house itself. These terraces are mostly not identifiable from the satellite image. Yet, they are to be considered as part of the house since they are intensively used as living spaces. Thus, they were integrated into the GIS, which required a ground check.

Figure 18.4 Examples of flat roofs with cantilevers
(left: the slum community of Kajlinagar, right: the community of Bhimraonagar. Photos: J. Wendel).

Also, the various types of construction materials used for the slum houses and the roofs in particular were a major problem for the interpretation of the satellite images. First, this mixture of materials used, like plastic tarpaulins, corrugated iron, bricks and clay bricks, tiles or thatch roofs prevents the use of automatic analysis tools to extract the buildings, for example using the IR-channel. Second, it complicates the visual interpretation, since the distinction between a roof build up from corrugated iron, plastic tarpaulins or clay bricks and the neighbouring loamy open space, or between a thatched roof and a tree is difficult and sometimes even impossible. Consequently, a certain error was to be expected, resulting from incorrect digitization of the feature edges, the omission of non identified features and the digitization of objects which did not really exist at all.

GIS applications as tools in urban poverty reduction – methodological aspects 431

Figure 18.5 Due to the climatic conditions, life mainly takes place outside of the buildings *Thus, terraces are to be considered as part of the building. (left: Shantinagar, right: Bhimraonager. Photos: J. Wendel, N. Sliwa).*

Figure 18.6 Slums: A, B, C Shantinagar, D Bhimraonagar
In the satellite image (A), neither the thatch roofed house nor its terrace are detectable (B). Pictures C and D give a good impression of the potpourri of construction materials used for the dwellings (Photos: J. Wendel, satellite image by European Space Imaging).

User caused errors. Last, the person interpreting the satellite image should be considered as a source of mistakes or rather as guarantor of a good quality. Past experience has shown that the quality of digitized data strongly depends on the digitizers' skills, imaginativeness and knowledge, in particular, knowledge of the research area. For someone who has never visited a slum it is hard to imagine the realities of such communities. As a result, misinterpretations of satellite images are more frequently made by persons with little knowledge of the study area or comparable areas. In that case, a good photo documentation is very helpful, providing a detailed impression of the sometimes unstructured and convoluted settlement with its unorthodox mixture of construction materials.

An important source of mistakes is the misinterpretations of shadows, which normally give good hints for object limitations. But depending on the orientation of gables and the insolation angle, it is difficult to distinguish between a shaded half of the roof and the shadow of the house itself (figures 18.7 and 18.8). Thus, sometimes buildings are digitized of smaller size than in reality. The same holds true for compound walls. Depending on their angle towards the insolation direction and their size, they may cast a shadow. If the shadow is too small, it might not be visible on the satellite image, since the shadow gets lost in a mixed pixel.

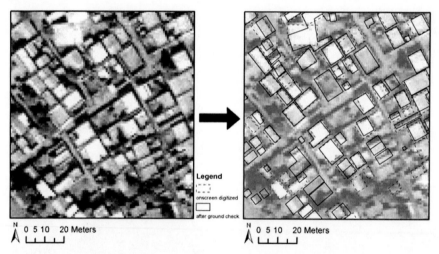

Figure 18.7 Mustuffunagar gives a good example of how helpful shadows are for the interpretation of satellite images

Due to the distinct structure of the slum and the excellent conditions of housing, the buildings and the compound walls are well recognizable and the slum was relatively easy to map. This is evidenced by the good accordance of the onscreen digitization with the ground check (satellite image: European Space Imaging).

Figure 18.8 In Bhimraonagar, the shadows are not as useful as in Mustuffangar
Bhimraonagar is more rural than Mustuffanagar, it is less densely built up and there are more open spaces and trees. In the left picture, only few buildings are well delimitable, some are only assumable, whereas compound walls are hardly recognizable. Thus, there is some discrepancy between the onscreen digitalization and the results of the ground check (satellite image: European Space Imaging).

18.3 Conclusion

The results of the onscreen digitizing from the satellite image are of a good quality. Approximately 80% of all larger buildings were covered, even some very small ones. Yet, small stables, storages or toilet houses less than one square meter are, for the most part, not detectable from the satellite image. These constructions, however, are not of interest for mapping purposes and thus were not covered, with exception of toilet houses, which are mapped as point features. In addition to the small sized features, the property boundaries and compound walls are poorly detectable from the satellite image even as a rough estimation. They can only be identified and integrated into the GIS-map by a ground check.

A major challenge of GIS-based slum mapping is the accuracy of the satellite-based GIS-map which always requires ground checking, hence labour and cost-intensive on-site work. Certainly, one does not need centimetre or millimetre accuracy in slum mapping as can be supplied by surveying methods. But this degree of accuracy is not needed anyway when one is collecting general survey data utilizing GIS-based maps. A hundred percent accuracy is neither required for fighting poverty in urban slums nor for most other developing and planning tasks. This is true for the accuracy of mapped floor spaces and for the features' geographical position. However, accurate mapping of topographies and spatial relations between the features is of high importance to assure the readability of a

GIS map. Thus, it is essential for the analysis of maps and the development of suitable actions based on real situation *in situ*. In terms of working steps of drawing up the inventory, analysis and development of actions, it does not matter whether a building is five or fifty centimetres longer or shorter. Neither does it matter whether or not it is positioned within the UTM grid a few seconds further to the West or the East. The coherence of the building structures, however, is crucial for analyzing the distribution patterns of survey data collected concomitantly with the mapping of the slum. But also, for infrastructural development like the installation of roads, whether with or without a GIS base map, a survey of the main coordinates of the housing is mandatory.

There is always a need for ground checking as Indian cities and particularly their slums feature high dynamics and are fast-growing. Thus, also a relatively new satellite image becomes rapidly outdated and completions are needed. Our experience shows that houses are built up or extended in a very short time, depending upon the needs of the occupants.

Furthermore, the ground check is required for data collection reasons as the satellite image gives no references with respect to the utilisation of a building, such as temples, mosques, housing or school. This information can only be collected by visiting the sites. Likewise, the plots are hardly recognizable in the images, since they are not always limited by compound walls but often by fences or hedges. Thus, the plot boundaries need to be integrated into the GIS after a ground check. Doing the ground check, one can then also integrate all further details in the GIS-maps, in example street lights or wells, since these important local features are much too small to been recognizable on the IKONOS image.

Most of these problems result from the small scales of objects covered by this pilot study - the slum buildings. This problem might be reduced using a QUICKBIRD image, since the resolution of thes images is approximately 70 centimetres. However, only one small advantage might be realized, since the 70 centimetres resolution is reached only by the pixels in the centre of the image and the problem of mixed pixels also exists with QUICKBIRD.

Finally, according to DR. VINOD K. SHARMA (NATIONAL CENTER FOR DISASTER MANAGEMENT, New Delhi) bringing GIS applications in the mainstream disaster management process is of top priority, since the scope of GIS is much beyond mapping and search and rescue tasks (SAR) in case of a disaster.

References

Banerjee, Anuradha, K.N. Reddy and P. Paul (2002): Application of Remote Sensing and GIS in Demographic and Socio-Economic Analysis of Dehradun City. In : Indian Cartographer, MUIP-06, p. 274-281,
www.incaindia.org/technicalpapers/46_MUIP06.pdf

Jakobsen, Karsten (2002): Comparison of High Resolution Mapping from Space. In Indian Cartographer, LSTM-01, p. 106-119,
www.incaindia.org/technicalpapers/19_LSTM01.pdf

Raju, Prasada, Sujata Ghosh, J. Saibaba and R. Ramachandran (2002): Large Scale Mapping versus High Resolution Imagery. In: Indian Cartographer, LSTM-03, p. 127-134
www.incaindia.org/technicalpapers/21_LSTM03.pdf

Shah, Shetal (year unknown): Application of mapping and GIS technologies initiated by EPC-Geographis to facilitate post-earthquake rehabilitation process - A case study of Gujarat earthquake.
www.gisdevelopment.net/application/natural_hazards/earthquakes/mi03202pf.htm

Sharma, Vinod K. (year unknown): Use of GIS related technologies for managing disasters in India: an overview. – National Center for Disaster Management, New Delhi
www.gisdevelopment.net/application/natural_hazards/overview/nho0003pf.htm

All web references: last check on July, 11th, 2005

Further links:
www.geographis.com
http://www.egovernments.org/index.htm

19 Socially differentiated urban slums – findings, problems, options for intervention

R. Schneider-Sliwa

19.1 Introduction

India, like Western societies, experiences increased social differentiation and polarisation of social milieus with new winners who are able to adjust to the changing globalising Indian economy and losers who do not have the means and capacity to adjust. That such processes may reach down to the lower caste urban slums has not been analyzed much. The implication of this, however, would be very interesting in terms of alleviating poverty.

Understanding whether or not, how and which factors in urban slums account for differentiation, in particular upward social mobility is important for a more effective, sustained and sustainable development, and for targeting scarce resources more efficiently towards the neediest of the poor.

In order to understand the forces of social differentiation and adaptive capacities at the level of the poorest, social differentiation was studied in a case study approach in selected urban slums of the Indian city of Bhuj (Gujarat):

- *horizontally* among the lowest castes, known in Western countries as the 'untouchables', and along religious background as represented in four different slum communities
- *vertically* along socioeconomic variables representative of social status and upward social mobility.

Both these dimensions were looked at with a view on identifying factors which assist or adversely affect one's ability to rise from or remain in extreme poverty. The analysis was, therefore, geared towards discovering social, spatial and behavioural patterns of distinction accounting for "landscapes of vulnerability" or "landscapes of adaptive capacities". For agencies concerned with development, this was intended to shed light onto the question of how and where to intervene more effectively and what type of local strength one might draw upon or try to strengthen. For social science research, this was to explore the question of which forces at the micro level seem to account for social differentiation in modern multicultural Indian society in which distinction along religious, class and ethnic characteristics persists and new distinctions along class and education emerges.

The City of Bhuj was selected for the case studies because it has experienced massive government investment and reconstruction after the earthquake of 2001. It also has a favourable climate of government and NGO cooperation in development efforts. Last, not least, the specific slum communities selected in the City of Bhuj were chosen because they do represent conditions and characteristics that were thought necessary to analyze the specific research question in mind, because they were areas of well established AIDMI efforts and thus, of high acceptance of foreign researchers working together with AIDMI.

Of course, not all expected findings would lend themselves easily to interpretation or well grounded theoretical explanation. For instance, social differentiation within urban slums can reflect the partial failure of government or NGO work, development efforts or policy of neglect or the lack of adaptive capacities of the population, to name only a few interpretations. Depending on the interpretation, one would focus on different strategies, for example, providing more infrastructure or focusing on the adaptive capacities that emerge from within.

In terms of its social science focus, the research, then, was based on
- the analysis of physical space in the context with social area analysis
- the micro level of the household
- a different a priori understanding of planning based on scientific action (actor research approach, cf. Reason & Bradbury 2001)
- a focus of impact orientation (how much of what is needed to help)
- an outcome orientation both of planning and the communities working together collectively in terms of developing "institutional thickness" (Amin & Thrift 1995), i.e. a well balanced institutional action, based on learning from the target groups and innovative management of problems.

This chapter will now provide a summary and synopsis by addressing the following aspects:

a. Findings - what should be noted from the survey in terms of
    - structural conditions (housing conditions, ownership issues, education and occupation)
    - basic needs (income, livelihood security, food security)
    - health and occupational hazards, access to health services
    - behavioural issues (demographic behaviour, willingness to contribute to the solution of problems, i.e. legalizing of land, payment for services)

b. Where are the most pressing problems in terms of the interrelated issues of
    - structural conditions
    - basic needs
    - behavioural variables?

c. What implications do socially differentiated urban slums have?
    - What do we do *not* know about sufficiently?
        - degrees of social differentiation

- degrees of objective slum environment (structural conditions) and social realities
- What is a matter of debate?
- What should be decided upon by public administration?
  - What is being overemphasized?
  - What is being insufficiently emphasized?

d. What are the leverages in terms of
- policies of social integration
- policies of designing public space and infrastructure
- participation
- local responsibility and action?

Based upon this conceptualization, the findings will now be summarized across the chapters and evaluated in terms of their relevance for planning and social science theory. A caveat is of note: all interpretations of social science research in this regional context and with this novel approach of conceptualizing social differentiation in slums is, by nature, only one of many ways of analyzing social processes in urban slums. Since it is difficult for Western researchers to take an insight perspective in the context of urban slum communities in India, it was very valuable to be able to heavily draw on the Indian partner's local development work.

19.2 Major findings – determinants of poverty and upward social mobility

Vicious cycles of education, occupation, incomes and livelihood security

The analysis of *education and occupation* showed that the level of education is a very important factor concerning the livelihood and general well-being of a family, not only in terms of income, but also in terms of job security and hazards. Though the results of the efforts of the government to increase the schooling and literacy levels of the population have shown a clear effect, there is still a high percentage of people who are illiterate – especially among the Scheduled Tribe and Scheduled Caste population. This remains a problem which needs to be tackled further in the future. This is especially important if one considers that education influences a whole range of livelihood factors such as livelihood security, employment opportunities, and last but not least, also the health and mental well-being of the population. It can be said in general that investments into education are of pivotal importance, and focus must be laid on the proper school enrolment of all children, and especially girl children as their numbers in the slums appeared to be striking during school hours when they were supposed to be in school. *Occupation, level of schooling, income* and *livelihood security* clearly emerge as prominent factors. Concerning the occupations of the slum dwellers, the high amount of people who work in the casual labour and construction sectors is striking and is related mostly to low educational standards. Casual labour generates casual income without social security and thus makes families more vulnerable to changing situations; especially members of the Scheduled Tribes, Scheduled Castes and other Backward Castes are often engaged in casual labour. Focus must be laid on these groups, especially to give them possibilities for a regular income via better schooling. Home based occupations tend to significantly increase the income of families, because all members of the household can be involved. In particular women who have to take care of their children in the traditional context could, through home based occupation, add up to the family income without leaving the house. In the case where old and dependent people live in the same household, they can also help to earn an additional income and relieve the financial situation of the family. Opportunities for home based occupation and the selling of the manufactured goods must thus be supported. Incomes and education have further multiplicator effects – they have a major impact on the *financial behaviour* with respect to *savings and debts*. The monthly savings value is an indicator which allows drawing conclusions on the foresight, rationality and financial possibilities of a family. Savings are important to absorb losses, crisis situations, illnesses and so on, when there is no guarantee to receive immediate help from the government. Concerning the savings behaviour of the slum dwellers, it was remarkable that only a very small percentage of the interviewed households was able to save small amounts. This situation creates a high vulnerability in the case of unforeseen expenses such as illnesses, accidents, or – as happened in 2001 – in the case of catastrophes. Given the low income occupations which result from low levels of schooling, the inability to save more is not surprising. It points, however, to the role of schooling as the base for all other improvements, or, vice versa, the lack of schooling as the deterrent of upward social mobility. Whereas this, of course, is not surprising in itself, it is of note that it is not caste or religion that figure as impediments to upward social mobility, but simply education. As for the debts of the households, one characteristic stands out: There is a relation between the amount of debts and the income of a family with families with a lower income having smaller debts, whereas families with a higher income are having higher debts. Households with lower incomes, then, seem to be more careful and efficient with their scarce resources and take care not to indebt themselves too much. Because of their frugality, assisting them with micro credit is especially meaningful as this supports self-help and self-responsibility to a greater extent than assisting households with higher incomes and an apparent tendency to overspending and indebtedness related thereto. Though the debts seem to be comparatively small for families with a lower income, they represent a huge financial burden for these families. This is often the case with families who have only casual income and thus have to continuously struggle to come up with the money for the interest payments. The high proportion of families who are indebted strongly indicates the need for small credits and micro credit financing, small and locally based financing agents, slum-based saving groups, micro-financing institutes as well as savings as self-help efforts such as rotating credit schemes.

Slum housing and slum conditions – vulnerability continues to be a fact of life

The most vulnerable suffer the most, and slums with the worst housing conditions to begin with are worst affected in case of disasters. Traditional kachcha housing was worst affected by the earthquake, thus most households who were already living in very poor circumstances also suffered the biggest impact from the earthquake. The next best form of housing does not give more options to escape vulnerability: semi-pucca houses have brick walls, their roofing structure is not always very stable and very likely consists of corrugated iron or other materials which collapse easily. Additionally, though semi-pucca houses are less expensive than pucca houses, many families still lack the proper financing to build a truly stable house – and the houses are more prone to suffer damages or collapse during an earthquake. Thus, it was the "poorer" slums (Shantinagar, Bhimraonagar) with high degrees of traditional and semi-traditional housing which were affected worst during the earthquake. Survey results indicated moreover, that despite better knowledge the traditional form of housing was still being built in order to save construction costs: kachcha houses are still built today because they are significantly cheaper than the brick pucca or semi-pucca houses, and because they offer a comparably higher living standard than temporary shelters made from cloth, corrugated iron or plastic sheets. Though most of the families have very limited financial means, they have mostly been able to rebuild their housing structures – almost all of them live in houses which they consider safe or which only show minor damages. An interesting trend could be made out: While families with a higher income were living in different houses than before the earthquake, families with a lower income were mainly still living in the same houses. This means that they have rebuilt their houses from the rubble, whereas wealthier families could move to another, new place.

Willingness to relocate

It is very clear that for only one third of the households, relocation for the sake of bettering their housing conditions is a viable option. Even for those willing to relocate, the trend to move over very short distances is obvious. It appears that relocation as such is not a prime choice for improving personal living conditions because a strong emphasis is placed upon living in familiar surroundings or family and neighbourhood contexts.

Public health issues

Food security and public health. Is striking that a large number of families own a BPL card – roughly half of the population (48.5%). Thus, in almost half of the families, the individual members have to get on with less than a poverty income. BPL cards are thus very important for a large share of the slum dwellers. The food the families got from the respective ration shop was mostly rated as average (86.6%). With only 2.2% of the family heads indicating that they were not able to feed their family, the survey indicates that the worst problem of human existence – hunger – is no longer a major concern and that there is room for progressing more strongly into more advanced issues of human existence. Considering the high amount of families who live below the poverty line, further research would have to be done to determine whether all of the family heads who answered that they are able to feed their family are also well-nourished, i.e. show no signs of malnutrition.

Occupational hazards and health

The assumption that there is a connection between income levels and the occurrence of illnesses was once again proven – and it seems to be even more striking in the slum context. All illnesses were much more frequent among the lower income classes, though there is still a pronounced difference between the lowest income classes and all other income classes. This pattern is visible across all four slum areas. Most households depend on government institutions for their health concerns – a fact that is surely due to the generally low income level of the surveyed. Thus, since a very large number of people depend on government hospitals, it is essential to further strengthen and support them. Most people visit the health centres for check-ups, but a significant number of people also use the government hospitals to buy medicine, due to the fact that quite a high proportion is ill and needs medicines regularly. A rather large number of interviewees indicated that they or their family have not been ill during the last year – though this is to some part also due to a changed perception on what the term "illness" means or whether or not certain illnesses are regarded as the "normal" condition. While working in the slums, a very high number of people – especially children – appeared to be ill with coughs and skin diseases. Thus, the survey results with respect to heath aspects represent a subjective state rather than an objective one – to gain objective statistical figures, more research would have to be done with skilled medical staff. Still, this is in the end not less meaningful – because the health status and well-being are always to a certain extent subjective. The study revealed once again that economical state and health/well-being are closely linked – and therefore have to be considered jointly for further action.

Problems of addiction

The percentage of addicted people is not very high and there is no evidence that this will change in the future. People are too poor to be able to spend large sums on drugs, and they are generally aware of that. Although illiterate people are more often addicted, they do not spend more on drugs than other people. Persons with higher wages spend more money on drugs or are also willing to pay for better quality. The lowest income group and women are least addicted and if they are, they spend their money on cheaper drugs such as tobacco and snuff. Addiction is not a wide spread problem and generally people are aware of their poverty and try to avoid expenses which might lead to even more impoverishment.

Participation in civil society and societal improvements

To what degree poor people invest themselves in changing their conditions of life is more than a monetary concern. Rather, it is important to what degree people use their means to exercise their will, engage themselves in society and be registered citizens. ***Tax bill ownership*** is such an indicator of engagement in civil society. It does not follow clear patterns with the exception that poorer households such as Scheduled Tribe households may have more to gain (and not much to lose) from having a tax bill registration. Engagement in civil society and investment of oneself in community concerns is a key factor in long lasting, sustained development. If the government is interested in larger proportions of the slum dwellers being registered with a tax bill, it is important to determine first what benefits are to be had from tax bill ownership and for what segments of the population this is of greatest relevance. Concerning the ***political participation*** of the slum dwellers, it is striking that less than half of the population own an ***election card.*** This can probably be attributed to the fact that a high proportion of the slum dwellers is illiterate and does, maybe because of this fact, not actively participate in politics. Still, the distribution of the election cards seems to indicate that the democratic rights of the people are guaranteed to the different slum dwellers in equal shares. This is not that surprising, since the poor make up a very significant part of the general population, and politics and politicians rely on the support of this section of society. However, the fact that no part of society is discriminated in the distribution of election cards in the surveyed area does not contain any information on whether or not some sections are discriminated during the votes.

Willingness to contribute towards infrastructural services

The slum households generally prefer to pay for better drinking water. To carry out physical work is only an option for poorer people who do not have the money for it but can work. The people showing significantly high percentages in this category were illiterates, Scheduled Tribes, casual labourers and in general people with a low income. To improve the services, it is important to take these differences into account and to ensure that everyone who wants improvements can take part in the contribution, be it with financial or physical power. It is also conceivable that people are more willing to invest in a service which they will have at home than in a service which would serve the whole community, like clearing up the waste water and rubbish.

Willingness to pay for the legalization of land

When investigating the question whether or not slum households can and want to contribute to infrastructural improvements – in particular access to good drinking water, drainage/sanitation and solid waste removal – it is obvious that people are very much willing to pay. The same is true for the willingness to pay their fair share towards legalising their land. This allows the conclusion that these are the problems with which people are most afflicted. Also, their illegal housing status seems to be an issue of grave concern. In general, people are also very much willing to invest in their houses, and thus improve their living conditions. This is a resource that needs to be better tapped by authorities. Most of the households indicate a high acceptance for shared financial responsibilities, in order to improve their living conditions. However, the amounts they are willing to invest depend to a large extent on their income levels. With income being the critical determinant and poverty being a fact of life for the largest share of the households, it is of no surprise that the greatest priority is given to compensation for wage losses due to the earner's illness, if the government was to create a new scheme of benefits.

Basic infrastructure – basic problems – the case of drinking water quality

As the case of drinking water quality shows, income and educational levels are pivotal elements in the improvement and maintenance of basic infrastructure. Especially the monthly income of a family seems to be a factor which partly explains the drinking water quality of a household. A higher monthly income may probably increase the drinking water quality of many households. Households with access to private water, toilet and sewerage facilities show a remarkable better drinking water quality than households which do not have access to such facilities. The availability of toilet and sewerage facilities are found to be even more important for safe drinking water than the water supply itself. This is probably due to the fact that the absence of a toilet and sewerage facility leads to further contamination of both clean and dirty water.

Another important factor to affect the quality of a household's drinking water is the education of its members. Families with a better educated household head showed better drinking water quality than families with an illiterate or poorly educated head. Highly educated families also stated to know about a relation between hygiene and health and showed more interest in improving their drinking water supply. These last two factors, the existence of hygienic infrastructure and the education, build the main indicator for the distribution of the water qualities among the sampled households. The hygienical infrastructure helps to protect the drinking water sources from contamination, and a certain educational level helps to use and maintain them right. Well educated people know the importance of hygienical behaviour and handle their drinking water carefully. It is therefore important not only to make such facilities available for all households, but also to teach the families about the use and maintenance of these facilities. Hygienic promotion and adequate sanitation facilities seem to be the key to sustainable good drinking water in slum communities.

19.3 Implications of socially differentiated urban slums

A major finding is that religion and class do not seem to account for much differences in socioeconomic patterns. Rather, the analysis of the GIS maps of structural patterns reveals a society at risk that seems to be independent of religion and caste but cuts across material existence: nobody seems to be a priori better or worse off because of caste or religion. At the micro level of the urban slum households, a similar phenomenon seems to be apparent that has become known as the world risk society (Bedford & Giddens 1996), where irrespective of class, family, background institutions and religious affiliation, everyone is increasingly forced to fend individually for their material existence, and knowledge how to do this and finding one's niche becomes more and more important. In other words, the globalizing Indian economy is gradually eliminating old forces of social differentiation and pushing everyone into the global risk society, making knowledge the distinctive factor of new social polarization. The following questions remain to be addressed:

19.3.1
What do we *not* know of sufficiently in terms of degrees of social differentiation, objective slum conditions and social realities?

Degrees of social differentiation – education, class and social context vs. caste and religion

Researchers from the developed world know too little of social differentiation among and within urban slums. As an example, of 18 Swiss young researchers on this project, none would have a priori known or even believed that the four communities in question were of the so called untouchable castes. This attests to the fact that in Western countries, clichés of a reality of lower castes prevail that may no longer represent today's multiple realities for this spectrum of society and concomitant social and development processes. Within often so-called untouchable communities, there are the well-off and the extremely poor, which makes differentiation therefore a key factor. The clichés of the "poor masses" have to be given up in order to understand the specific cases and differences within generally poor areas. This is what makes case studies so important. The objective of the studies in four slum communities that were all extensively communities of the lowest castes was exactly to bring out differences and mechanisms that enhance or prevent upward social mobility.

Understanding the multiple realities of the most vulnerable is important in the Western countries where many of the development projects for the most vulnerable are being launched. Not well understood by outsiders, for example, is how large the percentage of people in urban slums is who *do* benefit from government schemes.

Local planners, in turn, have not yet fully understood how NGOs working *in situ* strengthen local forces when assisting in their self help efforts. Because of the general lack of micro level data, planners' thinking may remain fixed in macro milieu planning and action rather than micro level constraints and adaptive capacities of households. Consider, for example, a policy to lift up an entire slum through infrastructural development which does not go any further than that. Infrastructure is, in many or most cases, a necessary and oftentimes desperately needed first step. When one leaves development at the level of infrastructure, however, it is no surprise when no further development will result or when in some slum communities like in Shantinagar, parallel societies persist with entirely different levels of development.

In order to understand why parallel societies exist although all segments of the poor are equally targeted by government schemes, one has to look at educational attainment, labour market practices and cultural milieus (for example affiliation to tribal groups) and environmental constraints pertaining to only specific groups of people (tribal areas in slums lacking running water), which may reflect a bias of public policy. It becomes apparent that infrastructure alone does not provide development, but also has to be accompanied by education and training and specific efforts geared towards tribals. It also becomes apparent that religion and caste are rather less distinctive but social situation is, hence religion and caste appear to be less important concepts than class, education and social context.

That class even at the lowest level of the social stratification may supersede traditional dividing mechanisms like caste and religion is a new finding or interpretation, as is the fact that this concept of class and social context represents no longer a social stratum defined by birth as was the case in Western societies. Rather, social differentiation even among the lowest caste urban slum communities depends on the means of accessing a certain social position in society – mostly defined by educational attainment and related achievements. The latter is, in urban slum communities, a matter of structural constraints, locally embedded mentalities, institutional regulations and sometimes even misconceptions about such mentalities (for example on the tribals that may falsely be assumed to be resistant to development efforts, but who have possibly been neglected in their particular needs).

Not fully understood, then, is an overlapping of the different dimensions of social inequality such as
- (remnants of) caste society
- upward and downward social mobility through education and the labor market
- micro milieus of self reinforcing solidarity systems
- actions and behaviour, adaptive capacity and resilience
- the manifestations of dimensions of a globalising Indian economy and inequality in local micro milieus
- differentiation and threshold values that indicate tipping points for losing communities to poverty or stabilizing them and their potential for upward social mobility.

Objective slum environment and social realities – "landscapes of vulnerability"

Too little attention is yet given to the fact that space itself and lack of access to facilities may reinforce conditions attributed to social behaviour and traditions. A case in point are Shantinagar's tribals who constantly infect themselves and their water supplies because they do not have enough water for both uses: at their outdoor toilets (in the bushes) and for washing their hands. As a consequence of washing their hands in their drinking water supplies – being aware of the connex between dirty hands and infections – they create the conditions of disease. Outsiders mistake this for ignorant behaviour: "They do not know how to use toilets", "If we built toilets for them they would still not know how to use them or would mess them up", "They prefer the outdoors to facilities that we would have to charge for".

In the example of Shantinagar's tribals, one might conclude that space structures behaviour, as has also been shown in urban slums of high income countries (cf. Wilson 1987). This has theoretically been treated by Lefebvre, Giddens and Bourdieu. The physical conditions of space then, show additional mechanisms at work not fully understood by planning: behaviours may not be so traditional (for example, tribals knowing that washing hands is important do this in their drinking water supplies). The deficits of the environment and the helplessness to ameliorate these deficiencies oneself, however, act as a double reinforcing mechanism of disease and socially undesirable conditions and behaviours. Certainly one might ponder this chicken and egg dilemma and the questions which came first. There is consensus in the social sciences, however, that space may be a means of social neglect, as "policies of neglect" (not providing necessary infrastructure) of certain areas and social milieus have amply been shown (so for example in the US context, cf. Frieden 1985). In the example of the missing toilets in Shantinagar, for instance, the question is not only one of provision of services, but also of providing the right type of facilities. This involves a social relation approach, the participation of the community in the decision making and the teaching of acceptance of responsibility for the maintenance, because it works both ways: If the facilities are not right and accepted, they will be neglected by those they should serve. Space is also an area where one can manifest one's discontent with policies and administrations as the abundant incidences of graffiti in public space of Western countries show. For improvements to occur, government has to provide the right facilities and the social relations approach of teaching acceptance of responsibility even needs to be intensified.

Hence, planners and public administrations should not ignore that space is *not* a container just to be filled with certain material things but that physical space also is a space of social relations, of social production and reproduction of physical and social space. In short: *physical space creates and perpetuates social conditions*. What has been shown for Western societies now must be understood in the micro contexts of urban poverty communities in Indian society as well. Social relations and conditions are structured by physical space which has a different manifestation in every case. What would planners gain by comprehending this? First, they gain an understanding that the social dimension and the social construction of space may well affect the success of the material planning (filling of space with material artefacts and infrastructure). This is quite relevant for the implication and efficiency of planning. Second, if planners understand the interrelation between space and social-behavioural processes, this will also favourably impact the target groups. For them, physical space is a world of daily experience that is also shaped by what is being or not being done and how it is done. The participation and willingness of both sides, planners and target groups, to engage in such a social process to planning that is based on the sharing of decisions and responsibilities is an important factor in achieving sustained development. Involving and integrating the target groups and the planning community is a worthwhile but difficult process. NGOs and/or the methods of GIS as a tool of urban poverty reduction have an important role in mediating the many challenges that arise.

19.3.2
What is a matter of debate?

Modern India has to face the same questions that rich Western countries are facing and have not sufficiently answered. Why do slum conditions exist and persist in countries that can launch space technology and that provide an ever growing global market with technical know how? In terms of urban slum communities, one may raise the question why many peripherally located and marginally integrated slums remain, why there are slums that 30 or 40 years after they were "established" still remain in conditions unacceptable by the standards of the Indian government that has target programs for such areas and their residents? Although many of these settlements were established voluntarily (and illegally), it is questionable whether or not the families and several generations remain there voluntarily or involuntarily by lack of opportunities, general policy neglect (lack of legalizing the settlement), or their own lack of means and motivation to change conditions somewhat.

How poverty and segregated life words should be seen and evaluated, what these manifest on the "supply side" (lack of government priorities, wrong planning) and the "demand side" of the slum communities (lack of educational and labor market opportunities, lack of motivation, wrong priorities) is by no means clear. Whether or not urban slums are a manifestation of unjust social regulations, quasi-acceptance of parallel societies, party policies that utilizes social issues during election times (but not otherwise), is a matter of concern both in rich countries as it is in emerging economies. As such, questions and debates on the persistence of poverty and the emergence of "new poverty" become similar in globalizing high and low income countries.

It is debatable, then, who is responsible for the continued plight of slum communities – the government, the slum dwellers, the planners etc. It is clear that each has a role to play in the development process. With two actors (government at all levels and slum communities) being often at opposing ends of opinions, the role of intermediaries such as NGOs doing educational, social activist and development work stands out eminently. As integrative forces pursuing a mutual learning process, listening to all sides, working at the grass roots, tapping government sources that exist and raising government's awareness for issues, they can truly provide leverages for self help and self sustaining development. Whereas many questions remain to be addressed, there is no doubt as to the role of NGOs in urban slums who for the most part can link public administration and people in such a way as to assist individual adaptive capacities, ameliorate social and economic situations through one's own efforts and established governmental and nongovernmental networks.

19.3.3
What should be decided upon by public administration? What is being overemphasized? What is being insufficiently emphasized?

This question addresses a *normative* aspect and was one of the starting points for this research. Of course, normative issues can be debated much. One thing is obvious and does not need much controversy because it is well accepted both in social science, development work and public administration officials with experience: infrastructural work, for example road construction, does not repair poverty and cannot build up a civil society that takes responsibility in its community issues. Poor, deficitary infrastructure, however, can impede societal development. Good infrastructure is a necessary condition for the betterment of social conditions.

When focusing on physical infrastructure, attention must be paid that local policy and planning are not accidentally disrupting well functioning communities and social solidarity systems as, for example, has been the case in Jayprakashnagar, where road construction physically removed the major social drivers of community development. Much needed physical infrastructure is not just about hardware but also about software: the upkeep and maintenance of it for present and future generations requires well functioning social networks, opinion leaders with a vision for the community and communities that allow themselves to take on responsibility.

What is frequently being overemphasized is the notion that on a global level development can be had for all: if millennium goals and other efforts start to take hold on a micro level, each household could catch up. What is being underemphasized is the fact that in an emerging country like India, there is a rapidly rising middle class with means of distinguishing themselves by the adoption of Western life styles and value systems, thus contributing to increasing polarization. The development of Indian society will rather show more differentiation and will make the plight of those who cannot be part of the New Indian society more obvious. With an emerging middle class that is living proof that one can get to means and wealth based on education, commerce/business and one's own achievement, the acceptance may be lowered for those who stay behind. A rapidly emerging Westernizing middle class may be prone to misunderstanding the less fortunate as being caught in traditional mentalities and behaviours.

What is frequently being underemphasized is that development is still being conceptualized top down and with an understanding that public administration knows in all cases what is best for the target groups. This ignores that the target groups have to do the coping in situ and perhaps have the adaptive capacities to do so. For those who voice concern with development and who are integrated in Western value systems, local adaptive capacities are a territory not well known.

Coping with being at the lower level of society is done locally in the slum communities and not in the regional capitals or the offices of public administration. In contemporary India, as is the case in Western countries, those with means can exercise their degrees of freedom of separating themselves in upper class residential areas, even gated communities, leaving those segments of population and areas lacking infrastructure and the empowerment for development behind. To sum up, India, like Western countries is globalizing and this may create new forms of polarizations between those fit for the global economy and those who are not. While this is a fact, it does not mean that these gaps cannot be overcome when appropriate efforts are being made.

19.4 What are the leverages in terms of public policies?

The prime goal is to set the frame for social development in slum communities. This is a matter of building housing, safe running water, mobilizing self-help and motivation to mobilize one's own physical and human resources and adaptive capacities. This set of measures, although no guarantee for social development per se, is a precondition. An example is given by the provision of drinking water.

Infrastructure for community residents

Safe drinking water supplies are the prime concern, at present, in communities lacking access thereof. Any other focus that promotes general growth of the City of Bhuj, for example, such as the ambitious road construction program that serves long term needs is not of prime importance in communities that on a daily basis have limited or no access to safe running water. As was shown by the water analyses, even where there is running water, however, this may not be safe or as safe as are the wells from which women carry head loads of water every day. Although many households do have running water, families prefer to get drinking water from wells because they perceive that this water is not so "heavy in the stomach". Running water from their own taps is regarded as "heavy" and as preventing food intake. High contamination levels, as were found in this project, indeed led credence to the observation that the frequent use of this water may yield a certain resistance to being constantly ill, but also that the body may reject food intake as a natural protective mechanism.

When water is supplied by authorities but runs out of the pipe in a muddy, brown colour, the question may be raised as to the priorities. On a more abstract level, one may question why a society that can race to space and develop satellite and computer capacity highly appreciated in the Western world cannot provide safe drinking water for all. On the micro level, then, India must face the same questions that the US, Germany or Switzerland are facing: Why is so much priority given to developing prestigious things and so little to the neediest of society? As a global player in the global market, India is developing global outreach and will be measured like the other global players in terms of their weakest members of society. The mixture of scales – macro/global and local/micro level – will be a measure of global-ness. India is not considered a poor country because it has developed space technology. Rather, *although* it has global engineering, computer and scientific capacity, India is considered poor because it has not developed its underdeveloped parts of society, cities and rural areas.

Infrastructure in public places

Whereas NGOs work for human development at the level of the slum household, government and public administration will always have major role in shaping public space and infrastructure towards more humane living conditions. In areas of deficits and living quarters of the disenfranchised, the potential for discontent is high. In situations of conflict that are not entirely unknown to Indian society, it is therefore not surprising that political unrest frequently unloads in those areas more than any others. It is of note that many religious or political conflicts took their greatest toll in areas of suboptimal, overcrowded urban slums. The planning of humane conditions and infrastructural investment necessary for everyday life (housing, water supplies, toilet facilities, etc.) is an investment in the integration of a multicultural society divided along multiple lines.

Participation and responsibility sharing

Participation is a much misunderstood term. That it means listening to the voice and vote of the poorest target groups and asking them to define their needs has only recently been accepted by authorities. The debate on participatory development is barely twenty years old and authorities dealing with development have yet to fully implement it.

Participation, however, does not only involve the target groups in the planning process. Rather, participation has also the dimension of responsibility sharing by the target groups. That, in turn, is poorly understood by communities. It is well documented that providing infrastructure and aid does not bring about development when local responsibility for maintaining this and paying for the services has not been activated. While that has become common knowledge among authorities, this has yet to be learned by many slum communities. The role of NGOs in raising awareness for shared responsibility and willingness to pay cannot be overemphasized.

There is, however, not yet consensus as to how much responsibility the poorest target groups can take. It is clear that shared responsibility has a financial dimension because at all levels of society and in all societies, responsibility in an era of constrained resources means setting priorities and putting one's (little) money where one's needs are felt. This has yet to be fully accepted by local communities, and surveys such as this one have aided in defining thresholds for particular communities. The shared responsibility of NGOs in this will be to raise acceptance, and this requires a communicative approach to development, a process of learning from each other in an output oriented communication. That NGOs can perform this task as intermediaries between communities and planning bodies is an issue that needs to be more appreciated by authorities.

This research and the case study approach support the notion of how relevant local NGOs are in leveraging self-help and self-responsibility by turning attention to the determinants of social differentiation within poverty such as education, willingness to share responsibility and to engage in self-help, as well as external factors impeding own initiatives.

List of Tables

Tab. 3.1	The sequencing and phasing of slum improvements	16
Tab. 4.1	Religion of family head, by slum.	26
Tab. 4.2	Religion, by slum.	26
Tab. 4.3	Caste of family head, by slum.	27
Tab. 4.4	Caste, by slum	27
Tab. 4.5	Age, by slum	28
Tab. 4.6	Occupation, by slum.	29
Tab. 4.7	Occupation of family head, by slum.	29
Tab. 4.8	Daily wages, by slum.	30
Tab. 4.9	Education, by slum.	31
Tab. 4.10	Study continue, by slum.	31
Tab. 4.11	Election card, by slum.	31
Tab. 5.1	Occupation, by slum.	46
Tab. 5.2	Occupation, by sex.	47
Tab. 5.3	Occupation, by religion.	48
Tab. 5.4	Occupation, by caste.	48
Tab. 5.5	Average daily wages of household members (in Rs.), by caste.	49
Tab. 5.6	Average daily wages of household members (in Rs.), by religion.	50
Tab. 5.7	Average daily wages of household members (in Rs.), by slum.	50
Tab. 5.8	Average daily wages of household members (in Rs.), by occupation of family head.	52
Tab. 5.9	Livelihood affected, by post earthquake housing status	51
Tab. 5.10	Livelihood affected by earthquake, by slum.	53
Tab. 5.11	Monthly savings (in Rs.) of household, by slum.	53
Tab. 5.12	Monthly savings (in Rs.) of household, by age of family head.	54
Tab. 5.13	Monthly savings (in Rs.) of household, by sex of family head.	54
Tab. 5.14	Monthly savings (in Rs.) of household, by education standard of family head	56
Tab. 5.15	Monthly savings (in Rs.) of household, by occupation of family head.	56
Tab. 5.16	Monthly savings (in Rs.) of household, by average daily wages of household members (in Rs.).	55
Tab. 5.17	Monthly savings (in Rs.) of household, by religion.	57
Tab. 5.18	Monthly savings (in Rs.) of household, by caste.	57
Tab. 5.19	Amount of debt (in Rs.) of household, by slum.	58
Tab. 5.20	Amount of debt (in Rs.) of household, by age of family head.	59
Tab. 5.21	Amount of debt (in Rs.) of household, by sex of family head.	59
Tab. 5.22	Amount of debt (in Rs.) of household, by education standard.	60
Tab. 5.23	Amount of debt (in Rs.) of household, by occupation of family head.	60

Tab. 5.24	Amount of debt (in Rs.) of household, by average daily wages of household members (in Rs.).	61
Tab. 5.25	Amount of debt (in Rs.) of household, by caste.	62
Tab. 5.26	Amount of debt (in Rs.) of household, by religion.	62
Tab. 6.1	Type of house, by slum.	74
Tab. 6.2	Average daily wages of household members (in Rs.), by type of house.	75
Tab. 6.3	Type of house, by year of arrival at this house.	75
Tab. 6.4	Affected livelihood through earthquake, by type of house.	76
Tab. 6.5	Post earthquake housing status, by type of house.	77
Tab. 6.6	Post earthquake housing status, by slum.	77
Tab. 6.7	Post earthquake housing status, by living in the same house as before the earthquake.	78
Tab. 6.8	Post earthquake housing status, by current housing status.	79
Tab. 6.9	Current housing status, by average daily wages of household members (in Rs.).	79
Tab. 6.10	Living in the same house as before the earthquake, by average daily wages of household members (in Rs.).	80
Tab. 6.11	Precaution to make the house earthquake proof, by average daily wages of household members (in Rs.)	81
Tab. 6.12	Precaution to make the house earthquake proof, by education standard of family head.	81
Tab. 6.13	Precaution to make the house earthquake proof, by caste.	82
Tab. 6.14	Precaution to make your house earthquake proof, by slum.	82
Tab. 6.15	Perception of efficiency of precautions measures, by education standard of family head.	83
Tab. 6.16	Investment to make shelter earthquake proof, by average daily wages of household members (in Rs.).	83
Tab. 6.17	Investment to make shelter earthquake proof, by slum (in Rs.).	84
Tab. 7.1	Ownership document, by age of family head.	96
Tab. 7.2	Ownership document, by slum.	96
Tab. 7.3	Ownership document, by religion.	97
Tab. 7.4	Ownership document, by caste.	97
Tab. 7.5	Ownership document, by average daily wages of household members (in Rs.).	98
Tab. 7.6	Ownership document, by education standard of family head.	98
Tab. 7.7	Ownership document, by sex of family head.	98
Tab. 7.8	Ownership document, by occupation of family head.	100
Tab. 7.9	Tax bill ownership, by age of family head.	99
Tab. 7.10	Tax bill ownership, by slum.	101
Tab. 7.11	Tax bill ownership, by religion.	101
Tab. 7.12	Tax bill ownership, by caste.	102
Tab. 7.13	Tax bill ownership, by average daily wages of household members (in Rs.).	102
Tab. 7.14	Tax bill ownership, by education standard of family head.	102
Tab. 7.15	Tax bill ownership, by sex of family head.	103
Tab. 7.16	Tax bill ownership, by occupation of family head.	100

List of Tables

Tab. 8.1	Ration card, by average daily wages of household members (in Rs.).	118
Tab. 8.2	Ration card, by caste.	119
Tab. 8.3	Ration card, by religion.	119
Tab. 8.4	Ration card, by illness of a family member in the last year.	119
Tab. 8.5	Ration card, by slum.	120
Tab. 9.1	Place for health check-up, by average daily wages of household members.	126
Tab. 9.2	Place for health check-up, by education standard of family head.	126
Tab. 9.3	Place for health check-up, by caste.	127
Tab. 9.4	Place for health check-up, by religion.	128
Tab. 9.5	Place for health check-up, by slum.	128
Tab. 9.6	Purpose of visiting health centre, by average daily wages of household members (in Rs.).	129
Tab. 9.7	Purpose of visiting health centre, by education standard of family head.	129
Tab. 9.8	Purpose of visiting health centre, by caste.	130
Tab. 9.9	Purpose of visiting health centre, by religion.	130
Tab. 9.10	Purpose of visiting health centre, by slum.	131
Tab. 9.11	Illness/death of a family member in the last year, by average daily wages of household members (in Rs.).	132
Tab. 9.12	Illness/death of a family member in the last year, by caste.	132
Tab. 9.13	Illness/death of a family member in the last year, by slum.	132
Tab. 9.14	Illnesses, by average daily wages of household members (in Rs.).	133
Tab. 9.15	Illnesses, by religion.	134
Tab. 9.16	Illnesses, by slum.	135
Tab. 9.17	Illnesses, by occupation of family head.	136
Tab. 9.18	Monthly expenses for medicine (in Rs.), by average daily wages of household members (in Rs.).	137
Tab. 9.19	Monthly expenses for medicine (in Rs.), by education standard of family head.	137
Tab. 9.20	Monthly expenses for medicine (in Rs.), by caste.	138
Tab. 9.21	Monthly expenses for medicine (in Rs.), by religion.	138
Tab. 9.22	Monthly expenses for medicine (in Rs.), by slum.	139
Tab. 10.1	Number of children between 0-7 years, by education standard of family head.	154
Tab. 10.2	Number of children between 8-17 years, by education standard of family head.	154
Tab. 10.3	Number of children between 0-7 years, by caste.	155
Tab. 10.4	Number of children between 8-17years, by caste.	155
Tab. 10.5	Number of children between 0-7 years, by religion.	156
Tab. 10.6	Number of children between 8-17 years, by religion.	156
Tab. 10.7	Number of children between 0-7 years, by slum.	157
Tab. 10.8	Number of children between 8-17 years, by slum.	157
Tab. 10.9	Number of children between 0-7 years, by age of family head.	158

Tab. 10.10	Number of children between 7-17 years, by age of family head....	158
Tab. 10.11	Number of children between 0-7 years, by average daily wages of household members (in Rs.).	159
Tab. 10.12	Number of children between 8-17 years, by average wages per person of whole family.	159
Tab. 10.13	Number of children between 0-7 years, by occupation of family head (with reference to families)	162
Tab. 10.14	Number of children between 0-7 years, by occupation of family head (with reference to single persons)	162
Tab. 10.15	Number of children between 8-17 years, by occupation of family head (with reference to families).	163
Tab. 10.16	Number of children between 8-17 years, by occupation of family head (with reference to single persons).	163
Tab. 10.17	Number of old people, by education standard of family head	165
Tab. 10.18	Number of old people, by caste.	165
Tab. 10.19	Number of old people, by religion.	166
Tab. 10.20	Number of old people, by slum.	166
Tab. 10.21	Number of old people, by age of family head.	167
Tab. 10.22	Number of old people, by average daily wages of household members (in Rs.).	170
Tab. 10.23	Number of old people, by occupation (with reference to families).	168
Tab. 10.24	Number of old people, by occupation (with reference to single persons)	169
Tab. 11.1	Education standard, by slum.	184
Tab. 11.2	Education standard, by age.	185
Tab. 11.3	Education standard, by sex.	186
Tab. 11.4	Education standard, by personal daily wages (in Rs.)	186
Tab. 11.5	Education standard, by religion.	187
Tab. 11.6	Education standard, by caste.	189
Tab. 11.7	Occupation, by age (-59).	190
Tab. 11.8	Occupation, by age (all ages).	192
Tab. 11.9	Occupation, by education standard.	192
Tab. 11.10	Home based occupation, by slum.	193
Tab. 11.11	Home based occupation, by education of family head	194
Tab. 11.12	Home based occupation, by occupation of family head	195
Tab. 11.13	Home based occupation, by average daily wages of household members (in Rs.).	196
Tab. 11.14	Home based occupation, by religion.	196
Tab. 11.15	Home based occupation, by caste.	197
Tab. 11.16	Possession of election card, by slum.	198
Tab. 11.17	Possession of election card, by personal daily wages (in Rs.).	198
Tab. 11.18	Possession of election card, by sex.	199
Tab. 11.19	Possession of election card, by religion.	199
Tab. 11.20	Possession of election card, by caste.	199
Tab. 12.1	Type of addiction, by slum.	206
Tab. 12.2	Type of addiction, by age.	206

List of Tables

Tab. 12.3	Type of addiction, by sex.	207
Tab. 12.4	Type of addiction, by education standard.	207
Tab. 12.5	Type of addiction, by personal daily wages (in Rs.).	208
Tab. 12.6	Type of addiction, by religion.	208
Tab. 12.7	Type of addiction, by caste.	209
Tab. 12.8	Daily expenses for addiction (in Rs.), by type of addiction.	209
Tab. 12.9	Daily expenses for addiction (in Rs.), by personal daily wages (in Rs.).	210
Tab. 12.10	Daily expenses for addiction (in Rs.), by education standard.	210
Tab. 13.1	Water facility in the house, by slum.	214
Tab. 13.2	Source of water, by slum.	214
Tab. 13.3	Water treatment, by slum.	215
Tab. 13.4	Method of water treatment, by slum	216
Tab. 13.5	Electricity facility in the house, by slum.	216
Tab. 13.6	Toilet facility in the house, by slum.	217
Tab. 13.7	Sewerage facility in the house, by slum.	218
Tab. 13.8	Water facility in the house, by occupation of family head.	219
Tab. 13.9	Source of water, by occupation of family head.	219
Tab. 13.10	Water treatment, by occupation of family head.	220
Tab. 13.11	Method of water treatment, by occupation of family head.	220
Tab. 13.12	Electricity facility in the house, by occupation of family head.	222
Tab. 13.13	Toilet facility in the house, by occupation of family head.	222
Tab. 13.14	Sewerage facility in the house, by occupation.	223
Tab. 13.15	Water facility in the house, by caste.	224
Tab. 13.16	If no in Tab. 15, source of water, by caste.	224
Tab. 13.17	Water treatment by caste.	225
Tab. 13.18	Method of water treatment, by caste.	225
Tab. 13.19	Electricity facility in the house, by caste.	226
Tab. 13.20	Toilet facility in the house, by caste.	226
Tab. 13.21	Sewerage facility in the house, by caste.	226
Tab. 13.22	Water facility in the house, by education standard of family head.	227
Tab. 13.23	If no in Tab. 22, source of water, by education standard of family head.	227
Tab. 13.24	Water treatment, by education standard of family head.	228
Tab. 13.25	Method of water treatment, by education standard of family head.	228
Tab. 13.26	Electricity facility in the house, by education standard of family head.	228
Tab. 13.27	Toilet facility in the house, by education standard of family head.	229
Tab. 13.28	Sewerage facility in the house, by education standard of family head.	229
Tab. 13.29	Water facility in the house, by average daily wages of household members (in Rs.).	230
Tab. 13.30	If no in Tab. 29, source of water, by average daily wages of household members (in Rs.).	230

Tab. 13.31	Water treatment, by average daily wages of household members (in Rs.).	231
Tab. 13.32	Method of water treatment, by average daily wages of household members (in Rs.).	231
Tab. 13.33	Electricity facility in the house, by average daily wages of household members (in Rs.).	232
Tab. 13.34	Toilet facility in the house, by average daily wages of household members (in Rs.).	232
Tab. 13.35	Sewerage facility in the house, by average daily wages of household members (in Rs.).	232
Tab. 13.36	Water facility in the house, by religion.	233
Tab. 13.37	If no in Tab. 36, source of water, by religion.	233
Tab. 13.38	Water treatment, by religion	233
Tab. 13.39	Method of water treatment, by religion.	234
Tab. 13.40	Electricity facility in the house, by religion.	234
Tab. 13.41	Toilet facility in the house, by religion.	234
Tab. 13.42	Sewerage facility in the house, by religion.	235
Tab. 13.43	Most necessary improvement of housing substance, by slum	235
Tab. 13.44	Most necessary improvement of drinking water supplies, by slum.	236
Tab. 13.45	Most necessary improvement of access to medical care, by slum.	236
Tab. 13.46	Most necessary improvement of food supplies, by slum.	236
Tab. 13.47	Most necessary improvement of sanitation facilities, by slum	237
Tab. 13.48	Most necessary improvement of housing substance, by occupation of family head.	238
Tab. 13.49	Most necessary improvement of drinking water supplies, by occupation of family head.	238
Tab. 13.50	Most necessary improvement of drinking water supplies, by education standard of family head.	239
Tab. 13.51	Most necessary improvement of sanitation facilities, by education standard of family head.	239
Tab. 13.52	Willingness to do something for better drinking water supply, by slum.	241
Tab. 13.53	Willingness to do something for better drinking water supply, by occupation of family head.	241
Tab. 13.54	Willingness to do something for better drinking water supply, by caste.	242
Tab. 13.55	Willingness to do something for better drinking water supply, by education standard of family head.	243
Tab. 13.56	Willingness to do something for better drinking water supply, by average daily wages of household members (in Rs.).	243
Tab. 13.57	Willingness to do something for better drinking water supply, by religion.	244
Tab. 14.1	Willingness to pay for good drinking water (per month in Rs.), by average daily wages of household members(in Rs.).	286

Tab. 14.2	Willingness to pay for drainage and sanitation (per month in Rs.), by average daily wages of household members(in Rs.)	287
Tab. 14.3	Willingness to pay for solid waste removal (per month in Rs.), by average daily wages of household members(in Rs.)	287
Tab. 14.4	Willingness to pay for good drinking water (per month in Rs.), by slum	288
Tab. 14.5	Willingness to pay for drainage and sanitation (per month in Rs.), by slum	288
Tab. 14.6	Willingness to pay for solid waste removal (per month in Rs.), by slum.	289
Tab. 14.7	Affordable amount of money to legalize the land (in Rs.), by average daily wages of household members (in Rs.).	289
Tab. 14.8	Affordable amount of money to legalize the land (in Rs.), by slum.	290
Tab. 14.9	Willingness to pay property tax (per month in Rs.), by average daily wages of household members (in Rs.).	291
Tab. 14.10	Willingness to pay property tax (per month in Rs.), by slum	291
Tab. 14.11	Willingness to pay property tax (per month in Rs.), by education standard	292
Tab. 14.12	Willingness to pay property tax (per month in Rs.), by average daily wages of household members (in Rs.).	292
Tab. 14.13	Willingness to pay property tax (per month in Rs.), by slum	293
Tab. 14.14	Willingness to pay water tax (per month in Rs.), by average daily wages of household members (in Rs.).	294
Tab. 14.15	Willingness to pay water tax (per month in Rs.), by slum.	294
Tab. 14.16	Willingness to invest in house when land is legalized, by average daily wages of household members (in Rs.).	295
Tab. 14.17	Willingness to invest in house when land is legalized, by slum.	296
Tab. 14.18	Priority benefit in new government scheme, compensation of daily wage loss, by average daily wages of household members	296
Tab. 14.19	Priority benefit in new government scheme, compensation of daily wage loss, by slum.	297
Tab. 14.20	Priority benefit in new government scheme: Improve housing condition, by slum.	297
Tab. 15.1	Relocation, by slum.	320
Tab. 15.2	Relocation, by religion.	320
Tab. 15.3	Relocation, by caste.	321
Tab. 15.4	Relocation, by average daily wage of household members (in Rs.).	321
Tab. 15.5	Relocation, by education standard.	322
Tab. 15.6	Relocation, by age of family head.	322
Tab. 15.7	Relocation, by occupation of family head.	323
Tab. 15.8	Willingness to move with the family, by slum.	324
Tab. 15.9	Willingness to move with the family, by religion.	324
Tab. 15.10	Willingness to move with the family, by caste.	325
Tab. 15.11	Willingness to move with the family, by average daily wage of household members (in Rs.).	325

Tab. 15.12	Willingness to move with the family, by education standard.	325
Tab. 15.13	Willingness to move with the family, by occupation of family head.	326
Tab. 15.14	Willingness to move with the family, by sex of family head.	327
Tab. 15.15	Maximum relocation distance (in km), by slum.	327
Tab. 15.16	Maximum relocation distance (in km), by religion.	328
Tab. 15.17	Maximum relocation distance (in km), by caste.	328
Tab. 15.18	Maximum relocation distance (in km), by average daily wage of household members (in Rs.).	329
Tab. 15.19	Maximum relocation distance (in km), by education standard.	329
Tab. 15.20	Maximum relocation distance (in km), by sex of family head.	329
Tab. 15.21	Maximum relocation distance (in km), by occupation of family head.	330
Tab. 15.22	Maximum relocation distance (in km), by age of family head.	331
Tab. 16.1	Receiving relief, by slum.	346
Tab. 16.2	Received relief, by religion.	346
Tab. 16.3	Received relief from other NGOs or similar, by caste.	347
Tab. 16.4	Received relief from other NGOs or similar, by slum.	347
Tab. 16.5	Received relief from other NGOs or similar, by religion.	347
Tab. 16.6	Received help to reconstruct house, by slums.	348
Tab. 16.7	Received help to reconstruct house, by caste.	349
Tab. 16.8	Received help to reconstruct house, by religion.	350
Tab. 16.9	Received help to reconstruct house, by occupation of family head.	351
Tab. 16.10	Type of relief received: material, by caste.	352
Tab. 16.11	Type of relief received: material, by religion.	352
Tab. 16.12	Type of relief received: cash, by caste.	353
Tab. 16.13	Type of relief received: cash, by religion.	353
Tab. 16.14	Type of relief received: cash, by slum.	354
Tab. 16.15	Type of relief received: information, by caste.	354
Tab. 16.16	Type of relief received: information, by religion.	355
Tab. 16.17	Type of relief received: information, by slum.	355
Tab. 16.18	Received relief from government, by slum.	356
Tab. 16.19	Received relief from government, by sex of family head.	356
Tab. 16.20	Received relief from government, by religion.	357
Tab. 16.21	Received relief from government, by caste.	357
Tab. 16.22	Received relief from government, by education standard of family head.	357
Tab. 16.23	Received relief from government, by age of family head.	357
Tab. 16.24	Received relief from AIDMI, by slum.	358
Tab. 16.25	Received relief from AIDMI, by caste.	359
Tab. 16.26	Linkages with AIDMI, by slum.	359
Tab. 16.27	Linkages with AIDMI, by religion.	360
Tab. 16.28	Linkages with AIDMI, by caste.	360
Tab. 16.29	Linkages with AIDMI, by sex of family head.	360
Tab. 16.30	Who helped the most, by sex of family head.	361
Tab. 16.31	Who helped the most, by religion.	362

Tab. 16.32	Who helped the most, by slum.	362
Tab. 17.1	Water quality (E.coli), by religion	389
Tab. 17.2	Water quality (E.coli), by caste	390
Tab. 17.3	Monthly income, by caste (only water sampled households)	390
Tab. 17.4	Water quality (E.coli), by number of family member	391
Tab. 17.5	Water quality (E.coli), by illness or death	392
Tab. 17.6	Illness or death, by food supply (ration shop)	393
Tab. 17.7	Water quality (E.coli), by place for health check up	394
Tab. 17.8	Monthly income, by place for health check-up (only water sampled households)	394
Tab. 17.9	Water quality (E.coli), by monthly expenses for medicine	395
Tab. 17.10	Water quality (E.coli), by monthly income of the family	396
Tab. 17.11	Water quality (E.coli), by knowledge about relation between hygiene and health	397
Tab. 17.12	Knowledge about the relation between hygiene and health, by education of family head (only water sampled households)	397
Tab. 17.13	Water quality (E.coli), by drinking water supplies as most important improvement	398
Tab. 17.14	Water quality (E.coli), by education of the family head	399
Tab. 17.15	Education, by drinking water supplies as most important improvement (only water sampled households)	399
Tab. 17.16	Water quality (E.coli), by water facility in the house	400
Tab. 17.17	Water quality (E.coli), by willingness to get involved towards achieving better drinking water	401
Tab. 17.18	Water quality (E.coli), by willingness to pay for good water	402
Tab. 17.19	Monthly income, by education of family head (only water sampled households)	402
Tab. 17.20	Simple frequency of treatment methods	403
Tab. 17.21	Water quality (E.coli), by water treatment	403
Tab. 17.22	Water quality (E.coli), by method of water treatment	404
Tab. 17.23	Water quality (E.coli), by toilet facility in the house	405
Tab. 17.24	Toilet facility, by water facility in the house (only water sampled households)	405
Tab. 17.25	Water quality (E.coli), by sewerage facility in the house	406
Tab. 17.26	Toilet facility, by sewerage facility in the house (only water sampled households)	407
Tab. 17.27	Water quality (E.coli), by slum	408
Tab. 17.28	Toilet facility in the house, by slum (only water sampled households)	408
Tab. 17.29	Sewerage facility, by slum (only water sampled households)	408
Tab. 17.30	Water quality (E.coli), by type of house	409
Tab. 17.31	Type of house, by slum	410
Tab. 17.32	Simple frequency of treatment methods	411
Tab. 17.33	Simple frequency of water quality when filtered by cloth	411

List of Maps

Map 4.1	The City of Bhuj, District of Kutch, Gujarat India viewed from the IKONOS satellite image	36
Map 4.2	The four study areas in the City of Bhuj, Gujarat - The slum communities of Bhimraonagar, Jayprakashnagar, Shantinagar and Mustuffunagar	37
Map 4.3	The slum community of Bhimraonagar, as viewed from the satellite (City of Bhuj, Gujarat)	38
Map 4.4	The slum community of Jayprakashnagar, as viewed from the satellite (City of Bhuj, Gujarat)	39
Map 4.5	The slum community of Jayprakashnagar after verification of the satellite based GIS-Map by means of *in situ* surveying	40
Map 4.6	The slum community of Shantinagar, as viewed from the satellite (City of Bhuj, Gujarat)	41
Map 4.7	The slum community of Mustuffunagar, as viewed from the satellite (City of Bhuj, Gujarat)	42
Map 4.8	The slum community of Mustuffunagar, after verification of the satellite based GIS-Map by means of in situ surveying	43
Map 5.1	Average daily wages of household members in Bhimraonagar	64
Map 5.2	Average daily wages of household members in Jayprakashnagar	65
Map 5.3	Average daily wages of household members in Mustuffanagar	66
Map 5.4	Average daily wages of household members in Shantinagar	67
Map 5.5	Households with livelihood affected by the earthquake in Bhimraonagar	68
Map 5.6	Households with livelihood affected by the earthquake in Jayprakashnagar	69
Map 5.7	Households with livelihood affected by the earthquake in Mustuffanagar	70
Map 5.8	Households with livelihood affected by the earthquake in Shantinagar	71
Map 6.1	Types of houses in Bhimraonagar	86
Map 6.2	Types of houses in Jayprakashnagar	87
Map 6.3	Types of houses in Mustuffanagar	88
Map 6.4	Types of houses in Shantinagar	89
Map 6.5	Post earthquake housing status in Bhimraonagar	90
Map 6.6	Post earthquake housing status in Jayprakashnagar	91
Map 6.7	Post earthquake housing status in Mustuffanagar	92
Map 6.8	Post earthquake housing status in Shantinagar	93
Map 7.1	Households reporting ownership of house, Bhimraonagar	104
Map 7.2	Households reporting ownership of house, Jayprakashnagar	105
Map 7.3	Households reporting ownership of house, Mustuffanagar	106
Map 7.4	Households reporting ownership of house, Shantinagar	107

Map 7.5	Households reporting ownership document of the house, Bhimraonagar	108
Map 7.6	Households reporting ownership document of the house, Jayprakashnagar	109
Map 7.7	Households reporting ownership document of the house, Mustuffanagar	110
Map 7.8	Households reporting ownership document of the house, Shantinagar	111
Map 7.9	Households reporting tax bill ownership, Bhimraonagar	112
Map 7.10	Households reporting tax bill ownership, Jayprakashnagar	113
Map 7.11	Households reporting tax bill ownership, Mustuffanagar	114
Map 7.12	Households reporting tax bill ownership, Shantinagar	115
Map 8.1	Households with ration card, Bhimraonagar	121
Map 8.2	Households with ration card, Jayprakashnagar	122
Map 8.3	Households with ration card, Mustuffanagar	123
Map 8.4	Households with ration card, Shantinagar	124
Map 9.1	Households reporting on their places for health check up, Bhimraonagar	140
Map 9.2	Households reporting on their places for health check up, Jayprakashnagar	141
Map 9.3	Households reporting on their places for health check up, Mustuffanagar	142
Map 9.4	Households reporting on their places for health check up, Shantinagar	143
Map 9.5	Spatial pattern of illness or death of a family member during the past year in Bhimraonagar	144
Map 9.6	Spatial pattern of illness or death of a family member during the past year in Jayprakashnagar	145
Map 9.7	Spatial pattern of illness or death of a family member during the past year in Mustuffanagar	146
Map 9.8	Spatial pattern of illness or death of a family member during the past year in Shantinagar	147
Map 9.9	Households reporting illnesses in Bhimraonagar	148
Map 9.10	Households reporting illnesses in Jayprakashnagar	149
Map 9.11	Households reporting illnesses in Mustuffanagar	150
Map 9.12	Households reporting illnesses in Shantinagar	151
Map 10.1	Households with children up to 7 years in Bhimraonagar	171
Map 10.2	Households with children up to 7 years in Jayprakashnagar	172
Map 10.3	Households with children up to 7 years in Mustuffanagar	173
Map 10.4	Households with children up to 7 years in Shantinagar	174
Map 10.5	Households with children between 8-17 years in Bhimraonagar	175
Map 10.6	Households with children between 8-17 years in Jayprakashnagar	176
Map 10.7	Households with children between 8-17 years in Mustuffanagar	177
Map 10.8	Households with children between 8-17 years in Shantinagar	178
Map 10.9	Households with dependent old people in Bhimraonagar	179

Map 10.10	Households with dependent old people in Jayprakashnagar	180
Map 10.11	Households with dependent old people in Mustuffanagar	181
Map 10.12	Households with dependent old people in Shantinagar	182
Map 11.1	Level of education of the family head in Bhimraonagar	201
Map 11.2	Level of education of the family head in Jayprakashnagar	202
Map 11.3	Level of education of the family head in Mustuffanagar	203
Map 11.4	Level of education of the family head in Shantinagar	204
Map 13.1	Water facilities in Bhimraonagar	245
Map 13.2	Water facilities in Jayprakashnagar	246
Map 13.3	Water facilities in Mustuffanagar	247
Map 13.4	Water facilities in Shantinagar	248
Map 13.5	Water sources in Bhimraonagar	249
Map 13.6	Water sources in Jayprakashnagar	250
Map 13.7	Water sources in Mustuffanagar	251
Map 13.8	Water sources in Shantinagar	252
Map 13.9	Households using water treatment, Bhimraonagar	253
Map 13.10	Households using water treatment, Jayprakashnagar	254
Map 13.11	Households using water treatment, Mustuffanagar	255
Map 13.12	Households using water treatment, Shantinagar	256
Map 13.13	Households with electricity, Bhimraonagar	257
Map 13.14	Households with electricity, Jayprakashnagar	258
Map 13.15	Households with electricity, Mustuffanagar	259
Map 13.16	Households with electricity, Shantinagar	260
Map 13.17	Households with toilets, Bhimraonagar	261
Map 13.18	Households with toilets, Jayprakashnagar	262
Map 13.19	Households with toilets, Mustuffanagar	263
Map 13.20	Households with toilets, Shantinagar	264
Map 13.21	Households with access to the sewerage system, Bhimraonagar	265
Map 13.22	Households with access to the sewerage system, Jayprakashnagar	266
Map 13.23	Households with access to the sewerage system, Mustuffanagar	267
Map 13.24	Households with access to the sewerage system, Shantinagar	268
Map 13.25	Felt need for the improvement of the housing substance, Bhimraonagar	269
Map 13.26	Felt need for the improvement of the housing substance, Jayprakashnagar	270
Map 13.27	Felt need for the improvement of the housing substance, Mustuffanagar	271
Map 13.28	Felt need for the improvement of the housing substance, Shantinagar	272
Map 13.29	Felt need for the improvement of drinking water supplies, Bhimraonagar	273
Map 13.30	Felt need for the improvement of drinking water supplies, Jayprakashnagar	274
Map 13.31	Felt need for the improvement of drinking water supplies, Mustuffanagar	275

List of Maps 465

Map 13.32	Felt need for the improvement of drinking water supplies, Shantinagar	276
Map 13.33	Felt need for the improvement of sanitation facilities, Bhimraonagar	277
Map 13.34	Felt need for the improvement of sanitation facilities, Jayprakashnagar	278
Map 13.35	Felt need for the improvement of sanitation facilities, Mustuffanagar	279
Map 13.36	Felt need for the improvement of sanitation facilities, Shantinagar	280
Map 13.37	Willingness to contribute towards better drinking water supplies, Bhimraonagar	281
Map 13.38	Willingness to contribute towards better drinking water supplies, Jayprakashnagar	282
Map 13.39	Willingness to contribute towards better drinking water supplies, Mustuffanagar	283
Map 13.40	Willingness to contribute towards better drinking water supplies, Shantinagar	284
Map 14.1	Willingness to pay towards good drinking water supply, Bhimraonagar	299
Map 14.2	Willingness to pay towards good drinking water supply, Jayprakashnagar	300
Map 14.3	Willingness to pay towards good drinking water supply, Mustuffanagar	301
Map 14.4	Willingness to pay towards good drinking water supply, Shantinagar	302
Map 14.5	Willingness to pay for drainage/sanitation, Bhimraonagar	303
Map 14.6	Willingness to pay for drainage/sanitation, Jayprakashnagar	304
Map 14.7	Willingness to pay for drainage/sanitation, Mustuffanagar	305
Map 14.8	Willingness to pay for drainage/sanitation, Shantinagar	306
Map 14.9	Willingness to pay for solid waste removal, Bhimraonagar	307
Map 14.10	Willingness to pay for solid waste removal, Jayprakashnagar	308
Map 14.11	Willingness to pay for solid waste removal, Mustuffanagar	309
Map 14.12	Willingness to pay for solid waste removal, Shantinagar	310
Map 14.13	Amount households would pay for the legalization of the land, Bhimraonagar	311
Map 14.14	Amount households would pay for the legalization of the land, Jayprakashnagar	312
Map 14.15	Amount households would pay for the legalization of the land, Mustuffanagar	313
Map 14.16	Amount households would pay for the legalization of the land, Shantinagar	314
Map 14.17	Amount households would invest into their houses after the legalization of land, Bhimraonagar	315
Map 14.18	Amount households would invest into their houses after the legalization of land, Jayprakashnagar	316
Map 14.19	Amount households would invest into their houses after the legalization of land, Mustuffanagar	317

Map 14.20	Amount households would invest into their houses after the legalization of land, Shantinagar	318
Map 15.1	Households willing to relocate, Bhimraonagar	332
Map 15.2	Households willing to relocate, Jayprakashnagar	333
Map 15.3	Households willing to relocate, Mustuffanagar	334
Map 15.4	Households willing to relocate, Shantinagar	335
Map 15.5	Households willing to relocate with parts of the community only, Bhimraonagar	336
Map 15.6	Households willing to relocate with parts of the community only, Jayprakashnagar	337
Map 15.7	Households willing to relocate with parts of the community only, Mustuffanagar	338
Map 15.8	Households willing to relocate with parts of the community only, Shantinagar	339
Map 15.9	Maximum distance willing to relocate, Bhimraonagar	340
Map 15.10	Maximum distance willing to relocate, Jayprakashnagar	341
Map 15.11	Maximum distance willing to relocate, Mustuffanagar	342
Map 15.12	Maximum distance willing to relocate, Shantinagar	343
Map 16.1	Households having received relief, Bhimraonagar	364
Map 16.2	Households having received relief, Jayprakashnagar	365
Map 16.3	Households having received relief, Mustuffanagar	366
Map 16.4	Households having received relief, Shantinagar	367
Map 16.5	Help for reconstructing the house, Bhimraonagar	368
Map 16.6	Help for reconstructing the house, Jayprakashnagar	369
Map 16.7	Help for reconstructing the house, Mustuffanagar	370
Map 16.8	Help for reconstructing the house, Shantinagar	371
Map 16.9	Type of relief received, Bhimraonagar	372
Map 16.10	Type of relief received, Jayprakashnagar	373
Map 16.11	Type of relief received, Mustuffanagar	374
Map 16.12	Type of relief received, Shantinagar	375
Map 16.13	Households with linkages with AIDMI, Bhimraonagar	376
Map 16.14	Households with linkages with AIDMI, Jayprakashnagar	377
Map 16.15	Households with linkages with AIDMI, Mustuffanagar	378
Map 16.16	Households with linkages with AIDMI, Shantinagar	379
Map 16.17	Most important source of help, Bhimraonagar	380
Map 16.18	Most important source of help, Jayprakashnagar	381
Map 16.19	Most important source of help, Mustuffanagar	382
Map 16.20	Most important source of help, Shantinagar	383
Map 17.1	Water quality, Bhimraonagar	420
Map 17.2	Water quality, Jayprakashnagar	421
Map 17.3	Water quality, Mustuffanagar	422
Map 17.4	Water quality, Shantinagar	423

List of Figures

Fig. 2.1	Indicators and thresholds for defining slums	9
Fig. 2.2	Inequality, poverty and slum formation	10
Fig. 3.1	Comprehensive approach to slum improvement.	14
Fig. 17.1	Water and sanitation related diseases	386
Fig. 17.2	Well No. 1 (Shantinagar)	412
Fig. 17.3	Hand pump (Mustuffanagar)	413
Fig. 17.4	Well No. 2 (Shantinagar)	413
Fig. 17.5	Water quality of well No1	414
Fig. 17.6	Water quality of well No. 2	414
Fig. 17.7	Water quality of handpump.	415
Fig. 17.8	Bottle on the roof top.	416
Fig. 17.9	Water quality of well No 1	416
Fig. 17.10	Water quality of well No. 2	417
Fig. 17.11	Water quality of handpump.	417
Fig. 18.1	IKONOS image of Bhuj, dated December 20th 2003 (European Space Imaging)	426
Fig. 18.2	The problem of "mixed pixels" and the blurring effect in the delimitation of boundaries	428
Fig. 18.3	Area A and Area B	429
Fig. 18.4	Examples of flat roofs with cantilevers	430
Fig. 18.5	Due to the climatic conditions, life mainly takes place outside of the buildings	431
Fig. 18.6	Slums: A, B, C Shantinagar, D Bhimraonagar	431
Fig. 18.7	Mustuffunagar gives a good example of how helpful shadows are for the interpretation of satellite images	432
Fig. 18.8	In Bhimraonagar, the shadows are not as useful as in Mustuffangar	433